A GUIDE
TO THE PAPERS OF
BRITISH CABINET MINISTERS
1900-1951

compiled by

CAMERON HAZLEHURST and CHRISTINE WOODLAND

LONDON

OFFICES OF THE ROYAL HISTORICAL SOCIETY
UNIVERSITY COLLEGE LONDON · GOWER STREET
LONDON WC1E 6BT

1974

ISBN 0 901050 23 7

Printed by TRUEXpress Oxford

CONTENTS

Page

Introduction and acknowledgements   vii

How to use the Guide   xiii

The Guide   1

Collections in institutions   157

Addenda   166

Index of Ministers   169

INTRODUCTION

Research workers in the field of modern British history have long been aware that there is no single source of information which gives details of the location, contents, and accessibility of the personal papers of politicians. Until recently, no systematic and comprehensive searches had been undertaken. The National Register of Archives contains extensive information about collections of papers in libraries and other public repositories, but its information on material in private hands is fragmentary and often out of date. Much time and money has been spent by individual researchers in their attempts to locate private papers. Even when their searches have led to a result, this has rarely been recorded in such a way as to be generally available, and individual efforts frequently have been duplicated.

By 1967 historians, archivists, and others were sufficiently perturbed by the problem to meet at Nuffield College, Oxford, to discuss possible courses of action. As a result of recommendations by a working party established at the Nuffield meeting, the Political Records Project was conceived early in 1968 as a pilot survey of the feasibility of a wider-ranging survey of papers relating to twentieth century politicians and political organizations. The Social Science Research Council financed the project from October 1968 until its completion. In October 1970, the Council agreed to extend its grant to permit the compilation of a guide for publication; and Nuffield College, Oxford, supplied both accommodation and supplementary financial assistance. The Council also agreed to sponsor a wider ranging project at the British Library of Political and Economic Science. The first volume of the results of this project, Chris Cook, with Philip Jones, Josephine Sinclair, and Jeffrey Weeks, *Sources in British Political History 1900-1951. vol. 1. A Guide to the Archives of Selected Organizations and Institutions,* will be published this year.

The aim of our project was first to locate, and then briefly describe, the private papers of every person of cabinet rank in the period 1900-1951. The names and dates of British Cabinet Ministers 1900-1951 are most readily available in David Butler and Jennie Freeman, *British Political Facts 1900-1960* (1963 and subsequent editions). We have included the various *ad hoc* wartime ministries even though there were periods when the conventional Cabinet was superseded by a War Cabinet. Rather than include in the survey only those individuals who actually served in the Cabinet, we have included *all* of the holders of those government offices which were in the Cabinet at any time during the period. Apart from four special cases which are mentioned in the succeeding section on 'How to use the Guide', the only exception to this was the subordinate office of Financial Secretary to the Treasury. W. Joynson-Hicks was given a seat in the Cabinet as Financial Secretary from May to October 1923. Joynson-Hicks subsequently held several other Cabinet offices, and is therefore included in this Guide. All Financial Secretaries and other junior ministers who did not achieve Cabinet rank will be included in another guide now being prepared at the British Library of Political and Economic Science under the direction of Dr C.P. Cook.

We drew up a list of 323 names, covering the period between the general elections of 1900 and 1951. A considerable body of information already existed about some collections, particularly those in institutions. Our first task was to scour the indices at the National Register of Archives and to obtain detailed information from the national and local repositories. For some Cabinet Ministers' papers, this was all that was needed. But even in these cases a useful centralization of information has been achieved. For example, there has not previously existed a single description of the papers of W. St John Brodrick, 1st Earl of Midleton, whose papers are scattered among the British Library, the Public Record Office, the Guildford Muniment Room, Duke University, North Carolina, U.S.A., the National Library of Ireland, and the family's solicitors. Many of the collections in institutions were (and still are) unlisted. We have tried to maintain contact over the last four years so that our information on such collections remains up-to-date.

The next step was to trace the families of the remaining Cabinet Ministers. For many ministers, this was a simple matter of turning to the current edition of Burke's *Peerage* or *Who's Who*. But for others, who died unmarried, childless, or without title, we devised our own procedure. First, works of reference — such as the *Dictionary of National Biography* and *Who Was Who* — were checked for general information: dates of birth and death, details of origins, marriage, children. Then, the catalogues of the British Library and Nuffield College Library were consulted for biographical and autobiographical works; any such works were read. If these searches failed to point to any obvious source of information we went to the Principal Probate Registry at Somerset House to read the Cabinet Ministers' wills and probate acts or letters of administration. Only a few wills specifically mentioned the disposal of a man's papers or appointed a literary executor: but all gave the full names, addresses, and occupations of executors or administrators, and many gave detailed information such as names and relationships of a minister's family, as well as the name and address of the family solicitor. These names were checked in the postal, geographical, and professional directories; and where an individual could still be found, a letter, asking for help, was sent.

If the executors could not be found, we tried to contact the firm of solicitors, a feat often only achieved by searching through successive volumes of the annual *Law List*. If the solicitors could not be found or could not help, then we went back to Somerset House to search for a minister's widow or other relations and their executors. As their dates of death were not usually known to us, and the registers at Somerset House are arranged annually, this involved a good deal of physical exercise; but it was rewarding. In only a few cases could we not trace a widow, and in such cases it must be assumed that either she is still alive or that she remarried or otherwise changed her name.

When this checking process failed to produce a lead, we used more oblique tactics — we wrote to the present constituency agent, to the local library, to the local newspaper, or to some person or institution with which the cabinet minister had had strong connections. Only when all these attempts failed, and we were unable to obtain leads from other interested scholars, was a file declared 'closed'. A description of our searches was compiled so that they need not be repeated by other researchers. It should be added, as a covering note, that in most cases it was thought neither necessary nor practicable to make exhaustive searches for any papers that may have been preserved by businesses, charities, or other institutions with which ministers were connected. Many of the relevant firms, newspapers, and other bodies are long defunct, or have been taken over in a complicated series of transactions that would take much time and specialist skill to unravel. However, scholars needing very detailed knowledge about the careers of individual ministers frequently will be rewarded if they pursue inquiries in corporate and institutional archives.

Where our letters elicited a positive result, we asked for permission to look at the papers. It should be emphasised that in the first half of the project we were only attempting to *locate* papers. It rapidly became apparent that to say nothing of the content of the papers would drastically limit the value of our survey, and, with the S.S.R.C.'s support, the scope of the project was expanded to include some description. Sometimes historians who were expert in a particular field and thus better able to quickly explore and assess a collection examined the papers on our behalf. Sometimes we relied on detailed handlists of papers that have been professionally arranged and catalogued. But most of the collections were personally examined by either or both of the investigators. Our method of examination, and the resulting descriptions, varied with the size of the collections: a small file can be properly examined in an hour; a large room full of papers will keep many of its secrets after several days' work. As our aim was to leave a collection as we had found it, we made our notes on small numbered cards which could be later shuffled to collate information. Often our notes said nothing more than 'bundle of letters 1880s-1890s from various politicians including . . .' Sometimes a particular letter or memorandum caught our eye and more detailed notes were taken. Obviously, the results of such searches can be little more than impressionistic; nevertheless, even this minimal examination and description represents a significant advance on what has hitherto been available.

Information about access to a collection is as important as a description of its contents. This raises difficult problems since one cannot expect all private individuals to try to cope with the flood of enquiries which publication of this survey might unleash. Owners of collections are now aware of the possible results of announcing that a collection is available for research. Consequently more than 30 collections, some of them large and important, have been deposited in libraries or record offices. In some cases, decisions have been taken that papers would not be made available, at least for the time being. There are other cases where access has been granted on an *ad hoc* basis to individual researchers although a collection remains formally 'not generally available'.

In a few cases no reply came to our letters. We wrote at least three times — and often sought to make contact through other channels — before we assumed that the person thus addressed was not going to reply. In such cases, our entry simply says that we were unable to make contact with a particular individual. In a few cases, the reply was, in effect, that whatever survived was none of our business — a perfectly legitimate attitude — which we have described in our entries as 'X was unable to help us'. All too often the reply came back that a minister's family had kept his papers for some years, usually till they moved house, and then, '. . . as no one seemed to think the papers important . . .' they had been thrown away. This was particularly true for the first Labour Cabinet ministers and is a sad reflection on the libraries and repositories that are now only too eager to collect whatever might have survived.

On the basis of our notes and discussions, a draft description was compiled and sent to the owners or custodians of the collections for their approval. Thus the Guide contains descriptions of the location, content, and accessibility of the papers, or of the searches which we unsuccessfully made for the papers, of 323 men and women: a unique, comprehensive source of information on the private papers of Cabinet Ministers of the first half of the twentieth century.

Until all of the papers are permanently housed in institutions, or they are proven never to have been kept, or to have been destroyed, this project must remain unfinished. Our searches ended in March 1974.

We have tried to find the papers of 323 Cabinet Ministers. When our survey began, the existence of some of the papers of 52 Cabinet Ministers was known. The results of our survey (*Addenda* included) may be summarized as follows:

1. Collections whose destruction or loss seems certain.................. 73
2. Collections in institutions and available for research 216
3. Collections in institutions but not available for research............. 24
4. Collections in private hands and available for research............... 56
5. Collections in private hands but not available for research 84
6. Collections whose fate has not been traced........................ 4

(Columns 1-6 yield a total of 443. Since in 73 cases it seems likely that the papers have been lost, and in 4 cases no trace was found, it is readily calculated that the papers of 245 Cabinet Ministers have been fragmented into 379 'collections'.)

We propose to undertake a constant process of revision, and will endeavour to publish in a scholarly journal a compendium of additions and alterations at two or three-yearly intervals. A revised edition of this volume will also be considered if the number of necessary changes, and the anticipated demand for copies, justify it.

In the meantime, some information about discoveries, institutional acquisitions, and sales of papers may be gleaned from the files and publications of the National Register of Archives and the Public Record Office (especially its annual reports which describe recent transfers and acquisitions in the category of 'Private Office' papers). *The Bulletin of the Institute of Historical Research* regularly records the 'migration' of manuscripts through auctions.

ACKNOWLEDGEMENTS

This Guide owes its existence to the foresight and beneficence of the Social Science Research Council, and the Warden and Fellows of Nuffield College, Oxford. We are indebted to the S.S.R.C. for bearing the main financial burden of the project, and to Nuffield College not only for housing the project for over four years but for assisting financially when our funds were exhausted. The personal encouragement and guidance of the Warden (Sir Norman Chester) and Dr R.M. Hartwell are greatly valued. We are also grateful for the unremitting help of the College Library staff, in particular Miss Christine Kennedy, Miss Julia Harrison, and Mr Tony Carr.

We wish to record our delight and gratitude for the quite astounding quantity and quality of help given in response to our inquiries. Almost all of the people to whom we wrote for information took great pains to help. Archivists, librarians, historians, and biographers responded generously. Many ex-ministers and their families were most hospitable as well as informative, and lightened the occasionally daunting labour of examining rooms full of papers that were often dusty and unsorted.

Acknowledgement is made in the main text of the Guide for advice and assistance in individual searches. But, in addition, we would like to thank a number of people upon whose time, skill, and good nature we repeatedly drew: Mr J.K. Bates, National Register of Archives, Scotland; Mr Alan Bell, National Library of Scotland; Mr Geoffrey Block, Conservative Research Department; Dr Philip Bull, Bodleian Library; Mr Martin Ceadel; Mr A.D. Childs, Churchill College; Dr C.P. Cook; Mr Edward David; Professor H.N. Fieldhouse; Mr R. Sharpe France, Lancashire Record Office; Mr Martin Gilbert; Miss M. Gollancz, Surrey County Record Office; Mr L.J. Gorton, British Library; Mr Les Hannah; Dr J. Harris; Professor R.F.V. Heuston; Miss Pat Jalland; Mr Richard Keiser; Mr Brendan Keith; Dr Felix Hull, Kent Archives Office; Mr Philip Jones; Dr Ross McKibbin; Dr Anthony Mason; Professor A. Temple Patterson; Mr D. S. Porter, Bodleian Library; Mr John Ramsden; Miss Felicity Ranger, National Register of Archives; Miss Angela Raspin, Churchill College; Professor Keith Robbins; Mrs Joanne Cooper-Scott; Miss Josephine Sinclair; Dr John Stubbs; Professor Hugh Thomas; Mr A.F. Thompson; Mr B. Trainor, Public Record Office of Northern Ireland; Mr Ian P. Watson; Professor D.C. Watt; Mr Jeffrey Weeks; Dr Edwin Welch; Dr Neville Williams, Public Record Office; Mr P.M. Williams; Mr F. Willis, Somerset House; and Dr Keith Wilson.

An immense volume of correspondence and filing, together with a wide range of research tasks in catalogues and reference works, and in the search room at Somerset House, were all undertaken by the project's successive secretaries: Mrs Sue Lloyd, Miss Christine Alabaster, Miss Susan Enever, and Mrs Mayling Stubbs. Most of the final manuscript was typed by Miss Janice Aldridge and Mrs Jan Hicks, and carefully scrutinised by Mrs Joan Lynravn, in the Department of History, Research School of Social Sciences, Australian National University. We are grateful for their cheerful fortitude.

Inevitably, our text will contain errors and omissions; and some of the information, especially that which relates to the custody of papers in private hands, will unavoidably become out-of-date. We trust that users of the Guide will draw our attention to mistakes, changes in the ownership or location of papers, and discoveries of hitherto unknown collections by writing to us c/o The Librarian, Nuffield College, Oxford OX1 1NF.

There would have been many more deficiencies in this work, had it not been for the dedication and resourcefulness of Christine Woodland. Although the Guide has been prepared jointly, the first of the undersigned compilers has exercised the privilege of paying a special tribute to, and recording his gratitude for, the outstanding contribution of his colleague.

March, 1974.

CAMERON HAZLEHURST
(Institute of Advanced Studies, Australian National University)

CHRISTINE WOODLAND
(Cambridge)

HOW TO USE THE GUIDE

The entries for all ministers (including those who became peers) are arranged in alphabetical order of family name. The index of ministers is on p. 169; it includes cross-references from titles and name-changes. Hyphenated names have been arranged by the name following the hyphen. Names beginning with 'Mac' or 'Mc' have all been treated as though they begin with 'Mac'. Where a minister changed his name the entry is under his last surname; there are cross-references in the index of names from his earlier surnames.

The title of each entry gives the minister's name on the day of his death, but it does not include his decorations. For consistency, we have referred to each minister by his family name throughout his entry, even if he inherited or was granted titles which required a change of name. If a peer was the only holder of his title, he is referred to in the entry heading as Viscount X, not the 1st Viscount.

The first paragraph of each entry is a brief biographical outline of the minister's political career. Where we know that a minister used a particular Christian name or nick-name, we have given it; otherwise we have given his full name. We have only included details of constituencies held, junior ministries, ministries, and titles granted or inherited. We have included details of governorships, embassies etc. only if papers relating to those offices have survived. We have only given details of the first and of the highest knighthoods granted. We have not included honours which do not involve a change in the style of address, or details of party offices. As all of the men and women covered by the guide were privy councillors, we have not given the date on which they were given that honour. Details of constituency names and dates were taken from J. Vincent and M. Stenton, *McCalmont's Parliamentary Poll Book, British Election Results 1832-1918* (Brighton, 1971), and F. W. S. Craig, *British Parliamentary Election Results 1918-1949, 1950-1970* (Glasgow, 1969; Chichester, 1971). Dates of offices were taken from David Butler and Jennie Freeman, *British Political Facts 1900-1968* (3rd edition, 1969) and the forthcoming Chris Cook and Brendan Keith, *British Historical Facts: 1830-1900* (Macmillan, 1974). We used the latter volume when it was still in manuscript form, and when some dates, particularly for junior ministries and Paymaster-Generals, had not been finally determined. For this reason we have not been able to give the precise dates of all offices held by ministers. Both books give the day, month, and year on which a minister entered his office; they do not say precisely when he left it. Usually the departure was only a few days, or even hours, before his successor took office; but as we cannot give the precise date, we have only given the month and the year. To save space, we have not given the month in which a minister took office, if he went immediately to that office from the preceding office; the month and year of departure are always given.

In the second and succeeding paragraphs we have indicated where the papers are, whether or not they are available, under what conditions, and from whom permission to use the papers must be obtained. Reference numbers are supplied if they exist. Succeeding paragraphs elaborate on the content of a collection. As many collections have been split (some might even be described as fragmented) we have described the main part of a minister's papers first, and then given at least a paragraph to each of the parts of the papers located elsewhere. Where a collection is not yet listed, and has no reference number, we have given the minister's name as its reference: for example, the Worthington-Evans Papers. We have given the principal biographical sources for a minister's career; unless otherwise indicated, the place of publication is London.

There is an entry for each minister, even if our searches produced no result. We have described our searches and the answers we received. In many cases, a minister's relative or solicitor said that he or she did not know of the existence of any papers. We have passed on this 'negative' information so that historians will not need to repeat our searches and the informants concerned will not be troubled again unnecessarily. In the cases where we received no reply to several letters or inquiries through other channels, we have said that we were unable to contact the individual addressed. To maintain the privacy of those private individuals who were unable to help, or whose collections are closed, we have not given their addresses. In only one case were we refused permission to disclose the existence of a 'closed' collection.

The list of 323 ministers was drawn up from the holders of the following offices (Butler and Freeman, *op.cit.*): Prime Minister; Lord President of the Council; Lord Chancellor; Lord Privy Seal; Chancellor of the Exchequer; Foreign Office; Home Office; Admiralty; Agriculture and Fisheries; Air; Aircraft Production; Attorney-General; Blockade; Civil Aviation; Colonial Office; Coordination of Defence; Defence; Dominion Office; Commonwealth Relations; Economic Warfare; Education; Food Control; Fuel and Power; India; Information; Ireland; Labour (and National Service); Duchy of Lancaster; Local Government Board; Health; Local Government and Planning; Materials; Munitions; Paymaster-General; Pensions; Minister without Portfolio; Postmaster-General; Reconstruction; Ministers Resident; Scotland; Shipping; Supply; Board of Trade; Transport; War Transport; War; Works.

We have not limited the guide to the papers of ministers who actually were in the cabinet; indeed we have included all of the ministers who held certain offices, even if a particular minister was not in the cabinet. Students of administrative history may find this comprehensive coverage particularly useful. There are, in addition, four entries not covered by this brief: Baron Ashbourne, who was a member of the cabinet as Lord Chancellor of Ireland; the 5th Earl Cadogan, who was a member of the cabinet as Lord Lieutenant of Ireland; the 1st Earl of Ypres, who was a member of the cabinet as Lord Lieutenant of Ireland; and J.C. Smuts, the South African politician, who was a member of the war cabinet 1917-1919.

The entries vary greatly in length. This is partly because of the varying size of the collections and of the length of time we were able to spend on them. Where only a few papers survived, we are able to give a fairly full description. But many collections are vast and disorganised. To have done more than sample their contents would have required far more time and human resources than were available. Consequently, descriptions of papers in private hands must be regarded as impressionistic. We deliberately concentrated our efforts on locating and describing collections that were not in institutions when we examined them. This has meant that collections in institutions, particularly those not yet listed, have had a much more cursory inspection. Usually, we have drawn up our descriptions of these papers by looking at whatever list or description was available, and by consulting the librarian or archivist concerned, rather than looking at the papers ourselves.

Full details (address, opening hours, and a list of collections mentioned in this guide) of the various libraries, record offices, and repositories are to be found in a list after the entries. The list is arranged alphabetically by the title of the various institutions; where the formal title of an institution is not generally used, we have given a cross-reference from the usual name. Most of the information in this list is based on the Royal Commission on Historical Manuscripts, *Record Repositories in Great Britain* (5th edn., 1973).

WILLIAM ADAMSON (1863-1936)

William Adamson was Labour M.P. for Fife (West) 1910-1931. He was Secretary (later Secretary of State) for Scotland January-November 1924 and June 1929-August 1931.

Adamson's son, Mr D.M. Adamson, informs us that neither he nor the rest of his brothers and sisters has any papers. Mr Adamson thinks that some papers were given by Adamson to a close friend sometime before his death, so that his friend might write a biography. The friend is now dead. He had no family and Mr Adamson has so far been unable to discover what happened to his father's papers.

CHRISTOPHER ADDISON, 1st VISCOUNT ADDISON (1869-1951)

Christopher Addison was Liberal M.P. for Shoreditch (Hoxton) 1910-1922, and Labour M.P. for Wiltshire (Swindon) 1929-1931, and 1934-1935. He was Parliamentary Secretary to the Board of Education August 1914-May 1915, Parliamentary Secretary to the Ministry of Munitions 1915-December 1916, Minister of Munitions 1916-July 1917, Minister of Reconstruction 1917-January 1919, President of the Local Government Board January-June 1919, Minister of Health 1919-April 1921, Minister without Portfolio April-July 1921, Parliamentary Secretary to the Ministry of Agriculture and Fisheries June 1929-June 1930, Minister of Agriculture and Fisheries 1930-August 1931, Secretary of State for Dominion Affairs August 1945-July 1947, Secretary of State for Commonwealth Relations July-October 1947, Lord Privy Seal 1947-March 1951, Paymaster-General July 1948-April 1949, and Lord President of the Council March-October 1951. He was created K.G. in 1946, Baron Addision in 1937, and Viscount Addison in 1945.

Addison's papers were deposited in the Bodleian Library in 1973 by his widow (ref. Addison Papers). They are not catalogued, but they were carefully arranged by Dorothy, Lady Addison, after Addison's death, and a box list was compiled. They fill 136 box-files.

One of Addison's earliest political interests was the 1911 National Insurance Bill; he was a strong supporter of Lloyd George's policies at that time. There are several files relating to his work for this bill, showing his more general interest in local government reform, the poor law, and health. Addison first stood as Liberal candidate for Hoxton in 1907; there are files of papers on this and succeeding election campaigns.

The largest part of the papers relates to Addison's work at the Ministry of Munitions. All aspects of the ministry's work are represented: there are files on various aspects of the ministry's employment of women — their health, salaries, and labour relations; on the supply of particular materials, including files on the sinking of individual ships; on the development of particular weapons; and on the government's attempt to control liquor consumption (mainly printed papers).

Addison was very interested in encouraging scientific and industrial research. The collection includes papers from the Privy Council's committee on this problem and early papers on the establishment and organization of the Medical Research Council 1918-1920. There are files from Addison's work at the Ministry of Health and, later, at Agriculture. As well as subject files, for example, on Ireland, on the 1916-1922 Coalition Government, and on the 1931 crisis, there are also files of correspondence with particular individuals, including letters to the King. There are only a few post-1945 papers. There are ten volumes of press cuttings. The collection also includes Addison's diary June 1914-February 1919. The diary was published by Addison, entitled *Four and a Half Years* (2 vols., 1934). The published version appears to be the same as the typed version in the Bodleian, as amended in manuscript. The manuscript amendments and deletions are usually on personal affairs or comments on contemporaries. Addison said in the published version that the diaries were usually dictated daily. There are also proofs, correspondence, and reviews of Addison's memoirs, *Politics from Within, 1911-1918* (2 vols., 1924). The papers were used for and are extensively quoted in R.J. Minney, *Viscount Addison. Leader of the Lords* (1958).

Dorothy, Lady Addison, has given a small collection of letters of condolence on the death of her husband to the Bodleian Library (ref. MS. Eng. lett. d.332).

Lady Addison has also given her own, very full diaries 1938-1958 to the British Library (ref. Reserved MS. 109/1-3). The diaries are closed until December 1990, when their closure will be reviewed.

SIR WILLIAM MAXWELL AITKEN, 1st Bt, 1st BARON BEAVERBROOK (1879-1964)

Max Aitken was Conservative M.P. for Ashton-under-Lyne 1910-1916. He was Chancellor of the Duchy of Lancaster and Minister of Information February 1918-February 1919, Minister of Aircraft Production May 1940-May 1941, Minister of State May-June 1941, Minister of Supply 1941-February 1942, Minister of War Production February 1942, and Lord Privy Seal September 1943-August 1945. He was knighted in 1911, created a baronet in 1916, and Baron Beaverbrook in 1917.

Several hundred boxes of Aitken's papers have been deposited in the Beaverbrook Library. They are being catalogued but applications for access will be considered.

There are 46 boxes of general correspondence (business, political, and family) for 1903-1910, and 161 for 1911-1964; these are arranged chronologically, then alphabetically within each year. At various stages during Aitken's life, correspondence with particular individuals was withdrawn from the general series and kept separately; there are 86 boxes of these special series.

There are nine boxes of constituency papers for 1910-1912, five boxes from Aitken's work for the Canadian government in the first world war, and twelve boxes of papers from the Ministry of Information. During the second world war Aitken's private and civil service secretaries accumulated two sets of overlapping files; fourteen boxes of the former, and 22 of the latter have survived. Aitken kept only War Cabinet papers relating to aircraft production. In addition to these official papers there are 27 boxes of unofficial correspondence and eight boxes of correspondence on political topics. There are also seventeen boxes concerning negotiations with the United States on the future of civil aviation, and four on oil supplies.

Aitken's newspaper work is amply represented, though most of what survives is post-second world war. There is one box of papers concerning the *Daily Express* up to 1928; 62 boxes for 1928-1964; one box concerning the *Evening Standard* up to 1928, twenty for 1928-1964. There are over twenty boxes of office files of the Empire Crusade, including correspondence with possible parliamentary candidates.

The visitors' books for Cherkley 1911-1964, and Aitken's engagement diaries 1922-1964 have survived. There are also private account books and 65 volumes of press cuttings. These include four volumes of articles by Aitken and eight of reviews of his various books. Material for his books was gathered both from his own papers and elsewhere and has been kept together to fill twenty boxes; there are two boxes of material for *Politicians and the War, 1914-1916* (2 vols., 1928-32; revised one vol. edition 1960). Other books by Aitken which contain either autobiographical material or quotations from original documents, are: *Politicians and the Press* (1926); *Friends. Sixty years of intimate personal relations with Richard Bedford Bennett. . . A personal memoir with an appendix of letters* (1959); *Men and Power: 1917, 1918* (1956); *The Decline and Fall of Lloyd George. And great was the fall thereof* (1963); and *My Early Life* (Fredericton, New Brunswick, 1965).

A.J.P. Taylor, *Beaverbrook* (1972) is based on the papers and quotes copiously from them.

ALBERT VICTOR ALEXANDER, EARL ALEXANDER OF HILLSBOROUGH (1885-1965)

Albert Victor Alexander was Co-operative M.P. for Sheffield (Hillsborough) 1922-1931 and 1935-1950. He was Parliamentary Secretary to the Board of Trade January-November 1924, 1st Lord of the Admiralty June 1929-August 1931, May 1940-May 1945, and August 1945-October 1946, Minister without Portfolio October-December 1946, Minister of Defence 1946-February 1950, and Chancellor of the Duchy of Lancaster 1950-October 1951. He was created K.G. in 1964, Viscount Alexander in 1950, and Earl Alexander of Hillsborough in 1963.

A collection of Alexander's papers has been deposited at Churchill College, Cambridge, by his daughter, Lady Beatrix Evison. The papers have been listed but not all of them are open for research; written application should be made to the Keeper of the Archives. The listed papers include reports and correspondence 1924-1951, but they are somewhat disappointing for information on the co-operative movement. There are no constituency letters. There are three fragments of diary: June 1942, March-June 1946 (concerning the Labour Party's Indian

ALBERT VICTOR ALEXANDER (cont.)

Mission), and April-August 1946. There are also press cuttings of articles by and about Alexander, and notes for speeches and broadcasts.

The papers of Alexander's local agent, Alderman Dr Albert Ballard, and of his constituency party have been deposited in the Sheffield Public Library (ref. Ballard papers and Co-operative Party Records). The papers have been listed; copies of the lists are available at Churchill College. Both collections include many letters from Alexander and his wife about local and national issues. The party records include analyses of Alexander's voting record, correspondence about his appointments, and press cuttings.

LEOPOLD CHARLES MAURICE STENNETT AMERY (1873-1955)

Leopold Stennett Amery was Conservative M.P. for Birmingham (South, later Sparkbrook) 1911-1945. He was Parliamentary Under-Secretary for the Colonies January 1919-April 1921, Parliamentary and Financial Secretary to the Admiralty 1921-October 1922, 1st Lord of the Admiralty 1922-January 1924, Secretary of State for the Dominions (an office he was instrumental in establishing) June 1925-June 1929, and Secretary of State for India May 1940-August 1945.

His papers are in the possession of his son, the Rt. Hon. Julian Amery M.P., 112 Eaton Square, London S.W.1. They are not generally available for research but Mr Amery hopes to publish extensive selections from them in the near future. Leo Amery had a very varied and active career and his large collection of papers (c. 230 box-files and 40 volumes of diary) reflects many aspects of it. Although the present arrangement is not permanent, a brief list of the papers has been compiled; the numbers in brackets refer to the box numbers.

There are seventeen box-files covering his early life: family letters, as well as his Harrow notebooks, Oxford notes, and some of his early articles. From 1899 to 1909 he worked for *The Times*. A box of correspondence with Valentine Chirol, foreign editor, survives (18). A great deal of correspondence survives from his reporting of the South African war and his part in writing *The Times'* History (18-21). There are another twenty boxes of papers from this period, mostly correspondence (arranged alphabetically within years) with a few separate series of 'special' correspondents such as Lord Milner (25), and Violet Markham (26). There are also a few subject files — press cuttings, pamphlets, notes, etc., as well as correspondence — mainly about the Army, National Service, and Tariff Reform (22, 36), and also papers from Amery's earliest attempts to enter Parliament (27, 39): he stood for Wolverhampton (East) in 1906, 1908, and January 1910, and for Bow and Bromley in December 1910.

The period 1910-1914 is covered by eight box-files. They include correspondence, speeches, articles and subject files on the Parliament Bill (47), Lloyd George's Insurance Act (47), the Army (52), Home Rule and the Curragh Crisis (49, 50, 53), and the Marconi Inquiry (51) (Amery was a member of the select committee).

Amery took both an administrative and military role in the first world war. His brother-in-law, Hamar Greenwood, wrote (4 September 1914) to Amery's wife describing how Amery had been able to persuade Kitchener to accept a scheme for processing recruits which the staff officers had been afraid to press. He was later sent to Flanders, the Balkans, Gallipoli, and Salonika as an intelligence officer. There is a small amount of correspondence from his fellow officers, in particular several letters from General Ian Hamilton who commanded the Dardanelles Expedition. On his return to England (3 November 1915) Hamilton asked Amery to use his influence to stop attacks on Hamilton's direction of the expedition, at least until he could write his report and put his case (57). Amery's active service meant that he was abroad during several political crises of the war, in particular that of December 1916. Very little political correspondence seems to have survived from this period, possibly because the ship on which Amery was returning home was sunk by a submarine. During 1917-1918 he served as an Assistant Secretary to the War Cabinet and took part in many of the conferences at Versailles. Memoranda, telegrams, and letters relating to his official work survive (69-72), as well as general correspondence, and various articles and speeches. There are two boxes (72, 73) of correspondence relating to his tenure of the Under-Secretaryship at the Colonial Office and at the Admiralty as well as material concerning his elections 1918-1935 (79), memoranda and subject files on Overseas Settlement (i.e. emigration) (81), Malta (81), and on the currency question 1920-1921 (81).

4

LEOPOLD CHARLES MAURICE STENNETT AMERY (cont.)

There are 30 box-files for the 1920s when Amery was Colonial and Dominions Secretary. In addition to general correspondence, there are sixteen files of correspondence with governors and governors-general. There are also subject files on the League of Nations, the Irish Boundary Question, the General Strike, and finance, as well as papers concerning his Empire tour of 1927-1928.

There are 30 box-files for the 1930s when Amery was out of office. The subject files for that period include the 1931 crisis, disarmament, India, unemployment, the Abdication, Austria 1938, and Czechoslovakia.

During the second world war Amery was Secretary of State for India and Burma. There are twenty boxes of telegrams, minutes to the Prime Minister, Cabinet memoranda, and correspondence with governors. There are also speeches and articles on India, as well as papers concerning Cripps's mission in 1942.

In 1945 Amery left office but 40 box-files reflect his continued and varied interests. There are several boxes of papers concerning the publication of his memoirs, including a draft for a fourth, unpublished volume (184, 185, 199, 200a, 200c), and also material for his *Thoughts on the Constitution* (1947) (222). There are also files on the Empire Industries Association 1948-1955, the Central Africa Federation 1952-1954, correspondence with Chaim Weizmann 1930-1955, and the Rhodes Trust 1939-1955 (Amery was Senior Trustee 1933-1955).

As well as these voluminous papers, Amery kept a diary from 1917 to 1955. It was dictated and then corrected by Amery. It is difficult to decide whether it was normally dictated daily, although on 5 March 1918 he talked of dictating arrears. The diary (as well as the other papers) is quoted extensively in Amery's memoirs, *My Political Life* (3 vols., 1953-55). Occasional annotations appear to have been added to the original text while the memoirs were being prepared. Against the entry for 16 July 1918, for example, he wrote: 'the omissions in my diary are often more vital than the inclusions!' There are, of course, gaps, for example in September 1918, when his secretary was on holiday. The entries for 1920, when his secretary was again away, are reminiscences and odd notes 'suggested by entries in my pocket book'. There are some notes for the period 1903-1914 compiled on the same basis. The main diary, where it exists, is a very detailed political record. Each volume, which covers approximately a year, has about 250 pages.

SIR JOHN ANDERSON, 1st VISCOUNT WAVERLEY (1882-1958)

John Anderson was Independent National M.P. for the Scottish Universities 1938-1950. He was Lord Privy Seal October 1938-September 1939, Secretary of State for Home Affairs 1939-October 1940, Lord President of the Council 1940-September 1943, and Chancellor of the Exchequer 1943-July 1945. He was created K.C.B. in 1919, G.C.B. in 1923, and Viscount Waverley in 1952.

His biographer, Sir John Wheeler-Bennett, informs us that Anderson was 'extremely reluctant to commit himself to paper'. Neither Anderson's widow nor his son, the present (2nd) Viscount Waverley, has any papers. Such material as Sir John found was in the archives of the Home, India and Irish Offices; no 'Anderson papers' have survived with his family, although Sir John does quote from letters by Anderson to his first and second wife, and to his father, in his biography, *John Anderson, Viscount Waverley* (1962).

A few fragments of Anderson's work as Joint Under-Secretary of State for Ireland 1918-1920 are available for research in the Public Record Office (ref. C.O. 904/188/1, 2). The first volume consists of papers connected with the attempted assassination of the Lord Lieutenant: witnesses' statements, etc. There are also copies of several letters to Sir Hamar Greenwood and A. Bonar Law. Anderson's view on the negotiations with the Irish and the Irish situation are given in several memoranda. The second volume mainly consists of miscellaneous correspondence with General Macready May 1920-September 1921. There are several letters and memoranda clarifying the truce terms agreed in 1921.

Also available at the Public Record Office is an incomplete set of papers of the Anderson Committee on pensions 1924 (ref. Pen. 1).

SIR JOHN ANDERSON (cont.)

Some of Anderson's papers as Lord President are still in the keeping of the Cabinet Office. They will be released to the Public Record Office in due course.

Two files of Anderson's personal papers are in the India Office Library (ref. MSS. Eur. D. 806). They include miscellaneous personal correspondence 1937-1941, and papers of the Royal Institute of International Affairs, Shanghai Study Group.

SYDNEY ARNOLD, BARON ARNOLD (1878-1945)

Sydney Arnold was Liberal M.P. for the West Riding of Yorkshire (Holmfirth, later Penistone) 1912-1921; he joined the Labour Party in 1922. He was Under-Secretary of State for the Colonies January-November 1924, and Paymaster-General June 1929-March 1931. He was created Baron Arnold in 1924.

Arnold died unmarried. His estate passed to his two brothers, Frederick Octavius Arnold, who died in 1953, and Lawrence Septimus Arnold, who died in 1954. Arnold's nephew, Mr Gerald Arnold, Messrs Seal Arnold & Co., Cavendish House, 30 Pall Mall, Manchester M60 2QX, has a very small collection of papers relating to Arnold's political career, including a copy of his letter of resignation 5 March 1931, a copy of a letter to J.R. MacDonald 27 September 1931 appealing to MacDonald not to go to the country as head of a national government, and the reply 29 September 1931, in which MacDonald reproached Arnold for not appreciating the necessity of his actions.

WILFRID WILLIAM ASHLEY, BARON MOUNT TEMPLE (1867-1939)

Wilfrid Ashley was Conservative M.P. for North Lancashire (Blackpool) 1906-1918, Lancashire (Fylde) 1918-1922, and Hampshire (New Forest) 1922-1932. He was Parliamentary Secretary to the Ministry of Transport October 1922-October 1923, Under-Secretary of State for War 1923-January 1924, and Minister of Transport November 1924-June 1929. He was created Baron Mount Temple in 1932.

Twenty-six boxes of Ashley's papers, a very small part of the Broadlands estate archive, have been deposited by the Broadlands Trustees in the Hampshire Record Office (ref. 27M60). The papers are being sorted (March 1974) but they are available for research. Applications should be made to the Hampshire County Archivist, who will forward them to the Trustees.

The bulk of the papers takes the form of correspondence. There is general correspondence for the years 1898-1912, 1914-1923, 1926-1938. This has been arranged alphabetically within years. A lot of correspondence with politicians has been separated from these letters and some of the letters from an individual put together in one bundle. For example, there are 90 letters from Sir W. Joynson-Hicks for the period 1909-1932, 35 from W.R.W. Peel 1901-1934, 26 from A. Bonar Law 1911-1923, 36 from Sir Anderson Montague-Barlow 1916-1930, 29 from Neville Chamberlain 1919-1935, 33 from Herbert Morrison 1929-1931 (mostly concerning the Road Traffic Bill), and 73 letters from Sir Arthur Steel-Maitland 1911-1932. There is a further series of letters from politicians arranged alphabetically within years. Apart from this correspondence, Ashley's political career is represented only by such fragments as speech notes 1929-1936, and a memorandum of a secret debate in the Commons in 1917.

Only a few papers have survived from Ashley's constituency work: there are printed election addresses for the 1906, 1910, and 1918 general elections, printed letters of thanks to canvassers, press cuttings, some photographs of Ashley campaigning, and a blue silk handkerchief which he wore on all his campaigns. Ashley was private secretary to Sir Henry Campbell-Bannerman for a short time after he resigned from the Guards in 1898, and a fragment of diary 22 April-3 May 1899 and 29 letters 1899-1908 survive for this period. Ashley made tentative efforts to gain a Liberal seat but was stopped by his father's refusal of funds unless he stood as a Conservative.

The only ministerial papers in this collection are Foreign Office Confidential Prints of reports by Max Muller on the situation in Austria-Hungary in 1917. A few subject files represent Ashley's interests: Ireland (he acted as a Brigade-Major in the Ulster Volunteer Force) mostly photographs, passes, posters, and a few letters from Ashley's Irish tenants; Germany (he was a member of the Anglo-German Fellowship but resigned in the thirties over the German treatment of Jews); and transport.

WILFRID WILLIAM ASHLEY (cont.)

Ashley's remaining papers are miscellaneous bank account books, various commissions and certificates, photographs, invitations, his letters to his first wife 1907-1910, and diaries 1884-1886, and for various trips abroad, *e.g.* to Morocco in 1894, and South Africa in 1898.

In addition to Ashley's own papers, the Broadlands Archive contains the papers of various members of his family. There are diaries, letters, and a press-cutting book relating to his father, the Rt. Hon. Evelyn Ashley, and his mother Sybella. Two large bundles of Sir Ernest Cassel's correspondence 1886-1921, including a bundle of letters from the Royal Family, are included in the collection. Cassel was the father of Ashley's first wife.

Some of Ashley's Private Office papers from the Ministry of Transport are now available in the Public Record Office (ref. M.T. 62/1). The papers include a file on the 1928 Cabinet Policy Committee on railway rating and motor taxation.

HERBERT HENRY ASQUITH, 1st EARL OF OXFORD AND ASQUITH (1852-1928)

Herbert Henry Asquith was Liberal M.P. for Fife (East) 1886-1918, and Paisley 1920-1924. He was Secretary of State for Home Affairs August 1892-June 1895, Chancellor of the Exchequer December 1905-April 1908, Prime Minister 1908-December 1916, and Secretary of State for War March-August 1914. He was leader of the Liberal Party 1908-1926. He was created K.G. and Earl of Oxford and Asquith in 1925.

One hundred and fifty-two volumes of Asquith's papers were given to Balliol College, Oxford, by his literary executors, his son, the Hon. Arthur Asquith, and Sir Maurice Bonham Carter. The papers were later given to the Bodleian Library, where they are available for research (ref. MSS. Asquith 1-152). The papers have been catalogued and an index compiled. They include a great wealth of material: for example Asquith's correspondence with King Edward VII and King George V; and drafts and copies of Cabinet letters to the kings, the main source for tracing Cabinet discussions and decisions until Lloyd George instituted Cabinet agenda and minutes in December 1916. This series of Cabinet letters is not complete; however, it does contain at least one letter not in the Royal Archives (ref. MS Asquith 5, ff. 86-7), dated 24 February 1909. There are letters, memoranda, and pamphlets on most of the political problems of Asquith's administration.

There are few papers from the period before Asquith became Prime Minister, and few constituency papers, except letters of congratulation on his victory at Paisley in 1920, and letters of condolence on his defeat in 1924. There are eight boxes of papers relating to the post-war Liberal Party, in particular, account books of party funds, and correspondence about the *Westminster Gazette,* in which the party had shares.

The *Life of Lord Oxford and Asquith* by J.A. Spender and Cyril Asquith (2 vols., 1932) and *Asquith* by Roy Jenkins (1964) both quote extensively from these papers. There are few personal recollections or documentary quotations in Asquith's *The Genesis of the War* (1923) and *Fifty Years of Parliament* (2 vols., 1926). Many personal letters, mostly by Asquith himself, are quoted in *Memories and Reflections 1857-1927* (2 vols., 1928); but these letters have not always been accurately transcribed, and, wherever possible, the originals should be consulted.

A letter from Winston Churchill to Asquith, 11 November 1915, conveying his resignation from the Cabinet, is among a collection of sixteen letters to Asquith's wife in the William R. Perkins Library, Duke University.

CLEMENT RICHARD ATTLEE, 1st EARL ATTLEE (1883-1967)

Clement Attlee was Labour M.P. for Stepney (Limehouse) 1922-1950, and Walthamstow (West) 1950-1955. He was Under-Secretary of State for War January-November 1924, Chancellor of the Duchy of Lancaster May 1930-March 1931, Postmaster-General March-August 1931, Lord Privy Seal May 1940-February 1942, Secretary of State for Dominion Affairs 1942-September 1943, Deputy Prime Minister 1942-May 1945, Lord President of the Council 1943-May 1945, and Prime Minister July 1945-October 1951. He was Deputy Leader of the Labour Party 1931-1935, and Leader 1935-1955. He was created K.G. in 1956, and Earl Attlee in 1955.

CLEMENT RICHARD ATTLEE (cont.)

Attlee gave 41 boxes of his papers to University College, Oxford. They are available to researchers after written application has been made to the Librarian and a letter of recommendation forwarded. The papers are not sorted but a rough list of the contents of each box is available. The papers fall into five main divisions: miscellaneous correspondence 1945-1951, arranged alphabetically; correspondence with Labour Party officials 1939-1944, including a memorandum by Attlee on the electoral truce (c. 28 March 1944); correspondence with Labour Party members 1945-1950, including messages and papers referring to tours, rallies, etc.; Labour Party Committee Papers; and speeches 1945-1951 (the largest section of the papers — 24 boxes). There is also a box of papers on the 1950 and 1951 general elections. There is no pre-war material.

Attlee gave two files of his papers to Churchill College, Cambridge; these are available to researchers after written application to the Keeper of the Archives. A list is available. The first file contains an incomplete draft of Attlee's memoirs *As It Happened* (1955). The drafts include personal comments left out of the published version. There are also notes from Attlee's diaries, and notes on his local government and parliamentary careers. The second file includes some correspondence with Churchill and Lady Megan Lloyd George, as well as miscellaneous notes on, for example, the organization of the Cabinet (c. 1932), and the making of appointments (mainly ecclesiastical) by the Prime Minister (c. 1951).

Lord Moyle, Attlee's literary executor, knows of no other surviving papers. Mr Kenneth Harris, 45 Molyneux Street, London W1H 5HW, Attlee's official biographer, has been entrusted with a small collection of personal papers which will not be available for research until the biography is finished. There are eighteen box-files which include 200 letters covering the years 1913-1960 from Attlee to his elder brother, Tom, who became a conscientious objector in World War I while his brother served in Gallipoli. There are also two boxes of genealogical papers and photographs, miscellaneous correspondence with various members of the Attlee family, a box of press cuttings, six boxes of miscellaneous correspondence with old friends, constituents, and former colleagues, and two volumes of family press cuttings. The future of these papers will be decided when the biography is completed. Neither Lord Moyle nor Mr Harris knows of any diary which may have been the source for the notes referred to in paragraph 3 above. Mr Harris hopes that his biography will be published in 1975.

SIR JOHN LAWRENCE BAIRD, 2nd Bt, 1st VISCOUNT STONEHAVEN (1874-1941)

John Lawrence Baird was Conservative M.P. for Warwickshire (Rugby) 1910-1922, and Ayr Burghs 1922-1925. He was Parliamentary Under-Secretary of State for Air December 1916-January 1919, Parliamentary Secretary to the Ministry of Munitions January 1919, Parliamentary Under-Secretary of State for Home Affairs April 1919-October 1922, Minister of Transport and 1st Commissioner of Works 1922-January 1924, and Governor-General of Australia 1925-1930. He succeeded his father as second baronet in 1920, and was created G.C.M.G. and Baron Stonehaven in 1925, and Viscount Stonehaven in 1938.

Baird's son, the present (2nd) Viscount Stonehaven, informs us that he has given most of his father's papers to the National Library of Australia (ref. MS 2127). He has retained only two large volumes of press cuttings 1925-1930 and a printed diary of Baird's travels in Abyssinia 1 November 1890-31 January 1891 and 24 April-20 May 1900.

The papers in the National Library of Australia have been divided into nine series: general correspondence; royal correspondence; advice given on Baird's becoming Governor-General of Australia; correspondence on Baird's resignation as Chairman of the Conservative Party; Committee of Imperial Defence Papers; papers on the powers of governors-general; diaries; press cuttings; and miscellaneous items.

The general correspondence has been arranged chronologically; it covers the period 1899-1940, but most of the letters are dated between 1926 and 1930. The series includes congratulations on Baird's appointment as Governor-General of Australia in 1925, letters concerning Baird's journey out to Australia, and Baird's comments on Australian politics, trade unionism, and socialism. The royal correspondence 1925-1937, mainly letters from royal secretaries,

SIR JOHN LAWRENCE BAIRD (cont.)

is closed until it is 60 years old. The letters are arranged in chronological order. Subjects covered include the 1926 Imperial Conference, and the 1926 General Strike, as well as comments on most aspects of Australian life.

The advice given on Baird's becoming governor-general was given by his predecessor, Lord Forster. It ranges from dress appropriate for the governor-general to laundry. The file also includes Baird's correspondence with Forster on the arrangements for a smooth succession. The file of papers on Baird's resignation as Chairman of the Conservative Party mostly comprises letters and press cuttings dated after his resignation (3 March 1936).

The Committee of Imperial Defence papers are mostly printed papers informing the Australian Government of information received by the British Government and of the decisions reached in the light of this information. The papers on the powers of governors-general are mostly drafts or copies of cables 1926-1927 exchanged between England, Australia, and New Zealand on the diminished powers resulting from the 1926 Imperial Conference.

There are diaries for 1919 and 1941. They include voluminous notes of conversations. The press cuttings cover 1892-1940 but mostly relate to Baird's period as Governor-General. The miscellaneous papers include itineraries, seating plans, and other ephemera.

PHILIP J. NOEL-BAKER (1889-   )

Philip Noel-Baker was Labour M.P. for Coventry 1929-1931, Derby 1936-1950, and Derby (South) 1950-1970. He was Parliamentary Secretary to the Ministry of War Transport February 1942-May 1945, Minister of State at the Foreign Office August 1945-October 1946, Secretary of State for Air 1946-October 1947, Secretary of State for Commonwealth Relations 1947-February 1950, and Minister of Fuel and Power 1950-October 1951. He was awarded the Nobel Peace Prize in 1959.

Mr Noel-Baker has preserved a considerable quantity of correspondence and other papers, particularly in relation to his work for the League of Nations and the United Nations, but these papers are not at present available for research. Mr Noel-Baker has not yet made any plans for the future disposition of his papers but he himself hopes to go through them and to use them as the basis for several books.

A volume of Mr Noel-Baker's correspondence concerning the League of Nations 1918-1919 is to be found in the Public Record Office (ref. F.O. 800/249).

STANLEY BALDWIN, 1st EARL BALDWIN OF BEWDLEY (1867-1947)

Stanley Baldwin was Conservative M.P. for Worcestershire (Bewdley or West till 1918, Bewdley from 1918) 1908-1937; he took over the seat on the death of his father who had held it from 1892. Baldwin was Joint Financial Secretary to the Treasury June 1917-April 1921, President of the Board of Trade 1921-October 1922, Chancellor of the Exchequer 1922-May 1923, Prime Minister 1923-January 1924, November 1924-June 1929 and June 1935-May 1937, and Lord President of the Council August 1931-June 1935. He was created K.G. and Earl Baldwin of Bewdley in 1937.

Baldwin bequeathed 'all my political papers, memoranda and correspondence' to the Cambridge University Library (ref. Baldwin Papers 1-233). There is a 33-page *Handlist to the Political Papers of Stanley Baldwin, First Earl Baldwin of Bewdley* (1973) by A.E.B. Owen. The papers were used by G.M. Young for his *Stanley Baldwin* (1952), by Keith Middlemas and John Barnes in *Baldwin* (1969), and by H. Montgomery Hyde, in *Baldwin, The Unexpected Prime Minister* (1973).

The papers have been listed and are open to researchers. The original arrangement of the papers — partly by subject, partly chronological — has been retained. To emphasize the subject basis of the arrangement, the papers have been put into the wide divisions of Home Affairs, Empire Affairs, Foreign Affairs, Letters, Personal, Speeches, and Papers Withdrawn. This last division consists of papers marked as being the property of H.M. Government and which were set aside to be returned to the Cabinet Office. After the documents had been reviewed, it was decided that they could be retained by the Library but this decision was made too late for

STANLEY BALDWIN (cont.)

their return to their original places in the various files. Vols. 176-178 contain correspondence with the Royal Family and their secretaries. They may be consulted only after the permission of H.M.'s Private Secretary has been obtained. Application for this should be made to the Royal Librarian, Windsor Castle.

The Cambridge collection contains only Baldwin's 'political' papers. No family or personal papers are included. (The 'Personal' section contains papers referring to the running of Chequers, the Prime Minister's country home, and the presentation of freedoms and honorary degrees.) Baldwin kept no diary and rarely wrote a memorandum, or a 'political' letter, or kept a copy of those he did write. There is hardly any material before 1923. The papers mainly relate to his first two administrations; there is very little relating to his period in opposition in 1924, only a little for his period as Lord President, and no official or departmental papers 1935-1937.

Some official papers still in Baldwin's possession at his death were returned to the Cabinet Office.

The present (3rd) Earl holds his father's personal papers, including a large box of Baldwin's letters to his mother 1889-1925. These letters are not at present available for research but Lord Baldwin has quoted from them extensively in his biography *My Father: The True Story* (1955). There are also some personal political papers which are not available for research. They include letters about Baldwin's gift to the Exchequer of £125,000 in 1919, Mrs Baldwin's account of the fall of the Coalition government in October 1922, copies of letters from Baldwin to his wife on the 1931 economic crisis and the formation of the National government, letters from J.C.C. Davidson on India (April 1932), and on a luncheon with Ribbentrop, the German Ambassador (November 1933), letters about the Abdication crisis, and letters from Neville Chamberlain May-October 1940.

The 3rd Earl's own papers are of special interest to the student of Baldwin because he interviewed and corresponded with many of his father's contemporaries when he was writing his biography. He has kept the correspondence and his notes of those interviews. These notes include a draft book on Baldwin and the rearmament question 1935-1937 by Sir Harold Graham Vincent K.C.M.G., Private Secretary to the Prime Minister 1928-1936, notes of interviews with Lord Citrine, Lord Davidson, Lord Hinchingbrooke, Lord Hankey, Lord Londonderry, Sir Horace Wilson, and James Stuart. There is also a collection of press cuttings, largely reviews or extracts from books by or about Baldwin and his contemporaries.

The papers referred to by Middlemas and Barnes as the 'J.P. Boyle manuscripts' were a few personal and family letters originally in the possession of Baldwin's eldest son, the 2nd Earl Baldwin. These have now been returned to the present Earl Baldwin.

Two volumes of notes of cases reviewed under Regulation 14 (B) by the Enemy Aliens Committee in the first world war, both of which belonged to Baldwin, are to be found in the papers of J.C.C. Davidson (*q.v.*).

SIR ARTHUR JAMES BALFOUR, 1st EARL OF BALFOUR (1848-1930)

Arthur James Balfour was Conservative M.P. for Hertford 1874-1885, Manchester (East) 1885-1906, and the City of London 1906-1922. He was President of the Local Government Board June 1885-February 1886, Secretary for Scotland August 1886-March 1887, Chief Secretary for Ireland 1887-November 1891, 1st Lord of Treasury 1891-August 1892 and June 1895-December 1905, Prime Minister July 1902-December 1905, 1st Lord of the Admiralty May 1915-December 1916, Secretary of State for Foreign Affairs 1916-October 1919, and Lord President of the Council 1919-October 1922 and April 1925-June 1929. He was created K.G. in 1922 and Earl of Balfour later in the same year.

Most of Balfour's political and philosophical papers have been deposited in the British Library (ref. Add. MSS. 49683-49962). The 280 volumes of papers have been divided into the following main groups: Royal Correspondence; Correspondence with Prime Ministers; Cabinet; Committee of Imperial Defence and Foreign Affairs papers; Papers as Lord President; Home Affairs papers; Family correspondence; General correspondence; and Literary manuscripts.

SIR ARTHUR JAMES BALFOUR (cont.)

The five volumes of royal correspondence include foreign royalty and visiting heads of state. The ten volumes of correspondence with Prime Ministers include four volumes of correspondence with the 3rd Marquess of Salisbury 1872-1902 (Balfour was his nephew and private secretary 1878-1880); one volume of correspondence with W.E. Gladstone, Lord Rosebery, Sir Henry Campbell-Bannerman, H.H. Asquith and D. Lloyd George; one volume of correspondence with A. Bonar Law; and one volume of correspondence with Stanley Baldwin, J.R. MacDonald and Winston Churchill.

The Cabinet and Committee of Imperial Defence papers include two volumes of Cabinet memoranda 1896-1928, three volumes of correspondence with General Sir G. Clarke 1904-1916, three volumes of correspondence with M.P.A. Hankey 1913-1929, and three volumes of correspondence with Admiral Fisher 1902-1916. There is one volume of correspondence and papers relating to Balfour's term as First Lord. There are seven volumes of Foreign Office papers 1878-1900, and 1902-1929, including three volumes of papers on the 1918-1919 Peace Conference. There are also five volumes of correspondence with Lord Lansdowne 1881-1922.

Four volumes of papers have survived from Balfour's term as Lord President of the Council. They include much material on the establishment of the scientific research councils, particularly the Medical Research Council.

Over 70 volumes of papers have survived relating to home affairs. They include six volumes of correspondence with Sir Bernard Mallet 1891-1915 on education reform, four volumes of correspondence with George Wyndham, and two volumes of memoranda on Ireland 1887-1902.

The six volumes of Balfour's family correspondence include four volumes of the Hon. Mrs Dugdale's papers collected for her work on Balfour's biography. Balfour himself had begun his autobiography in 1928; Mrs Dugdale edited this as *Chapters of Autobiography* (1930). She later published a two-volume biography *Arthur James Balfour* (1936) which quotes extensively from the papers. Kenneth Young, *Arthur James Balfour* (1963) and Sydney H. Zebel, *Balfour* (1973) are also based on these papers.

There are 32 volumes of general correspondence 1872-1929 and 20 volumes of letter books. Balfour's literary papers include his lectures, articles, books and speeches, including the two volumes of autobiography mentioned above.

Balfour's personal papers, and some of his political papers, remain at his family home, Whittingehame, in Scotland. Subject to Lord Balfour's permission they may be seen by arrangement at the National Register of Archives (Scotland), to whom all enquiries should be sent. A preliminary list of the papers is available but the papers have not been sorted or arranged. Intending researchers should consult the list (copies of which are available at the National Register of Archives, the Institute of Historical Research, and the Scottish universities) and should specify in their applications, as accurately as possible, the items which they wish to consult.

The papers at Whittingehame cover Balfour's entire life and should clearly be used in conjunction with those in the British Library. There are papers relating to his candidature at Hertford and Manchester (East), speech notes, drafts for articles and a good deal of correspondence. The latter includes correspondence with the 3rd Marquess of Salisbury on Lord Randolph Churchill's resignation in 1887, and correspondence on Ireland and the Empire with George Wyndham, Edward Grey, and Joseph Chamberlain. There is much correspondence with his political contemporaries from the 1920s; for example, with Lloyd George and Edward Grigg on closer union between the Coalition parties; with King George V and his secretaries — including a note by Balfour of an interview with Lord Stamfordham, 21 May 1923, on Bonar Law's resignation; with Lord Derby on Anglo-French relations; and with the 4th Marquess of Salisbury and M.P.A. Hankey on cabinet proceedings when Balfour was away from London in 1929. There is also some correspondence on Zionism 1919-1923, including correspondence with Dr Weizmann, Philip Kerr, and Lord Rothschild. The collection includes some Cabinet and Committee of Imperial Defence memoranda, particularly from the latter's invasion Sub-Committee 1907-1908.

SIR ARTHUR JAMES BALFOUR (cont.)

A further small collection of Balfour's papers is available at the Public Record Office (ref. F.O. 800/199-217). The collection includes a volume of correspondence with the King and the Prime Minister 1917-1918, two volumes of papers concerning the 1917 British War Mission to the U.S.A., four volumes of miscellaneous correspondence 1917-1919, and twelve volumes of correspondence 1916-1922 arranged alphabetically by country.

Balfour's papers as Chief Secretary for Ireland have been given to the Public Record Office (ref. P.R.O. 30/60, 1-13) but they are closed to research till various dates between 1990 and 2008.

An album of letters to Balfour 1882-1893 is available in the William R. Perkins Library, Duke University. Correspondents in this album include Joseph Chamberlain, Aretas Akers-Douglas, Lord Salisbury, and the Duke of Devonshire.

The papers of John Satterfield Sandars, Balfour's private secretary 1892-1915, are in the Bodleian Library (ref. Sandars Papers); they have only recently been opened for research but they were used before Sandars's death, most notably by J.L. Garvin in his biography of Joseph Chamberlain. The collection consists of 25 boxes of correspondence and memoranda, the greater part relating to the period of Balfour's premiership. The papers are particularly voluminous for 1903; they include a very considerable amount of material on the Cabinet crisis of that year. The collection is particularly important because of the extensive responsibilities given to Sandars by Balfour. Thus many letters, sent privately to Balfour, which might be expected to be found in his papers, were, in fact, kept by Sandars. Moreover, much of Sandars's own correspondence relates to important questions of government and, after 1905, opposition policy and tactics. The collection includes letters from the King and his private secretaries to Balfour, together with copies of Balfour's Cabinet letters to the King. But the papers also reveal the extent to which the Government's dealings with the Court were delegated to Sandars himself. Sandars's contacts with the Court persisted after the Conservatives had gone into opposition. These papers demonstrate how Sandars was used by various people, especially leading Conservatives, as an indirect approach to, and a means of gauging the opinion of, Balfour himself.

GERALD WILLIAM BALFOUR, 2nd EARL OF BALFOUR (1853-1945)

Gerald Balfour was Conservative M.P. for Leeds (Central) 1885-1906. He was Chief Secretary for Ireland July 1895-November 1900, President of the Board of Trade 1900-March 1905, and President of the Local Government Board March-December 1905. He succeeded his brother as 2nd Earl of Balfour in 1930.

Most of Balfour's papers remain at Whittingehame, his family home in Scotland. Like his brother's papers and under the same conditions, they may be seen at the National Register of Archives (Scotland). The papers have not been sorted or ordered and only a preliminary list is available. As well as a few letters from constituents 1900-1906 there are many bundles of papers on Ireland. They include correspondence with Lord Cadogan, the Irish Viceroy, 1899-1905; John Atkinson, the Irish Attorney-General, 1899-1907; Sir Henry Robinson, about the Irish Local Government Board, 1898-1909, and Sir Horace Plunkett 1899-1907.

Balfour's work at the Board of Trade is represented by a long correspondence 1902-1914 with Sir Francis Hopwood mostly on departmental business but also including general political subjects, such as the memorandum of a conversation between them, 21 May 1914, on the Government's attitude towards Home Rule. Balfour's correspondents also include S. Buxton and Keir Hardie on the 1905 Unemployment Bill and Sir F. Mowatt and Sir A. Bigge on the Port of London.

Not surprisingly there are several bundles of papers on tariff reform and the split it wrought in the Conservative and Liberal Unionist alliance. There is correspondence with his brother, A.J. Balfour, some enclosing correspondence with the Duke of Devonshire, from Joseph Chamberlain, and G.J. Goschen. There are also letters from Balfour to his wife, 1905-1906, on his brother's handling of the situation, and notes by Balfour himself on various aspects of the problem.

GERALD WILLIAM BALFOUR (cont.)

Another collection of Balfour's papers was given to the Public Record Office (ref. P.R.O. 30/60). Sections 13-35 contain further papers for Balfour's term at the Irish Office but they are closed till various dates between 1990 and 2008. Sections 36-44 contain Cabinet memoranda and Confidential Print 1897-1905. There are three volumes of Board of Trade papers 1901-1905, containing correspondence, memoranda, and pamphlets and further volumes on subjects of particular interest to the Cabinet — India, the War Office and the Committee of Imperial Defence, South Africa, and the redistribution of parliamentary seats.

A further five boxes of Balfour's papers, recently discovered at Whittingehame, are being calendared by the National Register of Archives (Scotland). They contain correspondence to Balfour from his wife from the late 1890s to the 1920s. Although personal and business affairs predominate, these letters also include much political comment. Enquiries should be addressed to the National Register of Archives (Scotland).

SIR HENRY CAMPBELL-BANNERMAN (1836-1908)

Henry Campbell-Bannerman (he assumed the additional name of Bannerman in 1872) was Liberal M.P. for Stirling Burghs 1868-1908. He was Financial Secretary to the War Office November 1871-February 1874 and May 1880-May 1882, Parliamentary Secretary to the Admiralty 1882-October 1884, Chief Secretary for Ireland 1884-June 1885, Secretary of State for War February-June 1886 and August 1892-June 1895, and Prime Minister December 1905-April 1908. He was Leader of the Liberal Party in the House of Commons 1899-1908. He was created G.C.B. in 1895.

Fifty-six volumes of his papers have been deposited in the British Library and classified in two series (Add. MSS. 41206-41252, and Add. MSS. 52512-52521). Both series are now open and have been divided under the following headings: (A) Royal and special correspondence; (B) General correspondence; (C) Notes and private correspondence; (D) Journals and diaries; (E) Letters and memoranda about Campbell-Bannerman. These papers were used by J.A. Spender for *The Life of the Right Hon. Sir Henry Campbell-Bannerman, G.C.B.* (2 vols.,1923). Spender stated (p. v) that Campbell-Bannerman never wrote much, particularly later in his life. They are also extensively quoted in John Wilson, *CB, A Life of Sir Henry Campbell-Bannerman* (1973).

Campbell-Bannerman's royal correspondence in the first series of papers includes letters from Queen Victoria and her secretaries 1886-1900, and two volumes of correspondence with King Edward VII and his secretaries. The 26 volumes of special correspondence include series of letters from the 1st Marquess of Aberdeen 1886-1908, H.H. Asquith 1893-1908, James Bryce 1886-1908, the Marquess of Lincolnshire 1899-1908, Lord Crewe 1905-1908, W.E. Gladstone, H.J. Gladstone, and Sir William Harcourt. There are eleven volumes of general correspondence 1871-1908.

In section 'C' of the papers there are several notes for speeches and lectures, especially on South Africa. There is also some family correspondence 1884-1908, and his wife's correspondence 1884-1906. This section also includes Campbell-Bannerman's own letters to his cousin James Campbell 1881-1900.

Campbell-Bannerman's diaries take the form of pocket diaries for 1886-1908, excepting 1891. His journals record various tours abroad, such as his tour in Europe 1850-1851, which he described in journal-letters to his sister Louisa, and which were published, edited by John Sinclair, Lord Pentland, *Early Letters of Sir Henry Campbell-Bannerman to his Sister Louisa* (1925). Lady Campbell-Bannerman's notebooks of tours are also included in this section.

The last section of the papers — 'E' — was formed in answer to requests by Lord Pentland, Campbell-Bannerman's executor, for autograph letters from Campbell-Bannerman. Campbell-Bannerman's own letters were put in their relevant place in the preceding series but the letters to Lord Pentland and several brief memoirs about Campbell-Bannerman are included in this section.

The ten volumes of the second series include Campbell-Bannerman's drafts of his Cabinet letters to the King, as well as further correspondence with the King and his secretaries. There are many letters from Sir Edward Grey 1905-1908, Lord Elgin 1906-1908, and Winston

SIR HENRY CAMPBELL-BANNERMAN (cont.)

Churchill, as well as three further volumes of general correspondence 1892-1895. There is one volume of Campbell-Bannerman's letters to his wife 1892-1895.

SIR (CLEMENT) ANDERSON MONTAGUE-BARLOW, Bt (1868-1951)

Sir Anderson Montague-Barlow (he changed his name from Montague Barlow by deed-poll in 1946) was Conservative M.P. for Salford (South) 1910-1923. He was Parliamentary Secretary to the Ministry of Labour April 1920-October 1922, and Minister of Labour 1922-January 1924. He was created K.B.E. in 1918, and a baronet in 1924.

No papers have survived from the politically active period of Sir Anderson's life. According to Lady Montague-Barlow, Sir Anderson destroyed a good deal of his own papers before his death and she herself destroyed his letters to her after she had read them. The only papers which have survived are the diaries Sir Anderson kept on five foreign tours he made after 1924. These diaries have been placed in Rhodes House Library (ref. MSS. Brit. Emp. T. 11-15). The diaries were kept in the form of letters to his sisters which were typed and bound up with photographs, a few letters, press cuttings, and other souvenirs. The original letters do not seem to have survived. The diaries contain a great number of tourist's observations but because Sir Anderson had been in the Cabinet, and, it may have been thought, might be a member of some future Cabinet, he met many of the leading politicians and administrators of the places he visited. It is for his impressions of these people and of the political, social and economic situation of the countries he visited, that the diaries are of special interest. There are also occasional retrospective references to cabinet discussions on colonial business, such as the decision in 1923 to give political concessions to Kenya (p. 15, January-April 1927 diary): Sir Anderson denies that the Cabinet were frightened by Lord Delamere's threats of secession.

The first diary (349 pages) covers a tour mainly of India, though Iraq, Palestine, Turkey, and Greece were also visited, from December 1924 till April 1925. Sir Anderson's widow describes his political views as 'Left of Centre Conservative' and this view is borne out by his remarks on India, particularly by his fears that the new policies of Indianization would be stultified by the old type of Indian Civil Service recruit. He met many of the leading Indians of the period and recorded his opinions of them.

The second diary (82 pages) covers a tour of Malaya, Ceylon, India, and Egypt, made between September 1925 and March 1926. It is chiefly concerned with Malaya and seems in part to have been a business diary.

The third diary (222 pages) covers a trip to East Africa made from January to April 1927. Again Sir Anderson's conversations and impressions of local people and situations are recorded, including his fears of problems to come:

... the fine type of gentleman settler will make a splendid whiteman's outpost in the Federation of E. Africa, which is bound to come ... but at the present I suspect they are rather conceited and contemptuous of many things, especially of native development and restrictions from home... (p. 23)

Another trip to Tanganyika and Kenya was made from December 1927 to March 1928. The diary for this trip (100 pages) indicates that Sir Anderson was negotiating for some electoral scheme, though whether officially is not clear. He certainly met the Hilton Young Commission and discussed electoral projects and systems of land holding.

The last diary describes a trip to South America from August till November 1932. It seems to be more of a tourist's diary than the other four and includes more photographs and press cuttings.

A portrait in oils is to be presented to Sir Anderson's college, King's, Cambridge.

Sir Anderson chaired the Royal Commission on the Location of Industry, 1938. One hundred and twenty eight files of the commission's papers are available in the Public Record Office (ref. H.L.G. 27). They are incomplete but it is not known if this is the result of contemporary weeding or of damage which may have occurred in the second world war.

ALFRED BARNES (1887-   )

Alfred Barnes was Labour Cooperative M.P. for East Ham (South) 1922-1931, and 1935-1955. He was Minister of Transport August 1945-October 1951.

Mr Barnes informs us that he has never kept any papers, press cuttings, speech notes or other records. However, some of Mr Barnes's Private Office papers from the Ministry of Transport are now available at the Public Record Office (ref. M.T. 62/125-129). They include policy papers on shipping, ship-building, and road haulage.

GEORGE NICOLL BARNES (1859-1940)

George Nicoll Barnes was Labour M.P. for Glasgow (Blackfriars; Glasgow Gorbals from 1918) 1906-1922. He was Minister of Pensions December 1916-August 1917 and Minister without Portfolio 1917-January 1920. He resigned from the Labour Party in 1918 when it withdrew from the Coalition so that he might take part in the Versailles negotiations.

According to Miss Jessie Barnes, his only daughter, all Barnes's papers were lost when his Herne Hill house was bombed during the second world war. In the preface to his autobiography *From Workshop to War Cabinet* (1924 [1923]), Barnes wrote that he never kept a diary and seldom kept letters.

SIR MICHAEL EDWARD HICKS BEACH, 9th Bt, 1st EARL ST ALDWYN (1837-1916)

Michael Edward Hicks Beach was Conservative M.P. for Gloucester (East) 1864-1885, and for Bristol (West) 1885-1906. He was Parliamentary Secretary to the Poor Law Board February-August 1868, Under-Secretary of State for Home Affairs August-December 1868, Chief Secretary for Ireland February 1874-February 1878 and August 1886-March 1887, Secretary of State for the Colonies February 1878-April 1880, Chancellor of the Exchequer June 1885-February 1886 and June 1895-August 1902, and President of the Board of Trade February 1888-August 1892. He succeeded his father as 9th baronet in 1854, was created Viscount St Aldwyn in 1906, and Earl St Aldwyn in 1915.

Hicks Beach's political papers have been deposited in the Gloucestershire County Record Office (ref. D2455). These papers are described on pages 1-97 of National Register of Archives' Report 3526, which is the only list of the papers. There are papers concerning Ireland, with much material about Irish education, and the 1892 Irish Local Government Bill, as well as copies of Hicks Beach's letters to Disraeli 1874-1881. The Colonial Office papers include copies of letters to Queen Victoria 1877-1885 and correspondence with Sir Bartle Frere about South African affairs 1878-1880. There is much material concerning the Zulu wars, including correspondence with Sir Garnet Wolseley 1879. There are also a few papers from the Board of Trade and a large number of Cabinet memoranda. There are a large number of Treasury papers, mostly concerning departmental estimates, particularly the army. There is correspondence with Hicks Beach's political contemporaries including W.E. Gladstone on the Transvaal 1881, the Irish boycott campaign 1885, and the reform of procedure 1886, correspondence with Lord Randolph Churchill 1884-1890, the Duke of Devonshire 1884-1905, Joseph and Austen Chamberlain, and the 3rd Marquess of Salisbury.

Some of Hicks Beach's estate and family papers are still in the possession of his grandson, the present (2nd) Earl St Aldwyn, Williamstrip Park, Cirencester, Gloucestershire. These papers include the letters written by Hicks Beach to his wife and family on political matters which are quoted in Lady Victoria A. Hicks Beach, *Life of Sir Michael Hicks Beach, Earl St Aldwyn* (2 vols., 1932). The remaining estate and family papers have been deposited in the County Record Office (ref. D2440).

(ISAAC) LESLIE HORE-BELISHA, BARON HORE-BELISHA (1893-1957)

Leslie Hore-Belisha (he assumed the additional surname Hore in 1912 when his mother re-married) was Liberal M.P. for Plymouth (Devonport) 1923-1945 (he became a Liberal National in 1931 and a Conservative in 1945). He was Parliamentary Secretary to the Board of Trade

(ISAAC) LESLIE HORE-BELISHA (cont.)

November 1931-September 1932, Financial Secretary to the Treasury 1932-June 1934, Minister of Transport 1934-May 1937, Secretary of State for War 1937-January 1940, and Minister of National Insurance May-July 1945. He was created Baron Hore-Belisha in 1954.

Hore-Belisha left his papers to his secretary, Miss Hilda Sloane. Miss Sloane informs us that his papers are not available for research.

R.J. Minney, in *The Private Papers of Hore-Belisha* (1960), stated that Hore-Belisha kept a diary daily for most of his life, as well as notes and memoranda on particular events. At the time of his death, Hore-Belisha was preparing a volume of autobiography to justify his work at the War Office; his diaries and notes for that period formed the basis of Mr Minney's book.

FREDERICK JOHN BELLENGER (1894-1968)

Captain Frederick John Bellenger was Labour M.P. for Nottinghamshire (Bassetlaw) 1935-1968 (he had been a Conservative until 1928). He was Financial Secretary to the War Office August 1945-October 1946 and Secretary of State for War 1946-October 1947.

His eldest son, Mr R.C. Bellenger, informs us that he is unable to be of any assistance regarding his father's papers.

WILLIAM WEDGWOOD BENN, 1st VISCOUNT STANSGATE (1877-1960)

William Wedgwood Benn was Liberal M.P. for Tower Hamlets (St. George's) 1906-1918, and Leith 1918-1927. He was Labour M.P. for Aberdeen (North) 1928-1931 and for Manchester (Gorton) 1937-1941. He was Secretary of State for India June 1929-August 1931, and Secretary of State for Air July 1945-October 1946. He was created Viscount Stansgate in 1942.

Most of Wedgwood Benn's papers were destroyed in a fire during the second world war. Those which survive are very badly charred and affected by damp. They were deposited by his widow and his eldest son in the House of Lords Record Office in 1973 (ref. Stansgate Papers). As some of the papers are in such a poor physical state, the collection will not be generally available for research until it has been repaired and listed.

The papers originally filled two rooms but the largest part of them consists of a unique collection of press cuttings. From 1920 onwards — if not before — Wedgwood Benn took two copies of *The Times* in order to take cuttings. He purchased the 'Royal edition' which was printed on good quality rag paper so that his cuttings have survived in very good condition. As well as keeping the cuttings Wedgwood Benn devised a decimal subject classification. A very detailed conspexus gives an outline of the system. Thus files numbered 1050, 1051, and 10511 contain cuttings about India, the North-west Frontier, and Pakistan. Almost every subject covered by *The Times* is represented. In addition, Wedgwood Benn made collections of the speeches and comments of his political contemporaries: there are four box-files of cuttings about D. Lloyd George 1908-1933, a box-file of cuttings about H.H. Asquith 1919-1922, a box-file of cuttings about Winston Churchill 1904-1914, and boxes of cuttings of Sir Edward Grey, Lord Rosebery, Lord Salisbury, A. Bonar Law, and Hamar Greenwood amongst many others.

Only a few boxes of more personal papers have survived. They include notes and rough drafts of a few chapters of autobiography: there is a chapter on Wedgwood Benn's early life, on parliament before 1914, and on being a whip. The chapter on his early life explains the history and purpose of his filing system. After reading Arnold Bennett, Wedgwood Benn kept a precise note of how he passed his time in a 'Job Book' and on various graphs; these have survived.

Probably the single most important item in this collection is Wedgwood Benn's diary. The surviving typed fragments cover January-May 1922, 1924, 1925, and 1926. They give a detailed account of Wedgwood Benn's activities in this period and show his increasing disillusion with Lloyd George. Later diaries have also survived, including a very detailed diary as President of the Inter-Parliamentary Union 1954-1958.

As well as the diaries there are draft notes on the political situation in the 1920s and on the circumstances of Wedgwood Benn's transfer of allegiance from the Liberal to the Labour

WILLIAM WEDGWOOD BENN (cont.)

Party in 1927. A file of correspondence and notes survives from that period, including Wedgwood Benn's letter of resignation to the Leith Liberals, and letters from politicians such as Lord Oxford, Christopher Addison, Philip Snowden, and Charles Trevelyan. There is also a draft of Wedgwood Benn's letter of application for the Stewardship of the Chiltern Hundreds and the letter appointing him to that post.

Before Wedgwood Benn joined the Labour Party he had been a leader of the Radical Group of Liberal M.P.s An annotated list of 'possible' Radicals invited to a dinner in November 1925 survives, as well as some miscellaneous correspondence, a note on the purpose of the group, and a 'Report of the Activities of the Parliamentary Radical Group, Easter to August 1926', which gives the dates of lunches held, their chief guests, and the subject discussed, as well as the group's division record and notes on points raised.

A few miscellaneous letters have survived including three from C.F.G. Masterman in 1920 — in a typescript note about Masterman, Wedgwood Benn describes him as an intimate friend. Wedgwood Benn's electoral addresses from 1918, October 1922, and October 1924, have also survived.

The collection includes no papers from Wedgwood Benn's tenure of office. Small fragments concerning his tenure of the Air Office are available at the Public Record Office (ref. Air 19/551, 552); they concern the amalgamation of common services between the R.A.F., the Navy, and the Army, and the future of aircraft production.

There are carbon copies of Wedgwood Benn's diary of the first Indian Round Table Conference 1930 in the papers of the then Lord Irwin (E.F.L. Wood, *q.v.*) in the India Office Library.

SIR HENRY BUCKNALL BETTERTON, Bt, BARON RUSHCLIFFE (1872-1949)

Henry Betterton was Conservative M.P. for Nottinghamshire (Rushcliffe) 1918-1934. He was Parliamentary Secretary to the Ministry of Labour March 1923-January 1924, and November 1924-June 1929, and Minister of Labour November 1931-June 1934. He was created G.B.E. in 1941, a baronet in 1929, and Baron Rushcliffe in 1935.

Neither of Betterton's two daughters, nor the son and executor of his second wife, knows of any papers.

ANEURIN BEVAN (1897-1960)

Aneurin Bevan was Labour M.P. for Monmouthshire (Ebbw Vale) 1929-1960. He was Minister of Health August 1945-January 1951, and Minister of Labour and National Service January-April 1951.

Bevan's papers were in the possession of Mr Michael Foot M.P., while Mr Foot wrote a full-scale biography of Bevan: *Aneurin Bevan, Volume I. 1897-1945* (1962); *Aneurin Bevan, Volume II. 1945-1960* (1973). Mr Foot informs us that the papers which have survived are in great disorder and are not available for research.

ERNEST BEVIN (1881-1951)

Ernest Bevin was Labour M.P. for Wandsworth (Central) 1940-1950, and for Woolwich (East) 1950-1951. He was Minister of Labour and National Service May 1940-May 1945, Secretary of State for Foreign Affairs August 1945-March 1951, and Lord Privy Seal March-April 1951.

A small collection of Bevin's wartime papers was deposited in 1967 by his daughter, Mrs S.E.R. Wynne, in the Library of Churchill College, Cambridge (ref. Bevin papers). These papers have not yet been listed and are therefore not generally available for research. The bulk of the papers consists of an alphabetically-arranged series of files. There are 33 boxes of 'Minister's Correspondence' but the series is incomplete. Bevin's political correspondents include C.R. Attlee, Lord Beaverbrook, Brendan Bracken, and R.A. Butler. There are miscellaneous papers on various problems facing the War Cabinet, including the 1944 Education Act, and a memorandum on

ERNEST BEVIN (cont.)

long term post-war policies. There are also papers relating to Bevin's Labour Party and trade union work. The latter include some papers from the 1930s on trade union attitudes to Fascism, Russia, and the League of Nations. There are three boxes of papers on Bevin's visits and tours 1940-1941, two boxes of speech notes 1940-1944, and six boxes of press cuttings 1940-1945. A box of miscellaneous papers includes papers on post-war plans 1943, a file on the 1945 general election, and a file of notes of meetings with lobby correspondents in 1942.

Bevin's pre-1940 union papers are in the possession of the Transport and General Workers' Union but we have been unable to discover anything about these papers.

Bevin's Foreign Office papers are still in the possession of the Foreign Office. There are 37 bound volumes entitled 'Private Papers of Mr Ernest Bevin 1945-1951'. They will be transferred to the F.O.800 class in the Public Record Office in 1982, thirty years after the date of the last paper. The collection only concerns Bevin's Foreign Office work.

Alan Bullock, *The Life and Times of Ernest Bevin* (2 vols., 1960-67) is based on these papers. He asks us to state that he has no Bevin papers in his possession; the material for his biography was assembled from the organizations with which Bevin was connected and from his friends. Francis Williams, *Ernest Bevin* (1952) is largely based on Francis Williams's own notes of his conversations with Bevin 1929-1951.

AUGUSTINE BIRRELL (1850-1933)

Augustine Birrell was Liberal M.P. for Fifeshire (West) 1889-1900 and for Bristol (North) 1906-1918. He was President of the Board of Education December 1905-January 1907 and Chief Secretary for Ireland 1907-July 1916.

A small collection of Birrell's papers has been deposited by his great-nephew and literary executor, Mr J.C. Medley, Kiln Bank, Nettlebed, Oxon., in the Bodleian Library (ref. Dep. c. 299-301). Mr Medley's written permission must be sought before the papers may be read. The papers refer almost exclusively to Ireland. They include Cabinet memoranda about most aspects of Irish administration. There is a large collection of letters from Sir Mathew Nathan 1914-1916 and a miscellaneous series of letters and memoranda, including suggestions for the exclusion of Ulster from the operation of any Home Rule bill, and the problems of administering the Defence of the Realm regulations in Ireland.

A further small collection of more personal Birrell papers has been deposited by his step-son, Sir Charles Tennyson, C.M.G. in the Liverpool University Library (ref. MS. 10. 1-3). There are three albums of approximately 250 letters to Birrell and his wife 1861-1912. An index of correspondents has been compiled. As well as letters, the albums contain some press cuttings, sketches and other printed material. A copy of the 1906 Education Bill bound up with relating memoranda is also available in the library (ref. K. 1. 32). Sir Charles has also deposited a small collection of letters from Birrell to various members of his step-family (ref. 8. 2-3).

Birrell's autobiography *Things Past Redress* (1937) appears to be based on personal reminiscence and does not quote from unpublished material.

MARGARET GRACE BONDFIELD (1873-1953)

Margaret Bondfield was Labour M.P. for Northampton 1923-1924, and Wallsend 1926-1931. She was Parliamentary Secretary to the Ministry of Labour January-November 1924, and Minister of Labour (the first woman Cabinet Minister) June 1929-August 1931.

We have been unable to trace any of Miss Bondfield's papers. She died unmarried, leaving her estate to the daughters of her sister, Mrs Harriet Farrant, and of her brother George Henry Bondfield. Mr D.A. Kershaw, one of Miss Bondfield's executors, did not know of the existence of any papers and informed us that another of the executors, Miss Florence Audrey Farrant, a niece of Miss Bondfield, was dead. Administration of Miss Farrant's estate was granted to her widowed sister, Mrs Doris Margaret Knight, but we have not been able to contact Mrs Knight.

In her autobiography *A life's work* (1941) Miss Bondfield quoted frequently from letters and diaries.

SIR ARTHUR SACKVILLE TREVOR GRIFFITH-BOSCAWEN (1865-1946)

Arthur Griffith-Boscawen was Conservative M.P. for Kent (Tunbridge) 1892-1906, Dudley 1910-1921, and Somerset (Taunton) 1921-1922. He was Parliamentary Secretary to the Ministry of Pensions December 1916-January 1919, Parliamentary Secretary to the Ministry of Agriculture and Fisheries 1919-February 1921, Minister of Agriculture and Fisheries 1921-October 1922, and Minister of Health 1922-March 1923. He was knighted in 1911.

A small file of his papers was given by his widow to the Bodleian Library (ref. MS. Eng. hist. c.396, ff 88-139). Most of the papers date from 1922; they shed much light on the break-up of the Coalition government and on the feelings of the Conservatives working with Lloyd George. These papers are not quoted in Griffith-Boscawen's *Fourteen Years in Parliament* (1907) or *Memories* (1925).

The papers include a collection of six letters dated 10-19 October 1922 relating to Griffith-Boscawen's threatened resignation. In his original letter to Austen Chamberlain (dated 10 October), Griffith-Boscawen emphasized that he was resigning over the lack of governmental action on agriculture. At first he was restrained by the critical state of the Conservative Party, but eventually he felt forced to resign by the feeling in the party of alienation from the Coalition, despite his loyalty to Austen Chamberlain: '. . . I should have to support the Party against any individuals'. Griffith-Boscawen wrote a four page memorandum on 'the Break Up of the Coalition — the Story of a Wonderful Week'. He also prepared a five page, undated, memorandum on policy for the new Bonar Law government.

Other papers are concerned with the Turkish crisis of September-October 1922. There are letters from Griffith-Boscawen to Curzon and Austen Chamberlain protesting that hostilities were being threatened before diplomacy had had a chance to do its job. Curzon's reply thanks Griffith-Boscawen for his support. Griffith-Boscawen had also protested that Ministers who returned to London in September had been bewildered by the attitude of Ministers who had been present during the summer. There are two letters from M.P.A. Hankey, Secretary to the Cabinet, dated 2 and 7 November 1922, which state that there had been no delegation of powers by the Cabinet to a Conference of Ministers during the summer, but that these Conferences had been called to advise the Ministers concerned in the crisis. Hankey listed the Cabinet Meetings and conferences of Ministers which had considered the crisis.

The only other document is a seven page memorandum by Griffith-Boscawen entitled 'Inland Transport After the War'. It is dated 21 February 1943.

JOHN THEODORE CUTHBERT MOORE-BRABAZON, 1st BARON BRABAZON OF TARA (1884-1964)

John Moore-Brabazon was Conservative M.P. for Rochester (Chatham) 1918-1929, and Wallasey 1931-1942. He was Parliamentary Secretary to the Ministry of Transport October 1923-January 1924, November 1924-January 1927, Minister of Transport October 1940-May 1941, and Minister of Aircraft Production 1941-February 1942. He was created G.B.E. in 1953, and Baron Brabazon of Tara in 1942.

Moore-Brabazon's papers have been deposited in the Royal Air Force Museum. They are being listed (March 1974) and are not yet available for research. They cover the period 1906-1964. They include material concerning different aspects of aviation including Moore-Brabazon's periods in office, and some political material: some papers on the General Strike, Moore-Brabazon's constituency, and some House of Lords speeches, as well as personal and sporting papers.

Moore-Brabazon's autobiography *The Brabazon Story* (1956) does not appear to quote from any papers.

BRENDAN RENDALL BRACKEN, VISCOUNT BRACKEN (1901-1958)

Brendan Bracken was Conservative M.P. for Paddington (North) 1929-1945, and Bournemouth (Bournemouth East from February 1950) 1945-1951. He was Minister of Information July 1941-May 1945, and 1st Lord of the Admiralty May-August 1945. He was created Viscount Bracken in 1952.

Mr Charles Lysaght, who is currently writing a biography of Bracken, informs us that Bracken systematically destroyed his papers during his life and that any remnants were destroyed, after his death, by his chauffeur. Bracken's books on English literary and political history were bequeathed to Sedbergh School.

WILLIAM CLIVE BRIDGEMAN, 1st VISCOUNT BRIDGEMAN (1864-1935)

William Bridgeman was Conservative M.P. for Shropshire (Oswestry) 1906-1929. He was Parliamentary Secretary to the Ministry of Labour December 1916-January 1919, Parliamentary Secretary to the Board of Trade 1919-August 1920, Parliamentary Secretary to the Board of Trade for the Mines Department 1920-October 1922, Secretary of State for Home Affairs 1922-January 1924, and 1st Lord of the Admiralty November 1924-June 1929. He was created Viscount Bridgeman in 1929.

Bridgeman's papers are in the possession of his son, the present (2nd) Viscount Bridgeman, Leigh Manor, Minsterley, Salop. Listing of the papers is not yet complete and they are consequently not generally open for research; however, a xerox copy has been made of most of Bridgeman's diary (a discontinuous series of notes on political events which covers the years 1906-1935). This, if available, will be lent to researchers on application to Lord Bridgeman and payment of a £5 deposit.

Salop County Record Office have a small collection of printed election papers for 1906, 1910, and 1924, and xerox copies of letters from Bridgeman to his third son, Maurice 1923-1935 (ref. S.R.O. 2225/1-40).

(WILLIAM) ST JOHN (FREMANTLE) BRODRICK, 1st EARL OF MIDLETON (1856-1942)

St John Brodrick was Conservative M.P. for Surrey (West) 1880-1885, and Surrey (South West or Guildford) 1885-1906. He was Financial Secretary to the War Office August 1886-August 1892, Under-Secretary of State for War July 1895-October 1898, Under-Secretary of State for Foreign Affairs 1898-November 1900, Secretary of State for War November 1900-October 1903, and Secretary of State for India 1903-December 1905. He succeeded his father as 9th Viscount Midleton in 1907 and was created K.P. in 1915, and Earl of Midleton in 1920.

For those interested in Brodrick's political and official career, the most important collection of his papers was deposited in the Public Record Office in 1967 by his daughter, Lady Moira Loyd (ref. P.R.O. 30/67). The class list of this collection has been published in the List and Index Society, vol. 70 *Public Record Office Gifts and Deposits. Supplementary List* (1971). A personal name index of correspondents and those mentioned in the papers has been compiled. The collection has been divided into two parts: papers concerning Brodrick's political career (P.R.O. 30/67, 1-26) and papers concerning his interest in Ireland (P.R.O. 30/67, 27-57).

Brodrick's political career is represented by papers from his term as Financial Secretary to the War Office. There are letters and minutes 1885-1891, including a challenge to a duel from T.M. Healy in 1893. There are also papers from Brodrick's term as Under-Secretary of State at the War and Foreign Offices including correspondence on the Boer War and the Boxer Rebellion. Brodrick's papers as Secretary of State for War include correspondence on the conduct of the Boer War and the subsequent reorganization of the War Office, and correspondence with the Sovereign November 1900-October 1903. The papers relating to Brodrick's term as Secretary of State for India include correspondence with Lords Kitchener and Roberts, and papers concerning the dispute between Lord Curzon and Lord Kitchener. In addition there are a few miscellaneous papers, including memoranda on Haldane as Secretary of State for War, Lloyd George as an arbitrator, and on the maladministration of the War Office by Kitchener as Secretary of State.

ST JOHN BRODRICK (cont.)

Brodrick was one of the most important English landowners in Ireland and a leader of the Southern Irish Unionists. His Irish papers cover Sinn Fein, the Easter Rebellion, and later attempts to solve England's Irish problem. There are working papers of the Irish Convention, including printed papers, correspondence (including letters from Lloyd George), and a memorandum of an interview with the War Cabinet in 1918. There are papers concerning the split in the Southern Unionists, the offer to Brodrick of the viceroyalty in 1918, and the 1920-1922 negotiations. There is also later correspondence about this period with historians, including Denis Gwynn.

None of Brodrick's papers were left to his son, the present (2nd) Earl of Midleton, but some were bequeathed to his second wife. Lord Midleton referred us to the family solicitors, Warrens, 34 John Street, London W.C.1, for further information. The only papers Warrens now have concerning Brodrick fill a tin trunk. The papers mostly relate to the marriage settlement of Brodrick and his daughter, and to personal financial and legal affairs.

Twenty boxes of estate papers from Warrens have been deposited in the Guildford Muniment Room (ref. 145). They range from the fifteenth to the twentieth century but they mostly date from the eighteenth and nineteenth centuries. They relate chiefly to the family's Surrey estates though there is material relating to Irish estates. A summary list of the collection has been made and a copy deposited in the National Register of Archives. The collection contains nothing relating to Brodrick's political career or personal life except for a few letters on estate and personal business. Researchers wishing to look at this collection should make an appointment to visit the Muniment Room.

Papers concerning the Brodricks' Irish estates and earlier members of the Brodrick family were purchased by the National Library of Ireland in 1954 (ref. MS. 8899). A description of them can be seen in R.J. Hayes, *Manuscript Sources for the History of Irish Civilisation* (Boston, Mass., 1965), iii, pp. 377-378.

Another small collection (one volume) of Brodrick's papers was purchased at Sotheby's in 1969 by the William R. Perkins Library, Duke University (ref. Midleton papers). There are 88 letters 1890-1933 probably collected for their autographs. They include letters from H.H. Asquith on his parliamentary election defeat (1919) and on his opinion of the Kaiser's memoirs (1922). There are nine letters from Joseph Chamberlain including one giving Chamberlain's views on tariff reforms (1903). There are eleven letters from Lord Cromer 1900-1905; a letter from Lord Grey of Fallodon on Lloyd George's conduct of foreign affairs in 1922; and eleven letters from Lord Rosebery 1890-1916.

Six volumes of Brodrick's correspondence with Lord Curzon as Secretary of State for India 1903-1906 have been deposited in the British Library (ref. Add. MSS. 50072-50077).

Brodrick's memoirs, Lord Midleton, *Records and Reactions 1856-1939* (1939) quote from letters and memoranda, including his own reports to King Edward VII on post-Boer War army reform. In May 1926 Brodrick wrote his version of the events leading up to Lord Curzon's removal from the viceroyalty in 1905, an account which was checked by the India Office, approved by A.J. Balfour, Prime Minister 1902-1905, and then printed as a State Paper. This account is available in the India Office Library (ref. MSS. Eur. B.189).

(ALFRED) ERNEST BROWN (1881-1962)

Ernest Brown was Liberal M.P. for Warwickshire (Rugby) 1923-1924 and Leith 1927-1945 (he was a Liberal National from 1931). He was Parliamentary Secretary to the Ministry of Health November 1931-September 1932, Secretary of the Mines Department 1932-June 1935, Minister of Labour (Labour and National Service from September 1939) 1935-May 1940, Secretary of State for Scotland 1940-February 1941, Minister of Health 1941-November 1943, Chancellor of the Duchy of Lancaster 1943-May 1945, and Minister of Aircraft Production May-July 1945.

We have been unable to trace any of Brown's papers. There were no children of his marriage. His executor, Mr C.R. Saunders, informs us that Brown requested that his papers be destroyed after his death, and, to the best of Mr Saunders's knowledge, this request was carried out. Brown gave a collection of eight cartoons to the Mayor of Torquay in 1961; they are now housed in the Torre Abbey Mansion.

GEORGE ALFRED BROWN, BARON GEORGE-BROWN (1914-   )

George Brown (he changed his surname to George-Brown in 1970 when he was created a life peer) was Labour M.P. for Derbyshire (Belper) 1945-1970. He was joint Parliamentary Secretary to the Ministry of Agriculture and Fisheries October 1947-April 1951, Minister of Works April-October 1951, 1st Secretary of State and Secretary of State for Economic Affairs October 1964-August 1966, and Secretary of State for Foreign Affairs 1966-March 1968. He was created Baron George-Brown (a life peerage) in 1970.

Lord George-Brown informs us that he brought no papers away from office and that his private papers are not available for research. He has recently published his memoirs *In My Way* (1971).

ALEXANDER HUGH BRUCE, 6th BARON BALFOUR OF BURLEIGH (1849-1921)

Alexander Hugh Bruce became the 6th Baron Balfour of Burleigh in 1869, when the act of attainder on his family was removed. He was created K.T. in 1901. He was a representative peer for Scotland 1876-1921. He was Parliamentary Secretary to the Board of Trade January 1889-August 1892, and Secretary for Scotland June 1895-October 1903.

Bruce's papers are in the possession of his grandson, the present (8th) Lord Balfour of Burleigh. They are being listed by the National Register of Archives (Scotland). Arrangements can be made for them to be seen at the Scottish Record Office. All enquiries about access to the papers should be addressed to the National Register of Archives (Scotland) (ref. MSS. *penes*), giving as much notice as is possible. See *Addenda*, p. 166, for further details of this collection.

VICTOR ALEXANDER BRUCE, 9th EARL OF ELGIN and 13th EARL OF KINCARDINE (1849-1917)

Victor Alexander Bruce, Lord Bruce from 1849 till he succeeded his father as 9th and 13th Earl in 1863, was Viceroy of India 1894-1898, and Secretary of State for the Colonies December 1905-April 1908. He was created K.G. in 1899.

Most of Bruce's papers are in the possession of his grandson, the present (11th and 15th) Lord Elgin and Kincardine, Broomhall, Dunfermline, Scotland. We were not able to examine them because they are being microfilmed by Queen's College, Kingston, Ontario, Canada. The papers, which cover most of Bruce's life, were used and are frequently quoted in Ronald Hyam, *Elgin and Churchill at the Colonial Office* (1968).

Bruce's papers as Viceroy of India were deposited in the India Office Library in 1956 by the 10th Lord Elgin (ref. MSS. Eur. F.84). There are 73 volumes of correspondence, including printed copies of correspondence with the Queen 1894-1898, originals and printed copies (with and index) of correspondence and telegrams with the Secretary of State, and correspondence with persons in England and in India. There are seven volumes of press cuttings. The collection also includes 44 volumes of Bruce's private secretary's correspondence, and sixteen volumes of miscellaneous papers and photographs.

JAMES BRYCE, VISCOUNT BRYCE (1838-1922)

James Bryce was Liberal M.P. for Tower Hamlets 1880-1885, and Aberdeen (South) 1885-1906. He was Under-Secretary of State for Foreign Affairs February-May 1886, Chancellor of the Duchy of Lancaster August 1892-March 1894, President of the Board of Trade 1894-June 1895 and Chief Secretary for Ireland December 1905-January 1907. He was British Ambassador to the United States 1907-1913. He was created G.C.V.O. in 1917, and Viscount Bryce in 1914.

Bryce's family gave his papers concerning Irish affairs to the National Library of Ireland (ref. 11,009-11,016). This collection includes approximately 1,000 documents dated 1878-1921 but most of the letters, memoranda etc. are from 1906, and relate to the 1907 Irish Council Bill. The main correspondent is Sir Anthony MacDonnell.

JAMES BRYCE (cont.)

The remainder of Bryce's papers were given to the Bodleian Library, Oxford (ref. Bryce papers). The papers were given in two parts; the first part has been catalogued in great detail, the second is uncatalogued but a brief list has been compiled. Both parts have been divided into American (that is, papers connected with Bryce's associations with the United States) and English papers. The catalogue of the first part is available at the National Register of Archives, list no. 6716.

The American papers include correspondence, embassy papers, and papers connected with the publication of Bryce's *The American Commonwealth* (3 vols., 1888). Series of correspondence with particular individuals, arranged alphabetically, are followed by miscellaneous correspondence arranged chronologically.

The English papers are also divided into correspondence with particular individuals, and miscellaneous correspondence. Bryce's English correspondents include Lord Acton, W.E. Gladstone, A.V. Dicey, G.O. Trevelyan, Sir Henry Campbell-Bannerman, H.H. Asquith, and other members of the post-1906 Liberal Cabinet. The second part of English papers includes political papers on Bryce's elections, and his constituency work. There are also three boxes of papers from his tenure of the Duchy of Lancaster, one box from the Board of Trade, and three boxes from the Irish Office, as well as boxes of printed papers. This part also includes some of Bryce's family's papers: the papers of his father, Dr James Bryce, and the papers of his wife, including Bryce's letters to her 1889-1903. There are also papers relating to Bryce's literary activities: manuscripts of articles, speeches, and books, as well as correspondence, agreements, and accounts with publishers. There are a few legal papers and briefs 1879-1919. Bryce's diaries for 1858-1859, 1875 and 1897 have also survived.

A further collection of Bryce's papers was purchased by the Bodleian Library in 1974 (ref. MSS. Addit. Bryce). The papers (mostly letters) will be arranged chronologically under their recipients. There are about 1000 letters, as well as pamphlets, photographs, and miscellanea, which cover Bryce's whole life. There are letters concerning his family, his education, and his legal career. There are letters about Ireland, and a large number of letters about the U.S.A., concerning Bryce's general interests, as well as his diplomatic career.

H.A.L. Fisher's biography, *James Bryce* (2 vols., 1927), quotes extensively from these papers and also from letters and recollections given him by Bryce's friends. Edmund Ions, *Bryce and American Democracy 1870-1922* (1968) is chiefly based on the Bodleian collection.

A further small collection of Bryce's papers has been deposited in the Public Record Office (ref. F.O. 800/331-335). It consists of four volumes of correspondence 1904-1921, and population maps of Hungary.

GEORGE BUCHANAN (1890-1955)

George Buchanan was Labour M.P. for Glasgow (Gorbals) 1922-1948. He was Joint Parliamentary Under-Secretary of State for Scottish Affairs August 1945-October 1947, and Minister of Pensions 1947-July 1948.

Buchanan's brother, Dr J.A. Buchanan, informs us that he has no papers belonging to Buchanan and that he could not suggest anyone else whom we might contact. Thus the small collection of papers, mainly relating to Buchanan's early life and personal affairs, that was used by R.K. Middlemas in *The Clydesiders* (1965), does not appear to have survived.

SIR STANLEY OWEN BUCKMASTER, 1st VISCOUNT BUCKMASTER (1861-1934)

Stanley Owen Buckmaster was Liberal M.P. for Cambridge 1906-1910, and Yorkshire (Keighley) 1911-1915. He was Solicitor-General October 1913-May 1915, and Lord Chancellor 1915-December 1916. He was knighted in 1913, created G.C.V.O. in 1930, Baron Buckmaster in 1915, and Viscount Buckmaster in 1933.

SIR STANLEY OWEN BUCKMASTER (cont.)

Buckmaster's papers are in the possession of his grandson, Mr H.D. Miller, 22 Milner Street, London S.W.7. They are mainly in the form of letters covering most of his life.

Buckmaster's daughter, the Hon. Mrs Barbara Miller, had intended to write a biography and she sorted the letters chronologically; the letters for each year have been put in a large envelope, and a list of contents, which includes the name of the correspondent and the subject of the letter, was sometimes written on the outside. Mrs Miller also began the compilation of a notebook on the events in Buckmaster's life and advertised in *The Times* for letters and recollections; a few replies are kept with Buckmaster's papers.

Most of the letters are 'political', though there are a few letters to his wife and daughter. The letters for 1914 include a typed note written in October 1914, justifying Buckmaster's activities as Press Censor in relation to Winston Churchill's trip to Antwerp, and copies of correspondence between Buckmaster and Edward Marsh, Churchill's secretary. There is also a memorandum justifying the suppression of the *Morning Post*'s references (18 January 1915) to the loss of the *Formidable*. Among the letters of congratulation written to Buckmaster in 1915 is a copy of his own letter to his predecessor as Lord Chancellor, Lord Haldane, expressing regret at the 'spite' which had led to Haldane's dismissal. There are no letters referring to the fall of Asquith's coalition government. There is, however, a typed memorandum, written by Buckmaster in January 1917, on those events; this is extensively quoted in R.F.V. Heuston, *Lives of the Lord Chancellors 1885-1940* (Oxford, 1964) as are many of the letters. The bundle of correspondence for 1917 includes a memorandum by Buckmaster on '. . . whether Asquith should come back . . .' which describes a meeting held by Asquith, Buckmaster, Samuel, McKenna, and Runciman (c. 21 February 1918) to discuss this question. There is also a memorandum for Asquith on war aims. The letters for 1918 include one from Austen Chamberlain on why he had joined the Government, and a letter from Buckmaster to Harcourt describing Asquith's state of mind (22 April 1918).

Apart from the correspondence, there are other papers representing many facets of Buckmaster's life. There are school reports, and examination papers; Oxford battels and receipts; several printed election addresses; a book of press cuttings; pamphlets on birth control; evidence given before the Coal Mining inquiry of 1924; notes of privy council judgements 1928-1930. There is also some correspondence of his father, J.C. Buckmaster.

EDWARD LESLIE BURGIN (1887-1945)

Edward Leslie Burgin was Liberal M.P. for Bedfordshire (Luton) 1929-1945 (he was a Liberal National from 1931). He was Parliamentary Secretary to the Board of Trade September 1932-May 1937, Minister of Transport 1937-April 1939, and Minister of Supply July 1939-May 1940.

A very small collection of papers survives in the possession of his widow, Mrs D. Burgin, 20 Amenbury Lane, Harpenden, Herts. Most of the papers which have survived concern a goodwill speaking-tour which Burgin undertook to America in 1944. There are draft speeches, memoranda, photographs, and press cuttings. There is a small collection of correspondence, mostly letters of sympathy to Burgin's widow, though also including six letters from Lord Simon, a close friend of Burgin. The beginnings of an autobiography, written during Burgin's last illness, have also survived.

JOHN ELLIOT BURNS (1858-1943)

John Burns was 'independent labour' M.P. for Battersea 1892-1895, and Liberal M.P. for the same constituency 1895-1918. He was President of the Local Government Board December 1905-February 1914, and President of the Board of Trade February-August 1914.

Burns died intestate and it seems clear that, in the confusion which followed his death, a large number of his papers were destroyed, many of them in the wartime salvage drives. A detailed account of what happened is to be found in a pamphlet by Mrs Y. Kapp 'John Burns's Library', *Our History*, pamphlet 16, Winter 1959. Nonetheless a large collection of Burns's papers was retrieved and presented to the British Library by his family in 1946 (ref. Add. MSS. 46281-46345). The collection comprises 65 volumes which were divided into six

JOHN ELLIOT BURNS (cont.)

main divisions: (A) royal correspondence; (B) special correspondence; (C) general correspondence; (D) speeches and memoranda; (E) diaries; (F) miscellaneous.

The single volume of royal correspondence includes letters from secretaries as well as various members of the royal family. The special correspondence includes series of correspondence from H.H. Asquith, D. Lloyd George, Winston Churchill, and J.R. MacDonald. There is an interesting series of letters from John Morley which includes a memorandum written by Burns about Morley in 1925. There is also correspondence reflecting Burns's trade union and labour activities, including letters from Keir Hardie and Robert Blatchford. There are seventeen volumes of general correspondence. An index has been compiled for the correspondence divisions.

The speeches and memoranda division includes Burns's press contributions and what may be drafts and notes for an autobiography. There are also some miscellaneous notes in diary form 1888-1928. There are 33 volumes of diary for 1888-1920. The miscellaneous division includes Burns's various diplomas and his autograph collection.

A further, small, uncatalogued collection of Burns's papers was purchased in 1971 by the Battersea District Library. They formed part of a collection of material on London made by Ernest Tyrrell. It is thought that Tyrrell, in his turn, acquired them from Burns's own library. Certainly Burns collected such material. As well as miscellaneous pamphlets, press cuttings, printed invitations, and a small notebook of names, addresses and expenditure, there is a bundle of 50 letters mostly from the period 1890-1912 but also including some letters from 1938 connected with Burns's work as a Trustee of the National Library of Wales. The letters are very miscellaneous in character: cases of injustice, etc., brought to Burns's attention; comments on speeches; Local Government Board private notices; invitations. There is a letter from James Bryce, then at the Local Government Board, dated 29 June 1894, asking for Burns's opinion on how to settle strikes; letters from Lord Thring 1895, on the use of prison labour; a letter from Sir Charles Dilke 24 June 1899 asking for Burns's cooperation in putting questions on labour and employment to Balfour in the debate on Home Office Estimates; several letters 1902-1912 from Frederick Rogers, organizing secretary of the National Committee of Organized Labour, and other members of his executive, asking for help in their campaign for Old Age Pensions.

The Battersea District Library also has a small collection of Burns's *memorabilia* lent by a Mrs Fuller. As well as ceremonial scrolls and keys, there is a collection of pamphlets by Burns, his 1895 election address, some press cuttings, and several photographs including one of his study at 106 Lavender Hill, and a press cutting of Burns and Morley leaving 10 Downing Street after their last Cabinet meeting.

Burns's family gave a large collection of his books on working-class history to his union, now the Amalgamated Union of Engineering Workers; these are housed in the library of the Trades Union Congress, Congress House, Great Russell Street, London WC1B 3LS. As Burns appears to have kept many of his papers inside related books, a small collection of his papers is also to be found there. There are 25 manilla envelopes containing a very miscellaneous collection of papers. The papers include receipts, photographs, and programmes for various ceremonial events, but the bulk of the papers are press cuttings 1894-1910, including cuttings on particular subjects such as the poor law and poverty. Rough notes by Burns include this comment on memoirs: 'I have read nearly all the memoirs, diaries, recollections, and revelations of the post-war period, and have found few worth remembrance, or even recognition . . .'

Burns's library on London was purchased by Lord Southwood for the London County Council in 1943. It is now part of the Greater London Council Library (Room 114) and is available for research. Burns's collection of prints and maps forms part of the Greater London Council's Map and Print Collection. Six box-files of Burns's papers are available in the Greater London Record Office (Room B.66). The collection is not catalogued but it mainly comprises pamphlets, press cuttings, copies and reports of speeches; none of the items dates from before 1888.

JOHN ELLIOT BURNS (cont.)

A further collection of 100 letters to Burns was purchased in 1972 by the Library of the California State University at Northridge (ref. DA 530 A3 C6 Special Collections). These papers were purchased from the estate of the late Dona Torr, the Marxist historian. Many of the letters concern Burns's pre-1914 activities, including a visit to Australia in 1903, and his correspondence with Australian labour leaders.

William Kent, *John Burns: Labour's Lost Leader* (1950) is based on the papers in the British Library and makes extensive quotations from them.

RICHARD AUSTEN BUTLER, BARON BUTLER OF SAFFRON WALDEN (1902-   )

Richard Austen Butler was Conservative M.P. for Essex (Saffron Walden) 1929-1965. He was Parliamentary Under-Secretary of State for India September 1932-May 1937, Parliamentary Secretary to the Ministry of Labour 1937-February 1938, Under-Secretary of State for Foreign Affairs 1938-July 1941, President of the Board and Minister of Education 1941-May 1945, Minister of Labour May-July 1945, Chancellor of the Exchequer October 1951-December 1955, Lord Privy Seal 1955-October 1959, Secretary of State for Home Affairs January 1957-July 1962, 1st Secretary of State and Deputy Prime Minister 1962-October 1963, and Secretary of State for Foreign Affairs 1963-October 1964. He was created K.G. in 1971, and Baron Butler of Saffron Walden (a life peerage) in 1965.

Lord Butler has arranged that, on his death, his papers will go to the Wren Library, Trinity College, Cambridge, where access will be controlled by trustees. At the moment his papers are completely closed for research. Lord Butler has quoted from his papers in his memoirs *The Art of the Possible* (1971).

NOEL EDWARD NOEL-BUXTON, 1st BARON NOEL-BUXTON (1869-1948)

Noel Buxton (he assumed the surname of Noel-Buxton prior to becoming a peer in 1930) was Liberal M.P. for the North Riding of Yorkshire (Whitby) 1905-1906 and Norfolk (North) 1910-1918; he was Labour M.P. for Norfolk (North) 1922-1930. He was Minister of Agriculture and Fisheries January-November 1924 and June 1929-June 1930. He was created Baron Noel-Buxton in 1930.

Buxton's son, the present (2nd) Lord Noel-Buxton, informs us that his father's papers are in the possession of his sister, the Hon. Mrs J.G. Hogg, Old Broad Oak, Brenchley, nr Tonbridge, Kent. Only a small collection, mainly of press cuttings, survives. There are seven books of cuttings on the electoral activities of various members of the Buxton family 1847-1910 (including Lady Noel-Buxton's electoral addresses 1918-1931), on the Balkans 1903-1907, on the passage of the 1911 Parliament Act, on the first Labour government (including a note from M.P.A. Hankey on the procedure for taking the oath of Privy Councillor), on the 1929 election, the second Labour government and Buxton's resignation because of ill-health, and on Norwich M.P.s 1937-1938. In addition, there is a small collection of letters from Buxton's Liberal contemporaries in 1915 on the Balkans (apart from a life-long interest in the Balkans, Buxton was sent to there to try to secure Balkan adherence to the Allied cause in 1914). There is also a file of papers on Buxton's wife's 1931 election campaign — notes of expenses, speeches, meetings, model answers, questionnaires, and some correspondence.

A second collection is in the William R. Perkins Library, Duke University. This collection was purchased from a dealer but Lord Noel-Buxton tells us that he does not know how the papers came to leave his family's possession. The Duke collection (ref. Noel-Buxton papers) consists of about 1000 miscellaneous letters 1896-1944. Buxton's correspondents include his brother, C.R. Buxton, and other members of his family, as well as many political colleagues. There is also a collection of press cuttings 1905-1944, particularly concerning Buxton's by-election at Whitby in 1905, the Balkans, women's suffrage, temperance; and some miscellaneous speech notes. There is a short description of this collection in the *National Union Catalog, Manuscript Collections, 1968* (Washington D.C., 1969), entry no. 1586.

A further collection is in the possession of Professor H.N. Fieldhouse, c/o the Principal's Office, Administration Building, McGill University, Montreal, P.Q., Canada. Part of this

NOEL EDWARD NOEL-BUXTON (cont.)

collection was purchased from a dealer and, again, Lord Noel-Buxton did not know how the papers had left his possession; the remainder were given to Professor Fieldhouse by Lord Noel-Buxton. Professor Fieldhouse is happy to allow access to the papers. The collection contains substantial amounts of material on the Balkans and the Balkan Committee 1896-1943, the Anti-Slavery Society, particularly in relation to Ethiopia 1932-1945, attempts to secure a 'peace without victory' 1916-1917, and attempts to secure a negotiated peace with Germany 1939-1942. There is also material on the pre-1914 Liberal Foreign Affairs Group, various peace movements between the wars, and colonial problems. The collection also contains some of Buxton's wife's papers, mainly on the Labour Party and domestic policy.

Mosa Anderson, *Noel Buxton, A Life* (1952) is based on the papers and quotes from autobiographical notes and reminiscences. Professor Fieldhouse hopes to edit these notes for publication. T.P. Conwell-Evans, *Foreign Policy from a Back Bench 1904-1918* (1932) also quotes fully from the papers, including a diary for 1914-1915.

SYDNEY CHARLES BUXTON, EARL BUXTON (1853-1934)

Sydney Buxton was Liberal M.P. for Peterborough 1883-1885, and for Tower Hamlets (Poplar) 1886-1914. He was Under-Secretary of State for Colonial Affairs August 1892-June 1895, Postmaster-General December 1905-February 1910, President of the Board of Trade 1910-February 1914, and Governor-General of the Union of South Africa 1914-1920. He was created G.C.M.G and Viscount Buxton in 1914, and Earl Buxton in 1920.

A large collection of Buxton's papers (they fill a large cupboard) is in the possession of his grand-daughter, Mrs E. Clay, Newtimber Place, Hassocks, Sussex, but these papers will not be generally available until a biography of Buxton has been written.

The bulk of the papers relates to Buxton's official career. There are 50 folders, beginning with Buxton's work for the London Schools Board 1876-1882, and including the 1886-1889 Royal Commission on Education, the 1889 Conciliation Committee for the dock strike, and his terms of office at the Colonial Office, the Post Office, and the Board of Trade. Buxton seems to have kept a large number of departmental and Cabinet papers, as well as correspondence with civil servants. There is a subject file for each month of his term of office at the Board of Trade.

In addition to these subject files there is a large collection of correspondence, much of it arranged chronologically. Some of the earlier correspondence refers to Buxton's work on the 1889 Conciliation Committee. There are letters from Campbell-Bannerman and Haldane in 1900 on party disunity, letters on fiscal policy 1904, and letters on various aspects of Buxton's official work, for example, a letter from Lloyd George in 1910 congratulating Buxton on his handling of a coal dispute in South Wales. There is a long series of letters (about 80) from Lord Ripon, Buxton's chief at the Colonial Office 1892-1895. They cover the years 1893-1909 but most of them are from the period 1893-1895 and they are in fact semi-official letters on Colonial Office daily business. Possibly of greatest interest are the letters from Buxton's friends during the period when Buxton was Governor-General of the Union of South Africa. Many of his friends wrote about the English political situation and the progress of the war. There is a series of letters from Sir Charles Hobhouse 1914-1916 and a large number of letters from Sir Edward Grey 1888-1932. Grey's letters are disappointingly sparse in political commentary, except for the period in 1924 when the problem of Grey's succession as Liberal Leader in the House of Lords was being discussed. There is also a file of letters from Sir George Barnes, mainly written in 1915, with detailed accounts of the progress of the war and the political situation.

Most of the papers relating to Buxton's term as Governor-General of South Africa fill a separate trunk. They have been arranged in approximately 25 folders and include some miscellaneous letters 1892-1913 and some relating to Buxton's term at the Colonial Office. The most important section of these South African papers contains fourteen files arranged chronologically and includes Buxton's correspondence with successive Colonial Secretaries, Asquith, the King's Secretaries, as well as officials and South African politicians such as Botha and Smuts. There is also a collection of press cuttings on Buxton's governor-generalship and three volumes of letters from his second wife to her mother.

SYDNEY CHARLES BUXTON (cont.)

In addition to these papers there are several volumes of press cuttings 1878-1888, 1896-1908, a volume of cuttings on the 1889 strike, two volumes of articles and pamphlets by Buxton, and a volume of reviews of these publications.

A testimonial album, presented to Buxton in March 1912 in commemoration of his 25 years as M.P. for Poplar, was donated to the Borough of Poplar in 1957. It is now part of the Tower Hamlets Local History Collection (item no. 60), which is housed in the Tower Hamlets Central Library.

GEORGE HENRY CADOGAN, 5th EARL CADOGAN (1840-1915)

George Henry Cadogan, known as Viscount Chelsea from 1864 until 1873, when he succeeded his father as 5th Earl Cadogan, was Conservative M.P. for Bath 1873. He was Under-Secretary of State for War May 1875-March 1878, Under-Secretary of State for the Colonies 1878-April 1880, Lord Privy Seal August 1886-August 1892, and Lord Lieutenant of Ireland (with a seat in the Cabinet) June 1895-August 1902. He was created K.G. in 1891.

About 1750 letters survive in the possession of Cadogan's grandson, the present (7th) Earl Cadogan, 28A Cadogan Square, London S.W.1. Many other papers were destroyed by a fire. This collection has been listed by the Historical Manuscripts Commission. A note about the contents of the collection appears in *Royal Commission on Historical Manuscripts. Report of the Secretary to the Commissioners 1970-1971* (1971), pp. 46-50.

There are very few letters in the collection covering Cadogan's early career, apart from his election campaign at Bath in 1873. The bulk of the letters dates from 1895-1900 and includes drafts of out-letters as well as memoranda. The letters reflect very fully the problems of Cadogan's term of office as Lord Lieutenant. They also include a series of letters from the Prince of Wales (with whom Cadogan was very friendly), and from Queen Victoria.

FREDERICK ARCHIBALD VAUGHAN CAMPBELL, 3rd EARL CAWDOR (1847-1911)

Frederick Archibald Vaughan Campbell, known as Viscount Emlyn from 1860 until 1898, when he succeeded his father as 3rd Earl Cawdor, was Conservative M.P. for Carmarthenshire 1874-1885. He was 1st Lord of the Admiralty March-December 1905.

Over 800 boxes of Cawdor family papers have been deposited in the Carmarthenshire County Record Office (ref. Cawdor papers). The collection mainly comprises family estate papers of the seventeenth to nineteenth centuries but it does include six boxes of papers relating to Campbell's political career (Cawdor 293-298). These boxes include correspondence with members of the Cabinet, the Admiralty Board, and officials in the Admiralty. There are Admiralty reports on coaling stations, submarines, Australian Naval Forces, and other subjects. There are three notebooks and various committee papers. There are also Cabinet memoranda. Cawdor 251 contains a notebook relating to some of Campbell's work as a director of the Great Western Railway (he was Chairman 1895-1905): there are notes on the costs of newspaper advertisements, a coal strike in South Wales, telegraph clerks, wages, and the costs of building locomotives.

A further bound volume of Campbell's papers — mostly printed official documents — is deposited in the Ministry of Defence Library (Navy) (ref. Cawdor papers).

SIR ARCHIBALD BOYD BOYD-CARPENTER (1873-1937)

Archibald Boyd-Carpenter was Conservative M.P. for Bradford (North) 1918-1923, Coventry 1924-1929, and Surrey (Chertsey) 1931-1937. He was Parliamentary Secretary to the Ministry of Labour November 1922-March 1923, Financial Secretary to the Treasury March-May 1923, Paymaster-General 1923-January 1924, Financial Secretary to the Admiralty May 1923-January 1924. He was knighted in 1926.

His son, Lord Boyd-Carpenter, knows of no papers.

CHARLES ROBERT WYNN-CARRINGTON, 3rd BARON CARRINGTON, MARQUESS OF LINCOLNSHIRE (1843-1928)

Charles Robert Carrington (he obtained a royal licence to spell his surname with only one 'r' in 1880, but assumed the surname Wynn-Carrington in 1896) was Liberal M.P. for Wycombe 1865-1868. He was Governor of New South Wales 1885-1890, President of the Board of Agriculture and Fisheries December 1905-October 1911, and Lord Privy Seal 1911-February 1912. He succeeded his father as 3rd Baron Carrington in 1868, and was created G.C.M.G. in 1886, K.G. in 1906, Earl Carrington in 1895, and Marquess of Lincolnshire in 1912.

His grandson, Brigadier A.W.A. Llewellen Palmer, D.S.O., M.C., of the Manor House, Great Somerford, Chippenham, Wilts., has a very large collection of his papers. They were very carefully sorted by Carrington's daughter, Lady Alexandra Palmer, in 1935. These papers have been microfilmed by the Bodleian Library (ref. MSS. Film 1097-1153) and the National Library of Australia. Written application to see the microfilm of the papers in the Bodleian should be made to Brigadier Llewellen Palmer.

Possibly the most important items in the papers are Carrington's diaries. They cover the period 1877-1928. The entries vary in length and detail. Carrington himself used the diaries as the basis for volumes of unpublished memoirs: three volumes on *King Edward VII as I knew Him 1855-1910*, two volumes on *Lord Rosebery .. 1878-1912*, and a volume of general recollections. The first-mentioned were used by Sir Sidney Lee for his biography of the king. The volumes also include press cuttings, menu cards, photographs, and transcripts of correspondence.

There are no official papers from Carrington's terms of office, but the collection includes a trunk of papers concerning his term of office as Governor of New South Wales. There are bundles of letters from fellow Governors — Lords Carnarvon, Hopetoun, Kintore, Loch, and Onslow — as well as correspondence from Australian politicians and officials, in particular several bundles of letters (1877-1894) from Sir Henry Parkes, Premier of New South Wales. There are manuscript and printed chapters by Carrington on the different aspects of his governorship, including the problems of Australian Federation and Chinese labour, and many notes for speeches, volumes of press cuttings and presentation volumes on his departure from Sydney. There are also a few official files and some correspondence with the Colonial Office.

Carrington was on close terms with King Edward VII and with other members of the Royal Family. A considerable correspondence reflects this relationship. In some transcripts of this correspondence, the individuals mentioned are identified, for example, in the transcripts of letters from the Prince of Wales to Carrington 1880-1885. As well as correspondence, there are scrapbooks and photograph albums, for example from the 1875-1876 Indian tour of the Prince, and from Carrington's mission in 1901 announcing the death of Queen Victoria in the capital cities of Europe. The latter includes Carrington's draft reports to both the King and to Lord Lansdowne. Carrington's relations with the court were strengthened by his position as Lord Great Chamberlain. There are several volumes relating to the coronation and funeral of King Edward VII, the marriage of the then Duke of York and Princess Mary of Teck, the coronation of King George V, and the investiture of the Prince of Wales. The volumes include not only press cuttings and souvenirs, but also Carrington's reminiscences, seating plans, rehearsal plans, and so forth. Telegrams from Queen Victoria for the period when Carrington was Lord Chamberlain of the Household have also survived.

There is much correspondence, both originals and transcripts. The bulk of it is arranged in alphabetical order. In particular there are two volumes of transcripts of some 'political' letters, letters of congratulation on being made a privy councillor, a cabinet minister, and an earl, as well as congratulations on the birth of his son, and on his 80th birthday. There are transcripts of Carrington's letters to his wife 1879-1918 and other family correspondence. The collection also includes letters of condolence on the death of Carrington's son, Viscount Wendover, after the battle of Cambrai. There are press cuttings and a memorial book, as well as Wendover's letters from the front.

In addition to various domestic papers, such as a list of Carrington's wedding guests and their gifts, invitation, engagement, and visitors' books, hunting diaries, game and stud books, valuations of family plate and porcelain, the collection includes some papers of other

CHARLES ROBERT WYNN-CARRINGTON (cont.)

members of the Carrington family: Lady Carrington's diaries and engagement books, letters to her from ladies-in-waiting to both Queen Alexandra and Queen Mary (Lady Carrington herself was a Lady-in-waiting to Queen Alexandra), and also letters from her daughter Victoria, who was a Woman of the Bedchamber to Queen Mary. There are also some papers of Carrington's younger brother William, who was equerry to Queen Victoria 1881-1901, and to King Edward VII 1902-1910, papers of his grandfather, the first Baron Carrington, and some papers of his mother. There are also some of Lady Alexandra Palmer's papers connected with the winding up of her mother's estate — including an inventory of the house contents.

The Mitchell Library, Sydney, holds a bound printed volume of contemporary notes by Carrington on Sir Henry Parkes's Federation Scheme 1889-1890 (ref. ML. 0342.901). The volume is in two parts. The first covers the period 15 June-29 November 1899 (23pp.); the second covers the period 31 December 1889-24 February 1890 (12 pp.). Both parts are headed 'Most Strictly Confidential'.

SIR EDWARD HENRY CARSON, BARON CARSON (1854-1935)

Edward Carson was Unionist M.P. for Dublin University 1892-1918 and for Belfast (Duncairn) 1918-1921. He was Irish Solicitor-General 1892, Solicitor-General May 1900-December 1905, Attorney-General May-November 1915, 1st Lord of the Admiralty December 1916-July 1917, and Minister without Portfolio 1917-January 1918. He was knighted in 1900, and created Baron Carson (a judicial life peerage) in 1921.

Many of Carson's papers were lost in the blitz so that, for example, nothing remains relating to his legal career. Such papers as survived, some 3000 documents, were purchased by the Public Record Office of Northern Ireland in 1962 (ref. D.1507). A description of the papers is to be found in Appendix C of the *Report of the Deputy Keeper of the Records for the years 1960-1965*, cmd. 521 (Belfast, 1968), pp. 189-190. A full catalogue of the papers has been made. The papers have been divided into five sections: 1. Correspondence 1896-1937 including seven separate series of Lady Carson's correspondence 1909-1949, and correspondence with Edward Marjoribanks and Ian Colvin, Carson's biographers, as well as reactions from various individuals after the volumes were published; 2. Cabinet papers, printed memoranda, etc., 1915-1917; 3. Ireland 1915-1923, including memoranda and correspondence on Home Rule, the Ulster Volunteer Force, and the 1921 settlement; 4. Admiralty papers 1916-1917 with some 200 subject files; 5. Miscellaneous. The collection also includes ten volumes of Lady Carson's diaries 1909-1949 (D. 1507/1/6/1-10).

Carson's son, the Hon. Edward Carson, informs us that he has retained none of his father's papers, but that he has placed them all in the Public Record Office of Northern Ireland.

Edward Marjoribanks and Ian Colvin, *The Life of Lord Carson* (3 vols., 1932-36) and H. Montgomery Hyde, *Carson, The Life of Sir Edward Carson, Lord Carson of Duncairn* (1953) were both based on Carson's papers and quote from them.

RICHARD GARDINER CASEY, BARON CASEY (1890-   )

Richard Casey, an Australian diplomat and Cabinet Minister, was Minister of State Resident in the Middle East and a member of the War Cabinet March 1942-December 1943, Governor of Bengal 1944-1946, and Governor-General of Australia 1965-1969. He was created G.C.M.G. in 1965, K.G. in 1969, and Baron Casey (a life peerage) in 1960.

Lord Casey informs us that he has preserved a large number of papers relating to his career, including a diary kept for many years, his correspondence, bound files of his public statements, and volumes of press cuttings.

The papers are not generally available for research, but several books have been based on them. A study of Lord Casey's father and grandfather, *Australian Father and Son* (1966), draws on voluminous family papers as well as Lord Casey's own recollections. There are some autobiographical passages relating to his period as Governor of Bengal in *An Australian in India* (1947). A fuller account of Lord Casey's wartime career, drawing on diaries containing 'over 700,000 words', is in *Personal Experience 1939-1946* (1962).

RICHARD GARDINER CASEY (cont.)

Lord Casey's period as Australian Minister for External Affairs is covered by *Australian Foreign Minister, the Diaries of R.G. Casey 1951-60*, ed. T.B. Millar (1972). The editor explains in his preface that Casey's diary was 'his personal account of the day's events, those with which he was concerned and other happenings of importance or interest, dictated each day either to a Secretary or into a recording machine to be typed out later. For the period ... 26 April 1951 to 22 January 1960, his total diary entries come to well over a million words'.

In 1967, Lord Casey presented a bound photocopy of his diaries as Governor of Bengal to the India Office Library (ref. Photo. Eur. 48). It will not be available for research until 1977.

RICHARD KNIGHT CAUSTON, BARON SOUTHWARK (1843-1929)

Richard Knight Causton was Liberal M.P. for Colchester 1880-1885 and for Southwark (West) 1888-1910. He was Paymaster-General December 1905-February 1910. He was created Baron Southwark in 1910.

We have been unable to trace any of Causton's papers. Causton left all his estate to his widow who died in 1931; there were no children by the marriage. We have contacted three of Causton's great-nephews (Mr J.W.F. Causton, Mr G.L.C.Elliston, and Mr E.E.N. Causton) but none of them knows of the existence of any papers or what might have become of the papers. Lady Southwark, in *Social and Political Reminiscences* (1913), did not quote from any papers but described her husband's electoral campaigns and their social and political life. Lady Southwark left all her estate to her sister, Miss Evelyn Fanny Chambers. Miss Chambers died in 1946; she divided her estate between three of her nieces and appointed one, Miss Kathleen Evelyn Chambers, as her sole executrix. We have not been able to trace Miss K.E. Chambers. The solicitors who acted for her were not able to give us a more recent address than 1948.

SIR GEORGE CAVE, VISCOUNT CAVE (1856-1928)

George Cave was Conservative M.P. for Surrey (Kingston) 1906-1918. He was Solicitor-General November 1915-December 1916, Secretary of State for Home Affairs 1916-January 1919, and Lord Chancellor October 1922-January 1924 and November 1924-March 1928. He was knighted in 1915, and created G.C.M.G. in 1920, and Viscount Cave in 1919.

Sir Charles Mallet, *Lord Cave. A Memoir* (1931), was based on Cave's papers then in the possession of his widow, and quoted frequently from the papers. Unfortunately some at least of these papers have been destroyed. Cave's niece, Mrs Margaret Story, informs us that many were burnt after Cave's death by his brother when he was clearing out Cave's home. Neither Mrs Story nor Cave's secretary, Mr R.W. Bankes, knows of the existence of any papers.

A large wooden box of papers (of which Mrs Story knew nothing) was deposited in the British Library by Cave's widow in 1932; but the papers are closed until 1982 (ref. Reserved Manuscripts 35).

SPENCER COMPTON CAVENDISH, 8th DUKE OF DEVONSHIRE (1833-1908)

Spencer Compton Cavendish, known as Lord Cavendish 1834-1858, and as the Marquess of Hartington from 1858 until he succeeded his father as 8th Duke in 1891, was Liberal M.P. for Lancashire (North) 1857-1868, Radnor 1869-1880, Lancashire (North-East) 1880-1885, and North Lancashire (Rossendale) 1885-1891. He became a Liberal Unionist in 1885 and joined in a coalition government with the Conservatives 1895-1903. He was Under-Secretary of State for War April 1863-February 1866, Secretary of State for War February-July 1866 and December 1882-June 1885, Postmaster-General December 1868-January 1871, Chief Secretary for Ireland 1871-February 1874, Secretary of State for India April 1880-December 1882, and Lord President of the Council June 1895-October 1903. He was asked to form a government three times — in 1880 and twice in 1886 — but refused. He was created K.G. in 1892.

A large collection of his correspondence is in the possession of the present (11th) Duke of Devonshire. Applications to read the papers should be made to the Keeper of the Devonshire

SPENCER COMPTON CAVENDISH (cont.)

Collections, Chatsworth, Bakewell, Derbyshire DE4 1PN. Nearly 4000 letters have survived. They have been arranged in chronological order except for letters from John Tilly at the Post Office 1868-1871, letters from Ireland 1870-1874, Lord Ripon's letter from India 1880-1883, 54 letters from Cavendish to the Duchess of Manchester, whom he later married, 1873-1887, and 110 letters from Sir Henry James 1886-1908. The calendar of the series, which exists in manuscript only at Chatsworth, gives an indication of the contents of each letter. The letters cover most of Cavendish's political career and his correspondents include the prominent politicians of his day.

Some of Cavendish's papers as Secretary of State for India are in the India Office Library (ref. MSS. Eur. D.604). They are not listed. The collection includes bound volumes of telegrams exchanged between Cavendish and the Viceroy April 1880-December 1882, and six boxes of printed Cabinet papers 1880-1885. Some of the latter are not included in the *List of Cabinet Papers 1880-1914* (Public Record Office Handbook no. 4) (1964). Very few of the Cabinet papers concern Indian affairs.

Bernard Holland, *The Life of Spencer Compton, 8th Duke of Devonshire* (2 vols., 1911), was based on Cavendish's papers and quotes extensively from letters and other documents.

VICTOR CHRISTIAN WILLIAM CAVENDISH, 9th DUKE OF DEVONSHIRE (1868-1938)

Victor Christian William Cavendish was Liberal Unionist M.P. for Derbyshire (West) 1891-1908. He was Financial Secretary to the Treasury October 1903-December 1905, Civil Lord of the Admiralty June 1915-July 1916, Governor-General of Canada 1916-1921, and Secretary of State for the Colonies October 1922-January 1924. He succeeded his uncle as 9th Duke of Devonshire in 1908. He was created G.C.V.O. in 1912, and K.G. in 1916.

A small collection of Cavendish's papers, mainly concerning the period when he was Governor-General of Canada, is in the possession of his grandson, the present (11th) Duke of Devonshire. Applications to read the papers should be made to the Keeper of the Devonshire Collections, Chatsworth, Bakewell, Derbyshire DE4 1PN. The papers have not been listed.

SIR FREDERICK CAWLEY, 1st Bt, 1st BARON CAWLEY (1850-1937)

Frederick Cawley was Liberal M.P. for South-East Lancashire (Prestwich) 1895-1918. He was Chancellor of the Duchy of Lancaster December 1916-February 1918. He was created a baronet in 1906 and Baron Cawley in 1918.

A small collection of his papers is in the possession of his grandson, the present (3rd) Baron Cawley, Openwood, Bagshot Road, Worplesdon, Guildford.

The collection is almost entirely composed of press cuttings, leaflets, and posters of Cawley's several election campaigns. There is nothing concerning his tenure of the Duchy. One of the earliest cuttings is from 1895; it describes Cawley's adoption meeting, and reports his speech giving his attitude to the topics of the day: he was in favour of Irish Home Rule, Welsh Disestablishment, various electoral reforms, abolition of the Lords' veto, and an eight-hour day for the miners.

The 1900 general election produced a spate of leaflets accusing Cawley of being pro-Boer; apart from his criticism of Chamberlain he had sent £20 to a peace committee, which, his opponents claimed, helped to harden the Boers' attitude. In retaliation Cawley published a silk handkerchief depicting himself and his four sons, all in uniform, to show his contribution to the war. The same type of electioneering tactic is revealed in the 1905 campaign. There is a full collection of cuttings about Cawley's opponent, W.T. Hedges, as well as posters accusing Cawley of aiming to close public houses at 9 pm and Cawley's emphatical denial. There is also a list of the questions Cawley was asked at different meetings. The list is analysed: out of 295 questions, 63 (the largest group) were described as 'Non Political'; 27 (the second largest) were asked on the fiscal question; 27 on working-class legislation; 26 on the land; and 21 on electoral and parliamentary reform. There are a few cuttings about the 1918 election campaign when his son, Harold, succeeded him in the seat.

SIR FREDERICK CAWLEY (cont.)

Two letters from Frederick Guest in February 1918 deal with Cawley's resignation from the government in order to make way for Lord Beaverbrook. A different version, in which his resignation is related to 'ill-health', is given in an undated 1000-word typescript note about Cawley's career. Though it is written in the third person, this document appears to have been written by Cawley himself.

(EDGAR ALGERNON) ROBERT GASCOYNE-CECIL, VISCOUNT CECIL OF CHELWOOD (1864-1958)

Robert Cecil (he became Lord Robert Cecil in 1868 when his father became 3rd Marquess of Salisbury) was Conservative M.P. for Marylebone (East) 1906-1910, and Independent Conservative M.P. for Hertfordshire (Hitchin) 1911-1923. He was Parliamentary Under-Secretary of State for Foreign Affairs December 1916-January 1919, Minister of Blockade December 1916-July 1918, Lord Privy Seal May 1923-January 1924, and Chancellor of the Duchy of Lancaster November 1924-October 1927. He was created Viscount Cecil of Chelwood in 1923.

Cecil himself presented 134 volumes of his papers to the British Library in 1954 (ref. Add. MSS. 51071-51204). The papers have been divided into three main groups: special correspondence; general correspondence; and literary papers.

Cecil's special correspondents (Add. MSS. 51071-51157) include A.J. Balfour 1906-1929, Sir Arthur Steel-Maitland 1911-1921, Sir Austen Chamberlain 1918-1936, and Cecil's brother, the 4th Marquess of Salisbury, 1906-1943. A volume of memoranda about the 1907 Education Bill and another volume of general political memoranda are also included in this division of the papers. The special correspondence section includes some official correspondence on foreign affairs 1915-1934. There are two volumes of Cabinet minutes 1917-1927, Foreign Office memoranda 1915-1918, and telegrams 1918-1930. Cecil's League of Nations papers are also included in this section — he was in charge of League of Nations' business as Lord Privy Seal and Chancellor of the Duchy. There are eight volumes of League papers, including minutes of League meetings, papers concerning the 1927 Naval Disarmament conference and some memoranda produced by the League of Nations Union 1930-1944. Cecil's diaries for the period 1917-1937, largely concerning his work for the League, are included in this division.

The general correspondence (Add. MSS. 51158-51192A, B) is arranged chronologically. The literary papers (Add. MSS. 51193-51204) are mainly correspondence concerning the publication of Cecil's numerous writings. Cecil published two volumes of memoirs, *A Great Experiment* (1941), and *All the Way* (1949), both of which quote from his papers. The former includes Cecil's '. . . Memorandum on Proposals for Diminishing the Occasion of Future Wars' (written in 1916, though not circulated to the Cabinet until 17 April 1917).

Four volumes of Cecil's miscellaneous Foreign Office correspondence 1915-1919 are available at the Public Record Office (ref. F.O. 800/195-198).

A further collection of some twenty boxes of Cecil's papers is in the possession of the present (6th) Lord Salisbury (ref. CHE 1-105). The collection includes correspondence, notes for speeches, memoranda, and articles by Cecil, mostly concerning League of Nations and international affairs 1876-1965. There are also family and personal letters, some of which are not available for research. The remainder of the papers in this collection will only be made available for research when they are at least fifty years old. Written application should be made to the Librarian, Hatfield House, Hatfield, Herts., stating the nature of the research being undertaken. Permission to read the papers is only granted on the condition that all references to or extracts from the papers will be submitted to Lord Salisbury for his permission to publish. No photographic reproduction of the papers is allowed. At the present time the strong rooms at Hatfield House are being reorganized and no access at all is being granted to any of the manuscripts there. It is hoped that the reorganization will be completed by the summer of 1974.

JAMES EDWARD HUBERT GASCOYNE-CECIL,
4th MARQUESS OF SALISBURY (1861-1947)

James Edward Hubert Gascoyne-Cecil, Viscount Cranborne 1868-1903, was Conservative M.P. for North-East Lancashire (Darwen) 1885-1892 and for Rochester 1893-1903. He was Under-Secretary of State for Foreign Affairs November 1900-October 1903, Lord Privy Seal 1903-December 1905 and November 1924-June 1929, President of the Board of Trade March-December 1905, Chancellor of the Duchy of Lancaster October 1922-May 1923, and Lord President of the Council October 1922-January 1924. He succeeded his father as 4th Marquess of Salisbury in 1903. He was created G.C.V.O. in 1909, and K.G. in 1917.

Cecil's papers are in the possession of his grandson, the present (6th) Marquess of Salisbury. They will not be made available for research until the collection is catalogued — a process which will take at least two more years. Papers will then be released subject to a fifty year rule. The collection has been arranged chronologically within such major divisions as General Correspondence, Private Family Correspondence, Estate Papers, and some subject divisions such as India, and Honours. The General Correspondence 1889-1947 is probably the most important part of the collection. Applications, stating the reason for wishing to read these papers, should be made in writing to the Librarian, Hatfield House, Hatfield, Herts. Access will be granted on the condition that any reference to or quotation from the papers may only be made after Lord Salisbury's permission has been obtained.

ROBERT ARTHUR JAMES GASCOYNE-CECIL,
5th MARQUESS OF SALISBURY (1893-1972)

Robert Arthur James Gascoyne-Cecil, Viscount Cranborne 1903-1947, was created K.G. in 1946, and Baron Cecil of Essendon in 1941; he succeeded his father as 5th Marquess in 1947. He was Conservative M.P. for Dorset (South) 1929-1941. He was Parliamentary Under-Secretary of State for Foreign Affairs August 1935-February 1938, Paymaster-General May-October 1940, Secretary of State for Dominion Affairs 1940-February 1942 and September 1943-July 1945, Secretary of State for Colonial Affairs February-November 1942, Lord Privy Seal November 1942-September 1943 and October 1951-May 1952, Secretary of State for Commonwealth Relations May-November 1952, Lord President of the Council 1952-January 1957, and Acting Secretary of State for Foreign Affairs June-October 1953.

Cecil's papers are completely closed for research at present and no date for opening them is yet envisaged. None of his papers will be made available until they are 50 years old.

One volume of miscellaneous general correspondence 1935-1938, from Cecil's work at the Foreign Office, is available in the Public Record Office (ref. F.O. 800/296).

ROBERT ARTHUR TALBOT GASCOYNE-CECIL,
3rd MARQUESS OF SALISBURY (1830-1903)

Lord Robert Arthur Talbot Gascoyne-Cecil, known as Viscount Cranborne from 1865 till he succeeded his father as 3rd Marquess in 1868, was Conservative M.P. for Stamford 1853-1868. He was Secretary of State for India July 1866-March 1867 and February 1874-April 1878, Secretary of State for Foreign Affairs 1878-April 1880, June 1885-January 1886, January 1887-August 1892, and June 1895-October 1900, Prime Minister June 1885-January 1886, July 1886-August 1892, June 1895-July 1902, and Lord Privy Seal October 1900-July 1902. He was created K.G. in 1878.

Cecil's papers have been deposited in the Library of Christ Church, Oxford. Permission to use the papers must be obtained from the Governing Body of Christ Church and is only granted on acceptance of the condition that all reference to or extracts from the papers shall be submitted to the present Marquess for his permission to publish. No photographic reproduction of the papers is allowed. The papers will be returned to the present (6th) Lord Salisbury in 1974. Written application should then be made to the Librarian, Hatfield House, Hatfield, Herts., stating the nature of the research being undertaken. Permission to read the papers is only granted on the same condition which applied when the papers were at Christ Church.

34

ROBERT ARTHUR TALBOT GASCOYNE-CECIL (cont.)

Cecil's papers have been divided into 27 classes, each of which is identified by a letter of the alphabet, and which fall into the following groups: (A) Foreign Office papers; (B) Cabinet papers; (C) letter books and copies of letters from Cecil; (D) twenty volumes of copies of letters from Cecil collected by Lady Gwendolen Cecil; (E-L) special correspondence; (M-Z) miscellaneous correspondence; (AA) Cinque Port papers; (BB) dinners, receptions etc.; and (CC) papers collected by Lady Gwendolen Cecil, including summaries and extracts from Cecil's articles for the *Quarterly Review*.

As would be expected, one of the largest groups is the Foreign Office papers. There are 140 volumes, a two-volume calendar of which has been produced and distributed by the National Register of Archives. Another major group is the special correspondence which fills 217 boxes. The main series of this correspondence (174 boxes) is arranged alphabetically by correspondent but there are also twenty volumes of correspondence with the royal family and its household, three volumes of foreign correspondence, seven volumes of ecclesiastical correspondence, three volumes of university correspondence, two volumes of Great Eastern Railway correspondence, and eight volumes of household and estate papers. This group of special correspondence is probably the most interesting for English political history. A card index of persons has been compiled.

Cecil's period at the India Office is represented by four letter-books (C/1-4) and four boxes of papers (Q). A microfilm copy of some of these papers is available at the India Office Library (ref. I.O.L. Reels 805-822).

The miscellaneous correspondence has been divided into the following subgroups: 47 boxes of miscellaneous political correspondence 1866-1903 (M); 32 boxes of household, estate and county correspondence 1852, 1862, 1866-1903 (N); 35 boxes of personal correspondence 1852, 1860-1903 (O); one bundle of papers concerning Cecil's constituency work at Stamford 1855-1868 (P); three boxes of papers connected with the Great Eastern Railway mainly 1868-1870 (R); three boxes of papers concerning universities 1869-1903 (S); five boxes of papers concerning Conservative Associations 1882-1888 (T); six boxes of papers concerning ecclesiastical preferment (V); papers about parliamentary bills (W); deputations (W); honours (Y); and Lord Lieutenants (Z).

The Library is adding to the collection made by Lady Gwendolen Cecil of copies of letters by Cecil and arranging them chronologically (C). The twenty volumes of copies collected by Lady Gwendolen (D) have been arranged alphabetically by correspondent. None of the copies is later than 1892. An index of correspondents has been compiled. Lady Gwendolen Cecil, *Life of Robert, Marquess of Salisbury* (4 vols., 1921-32) quotes from many of these papers but Lady Gwendolen deliberately excluded any work on the official papers.

(ARTHUR) NEVILLE CHAMBERLAIN (1869-1940)

Neville Chamberlain was Conservative M.P. for Birmingham (Ladywood) 1918-1929 and Birmingham (Edgbaston) 1929-1940. He was Postmaster-General October 1922-March 1923, Paymaster-General February-March 1923, Minister of Health March-August 1923, November 1924-June 1929, and August-November 1931, Chancellor of the Exchequer August 1923-January 1924 and November 1931-May 1937, Prime Minister 1937-May 1940, and Lord President of the Council May-November 1940.

A large collection of Chamberlain's papers has been deposited by his family in the Birmingham University Library (ref. Neville Chamberlain papers) but these papers are closed to research. It is hoped to be able to open them at the end of 1974 but no definite date has yet been set. These papers are frequently quoted in Keith Feiling, *Life of Neville Chamberlain* (1946, reissued 1970) and Iain Macleod, *Neville Chamberlain* (1961). A new biography based on the papers is being written by Professor David Dilks of Leeds University and Mr A.J. Beattie of the London School of Economics. The biographers hope that one volume of biography and one volume of extracts from the papers will be published by Eyre Methuen by 1974-1975.

(ARTHUR) NEVILLE CHAMBERLAIN (cont.)

Perhaps the outstanding items in Chamberlain's papers are his political diaries 1913-1940. There are also many diaries or journals of visits abroad, for example to India 1904-1905. As well as 33 boxes of miscellaneous correspondence 1910-1940, there is a great deal of family correspondence — not only letters to Neville but his letters to his brother Austen 1915-1936, his sister 1891-1940, his wife 1911-1938, and his children 1927-1939.

The collection includes various papers relating to Joseph Chamberlain: his birth and death certificates; some early family letters; letters of condolence on the death of his first wife in 1875; and various printed papers. There are also 128 letters from Neville to Joseph Chamberlain 1890-1914 and 36 from Joseph to Neville 1891-1904. There is correspondence to and from J.L. Garvin 1928-1934 concerning his biography of Joseph Chamberlain, and correspondence between Neville Chamberlain and Sir Charles Petrie 1938-1939 concerning the latter's *The Chamberlain Tradition* (1938).

Apart from these diaries and correspondence, notes of speeches and broadcasts, and 41 boxes of press cuttings, the various stages of Chamberlain's life are well represented in other ways. There are several papers — including a diary, correspondence and accounts — from Chamberlain's attempt to work a sisal plantation in the Bahamas. Chamberlain's municipal activities are well represented: as well as correspondence about the city's hospital, bank, and university, there are papers concerning Chamberlain's election as mayor 1916-1917, the local Unionist Association, and Chamberlain's parliamentary elections, as well as constituency correspondence from the 1920s.

Chamberlain's official career at national level began in December 1916 when he was appointed director-general of the National Service Department. General correspondence, printed papers, and some letters of congratulation on his appointment and commiseration on his resignation have survived. Chamberlain's tenure of the Ministry of Health is amply represented by eleven bound volumes of the acts for which he was responsible and the speeches he made in their support which were presented by the Ministry's officials in June 1929. The volumes include the 1925 Widows, Orphans and Old Age Contributory Pensions Bill, the 1925 Rating and Valuation Bill, and the 1928 Local Government Bill.

Chamberlain's terms of office as Chancellor of the Exchequer are represented by congratulations on his appointment in 1923, tables on defence expenditure 1920-1934, papers on the 1931 financial crisis, and letters of congratulation on various budgets or particular bills. There are also files on more general political issues such as correspondence 1930-1931 with Stanley Baldwin concerning Baldwin's conduct of the party, on Conservative party matters 1935-1940, correspondence with Winston Churchill 1927-1940, on the 1931 political settlement, and on King Edward VIII's abdication.

Very little seems to have survived from Chamberlain's tenure of the premiership but that little is of great importance. There is a note by Chamberlain of his discussions with Hitler at Berchtesgaden in 1938, notes by Sir Horace Wilson of the same event, and a notebook of conversations between Hitler and Chamberlain in September 1938. Details of Chamberlain's itinerary and drafts of the messages Chamberlain sent to Hitler and Mussolini have also survived, and there are papers relating to Chamberlain's visits to Paris in 1938 and Italy in 1939. There is correspondence relating to the rumours about Chamberlain's shares in armaments firms 1939-1940, the resignation of Leslie Hore-Belisha in 1940, and notes for the Norway debate in May 1940. There are guest lists and lunch books for 10 Downing Street 1937-1940, and many letters of congratulation in 1937 and of support 1938-1940.

The collection also includes Mrs Neville Chamberlain's papers. There is some miscellaneous correspondence 1916-1955, diaries for 1940, correspondence concerning various charities and functions, and correspondence 1941-1946 with Keith Feiling concerning his biography. Obituary notices, and papers concerning Chamberlain's funeral and will, complete the collection.

JOSEPH CHAMBERLAIN (1836-1914)

Joseph Chamberlain was Liberal M.P. for Birmingham (Birmingham West from 1885) 1876-1886; he became a Liberal Unionist in 1886 and held the seat till his death. He was President of the Board of Trade May 1880-June 1885, President of the Local Government Board February-March 1886, and Secretary of State for the Colonies June 1895-October 1903.

A large collection of Chamberlain's papers has been deposited in the University of Birmingham Library (ref. Joseph Chamberlain papers). A list of the papers is available. Applications to see the papers should be made in writing to the Rare Books Librarian and should enclose a character reference. The collection covers most aspects of Chamberlain's political career. There are family papers, including Chamberlain's letters to his various relations, typed extracts from the diary of Mary, his third wife, 1901-1914, and some papers relating to his home and domestic finances. There are papers and correspondence relating to Chamberlain's various election campaigns. Papers on most of the political problems of the time, domestic and foreign, have survived. There are, in particular, many papers and a great deal of correspondence on Ireland. There is correspondence, memoranda, and draft bills from Chamberlain's term of office at the Board of Trade: for example, on bankruptcy, Employers' Liability, and merchant shipping. There are many papers deriving from his part in the conference with the United States on the Newfoundland Fisheries 1887-1888.

Chamberlain's role in Salisbury's government is fully represented by papers on Colonial and Imperial affairs, including papers on the Jameson raid, and on the reasons for his resignation in 1903. His entire political and official career is reflected in a general correspondence series and press cuttings. Chamberlain seems not to have kept a diary but there is a memorandum of events 1880-1892 (J.C. 8/1/1) which was published as *A Political Memoir 1880-1892*, ed. C.H.D. Howard (1953). There are diaries he kept on various foreign tours. The collection also includes Sir Charles Dilke's diary 1880-1885, and correspondence of the 1920s and 1930s when J.L. Garvin was writing the first three volumes of an official *Life*. The biography was completed by the Rt. Hon. Julian Amery and quotes extensively from the papers: *Life of Joseph Chamberlain* (6 vols., 1932-69). Peter Fraser, *Joseph Chamberlain: Radicalism and Empire* (1966) also makes extensive use of the papers.

Original correspondence and a register of correspondence 1902-1903 concerning Chamberlain's tour of South Africa while he was Secretary of State for the Colonies is in the Public Record Office (ref. C.O. 529 and C.O. 638). (See also *Addenda*, p. 166.)

SIR (JOSEPH) AUSTEN CHAMBERLAIN (1863-1937)

Austen Chamberlain was Liberal Unionist M.P. for Worcestershire (East) 1892-1914 (he became a Conservative in 1906) and Conservative M.P. for Birmingham (West) 1914-1937. He was a Civil Lord of the Admiralty July 1895-November 1900, Financial Secretary to the Treasury 1900-August 1902, Postmaster-General 1902-October 1903, Chancellor of the Exchequer 1903-December 1905, and January 1919-April 1921, Secretary of State for India May 1915-July 1917, Minister without Portfolio in the War Cabinet April 1918-January 1919, Lord Privy Seal and Leader of the Conservative Party March 1921-October 1922, Secretary of State for Foreign Affairs November 1924-June 1929, and 1st Lord of the Admiralty August-October 1931. He was created K.G. in 1925.

Many of Chamberlain's papers have been extensively quoted in print: in his autobiography, *Down the Years* (1935), Chamberlain said that while he kept no diary, he had referred to occasional memoranda and letters. *Politics from Inside. An Epistolary Chronicle, 1906-1914* (1936), was based on Chamberlain's letters to his wife, many of which were intended to be read to his father in order to keep him up to date with political events. Sir Charles Petrie, *The Life and Letters of the Right Hon. Sir Austen Chamberlain* (2 vols., 1939-40), also quotes extensively from the papers.

A large collection of Chamberlain's papers was deposited in the Birmingham University Library (ref. Austen Chamberlain papers). Applications to see the papers should be made in writing to the Rare Books Librarian and should enclose a character reference. These papers have been listed. They seem to throw light on all of Chamberlain's career, and include a good deal of family correspondence. As well as Chamberlain's letters to his wife and her replies,

SIR (JOSEPH) AUSTEN CHAMBERLAIN (cont.)

there are many letters to and from his sisters and his half-brother Neville. There is a series of letters from Chamberlain to his father 1908-1912 and there are many of Joseph Chamberlain's papers in this collection: as well as papers concerning the Chamberlain family tree, there is Joseph Chamberlain's own marriage certificate, miscellaneous correspondence 1896-1913, a play by him entitled 'Politics, a political comedy', and other farces and miscellaneous papers.

Chamberlain's early political career is reflected by correspondence 1892-1908 and papers concerning the 1906 general election. His role in Unionist affairs is reflected by papers on subjects such as Home Rule and Tariff Reform. There are also papers related to his candidature for the party leadership in 1911, his activities in July and August 1914, the formation of the May 1915 and December 1916 Coalition governments, the growth of Unionist discontent with the Coalition, the defeat of the Coalition in October 1922, and the reunification of the Conservative Party in 1923.

Chamberlain's official career is also represented: there are many Cabinet papers 1903-1905 on various topics, and some correspondence, for example, with George Wyndham on Ireland. There are also many papers relating to India, including correspondence with Lords Chelmsford and Hardinge 1913-1917, and also papers concerning E.S. Montagu's resignation in 1922. There are a great many papers concerning military operations in Mesopotamia during the first world war, the mismanagement of which caused Chamberlain to resign. There seem to be few official papers for his tenure of the Foreign Office but there is a vast correspondence for the years 1920-1937. There is also correspondence concerning the publication of his books.

Eight volumes of Chamberlain's miscellaneous correspondence as Secretary of State for Foreign Affairs have been deposited in the Public Record Office (ref. F.O. 800/256-263).

HENRY CHAPLIN, 1st VISCOUNT CHAPLIN (1840-1923)

Henry Chaplin was Conservative M.P. for Mid-Lincolnshire (Lincolnshire, Sleaford from 1885) 1868-1906, and Surrey (Wimbledon) 1907-1916. He was Chancellor of the Duchy of Lancaster June 1885-February 1886, President of the Board of Agriculture September 1889-July 1892, and President of the Local Government Board June 1895-November 1900. He was created Viscount Chaplin in 1916.

Chaplin's grandson, the present (3rd) Viscount Chaplin, informs us that he has no papers relating to Chaplin's life and career. He suggested that his cousin, Lady Mairi Bury, might be able to give us further information, but we have not been able to contact her. Lady Mairi's mother, Chaplin's elder daughter, published selections from Chaplin's papers: Edith H. Vane-Tempest-Stewart, Marchioness of Londonderry, *Henry Chaplin* (1926). Lady Londonderry said, in her introduction, that her father wanted some account of his political and sporting career to be published and, with this end in view, he prepared several letters and memoranda which she included in her book. It is suggested that researchers should write to the Public Record Office of Northern Ireland for current information about papers in Lady Mairi's possession.

Some of Chaplin's papers are included in the Londonderry papers in the Durham Record Office (ref. D/Lo/F/626-632). A full description of the entire collection is to be found in S.C. Newton, *The Londonderry Papers* (Durham, 1969). There are no personal or political papers apart from the papers used for Lady Londonderry's memoir. There are eight files of draft chapters, letters and memoranda about Lady Londonderry's work, and press cuttings about Chaplin's 1907 election for Wimbledon.

Another small collection of Chaplin's papers is available in the Lincolnshire Record Office (ref. B. 5. 13). The papers were included in a collection deposited by Mossop Barton & Co., solicitors. The papers almost all concern the management of Chaplin's Lincolnshire estates: audits, accounts, agreements, and draft contracts; but there are a few, miscellaneous political papers: press cuttings about Chaplin's House of Commons' activities; the 1881 Land Bill; and a printed speech about Ireland.

HENRY CHAPLIN (cont.)

Some letters 1875-1890 from Chaplin and his children to his sister-in-law, Lady Alexandra Leveson-Gower, are available in the Sutherland collection in the Staffordshire Record Office (ref. D 593/P/29/1/4,8).

SIR (ALFRED) ERNLE MONTACUTE CHATFIELD, 1st BARON CHATFIELD (1873-1967)

Ernle Chatfield was Minister for the Coordination of Defence January 1939-April 1940. He was created K.C.M.G. in 1919, G.C.B. in 1934, and Baron Chatfield in 1937.

Chatfield's papers were deposited in the National Maritime Museum in 1973 (ref. CHT/1-9). A preliminary list of the papers is available.

The collection (it filled ten box-files) has been divided into seven groups: papers concerning Chatfield's early life; his Atlantic and Mediterranean Commands; his term of office as 1st Sea Lord; his work on the Indian Defence Committee 1938-1939; his term as Minister; his later life; and photograph albums.

The papers concerning Chatfield's early life consist of family genealogy. The Atlantic and Mediterranean Command papers include some relating to the 1931 Invergordon Mutiny. Chatfield's 1st Sea Lord papers include papers on the 1935 Naval Conference, a visit to the Combined Fleets, Gibraltar in 1938, and his promotion to Admiral of the Fleet. As well as general correspondence for the period, there is correspondence with Winston and Randolph Churchill 1936-1942, Sir Robert Vansittart, Sir Warren Fisher, Lord Beatty, and senior admirals.

Chatfield's Ministry papers do not reflect his activities particularly well. They have been divided into general papers and papers concerning Anglo-American relations 1937-1940.

Chatfield's later papers include three boxes of speech and broadcast notes, press cuttings, and correspondence with Professor Arthur Marder. They also include the manuscripts for Chatfield's two volumes of autobiography: *The Navy and Defence* (1942) and *It might happen again* (1947). These are particularly interesting for they show the deletions made in the published version, for example, about the 1922 Washington Naval Conference. The National Maritime Museum operates a 30-year rule, so that post-war papers in the collection are not yet available for research.

Chatfield's widow has retained his letters to her. They are not available for research, but they were used for the forthcoming biography of Chatfield by Professor A. Temple Patterson.

CHARLES RICHARD JOHN SPENCER-CHURCHILL, 9th DUKE OF MARLBOROUGH (1871-1934)

Charles Spencer-Churchill, Earl of Sunderland till 1883 and Marquess of Blandford 1883-1892, succeeded his father as 9th Duke in 1892. He was created K.G. in 1902. He was known all his life as 'Sunny', and so signed many letters. He was Paymaster-General 1899-March 1902, Under-Secretary of State for the Colonies July 1903-December 1905, and Joint Parliamentary Secretary to the Board of Agriculture and Fisheries February 1917-March 1918.

The Library at Blenheim Palace has only a small box of his papers; it contains a fragment of diary written during the South African War and a few letters on family financial affairs. The only other surviving items are the Blenheim visitors' book, and some photograph albums. None of these is generally available.

SIR WINSTON LEONARD SPENCER-CHURCHILL (1874-1965)

Winston Churchill was Conservative M.P. for Oldham 1900-1904. He became a Liberal in 1904 and continued as M.P. for Oldham till 1906. He was Liberal M.P. for Manchester (North-West) 1906-1908, Dundee 1908-1922. He was Conservative M.P. for Essex (Epping) 1924-1945, and for Woodford 1945-1964. He was Under-Secretary of State for the Colonies December 1905-April 1908, President of the Board of Trade 1908-February 1910, Secretary of State for Home Affairs 1910-October 1911, 1st Lord of the Admiralty 1911-May 1915 and September 1939-May 1940, Chancellor of the Duchy of Lancaster May-November 1915, Minister of Munitions July 1917-January 1919, Secretary of State for War and Air 1919-

SIR WINSTON LEONARD SPENCER-CHURCHILL (cont.)

February 1921, Secretary of State for the Colonies 1921-October 1922, Chancellor of the Exchequer November 1924-June 1929, Prime Minister May 1940-July 1945 and October 1951-April 1955, Minister of Defence May 1940-July 1945 and October 1951-March 1952, and Leader of the Opposition July 1945-October 1951. He was created K.G. in 1953.

The rights of use and the copyright to Churchill's papers are owned by C. & T. Publications Ltd., c/o J. McCracken, Fladgates, Waterloo Place, London S.W.1. The papers have been sorted and arranged by the Public Record Office. While an official biography is being written the papers are closed to other researchers; limited access to those sections of the papers already used in the biography may be granted on application to C. & T. Publications Ltd. Ultimately the papers will be deposited in the library of Churchill College, Cambridge. The first instalment of Churchill's personal papers (c. 1874-1900) has been transferred to Churchill College; further transfers are expected. No decision has yet (March 1974) been made on conditions of access, but it is not anticipated that the papers will be opened for some time. A microfilm of the papers has been made by the Public Record Office and will be opened when the papers themselves are opened (ref. P.R.O. 31/19). In the meantime the published volumes of the official biography, and in particular the *Companion Volumes* of documents, contain extensive selections from the Churchill papers: Randolph S. Churchill, *Winston S. Churchill, Volume I Youth 1874-1900* (1966); *Companion Volume I, part 1, 1874-1896, part 2, 1896-1900* (1967); *Volume II Young Statesman 1901-1914* (1967); *Companion Volume II, part 1, 1901-1907, part 2, 1907-1911, part 3, 1911-1914* (1969); Martin Gilbert, *Volume III 1914-1916* (1971); *Companion Volume III, part 1, July 1914-April 1915, part 2, May 1915-December 1916* (1972). Churchill's own numerous publications, including *The World Crisis* (6 vols., 1923-31) and *The Second World War* (6 vols., 1948-54), also contain much documentary material.

Churchill's papers have been divided into three parts. The first — Chartwell Trust papers — consists of all his papers up to 27 July 1945, which were presented by Sir Winston to the Chartwell Trust. The second part — Churchill papers — are Churchill's papers from 1945 till his death. The third part were regarded by the Public Record Office as being official 'Private Office Papers', and as such have been retained in official custody; they will be opened for research in accordance with the Public Records Act and form part of the class entitled 'Premier'.

Within these three physical divisions, the papers were arranged under the following headings: personal; public and political: general; political: constituency; literary; official; speeches; acquired papers; miscellaneous; obsolete lists. Obviously there is a great deal of overlapping between these headings. For example, some early Oldham constituency papers appear under the 'Personal' heading; papers from the 1916 Dardanelles Commission include a large number of Admiralty papers removed by Churchill himself when preparing his evidence for the Commission; the 'Literary' heading is particularly rich in papers removed by Churchill from other files for reference when writing his various histories. Within these headings the papers have been arranged chronologically.

In the Chartwell papers there are 394 files of Personal papers, 569 files of Public and General papers — including files on the General Strike, the Abdication crisis, and on India. The acquired papers include the papers of Lord and Lady Randolph Churchill, and John Spencer-Churchill.

ROBERT GEORGE WINDSOR-CLIVE, 14th BARON WINDSOR, 1st EARL OF PLYMOUTH (1857-1923)

Robert George Windsor-Clive succeeded his grandmother as 14th Baron Windsor in 1869. He was created G.B.E. in 1918, and Earl of Plymouth in 1905. He was Paymaster-General 1891-July 1892 and 1st Commissioner of Works August 1902-December 1905.

His grandson, the present (3rd) Earl of Plymouth, knows of no papers; neither does his grand-daughter by his only daughter, Miss Melissa Benton.

JOHN ROBERT CLYNES (1869-1949)

John Robert Clynes was Labour M.P. for Manchester (North-East; Platting from 1918) 1906-1931 and 1935-1945. He was Parliamentary Secretary to the Ministry of Food July 1917-July 1918, Food Controller 1918-January 1919, Lord Privy Seal January-November 1924, and Secretary of State for Home Affairs June 1929-August 1931.

Clynes's daughter-in-law, Mrs G.E. Clynes, has only a very small collection of his papers; these papers are not generally available for research. Mrs Clynes thinks that any other papers were probably destroyed during successive house-removals; she informs us that neither of Clynes's grand-children (who live in the U.S.A.) has any papers.

The papers in Mrs Clynes's possession consist almost entirely of press cuttings and printed material; the only other papers are invitations, short social notes, correspondence concerning Clynes's swearing-in as a Privy Councillor, and a letter from Clynes to his daughter describing the latter ceremony. A letter from Mrs Clynes to her daughter describes her first visit to Windsor Castle. There is one album of press cuttings, almost all of which describe speeches and social functions during the first Labour Government of 1924. There are several loose cuttings of articles by Clynes, including one from the *News of the World* 14 September 1947, describing the 1931 crisis, and many for the journal of the National Union of General and Municipal Workers. The collection also includes two records of speeches for the 1929 general election campaign and Clynes's election addresses for his 1906, 1910, 1918, 1922, 1923, and 1935 election campaigns.

Clynes's views of contemporary Labour politicians are to be found in short biographical articles in *The British Labour Party*, ed. Herbert Tracey (1948). His own *Memoirs* (2 vols., 1937) quote from very few documents.

SIR GODFREY PATTISON COLLINS (1875-1936)

Godfrey Collins was Liberal M.P. for Greenock 1910-1936; he was a Liberal National from 1931. He was Secretary of State for Scotland September 1932-October 1936. He was created K.B.E. in 1919.

Collins's son, William Hope Collins (who died in 1967), informed us that Collins rarely kept any papers; his business habit was to write his decision or comment on whatever was sent to him and return the document to the sender. Mr W.H. Collins did have some personal papers about the break-up of the Liberal Party in the 1920s (Collins was Liberal Chief Whip 1924-1926) and the work done by Collins on the Army Council. Unfortunately these papers can no longer be found and Mr James Collins, the son of W.H. Collins (W. Collins Sons & Co. Ltd., 144 Cathedral Street, Glasgow G4 ONB), has only a volume of press cuttings. The cuttings are all from June-December 1935 and are taken from Scottish newspapers; they include coverage of the November 1935 general election when Collins was not expected to be returned. Collins's daughter, Mrs Elspeth Barry, of Fairfield House, St Martin, Jersey, Channel Islands, has a comprehensive collection of Collins's obituary notices made by his secretary. Mrs Barry also has cuttings concerning the 1929, 1931 and 1935 elections, Collins's becoming a privy councillor, and his becoming a cabinet minister in 1932. Her collection also includes cuttings on a Scottish Education Bill, as well as numerous invitations and programmes for various functions.

Neither Mrs Barry nor Mr James Collins knows what became of the papers known to exist in 1966 nor of the existence of any other papers. David Keir, *The House of Collins* (1952), includes an account of Collins's career but it does not quote from documents.

SIR (DAVID) JOHN COLVILLE, 1st BARON CLYDESMUIR (1894-1954)

John Colville was Conservative M.P. for Midlothian and Peebleshire (Northern) 1929-1943. He was Parliamentary Secretary for the Overseas Trade Department of the Board of Trade November 1931-November 1935, Parliamentary Under-Secretary of State for Scotland 1935-October 1936, Financial Secretary to the Treasury 1936-May 1938, and Secretary of State for Scotland 1938-May 1940. He was created G.C.I.E. in 1943 and Baron Clydesmuir in 1948.

Colville's son, the present (2nd) Lord Clydesmuir, informs us that he has no papers concerning his father's political career. Lord Clydesmuir adds that his father destroyed many

SIR JOHN COLVILLE (cont.)

private papers before taking up the governorship of Bombay 1943-1948. Colville's elder daughter, the Hon. Mrs Dalrymple-Hamilton, has only a few prints and press cuttings relating to the site of what is now St Andrew's House, the building which houses the Scottish Office in Edinburgh. Colville's younger daughter, the Hon. Mrs Whitcombe, has no papers relating to her father's career.

SIR ALFRED DUFF COOPER, 1st VISCOUNT NORWICH (1890-1954)

Alfred Duff Cooper was Conservative M.P. for Oldham 1924-1929, and for Westminster (St George's) 1931-1945. He was Financial Secretary to the War Office January 1928-June 1929, and September 1931-June 1934, Financial Secretary to the Treasury 1934-November 1935, Secretary of State for War 1935-May 1937, 1st Lord of the Admiralty 1937-October 1938, Minister of Information May 1940-July 1941, Chancellor of the Duchy of Lancaster 1941-November 1943, and Representative of the British Government with the French Committee for National Liberation 1943-1944. He was created G.C.M.G. in 1948 and Viscount Norwich in 1952.

Cooper left his papers to his literary executor, Sir Rupert Hart-Davis. Sir Rupert informs us that the papers are closed for the foreseeable future. He adds that there are very few 'political' papers, except for the period when Cooper was British Representative in Algiers. Most of the papers, which include a diary, are of a personal, social, and literary nature. Sir Rupert, in his will, has left the papers to his cousin, the present (2nd) Viscount Norwich.

Cooper copied his diaries for 1952 and 1953 for Lady Caroline Duff, wife of Sir Michael Duff, 3rd Bt; he also returned to Lady Caroline her letters to him. She has presented the copies of the diaries and her correspondence 1931-1951 (that is both her letters to Cooper and his to her) to the British Library, but the papers will remain closed until 2009 or the death of Lady Caroline's son, whichever is the later (ref. Reserved MS. 94).

Some papers concerning Cooper's work with the French Committee of National Liberation in Algeria are available at the Public Record Office (ref. F.O. 660/106-199). They include reports on the political situation and the various resistance groups, as well as social papers connected with the Prime Minister's visit to Algeria.

In *Old Men Forget* (1953) Cooper quoted from many letters and from his diaries. His wife, Lady Diana Cooper, also quotes from his diaries and from his letters to her in her memoirs *The Rainbow Comes and Goes* (1958), *The Light of Common Day* (1959), and *Trumpets from the Steep* (1960).

SIR CHARLES ALFRED CRIPPS, 1st BARON PARMOOR (1852-1941)

Charles Alfred Cripps was Conservative M.P. for Gloucestershire (Stroud) 1895-1900, South-East Lancashire (Stretford) 1901-1906 and Buckinghamshire (Wycombe) 1910-1914. He was Lord President of the Council January-November 1924 and June 1929-August 1931. He was British Representative on the Council of the League of Nations 1924. He was created K.C.V.O. in 1908, and Baron Parmoor in 1914.

According to his son, the present (2nd) Baron Parmoor, all Cripps's papers were given to his youngest son, Sir Stafford Cripps. Sir Stafford's widow, Dame Isobel Cripps, has no recollection of this nor does she know where any Parmoor papers might be found. The house to which the papers may have been sent was burned down during the war and many valuable papers were certainly lost then, a loss which possibly includes the Parmoor papers.

In his autobiography, *A Retrospect* (1936), Cripps quoted from several letters including correspondence with J.R. MacDonald on the formation of the first Labour Government in 1924.

SIR (RICHARD) STAFFORD CRIPPS (1889-1952)

Stafford Cripps was Labour M.P. for Bristol (East) 1931-1950 and Bristol (South-East) February-October 1950. He was Solicitor-General October 1930-August 1931, Lord Privy Seal February-November 1942, Minister of Aircraft Production 1942-May 1945, President of the Board of Trade July 1945-September 1947, Minister of Economic Affairs September-November 1947, and Chancellor of the Exchequer 1947-October 1950. Cripps was knighted in 1930.

A large number of Cripps's papers are in the possession of his widow, Dame Isobel Cripps, but they are not available for research until Mr Maurice Shock has completed a biography (approximately 1981). In the meantime only the papers deposited by Dame Isobel in the library of Nuffield College, Oxford, are available (ref. Cripps papers).

These papers fill three bays of shelving, and only a very rough, preliminary list has been compiled. The papers fall into two main types: subject files and speech files; this division is reflected by two series of descriptive entries, both arranged in approximate chronological order, and both ranging over Cripps's political life 1930-1950.

The speech files include copies of speeches, notes, and information used for a particular speech. Articles for the press and broadcasts are included in this section. In many cases the speeches contain the only reference in the collection to particular events in Cripps's life: for example, the only official papers in the collection come from the Ministry of Aircraft Production and relate to Cripps's visits to factories and the speeches he made there. The only reflections of Cripps's period as British Ambassador in Moscow 1940-1942 and his mission to India 1942 are in the text of several speeches and broadcasts made on his return.

The subject files include much material from Cripps's work in his constituency. There are files on the 1931 by-election, and the 1931, 1935, and 1945 general elections. There are several files of correspondence on constituency 'cases' — including many instances of constituents asking for help in revising their means test assessment. There are also several files on the Labour Party's annual conferences, particularly those at which the issues of membership in the Socialist League and the Popular Front were raised. Cripps's earlier, more harmonious, contacts within the party are represented by a file of papers on a proposal to market cigarettes to help the party's funds. There are a few papers on the founding of *Tribune* in 1936 but the collection is disappointing on the Socialist League and Popular Front. As well as Cripps's own activities there are files on such subjects as Spain, Germany, and the West Indies. There are also fifteen books of press cuttings, mostly post-1940. There are very few papers from the post-war period.

Colin Cooke, *The Life of Richard Stafford Cripps* (1957) and Eric Estorick, *Stafford Cripps* (1949), were both based on all of Cripps's papers and contain many quotations from the diary Cripps began to keep in 1938, as well as some of Cripps's correspondence. *The Transfer of Power 1942-1947. Volume I. The Cripps Mission January-April 1942*, ed. Nicholas Mansergh (1970) prints a large number of documents concerning Cripps's first mission to India, including Cripps's own record of interviews with Indian leaders. These notes were deposited in the India Office in 1942 and are now available in the India Office Library (ref. IOR: L/P & J/10/4).

HARRY FREDERICK COMFORT CROOKSHANK, VISCOUNT CROOKSHANK (1893-1961)

Captain Harry Crookshank was Conservative M.P. for Lincolnshire (Gainsborough) 1924-1956. He was Parliamentary Under-Secretary of State for Home Affairs June 1934-June 1935, Parliamentary Secretary for Mines 1935-April 1939, Financial Secretary to the Treasury 1939-February 1943, Postmaster-General December 1942-August 1945, Minister of Health October 1951-May 1952, Lord Privy Seal 1952-December 1955, and Leader of the House of Commons 1951-1955. He was created Viscount Crookshank in 1956.

A small collection of his papers was given to the Bodleian Library (ref. MSS. Eng. hist. b.223; c.596-605; d.359-361) by the executors of his nephew, the late Lt Col. P.R.H. Crookshank. The papers (five boxes) are mainly notes for speeches covering the whole of Crookshank's political life, speeches made both in and out of Parliament. One of the few letters in the collection is what appears to be a draft letter to the Prime Minister (5 December 1936) giving the reaction

HARRY FREDERICK COMFORT CROOKSHANK (cont.)

of Crookshank's constituents to the Abdication. Perhaps of greatest interest is a resignation speech drafted in October 1938 but marked 'not used'. A carbon of Crookshank's proposed letter of resignation is marked 'letter sent but afterwards "lay on the table" '. For his proposed speech Crookshank wrote that at Munich '. . . we did in fact yield to force and not to reason' and '. . . if he [the Prime Minister] can speak of what happened last week as peace with honour, then I can only say that in the realm of foreign affairs he is using a language I cannot understand'. As well as political speeches there are notes which show the religious aspect of Crookshank's character: a speech to Unitarians in 1938, and an address in St Mary's, Cambridge, in 1948 on 'My Faith and My Job'. There is a number of press cuttings on Crookshank's political activities. There are also appointment diaries for the years 1943-1961.

The most important item in the collection is Crookshank's diary for July 1934-October 1951, and 1955-1958. The diary was kept on loose-leaf notepaper, which has allowed considerable variation in the length of the entries. Most of the entries are purely social but there is some political comment, for example on the changes made in the government in 1942. The entries for this period include copies of letters written by Crookshank to Churchill when the Prime Minister offered him the Ministry of Works and a peerage, and Crookshank's letter to James Stuart, the Conservative Whip, and the latter's reply.

Two large scrap-books were given by Crookshank to the Lincolnshire Record Office. They contain press cuttings and invitations mainly concerning Crookshank's political career.

SIR RICHARD ASSHETON CROSS, 1st VISCOUNT CROSS (1823-1914)

Richard Assheton Cross was Conservative M.P. for Preston 1857-1862, Lancashire (South-West) 1868-1885, and South-West Lancashire (Newton) 1885-1886. He was Secretary of State for Home Affairs February 1874-April 1880 and June 1885-February 1886, Secretary of State for India August 1886-August 1892, Chancellor of the Duchy of Lancaster June-July 1895, and Lord Privy Seal June 1895-November 1900. He was created G.C.B. in 1880, and Viscount Cross in 1886.

Fifty-seven volumes of Cross's papers as Secretary of State for India have been deposited in the India Office Library (ref. MSS. Eur. E. 243). They consist of correspondence with successive viceroys, governors of Madras, governors of Bombay, and telegrams. Sixteen volumes of original index are included in the collection.

The remainder of Cross's papers were given to the British Library by his grandson, the present (3rd) Viscount Cross, in 1962 (ref. Add. MSS. 51263-51289). The 27 volumes of papers have been divided into special correspondence, general correspondence, and family correspondence. The six volumes of special correspondence include two volumes of correspondence with the 3rd Marquess of Salisbury and his family 1874-1907, as well as correspondence with Disraeli and Northcote. The thirteen volumes of general correspondence cover the years 1846-1913. There are five volumes of family correspondence including Cross's letters to his mother 1842-1849, his letters to his wife 1859-1881, and letters of condolence on the death of his wife and son.

A further small collection of papers has been deposited in the Lancashire Record Office (ref. DDX 841). The collection includes letters on local politics 1857-1862, 1868, 1871, some press cuttings, electoral addresses for 1857, and a letter to the Preston electors giving the reasons for his resignation in 1862. There are also some genealogical and estate papers.

In his *A Political History* (1903) Cross described for his children his political and official career and quoted from a few letters, particularly from Queen Victoria.

SIR RONALD HIBBERT CROSS, Bt (1896-1968)

Ronald Hibbert Cross was Conservative M.P. for Rossendale 1931-1945, and for Lancashire (Ormskirk) 1950-1951. He was Parliamentary Secretary to the Board of Trade May 1938-September 1939, Minister of Economic Warfare 1939-May 1940, and Minister of Shipping 1940-May 1941. He was created K.C.V.O. in 1954, K.C.M.G. in 1955, and a baronet in 1941.

SIR RONALD HIBBERT CROSS (cont.)

Cross's daughter, the Hon. Mrs N.D. Campbell, informs us that she is unable to find any papers relating to her father's political and official career.

SIR SAVILE BRINTON CROSSLEY, 2nd Bt, 1st BARON SOMERLEYTON (1857-1935)

Savile Brinton Crossley was Liberal M.P. for Suffolk (North) 1885-1892, and Liberal Unionist M.P. for Halifax 1900-1906. He was Paymaster-General March 1902-December 1905. He succeeded his father as second baronet in 1872 and was created K.C.V.O. in 1909, G.C.V.O. in 1922 and Baron Somerleyton in 1916.

Crossley's grandson, the present (3rd) Lord Somerleyton, has been unable to find any of his grandfather's papers.

GEORGE NATHANIEL CURZON, 5th BARON SCARSDALE, MARQUESS CURZON OF KEDLESTON (1859-1925)

George Nathaniel Curzon was Conservative M.P. for South-West Lancashire (Southport) 1886-1898. He was Under-Secretary of State for India November 1891-August 1892, Under-Secretary of State for Foreign Affairs June 1895-October 1898, Viceroy and Governor-General of India 1898-1905, Lord Privy Seal May 1915-December 1916, President of the Air Board May-December 1916, Lord President of the Council 1916-October 1919 and November 1924-March 1925, a member of the War Cabinet December 1916-October 1919, and Secretary of State for Foreign Affairs October 1919-January 1924. He was an Irish Representative Peer in the House of Lords 1908-1916 and Leader of the House of Lords 1916-1924. He was created G.C.I.E. in 1898, K.G. in 1916, Baron Curzon of Kedleston (an Irish peerage) in 1898, Earl Curzon of Kedleston in 1911, and Marquess Curzon of Kedleston 1921; he succeeded his father as 5th Baron Scarsdale in 1916.

A very large collection of Curzon's papers has been deposited in the India Office Library in two parts. The first part (ref. MSS. Eur. F. 111) mainly covers Curzon's Indian activities; it is listed and generally available. The second part (ref. MSS. Eur. F. 112) covers the rest of Curzon's private and public life including his terms in office. A list is being prepared, and the papers will be available when it is completed.

MSS. Eur. F. 111 is divided into four main divisions: papers concerning Curzon's life before he became Viceroy; papers related to Curzon's term of office as Viceroy; papers concerning India after Curzon was Viceroy; and printed volumes. The first section includes many papers relating to Curzon's early travels: pamphlets, press cuttings and correspondence concerning tours in Afghanistan, Persia and the Far East including letters from the Amir of Afghanistan 1895-1898. There are also many papers about different aspects of the Indian Frontiers. There is a considerable amount of correspondence, divided into general correspondence, letters from individuals, and letters from individual politicians. There are albums and scrapbooks of press cuttings about Curzon and about the 'Souls'. There are also many literary papers, including Curzon's reminiscences of meeting famous men such as H.M. Stanley, General Gordon, and W.E. Gladstone.

The second section of MSS. Eur. F. 111 consists mainly of correspondence. It is divided into 'demi-official' and private correspondence. The former includes correspondence with the Sovereign, with the Secretary of State for India, with '. . . persons in England', '. . . persons in India', and private telegrams. This correspondence has been bound and printed; the printed volumes include Curzon's 'out' letters. The private correspondence is divided into general correspondence arranged chronologically, and correspondence with particular individuals such as A.J. Balfour, and Lords Selborne and Knollys.

The papers related to Curzon's continued interest in India after he had ceased to be Viceroy are mainly arranged by topic. They include minutes, memoranda, press cuttings, and correspondence. The dominating topic is defence in its many aspects: the frontiers — Tibet, Persia,

GEORGE NATHANIEL CURZON (cont.)

the North West Frontier district; and Curzon's dispute with Lord Kitchener about civil control of the military in India. There are also papers concerned with Curzon's resignation and with the publication of various books on India.

The final section of MSS. Eur. F. 111 contains printed volumes. They include the vast 'summary' of Curzon's administration arranged by the various departments of the Indian government. There are also five volumes of speeches by Curzon, archaeological survey reports, and census reports.

MSS. Eur. F. 112 consists of a few papers from Curzon's Under-Secretaryship at the Foreign Office 1895-1898, and a mass of papers, memoranda and correspondence, relating to his career after his return from India. There are a great number of papers on political matters from the period 1905-1915 when Curzon was out of office: Unionist party policy; women's suffrage; the 1911 parliamentary crisis. There are papers from Curzon's terms of office as Lord Privy Seal including papers concerning the compulsory service debate and unprinted (and therefore very secret) War Cabinet minutes. There are voluminous papers from his term of office as Foreign Secretary: official papers and correspondence. There are, in addition, political papers including memoranda by Curzon on his relations with Lloyd George, the fall of the Coalition in October 1922, and the succession to Bonar Law in May 1923.

There is material concerning his trusteeship of the National Gallery and his term as President of the Royal Geographical Society; the latter includes correspondence about Captain Scott's 1911 Antarctic Expedition.

Much of the correspondence, including Curzon's letters to his contemporaries, is quoted in the authorized biography by the Earl of Ronaldshay, *The Life of Lord Curzon* (3 vols., 1928). The Indian papers are extensively quoted in David Dilks, *Curzon in India* (2 vols., 1969-70). Two other works have been based on the papers now in the India Office Library: Leonard Mosley, *Curzon. The End of an Epoch* (1960), and Kenneth Rose, *Superior Person, A Portrait of Curzon and his Circle in late Victorian England* (1969).

Curzon's electoral address of June 1886 to the electors of Southport is in the Southport Public Library (ref. 942.72 Sa.). That library also holds copies of speeches published by Curzon on general political matters 1891 (ref. 825.91 S.) and on the fisheries question 1892 (ref. 629.2 Sa [Pamph]), and a collection of press cuttings and cartoons about Curzon (ref. B.20. S.).

A small collection relating to Curzon's terms of office as Under-Secretary and Secretary of State at the Foreign Office has been deposited in the Public Record Office (ref. F.O. 800/ 28, 147-158). It includes correspondence 1886-1887 (F.O. 800/28), 1895-1898 (F.O. 800/ 147-148), volumes 15-21 of Curzon's general correspondence 1919-1924, and three volumes of correspondence 1919-1923 arranged by subject.

Curzon's nephew, the present (2nd) Viscount Scarsdale, has further personal papers, in particular Curzon's letters to his second wife. These papers are not available for research. They include Curzon's autobiographical notes on his early life; his correspondence with his mother 1869-1875; letters from the Royal Family for the period of his official life; papers on financial matters; and papers on the management and history of Curzon's houses.

Curzon's correspondence with his first wife is in the possession of their youngest daughter, Lady Alexandra Metcalfe. These letters are not available for research, but they will be used in Mr Nigel Nicolson's forthcoming biography of Curzon.

(EDWARD) HUGH (JOHN NEALE) DALTON, BARON DALTON (1887-1962)

Hugh Dalton was Labour M.P. for Camberwell (Peckham) 1924-1929 and for Durham (Bishop Auckland) 1929-1931 and 1935-1959. He was Under-Secretary of State for Foreign Affairs June 1929-August 1931, Minister of Economic Warfare May 1940-February 1942, President of the Board of Trade 1942-May 1945, Chancellor of the Exchequer July 1945-November 1947, Chancellor of the Duchy of Lancaster May 1948-February 1950, Minister of Town and Country Planning 1950-January 1951, and Minister of Local Government and Planning January-October 1951. He was created Baron Dalton (a life peerage) in 1960.

HUGH DALTON (cont.)

Approximately twelve linear feet of Dalton's papers have been deposited in the British Library of Political and Economic Science (ref. Dalton papers); a list of the papers is available. The papers have been divided into three sections: diaries; subject files; and miscellaneous papers.

There are 56 volumes of diary covering the years 1916-1960. Not all of the diaries are presently open for research; but where only part of a volume is closed, the open section has been xeroxed and the xerox copy made available to researchers, for example the diary for April 1931-October 1932 and December 1932-February 1934. Dalton himself quoted frequently both from his diaries and his correspondence in his three volumes of memoirs, *Call Back Yesterday, The Fateful Years,* and *High Tide and After* (1953-62).

Dalton's subject files include notes on the suspension of thirteen Socialist M.P.s in April 1926, press cuttings on the General Strike, papers on the 1929 Bishop Auckland by-election, papers for the 1936, 1937 and 1940 party conferences, papers on defence 1938-1939, including some from the Labour Party's defence sub-committee, some papers from the Ministry of Economic Warfare, press cuttings on the 1945 budget, and a file on 'cheap' money. There are also letters of congratulation of Dalton's various appointments, and eight files of letters written after his resignation as Chancellor following a leak of the impending budget proposals. The miscellaneous papers are arranged in chronological order. They are currently being sorted.

SIR JOHN COLIN CAMPBELL DAVIDSON, 1st VISCOUNT DAVIDSON (1889-1970)

John Colin Campbell Davidson was Conservative M.P. for Hertfordshire (Hemel Hempstead) 1920-1923 and 1924-1937. He was Chancellor of the Duchy of Lancaster May 1923-January 1924 and November 1931-May 1937, and Parliamentary and Financial Secretary to the Admiralty November 1924-December 1926. He was created G.C.V.O. in 1935 and Viscount Davidson in 1937.

Approximately 40 linear feet of his papers have been deposited in the Beaverbrook Library. They have not yet been sorted and no list is available. Applications for access should be made to the Librarian. There are many boxes of general correspondence from 1911 to the 1960s, as well as series of correspondence with individuals, such as Bonar Law and Beaverbrook, and subject files. The latter best reflect Davidson's work: they begin in 1911, when he was private secretary to the Secretary of State for the Colonies, and include correspondence between Sydney Buxton and Bonar Law in 1915 about the political situation in South Africa. There are also two volumes of cases reviewed by the Enemy Aliens Committee under regulation 14 (B) 1915-17 and some printed reports of Board of Trade Committees on the position of industries after the war. There are files on manpower and recruiting, railways, Poland and Russia 1917, reparations, the Genoa Conference, and coal reparations. There appear to be no papers concerning Davidson's ministerial duties. From 1926 to 1930 he was Chairman of the Conservative Party; one box of papers represents this period.

Selections from the Davidson papers were published by Robert Rhodes James in *Memoirs of a Conservative: J.C.C. Davidson's Memoirs and Papers* (1969). Mr Rhodes James informs us that a few non-political papers were retained by Davidson's family, and that other papers, lent some years ago to a researcher who failed to return them, are now being traced by the family. The missing papers are mainly copies of intercepted and decoded telegrams between various Russian leaders. Some of them are quoted in R.H. Ullman, *Anglo-Soviet Relations,* iii (Princeton, N.J., and London, 1973).

A further collection of Davidson's papers was given by his widow to the Bodleian Library in 1971 (ref. MSS. Eng. hist. b.219-222; c.557-587; d.344-355). A list and index of the papers have been compiled. The papers relate almost entirely to the period 1931-1939 when Davidson was Chairman of the Indian States Enquiry Committee (Financial) — a committee which was set up by the Round Table Conference. The papers have been divided into correspondence and general papers 1931-1939, miscellaneous files, files concerning particular Indian states, blue books, and miscellaneous papers (mostly photographs).

SIR JOHN COLIN CAMPBELL DAVIDSON (cont.)

The first section of the papers includes correspondence with Davidson's contemporaries including J.R. MacDonald and Lord Percy, as well as leading Indian politicians. There are also reports of the committee's meetings and papers which it prepared for the Cabinet Committee on India. The miscellaneous papers include diaries kept by Davidson and his wife on their Indian tour January-May 1932, notes of interviews and discussions, as well as printed memoranda on the various schemes put to the Committee.

The files on particular Indian states include submissions to the committee by state governments and individuals, as well as committee minutes concerning these submissions. The Blue Books are nearly all concerned with Indian constitutional reform in the 1930s; some are annotated.

ARETAS AKERS-DOUGLAS, 1st VISCOUNT CHILSTON (1851-1926)

Aretas Akers-Douglas (known as Aretas Akers till 1875) was Conservative M.P. for Kent (East; St Augustine's from 1885) 1880-1911. He was Patronage Secretary to the Treasury June 1885-January 1886, July 1886-August 1892 and July 1895, 1st Commissioner of Works 1895-August 1902, and Secretary of State for Home Affairs 1902-December 1905. He was created G.B.E. in 1920, and Viscount Chilston in 1911.

A very large collection of his papers has been deposited in the Kent Archives Office (ref. U. 564; National Register of Archives list no. 9550). A two-volume catalogue of the papers has been compiled. A brief description is included in the printed *Guide to the Kent County Archives Office*, ed. Felix Hull (Maidstone, 1958), pp. 166-167. The papers are now generally available. The bulk of the collection consists of correspondence. There are almost 600 separate correspondence series with individuals; the most important are those with the 3rd Marquess of Salisbury (55 letters, 1885-1900), A.J. Balfour (25 letters, 1887-1911), and W.H. Smith (174 letters, 1885-1891). Akers-Douglas's political letter books 1885-1911 and estate and personal letter books 1875-1911 have also survived. There are fifteen volumes of press cuttings, and Akers-Douglas's diaries for 1873-1925, though these are mainly engagement diaries. One of the letter books of Richard Middleton, Conservative Chief Party Agent 1885-1902, has also survived in the collection.

There are extensive quotations from the collection in *Chief Whip: The Political Life and Times of Aretas Akers-Douglas, 1st Viscount Chilston* by his grandson, Eric Alexander Akers-Douglas, 3rd Viscount Chilston (1961).

SIR HENRY EDWARD DUKE, 1st BARON MERRIVALE (1855-1939)

Henry Edward Duke was Conservative M.P. for Plymouth 1900-1906, and Exeter 1910-1918. He was Chief Secretary for Ireland July 1916-May 1918. He was a lord of appeal 1918-1919, and President of the Probate, Divorce and Admiralty Division 1919-1933. He was knighted in 1918, and created Baron Merrivale in 1925.

A small collection of his papers is in the possession of his grandson, the present (3rd) Baron Merrivale, 16 Brompton Lodge, 9-11 Cromwell Road, London S.W.7. The collection mainly consists of letters of congratulation to Duke on his election for Plymouth in 1900, on his appointment as a lord of appeal in 1918, on his appointment as President of the Probate, Divorce and Admiralty Division in 1919, on his peerage in 1925, and on his retirement in 1933. There is, however, a small bundle of miscellaneous correspondence from his term of office as Chief Secretary, especially for 1916-1917, including letters from Asquith, Walter Long, Lord Wimborne, and General Maxwell.

SIR ANDREW RAE DUNCAN (1884-1952)

Andrew Duncan was National M.P. for the City of London 1940-1950. He was President of the Board of Trade January-October 1940, and June 1941-February 1942, and Minister of Supply October 1940-June 1941 and February 1942-July 1945. He was knighted in 1921, and created G.B.E. in 1938.

SIR ANDREW RAE DUNCAN (cont.)

The only papers in the possession of Duncan's surviving son, Mr Gordon Duncan, are copies of the reports of some of the Royal Commissions on which Duncan served, and a volume of obituary notices privately printed by the British Iron and Steel Federation.

LAWRENCE JOHN LUMLEY DUNDAS, 2nd MARQUESS OF ZETLAND (1876-1961)

Lawrence Dundas, known as Lord Dundas 1876-1892 and as the Earl of Ronaldshay from 1892 until he succeeded his father as 2nd Marquess of Zetland in 1929, was Conservative M.P. for Middlesex (Hornsey) 1907-1916. He was Governor of Bengal 1917-1922, Secretary of State for India June 1935-May 1940, and Secretary of State for Burma 1937-May 1940. He was created G.C.I.E. in 1917, and K.G. in 1942.

A large collection of Dundas's papers has been deposited in the North Riding of Yorkshire Record Office (ref. ZNK X 10). Most of the papers have now been sorted and arranged but the listing of the papers is not yet complete. Permission to quote from the collection must be obtained through the Record Office. The collection contains almost no papers relating to Dundas's term at the India Office or to his work on the Round Table Conference 1930-1931, but it does contain a large number of papers relating to his long interest in Indian affairs and especially to his Governorship of Bengal.

Long before his official interest in India began, Dundas made several tours both of India, Persia, and the Far East. Notebooks and diaries survive from some of these tours, for example a tour of Ceylon in 1898, and of China and Japan in 1906. Dundas was a member of the Royal Commission on Public Services in India 1912-1914. His diary for a visit to India 12 December 1912-16 April 1913, his notebooks of evidence, and memoranda survive, as well as printed Minutes of Evidence, and papers on the recruitment, training, pay, and organization of the various departments.

Dundas's papers as Governor of Bengal include 120 letters to and from the successive viceroys, letters from the Secretaries of State for India, and copies of three letters to the King written in 1921, including a long account of Gandhi's non-cooperation movement. There are also papers on the 1917-1918 'outrages', memoranda on several Bengali revolutionary organizations, intelligence reports, translations of revolutionary literature, and statements made by persons questioned. There are also fortnightly reports on the Bengal political situation June 1920-February 1922. There are many official and unofficial printed papers including reports for 1916-1920 on publications registered under Act XXV of 1867, on agriculture, and on the anti-malaria campaign. There is also a file — mainly of press cuttings — on Gandhi's activities. Dundas's interests also ranged from a study of Islam and Eastern philosophy to the problems of the North West Frontier.

The collection also contains the manuscripts of Dundas's various publications and notes for speeches, lectures, and articles, many of which were about India. There is also a series of approximately 1000 'Selected Letters' arranged by Dundas himself in alphabetical order. Dundas's post-war papers have also been deposited with the record office but they have not yet been sorted and are therefore closed to research. On preliminary inspection they do not appear to contain material of political interest; they are mainly about personal and estate finance and Dundas's personal interests such as horse-racing. No more papers have been retained by Dundas's family.

A further nineteen volumes of Dundas's papers have been deposited in the India Office Library (ref. MSS. Eur. D. 609). They consist of some of Dundas's correspondence and papers as Governor of Bengal, as Secretary of State for India and Burma, and as a member of the Round Table Conference. The collection includes Dundas's diaries February 1917-March 1922. The diaries were kept at irregular intervals but contain fairly full descriptions of his activities and opinions.

A further collection of Dundas's papers has just (May 1973) been discovered by his family. This will be added to the papers already in the India Office Library. The collection includes manuscript and typed drafts of Dundas's life of Curzon, a few miscellaneous letters, and about twenty photograph albums covering his travels and his term of office in Bombay.

LAWRENCE JOHN LUMLEY DUNDAS (cont.)

In his volume of memoirs, *Essayez* (1957), Dundas quoted from many of his letters and from his diaries.

JAMES CHUTER EDE, BARON CHUTER-EDE (1882-1965)

James Chuter Ede was Labour M.P. for Surrey (Mitcham) March-November 1923, and South Shields 1929-1931 and 1935-1964. He was Parliamentary Secretary to the Ministry of Education May 1940-May 1945, and Secretary of State for Home Affairs August 1945-October 1951. He was created Baron Chuter-Ede (a life peerage) in 1964.

After his death, Chuter Ede's papers were carefully examined and divided by his executors. A few papers were removed by the Cabinet Office; correspondence with the B.B.C., the British Museum, and the County Councils Association was returned to them. It seems probable that papers of an 'ultra-confidential' nature — such as correspondence with ex-prisoners — was destroyed. Certainly three Home Office files were destroyed. Chuter Ede's library, literary writings, photographs, and newspaper cuttings were deposited in Epsom Borough Library. Most of the press cuttings and photographs are unlisted and kept in store outside the library, so that several days' notice is required for them to be produced. Fourteen volumes of Chuter Ede's diaries for 1941-1945 and 1952 and a few other papers have been deposited in the British Library. They contain a day-by-day description of the passage of the 1944 Education Act and will be available for research in 1976 (ref. Reserved MS. 128). Other papers relating to education were returned to the Department of Education and Science. They are now available at the Public Record Office among the department's Private Office papers (ref. Ed. 136). Some papers were also returned to the Home and Colonial Offices. The correspondence returned to the B.B.C. is now available at the B.B.C.'s Written Archives Centre. The letters refer to Chuter Ede's participation in, and reactions to, radio and television programmes 1959-1964. As well as Chuter Ede's own papers, the B.B.C. has, amongst its archives, papers relating to Chuter Ede, including a series of press cuttings. There are also transcripts of his broadcasts including an interview, transmitted in 1960, which he gave to George Scott, Mrs D. Pickles and Mrs J. Hubback, in which he answered questions relating to his career and beliefs.

His remaining papers were deposited in the Surrey Record Office. They include some South Shields constituency papers, papers relating to his work with the National Union of Teachers and with Surrey County Council, some general correspondence, diaries for 1946, 1-7 January 1948, and 1949 (references to Cabinet business are still restricted) and some early personal papers — applications for teaching posts and testimonials 1903-1910, and a letter written to his parents on the eve of his departure for France, September 1914. These papers have not yet been listed. Permission to see them must be obtained from Mr A.F.S. Cotton, Theodore Bell, Cotton & Co., 16 Waterloo Road, Epsom, Surrey.

No papers remain with Chuter Ede's sister, his sole surviving relation.

SIR (ROBERT) ANTHONY EDEN, 1st EARL OF AVON (1897-)

Anthony Eden was Conservative M.P. for Warwickshire (Warwick and Leamington) 1923-1957. He was Parliamentary Under-Secretary of State for Foreign Affairs September 1931-December 1933, Lord Privy Seal 1933-June 1935, Minister without Portfolio for League of Nations Affairs June-December 1935, Secretary of State for Foreign Affairs 1935-February 1938, December 1940-July 1945 and October 1951-April 1955, Secretary of State for Dominion Affairs September 1939-May 1940, Secretary of State for War May-December 1940, Prime Minister April 1955-January 1957. He was created K.G. in 1954 and Earl of Avon in 1961.

Lord Avon informs us that he hopes that all his papers will, eventually, be deposited in the library of Birmingham University. But at the moment this process is still under way — it is likely to take some years — and his papers are not yet available for research. In his three volumes of memoirs, *Full Circle, Facing the Dictators* and *The Reckoning* (1960-65), Lord Avon quoted frequently from his notes, diaries and correspondence.

NESS EDWARDS (1897-1968)

Ness Edwards was Labour M.P. for Glamorganshire (Caerphilly) 1939-1968. He was Parliamentary Secretary to the Ministry of Labour and National Service August 1945-February 1950, and Postmaster-General 1950-October 1951.

Edwards's son, Mr R.M. Edwards, informs us that his father's papers are not available for research and that he can foresee no time at which they will be made available.

WALTER ELLIOT ELLIOT (1888-1958)

Walter Elliot was Conservative M.P. for Lanarkshire (Lanark) 1918-1923, Glasgow (Kelvingrove) 1924-1945, and 1950-1958, and the Scottish Universities 1946-1950. He was Parliamentary Secretary and Minister of Health for Scotland January 1923-January 1924 and November 1924-July 1926, Parliamentary Under-Secretary of State for Scotland 1926-July 1929, Financial Secretary to the Treasury September 1931-September 1932, Minister of Agriculture and Fisheries 1932-October 1936, Secretary of State for Scotland 1936-May 1938, and Minister of Health 1938-May 1940.

Elliot's papers are in the possession of his widow, the Baroness Elliot of Harwood. They are being sorted and listed by the National Library of Scotland, to whom all enquiries about access should be addressed. The papers have not yet (March 1974) been collected together, so that it is not possible to give any idea of their bulk or content, but they include some 40 volumes of press cuttings and collections of articles.

Sir Colin R. Coote, *A Companion of Honour* (1965), quotes from a number of letters in Elliot's papers.

ALFRED EMMOTT, BARON EMMOTT (1858-1926)

Alfred Emmott was Liberal M.P. for Oldham 1899-1911. He was Chairman of Ways and Means in the House of Commons 1906-1911, Under-Secretary of State for the Colonies October 1911-August 1914, and 1st Commissioner of Works 1914-May 1915. He was created G.C.M.G. in 1914, G.B.E. in 1917, and Baron Emmott in 1911.

A small collection of his papers was deposited in 1968 by his grand-daughter, Mrs J. Simon, in the Library, Nuffield College, Oxford (ref. Emmott papers). Mrs Simon informs us that many papers were probably destroyed when Lady Emmott moved house many years ago. The papers now in Nuffield were inherited by Emmott's elder daughter, Mrs Simon's mother.

The most important items in this collection are probably two volumes of diary for 24 February 1907 to 3 October 1915. Mrs Simon's permission must be obtained for quotations from the diaries. The correspondence has been arranged in a single chronological series 1890-1927. The only exception to this arrangement is a file of papers from the Foreign Office Committee on the political situation in Russia which Emmott chaired 1920-1921. The collection has some interesting correspondence on the discontent of some Liberals with Campbell-Bannerman's leadership of the party 1900-1901, correspondence on the Congo Reform Association 1904-1908, and on the War Trade Department which Emmott organised and ran 1915-1919. There is also a considerable collection of press cuttings arranged in chronological order, and letters of condolence to Emmott's widow. There are also notes by Mrs Simon on the provenance of these papers, on Emmott's family and early life, and extracts from some letters by Emmott to his elder daughter 1906-1926 (the originals of these letters are not available for research).

A further four files of Emmott's papers have been deposited in the House of Lords Record Office (ref. Emmott papers). They include letters and memoranda concerning Winston Churchill 1900-1911 (typed copies of some of these are included in the Nuffield collection), election manifestos, photographs, press cuttings 1905-1922, a note of Emmott's voting record in the House of Commons 1899 and 1900, and letters and memoranda concerning Emmott's work as Chairman of Ways and Means 1906-1911.

Three letters between Emmott and H.H. Asquith in 1911 on the question of honours for women have been deposited in the Fawcett Library.

SIR LAMING WORTHINGTON-EVANS, 1st Bt (1868-1931)

Laming Worthington-Evans was Conservative M.P. for Colchester (Essex, Colchester from 1918) 1910-1929, and for Westminster (St George's) 1929-1931. He was Parliamentary Secretary to the Ministry of Munitions December 1916-May 1918, Minister of Blockade July 1918-January 1919, Minister of Pensions 1919-April 1920, Minister without Portfolio 1920-February 1921, Secretary of State for War 1921-October 1922, and November 1924-June 1929, and Postmaster-General May 1923-January 1924. He was created G.B.E. in 1922, and a baronet in 1916; at that time he assumed the additional surname of Worthington.

Twenty boxes of his papers were given to the Bodleian Library by his son, the late Sir Shirley Worthington-Evans, in 1972 (ref. Worthington-Evans Papers). A large number of Cabinet papers were removed by the Cabinet Office in 1935; a list of these papers survives but the papers themselves have either been lost or destroyed. The papers which remain are entirely political: there are no papers concerning Worthington-Evans's early life, his years as a solicitor, or any later personal papers.

Worthington-Evans first stood (unsuccessfully) for Parliament in 1906. A file of receipts and a return of expenses survive from this contest. Press cuttings, posters, buttons, election addresses, and other printed ephemera survive from his later election campaigns as well as some accounts, memoranda on the organization of the constituency workers, canvas returns, and the reports of political 'missionaries', and some constituency correspondence.

Very little survives relating to Worthington-Evans's activities as a back bencher. There are some press cuttings on State Insurance and the Insurance Act 1912-1914. From 1915-1916 some press cuttings survive, many concerning the commandeering of American securities and other aspects of war financing, such as the Women's War Loan scheme. There is also some correspondence dating from 1915-1916. There are few papers relating to his terms of office at the War and Foreign Offices and the Ministry of Munitions; there are no papers relating to his terms of office as Minister of Blockade or Pensions.

There are several files concerning Ireland 1918-1925. There is a list of contents to several of these files. They include Cabinet Memoranda and, for 1921 and 1922, some weekly surveys of the situation by the Chief Secretary and by the General Officer Commanding. The papers include minutes of six meetings May-November 1920 of the Amendments Committee for the Government of Ireland Bill, minutes of conferences and notes of meetings with Irish leaders October-November 1921, a printed report of the proceedings of the Irish Convention, drafts of bills from 1914 to 1920, and the Articles of Agreement of the Irish Treaty. Much material exists relating to an Arbitration Committee to decide on the contributions and compensations of the English and Irish Governments. The committee appears to have sat from 1923 (at least) until 1925. Its papers include memoranda, correspondence, transcripts of meetings, reports, and a Final Report. There is also a copy of a drawing of Arthur Griffith by Paul Henry which was given to the Irish Free State in 1923. In a file of War Office papers there are several memoranda on the Irish military situation, the activities of Sinn Feiners after the 'truce', and the need to minimise the risk of misunderstanding about the terms of the truce.

There are many files on various aspects of finance and related problems for the period 1920-1930; the Imperial Exchange and Currency, the Geddes committee's recommendations, a turnover tax, unemployment, various types of State Insurance, and political levies, are all considered in Cabinet memoranda, notes, articles, and correspondence. The problems of reparations and interallied indebtedness are also represented; these papers include a proposal by Worthington-Evans to neutralize the advantage to Germany of a depreciated mark by an exports tax. There are two box files on the Genoa Conference of 1922; they contain verbatim reports, notes on the delegates, Cabinet memoranda, and a letter from R.S. Horne, then Chancellor of the Exchequer, 28 April 1922, written in response to pressure from the King, urging that the negotiations with the Russians be conditional on an end to Bolshevik propaganda. There are also Cabinet memoranda on Iraq and Palestine 1921, 1922, and some correspondence with Lord Robert Cecil August 1922 on the implementation of the disarmament clauses of the peace treaties.

SIR LAMING WORTHINGTON-EVANS (cont.)

There are very few papers directly concerning Worthington-Evans's work at the War Office and the Post Office. There is a draft note on administering and accounting for expenditure at the War Office in 1923, and some Cabinet memoranda on attempts to reduce expenditure after the Geddes report. There is a file of private correspondence received while Worthington-Evans was at the War Office, and a file (mentioned above) on the military situation in Ireland. For a few days in March 1922 Worthington-Evans acted as Secretary of State for India. There is correspondence on Indian railways, copies of telegrams exchanged with the Viceroy, and some correspondence with the succeeding Secretary of State, Viscount Peel. There are several files of speeches from 1920 until 1930.

There are some papers concerning national politics, in particular Baldwin's election as leader of the Conservative Party and his decision to call a general election on tariff reform. There are letters from Austen Chamberlain in May 1923 and a memorandum on the events of May and June of that year. Worthington-Evans also wrote a 22 page memorandum on the events of October 1923. He was on various Unionist Party committees and, particularly for 1924, there are memoranda and minutes of meetings. In 1928 he was on the Cabinet committee which considered Conservative policy proposals, and some memoranda, minutes, and correspondence of this committee have been preserved.

Some of Worthington-Evans's papers as Parliamentary Secretary at the Ministry of Munitions have survived with official papers and are to be seen at the Public Record Office (ref. MUN/4/396-451). They include papers of the War Priorities Committee on commercial intelligence, supplies of various chemicals, and minutes of meetings with heads of departments 1917-1918. These papers would appear to be those described in a list compiled at the Ministry in 1918 and now found in the Public Record Office (ref. MUN/5/25/262.1/25).

SIR AILWYN EDWARD FELLOWES, 1st BARON AILWYN (1855-1924)

Ailwyn Edward Fellowes was Conservative M.P. for Huntingdonshire (North) 1887-1906. He was President of the Board of Agriculture March-December 1905. He was created K.C.V.O. in 1911, and Baron Ailwyn in 1921.

Neither Fellowes's son, the present (3rd) Lord Ailwyn, nor the widow of the 2nd Baron knows of any papers other than a volume of speeches made by Fellowes when he was President of the Board of Agriculture.

SIR RONALD CRAUFORD MUNRO-FERGUSON, VISCOUNT NOVAR (1860-1934)

Ronald Munro-Ferguson was Liberal M.P. for Ross and Cromarty 1884-1885 and Leith Burghs 1886-1914. He was Governor-General of Australia 1914-1920, and Secretary for Scotland October 1922-January 1924. He was created G.C.M.G. in 1914, K.T. in 1926, and Viscount Novar in 1920.

Three box-files of Munro-Ferguson's letters to his wife 1891-1913 are being calendared by the National Register of Archives (Scotland) (ref. Novar papers). The letters are owned by Munro-Ferguson's nephew, Mr A.B. Munro-Ferguson. The letters are full of uninhibited discussion of political affairs, particularly concerning relations between Lord Rosebery and Sir William Harcourt. Inquiries concerning access to these papers should be addressed to the National Register of Archives (Scotland).

A collection of Munro-Ferguson's papers (seven foot run) relating to his term-of-office as Governor-General of Australia was deposited by his trustees in the Manuscript Section of the National Library of Australia in 1961 (ref. MS. 696). A detailed list and name index of the collection have been compiled. The collection includes Munro-Ferguson's personal and official dispatches to the King, his personal and official correspondence with successive Secretaries of State for the Colonies, and his correspondence with Australian Prime Ministers, as well as correspondence with Australian politicians and officials. There are also a large number of subject files covering a wide range of subjects: from constitutional issues, and the question of channels of communication with England, to the visit in 1920 of the Prince of Wales. The National Register of Archives (Scotland) has a copy of the list of these papers.

SIR RONALD CRAUFORD MUNRO-FERGUSON (cont.)

In 1935 Lady Novar presented three bundles of her husband's letters, totalling approximately nine shelf inches, to the Australian War Memorial (ref. D.R.L. No. 2574, 3rd Series). The three groups are (1) copies of letters from Munro-Ferguson to the King 1914-1920; (2) copies of letters from Munro-Ferguson to Sir William Birdwood 1915-1920; and (3) letters from Sir William Birdwood to Munro-Ferguson 1915-1920. Permission to read the letters to the King must be obtained from the Keeper of the Royal Archives. The letters exchanged between Munro-Ferguson and Birdwood are open for research, but readers must sign an agreement indemnifying the Australian War Memorial against any legal action that may arise as a result of publication of material in the collection.

SIR ROBERT BANNATYNE FINLAY, 1st VISCOUNT FINLAY (1842-1929)

Robert Finlay was Liberal M.P. for Inverness Burghs 1885-1886; he became a Liberal Unionist in 1886 and held the seat 1886-1892 and 1895-1906; he was Conservative M.P. for Edinburgh and St Andrews Universities 1910-1916. He was Solicitor-General August 1895-May 1900, Attorney-General 1900-December 1905, and Lord Chancellor December 1916-January 1919. He was knighted in 1895, and created G.C.M.G. in 1904, Baron Finlay in 1916, and Viscount Finlay in 1919.

Finlay's grand-daughter, the Hon. Lady Hayes, of Arabella House, Nigg, Ross-shire, Scotland, has a very small collection of papers. They include press cuttings, menu cards, and a few letters commiserating with Finlay when he was not appointed Lord Chancellor in May 1915 and congratulating him when he was appointed in December 1916. Some of the latter are quoted in R.F.V. Heuston, *Lives of the Lord Chancellors 1885-1940* (Oxford, 1964).

A further collection of papers, formerly in the possession of Finlay's solicitors, has recently been added to the collection held by Lady Hayes. Most of these papers concern Finlay's various estates and property but there are also some papers of legal and political interest. There is a memorandum written by Finlay in December 1910, describing the negotiations between government and opposition over the Parliament Bill. A copy of this memorandum is available in Austen Chamberlain's papers (ref. AC 10/2/57); it is quoted in Chamberlain's *Politics from Inside. An Epistolary Chronicle, 1906-1914* (1936), pp. 295-297. There are also some papers relating to Finlay's work on the 1903 Alaskan boundary dispute, his views on how to deal with the 1912 strikers, and his opinion on the need for re-election of Ministers brought into the government or given new portfolios 1915-1916.

HERBERT ALBERT LAURENS FISHER (1865-1940)

Herbert Albert Laurens Fisher was Liberal M.P. for Sheffield (Hallam) 1916-1918, and for the English Universities 1918-1926. He was President of the Board of Education December 1916-October 1922.

Forty-five boxes of his papers were given to the Bodleian Library (ref. Fisher papers). A rough list of the papers has been compiled.

Most of Fisher's life was spent in the academic, rather than the political, world and his papers reflect this balance: there are lecture notes, bibliographies, articles, reviews, manuscripts, and reviews of Fisher's books. These include the manuscript of his unfinished memoirs published in 1940, entitled *An Unfinished Autobiography*. There are, however, several boxes of papers derived from his official career. These include Board of Education memoranda, and papers relating to the 1918 Education Act. There are also Cabinet papers on various topics, including liquor control 1920, gas warfare, the League of Nations, and Ireland. Fisher kept a diary for part of his term in office 21 November 1917-14 December 1922 and subsequently, from 8 February 1923-8 December 1924; this is included in the collection. There are also diaries for various tours he made, for example to Holland in 1910, and to the U.S.A. in 1930. There are also notes made by Fisher of conversations with Lord Rosebery in 1909, with Lord Morley in 1911, and with Lloyd George in 1916.

HERBERT ALBERT LAURENS FISHER (cont.)

Apart from his work at the Board of Education, Fisher served on several committees and commissions. There is correspondence on the 1912 Royal Commission on Indian Public Services, and memoranda on alleged German war atrocities.

There are several boxes of general correspondence covering Fisher's entire life, including letters to his wife 1907-1940, and letters to Gilbert and Lady Mary Murray 1890-1939.

David Ogg, *Herbert Fisher* (1947), quotes from the papers.

WILLIAM HAYES FISHER, BARON DOWNHAM (1853-1920)

William Hayes Fisher was Conservative M.P. for Fulham 1885-1906, and 1910-1918. He was Financial Secretary to the Treasury August 1902-April 1903, Parliamentary Secretary to the Local Government Board May 1915-June 1917, President of the Local Government Board 1917-November 1918, and Chancellor of the Duchy of Lancaster 1918-January 1919. He was created Baron Downham in 1918.

A small bundle of Hayes Fisher's letters have survived in the possession of his grandson, Mr Peter Hayes Fisher, Cock Farm, Stonegate, Wadhurst, Sussex.

There are few papers relating to Hayes Fisher's official career. There is a letter from A.J. Balfour in November 1905, explaining why Hayes Fisher could not be offered a Privy Council-lorship (see R.F.V. Heuston, *Lives of the Lord Chancellors 1885-1940* (Oxford, 1964), pp. 254-255 and 366). Hayes Fisher was finally created a Privy Councillor in July 1911; Asquith's letter informing him that the King had approved the granting of the honour, and the official notice of his taking the oath, with a covering letter from the Privy Council's clerk, have all survived. There is also a three-page typed memorandum about Hayes Fisher's appointment as Parliamentary Secretary to the Local Government Board with some relevant telegrams.

The remaining papers are miscellaneous letters, including three letters from Princess Louise about charity work, 1903 and 1916, a summons to attend Parliament 1886, and a letter from Balfour about the Royal Patriotic Fund Corporation December 1903.

GEOFFREY WILLIAM RICHARD HUGH FITZCLARENCE,
5th EARL OF MUNSTER (1906-   )

Geoffrey William Richard Hugh FitzClarence succeeded his uncle as 5th Earl of Munster in 1928. He was made K.B.E. in 1957. He was Paymaster-General June 1938-January 1939, Parliamentary Under-Secretary of State for War January-September 1939, Parliamentary Under-Secretary of State for India and Burma January 1943-October 1944, Under-Secretary of State for Home Affairs 1944-July 1945, Under-Secretary of State for Colonial Affairs October 1951-November 1954, and Minister Without Portfolio 1954-June 1957.

The Earl of Munster informs us that he has no papers of interest.

EDMOND GEORGE PETTY-FITZMAURICE,
BARON FITZMAURICE (1846-1935)

Edmond Fitzmaurice (he became Lord Edmond Fitzmaurice in 1863 when his father became 4th Marquess of Lansdowne) was Liberal M.P. for Calne 1868-1885, and Wiltshire (Cricklade) 1898-1905. He was Under-Secretary of State for Foreign Affairs January 1883-June 1885, and December 1905-October 1908, and Chancellor of the Duchy of Lancaster 1908-June 1909. He was created Baron Fitzmaurice in 1905.

Eleven box-files of his papers are in the possession of his great-nephew, the present (8th) Marquess of Lansdowne, Bowood Estate Office, Bowood, Calne, Wiltshire. Fitzmaurice had himself sorted through his papers — as an historical biographer he must have been well aware of the problems of historians — and some of his papers have explanatory notes or comments by him. He arranged the papers, most of which take the form of correspondence, by writer and then in date order, with a few subject and miscellaneous files. This original arrangement has been retained.

EDMOND GEORGE PETTY-FITZMAURICE (cont.)

There is one box-file of 'general correspondence', that is, correspondence consisting of less than five letters to or from an individual. This general correspondence is arranged alphabetically by the writers' names; it was not possible to check whether a particular writer occurs under his family name, courtesy title, or last title so all these names should be checked. The exception to this is the Fitzmaurice or Lansdowne family itself who are all grouped together under Fitzmaurice rather than being scattered between the two names. It is remarkable that the collection includes only four letters to Fitzmaurice from his brother, the 5th Marquess of Lansdowne, despite their mutually overlapping and long political lives. The four, which are in the general correspondence in this collection, were written in June 1909, when Fitzmaurice resigned because of his ill-health, and they bear witness to a close personal relationship. The outside of each file in this section gives the names of the correspondents and the dates of their letters.

Fitzmaurice's 'Special', or extensive, correspondence fills seven box-files. A list of the dates of the letters is on the outside of the file for each correspondent. There are long series of correspondence with Sir Henry Campbell-Bannerman 1900-1907, James Bryce 1900-1921, Lord Crewe 1906-1933, Sir Charles Dilke 1876-1908, Lord Eversley 1912-1928, W.E. Gladstone 1874-1898, Lord Granville 1880-1898, Lord Granville 1880-1889, Sir Edward Grey 1905-1908, Lord Ripon 1905-1909, the 6th Earl Spencer 1910-1922, and J.A. Spender 1905-1935. The last two series in particular are full of political discussion.

The three box-files of subject files include correspondence 1876-1877 to Frank H. Hill, Political Editor of the *Daily News*, on the Balkan situation, a few Foreign Office printed memoranda and correspondence, some drafts of Foreign Office letters and memoranda by Fitzmaurice, and correspondence 1907-1908 about Congo Reform with Lord Cromer, E.D. Morel, and John Harris. The miscellaneous files include press cuttings, 1898 election leaflets, and some verses by Fitzmaurice.

Following Fitzmaurice's death, his family returned to Brigadier-General J.H. Morgan a large group of letters, which he had written to Fitzmaurice (J.H. Morgan, *Assize of Arms, Being the Story of the Disarmament of Germany and her Rearmament [1919-1939]* [2 vols., 1945], i, p. 34). It has not been possible to determine whether these letters have survived, as the whereabouts of Morgan's own papers are now uncertain.

HENRY CHARLES KEITH PETTY-FITZMAURICE, 5th MARQUESS OF LANSDOWNE (1845-1927)

Henry Charles Keith Petty-Fitzmaurice was known as Viscount Clanmaurice 1845-1863, and as the Earl of Kerry from 1863 till he succeeded his father as 5th Marquess of Lansdowne in 1866. He was created G.C.M.G. in 1884, and K.G. in 1895. He was Under-Secretary of State for War April 1872-February 1874, Under-Secretary of State for India April-July 1880, Governor-General of Canada 1883-1888, Viceroy of India December 1888-January 1894, Secretary of State for War June 1895-November 1900, Secretary of State for Foreign Affairs 1900-December 1905, and Minister without Portfolio May 1915-December 1916.

A large collection of Petty-Fitzmaurice's papers is in the possession of his grandson, the present (8th) Marquess, but the collection is closed until a projected biography is completed. The papers were, however, extensively used and quoted in Lord Newton, *Lord Lansdowne, A Biography* (1929).

Petty-Fitzmaurice's papers as Viceroy of India have been given to the India Office Library (ref. MSS. Eur. D. 558). They consist of 26 volumes of correspondence and telegrams, as well as summaries of Petty-Fitzmaurice's actions as Viceroy, arranged by department, and two volumes of speeches. The correspondence has been arranged in the usual viceregal order: correspondence with the Queen (one volume), correspondence and telegrams with the Secretary of State for India (nine volumes), correspondence with persons in England (five volumes), and correspondence with persons in India (eleven volumes). Printed copies of this correspondence are also to be found in the Printed Books Department of the British Library.

Some of Petty-Fitzmaurice's papers as Secretary of State for Foreign Affairs are available in the Public Record Office (ref. F.O. 800/115-146). The papers include two files of general

HENRY CHARLES KEITH PETTY-FITZMAURICE (cont.)
correspondence 1898-1905. The remainder of the papers are arranged alphabetically by
country and cover the years 1900-1906, although the box of papers concerning Germany
includes some for 1920-1924. A subject index has been compiled.

Microfilm copies of those of Petty-Fitzmaurice's papers which relate to his term of office
as Governor-General of Canada have been made by the Public Archives of Canada (ref. MG27
I B6).

REGINALD THOMAS HERBERT FLETCHER, BARON WINSTER (1885-1961)

Reginald Thomas Herbert Fletcher was Liberal M.P. for Hampshire (Basingstoke) 1923-
1924 and Labour M.P. for Warwickshire (Nuneaton) 1935-1942. He was Minister of Civil
Aviation August 1945-October 1946 and Governor of Cyprus 1946-November 1948. He was
created K.C.M.G. in 1948 and Baron Winster in 1942.

Fletcher left most of his estate to his widow; she died shortly after him. She left their
home in Crowborough — Winster Lodge — and its contents to the Bishop of Chichester for
the benefit of Anglican clergy. Only five volumes of press cuttings have survived in the house,
in the charge of a Management Committee. Researchers wishing to see these volumes should
apply to The Resident Warden, Winster Lodge, Stone Cross, Crowborough, Sussex TN6 3SJ.
Most of the volumes cover Fletcher's post-1945 activities but one volume is solely devoted
to the Gallipoli campaign of 1915 (in which Fletcher fought). One volume contains cuttings
relating to Fletcher's term as Governor of Cyprus. As well as reports on social activities and
tours there are several pages of cuttings from the British and Cypriot press on the British proposals for limited self-government in Cyprus. The rejection of these terms led to Fletcher's
resignation. Fletcher's log-book as a midshipman September 1901-July 1903 is included in
this collection, as well as the visitors' book for his homes from 1910 onwards.

Fletcher's surviving executor, the National Westminster Bank, does not know of the
existence of any papers. Fletcher left some books and prints to the Royal Naval College,
Greenwich, but his bequest did not include any papers. The National Maritime Museum
does not know of the existence of any papers.

HUGH OAKELEY ARNOLD-FORSTER (1855-1909)

Hugh Oakeley Arnold-Forster (he assumed the name Arnold-Forster in 1877) was Liberal
Unionist M.P. for Belfast (West) 1892-1906, and Conservative M.P. for Croydon 1906-1909.
He was Parliamentary Secretary to the Admiralty November 1900-October 1903, and
Secretary of State for War 1903-December 1905.

Eighty-three volumes of Arnold-Forster's papers were presented by his son to the British
Library in 1961 (ref. Add. MSS. 50275-50357). They have been divided into four main
groups: Admiralty papers; War Office papers; diaries; and miscellaneous.

Arnold-Forster's Admiralty papers (Add. MSS. 50275-50299) include printed, typed, and
manuscript papers on staff appointments and salaries, ships' boilers, consumption of water
and coal, education, and annual estimates 1901/2-1904/5. An original index to these papers
has survived.

Arnold-Forster's War Office papers (Add. MSS. 50300-50334) cover such topics as the
Committee of Imperial Defence 1903-1904, and the Esher Committee. There are also submissions to the King 1904-1905. Again, an original index survives.

Arnold-Forster's diaries (Add. MSS. 50335-50353) cover 1903-1908. According to a note
by Arnold-Forster himself, they were dictated daily; when he was away from home he wrote
the entries himself and forwarded them for transcribing. The diaries exist both in typescript
and manuscript. The miscellaneous papers include various pamphlets and the 1901 report
and press cuttings of the Lands Settlement Committee which Arnold-Forster had chaired.

His wife, Mary Arnold-Forster, in *Memoir of H.O. Arnold-Forster* (1910), quoted from
many letters especially to his mother, and also compiled a list of his books and articles.

SIR HENRY HARTLEY FOWLER,
1st VISCOUNT WOLVERHAMPTON (1830-1911)

Henry Hartley Fowler was Liberal M.P. for Wolverhampton (Wolverhampton, East from 1885) 1880-1908. He was Under-Secretary of State at the Home Office December 1884-June 1885, Financial Secretary to the Treasury February-July 1886, President of the Local Government Board August 1892-March 1894, Secretary of State for India 1894-June 1895, Chancellor of the Duchy of Lancaster December 1905-October 1908, and Lord President of the Council 1908-June 1910. He was created G.C.S.I. in 1895, and Viscount Wolverhampton in 1908.

Fowler had one son and two daughters. His son, the 2nd Viscount Wolverhampton, died in 1943 leaving no issue. The widow of the 2nd Viscount died in 1947; her family know of no papers. Fowler's elder daughter married Alfred L. Felkin who wrote the biography of Fowler in the *D.N.B.* She died in 1929, her husband in 1942. He appointed the Fowler family law-firm and his brother-in-law as executors. The younger daughter, Edith Henrietta Fowler, married the Rev. William R. Hamilton. In *The Life of Henry Hartley Fowler, 1st Viscount Wolverhampton* (1912) she quoted from several letters. There are two sons of this marriage but they do not know of any papers, nor does the family law-firm, Messrs Fowler, Langley & Wright of Wolverhampton.

Some years ago the India Office Library purchased three volumes of correspondence from Mr Edward Hall, the antiquarian, but he is unable to give any details of the provenance of these volumes. The volumes (ref. MSS. Eur. C. 145) consist of printed and manuscript correspondence 1894-1895 with the Viceroy, Lord Elgin.

SIR JOHN DENTON PINKSTONE FRENCH, 1st EARL OF YPRES (1852-1925)

John French was Lord Lieutenant of Ireland May 1918-April 1921. He was created K.C.B. in 1900, K.P. in 1917, Viscount French in 1916, and Earl of Ypres in 1922.

Ownership of French's papers is at present the subject of a case before the High Court. The ownership is disputed by the present (3rd) Earl of Ypres, and the representatives of his late uncle, the Hon. E. Gerald French (Lady Patricia Kingsbury and Mrs Muriel Nash). It is hoped that the case will be decided by the end of 1974.

A small fragment of French's diary for June 1919-August 1920 was bought by the National Library of Ireland in 1955 (ref. MS. 2269). There are 76 pages of manuscript entries, some of which are badly torn.

Long selections from French's papers, in particular his almost daily diary entries, have been published by French himself and by his son, the Hon. E. Gerald French. French's account of the first months of World War I and the effectiveness of British military preparations are to be found in his *1914* (1919). The Hon. E. Gerald French has written *The Life of F.M. Sir John French, 1st Earl of Ypres* (1931), *French Replies to Haig* (1936), *Some War Diaries, Addresses, and Correspondence* (1937) and *The Kitchener-French Dispute. A Last Word* (Glasgow, 1960); all of which were based on his father's papers.

SIR DAVID PATRICK MAXWELL-FYFE, EARL OF KILMUIR (1900-1967)

David Patrick Maxwell-Fyfe was Conservative M.P. for Liverpool (West Derby) 1935-1954. He was Solicitor-General March 1942-May 1945, Attorney-General May-August 1945, Secretary of State for Home Affairs October 1951-October 1954, and Lord Chancellor 1954-July 1962. He was knighted in 1942, and created G.C.V.O. in 1953, Viscount Kilmuir in 1954, and Earl of Kilmuir in 1962.

Maxwell-Fyfe's literary trustees have deposited a collection of his papers in Churchill College, Cambridge. A list has been compiled but not all of the papers are open, particularly the most recent. The papers are almost all post-1942 — some of Maxwell-Fyfe's papers were destroyed by the bombing of both his house and his chambers in the second world war. In the preface to his memoirs, *Political Adventure* (1964), Maxwell-Fyfe stated that he had never 'harboured' documents but that he had written memoranda after what he considered were important events in which he had taken part. These memoranda or notes were used as

SIR DAVID PATRICK MAXWELL-FYFE (cont.)

the basis of his book but they are not in the collection deposited in Churchill College. A few letters are also quoted in the book. Maxwell-Fyfe's widow, the Countess De La Warr, informs us that she does not know what became of the notes.

The papers deposited at Churchill have been divided into six groups: 1. diaries; 2. press cuttings; 3. speeches; 4. photographs; 5. correspondence; 6. miscellaneous. The diaries cover 1954-1961 but they are only engagement diaries except for 1/5, which describes the events of July-December 1956. The press cuttings cover 1942-1951. They include cuttings made during his tenure of the Solicitor-Generalship, as well as his period in opposition 1945-1951, and his part in the Nuremberg War Criminal trials (he was Deputy Chief Prosecutor). The correspondence is mainly from the periods 1949-1952 and 1955-1962, including letters relating to his memoirs. There are also letters concerning his legal activities, his wartime services, the Nuremberg trials and a few papers relating to his unsuccessful candidacy at Wigan in 1924.

HUGH TODD NAYLOR GAITSKELL (1906-1963)

Hugh Gaitskell was Labour M.P. for Leeds (South) 1945-1963. He was Parliamentary Under-Secretary to the Ministry of Fuel and Power May 1946-October 1947, Minister of Fuel and Power 1947-February 1950, Minister of State for Economic Affairs February-October 1950, and Chancellor of the Exchequer 1950-October 1951. He was Leader of the Labour Party 1955-1963.

A very large collection of his papers, inherited by his widow, Lady Gaitskell, is temporarily in the possession of Mr Philip Williams, Nuffield College, Oxford. The papers are closed to researchers while Mr Williams is writing a biography of Gaitskell. Gaitskell's literary executors are the Rt. Hon. Roy Jenkins, M.P. and the Rt. Hon Anthony Crosland, M.P.

Most of the surviving papers are post-war but there are a few papers from Gaitskell's unsuccessful attempts to win a seat at Chatham in the 1930s. There are also papers from Gaitskell's pre-war political activities in Leeds, including a long series of correspondence with his political agent. There are also lecture notes and drafts for articles and books on economics. There are very few official papers apart from some Ministry of Fuel papers, and congratulations on his various appointments and on his budget. The bulk of the collection — in the form of letters, committee papers, speech notes, memoranda, pamphlets, and press cuttings — derives from the 1950s.

There are twelve box files of constituency papers, including correspondence about visits, party meetings, particular cases, and a long correspondence with Gaitskell's agent. Gaitskell's Labour Party papers include drafts of party publications and material from the party's conferences, meetings, and general elections. There are also several boxes of correspondence with M.P.s and politicians, especially Sir Stafford Cripps and Hugh Dalton. There are many subject files of press cuttings, memoranda, and pamphlets.

SIR AUCKLAND CAMPBELL GEDDES, 1st BARON GEDDES (1879-1954)

Auckland Campbell Geddes was Unionist M.P. for Hampshire (Basingstoke) 1917-1920. He was Minister of National Service August 1917-August 1919, President of the Local Government Board November 1918-January 1919, Minister of Reconstruction January-May 1919, and President of the Board of Trade 1919-March 1920. He was Ambassador to Washington 1920-1924. He was created K.C.B. in 1917, G.C.M.G. in 1922, and Baron Geddes in 1942.

According to his son, the present (2nd) Baron Geddes, Geddes was very methodical in destroying both official and business papers and after his death none were found. In his book, *The Forging of a Family* (1952), Geddes devoted some 50 pages to his own career, written in the third person; conversations are quoted, but very few letters are mentioned.

SIR ERIC CAMPBELL GEDDES (1875-1937)

Sir Eric Geddes was Unionist M.P. for Cambridge 1917-1922. He was 1st Lord of the Admiralty July 1917-January 1919, Minister without Portfolio January-May 1919, and Minister of Transport August 1919-November 1921. He was knighted in 1916, and created G.B.E. in 1919.

Geddes's son, Sir Reay Geddes, informs us that his father kept no papers.

Geddes's Private Office papers as Controller (May-September 1917) and 1st Lord of the Admiralty are available at the Public Record Office (ref. Adm. 116/1804-10). Adm. 116/1804 is an index of the correspondence. His Ministry of Transport papers are also available at the Public Record Office (ref. M.T. 49). The bulk of these papers is concerned with the drawing up and passage of the 1921 Railways Act which amalgamated 123 separate railway companies. There are notes of meetings, proposals, and deputations from the different groups. There is also much material on railway administration, the revision of the 1921 season ticket rates for the Underground, and the 1919 strike. There are also papers concerning canals, ferries, ports, roads, and traffic — for example on the use of road works to alleviate unemployment. The Public Record Office also has papers connected with Geddes's work as Deputy Director-General of Munitions Supply (1915) including correspondence and minutes (ref. MUN 4/1733-6). A list of Geddes's own papers from the Ministry of Munitions period, drawn up in 1919, is to be found in the Public Record Office (ref. MUN 5/26/262. 1/49). These munitions papers are now lost, though they were used by the official historians of the Ministry of Munitions.

In *The Forging of a Family* (1952), Geddes's brother, the 1st Baron Geddes, devoted thirty pages to E.C. Geddes's career; only a few letters are quoted but there are also occasional descriptions of conversations.

DAVID LLOYD GEORGE, 1st EARL LLOYD-GEORGE OF DWYFOR (1863-1945)

David Lloyd George was Liberal M.P. for Caernarvon Boroughs 1890-1945; he styled himself an Independent Liberal from 1931. He was President of the Board of Trade December 1905-April 1908, Chancellor of the Exchequer 1908-May 1915, Minister of Munitions 1915-July 1916, Secretary of State for War July-December 1916, and Prime Minister 1916-October 1922. He was created Earl Lloyd-George of Dwyfor in 1945.

One thousand and forty one boxes of Lloyd George's papers were purchased by Lord Beaverbrook in 1949. They are now owned by the First Beaverbrook Foundation and housed in the Beaverbrook Library. The papers have been listed and are divided into the following series: (A) papers as an M.P. to 1905, thirteen boxes; (B) papers as President of the Board of Trade, five boxes; (C) papers as Chancellor, 36 boxes; (D) papers as Minister of Munitions, 27 boxes; (E) papers as Secretary of State for War, ten boxes; (F) papers as Prime Minister, 254 boxes; (G) papers for 1922-1945, 264 boxes; (H) press cuttings, arranged in alphabetical order and mostly after 1922, 390 boxes; (I) personal papers, 42 boxes.

Series A-G have been divided into correspondence and papers. The correspondence has been subdivided into semi-official, special (that is, with particular individuals), foreign (arranged by country), general, and Cabinet notes. The papers have been divided into semi-official, Cabinet, and general. They include speech notes, briefs for speeches made during his premiership, and notes on deputations. Series F and G have 'secretarial' sections, that is papers produced by Lloyd George's secretaries. They include notes on the political situation 1939-1945 made by A.J. Sylvester, Lloyd George's secretary, when Lloyd George was away from Westminster. Series G includes articles and books by Lloyd George, correspondence about their publication, and material used in them including papers removed from Lloyd George's own and other people's papers.

A card index of every reference to any person or subject (except in the printed papers) has been made for series A-E, and partly for F and G.

Large portions of Lloyd George's papers have been published, initially in his own *War Memoirs* (6 vols., 1935-36), and *The Truth About the Peace Treaties* (2 vols., 1938). Two biographies have been based on the papers: *David Lloyd George* by Malcolm Thomson (1948);

DAVID LLOYD GEORGE (cont.)

and *Tempestuous Journey* by Frank Owen (1954). John Grigg, *The Young Lloyd George* (1973), is based on the papers in the Beaverbrook Library, those in the National Library of Wales (see below), and some still in the possession of members of the Lloyd George family.

A collection of over 3,500 letters to his wife and other members of his family was purchased by the National Library of Wales in 1969 (ref. N.L.W. MSS. 20403-20493). A selection has been edited by Dr Kenneth Morgan: *Lloyd George, Family Letters 1885-1936* (Cardiff and London, 1973). These papers are now open for research on the condition that nothing relating to the private life of the Lloyd George family may be published without the prior permission of the Librarian and/or surviving members of the family.

Some early letters and diaries of Lloyd George, together with a large number of letters to his brother, William George, are in the possession of his nephew, Mr W.R.P. George of Criccieth, but they are not at present open to scholars. They were, however, used in Herbert du Parcq, *Life of David Lloyd George* (4 vols., 1912-14), and William George, *My Brother and I* (1958).

Lloyd George's grandson, the 3rd Earl Lloyd-George, has one box of letters and photographs relating to his grandfather's career, but these are not generally available for research.

GWILYM LLOYD GEORGE, 1st VISCOUNT TENBY (1894-1967)

Major Gwilym Lloyd George was Liberal M.P. for Pembrokeshire 1922-1924 and 1929-1950, and Conservative M.P. for Newcastle-upon-Tyne (North) 1951-1957. He was Parliamentary Secretary to the Board of Trade September-November 1931, and September 1939-February 1941, Parliamentary Secretary to the Ministry of Food October 1940-June 1942, Minister of Fuel and Power 1942-August 1945, Minister of Food October 1951-October 1954, and Secretary of State for Home Affairs 1954-January 1957. He was created Viscount Tenby in 1957.

A small, miscellaneous collection of his papers is in the possession of his younger son, the Hon. William Lloyd George. They are not generally available for research. The bulk of the collection consists of congratulations on entering office and on Lloyd George's various honours. These have been weeded and only those from prominent individuals or of personal importance retained. There are a few notes for speeches: on capital punishment; on Suez (3 December 1956); and on being given the freedom of Cardiff in 1956. There are a few letters from Winston Churchill, most of them simply offering posts in the government. There are some papers concerning the 1951 election campaign, including campaign material and letters of support from Winston Churchill and Lord Beaverbrook. There is a large file of papers relating to a law suit brought against Lloyd George in 1957 by a Mr Marrinan, for granting authorization (as Secretary of State for Home Affairs) to the police in 1956 to tap Marrinan's telephone. Lloyd George won the case but had to pay most of his own costs. Perhaps of greatest interest is a note on the visit made by Lloyd George with his father to Hitler in 1936. Lloyd George says that the visit was made solely to study what the Germans were doing to meet their unemployment problem. There are also a few pages of typed notes which were the beginnings of a volume of memoirs never completed. They include Lloyd George's impressions of political contemporaries, such as Stanley Baldwin, Neville Chamberlain, and Sir John Simon, as well as childhood, family and parliamentary reminiscences.

EDWARD GIBSON, 1st BARON ASHBOURNE (1837-1913)

Edward Gibson was Conservative M.P. for Dublin University 1875-1885. He was Irish Attorney General 1877-1880 and Lord Chancellor of Ireland with a seat in the Cabinet 1885-1886, 1886-1892, June 1895-December 1905. He was created Baron Ashbourne in 1885.

A considerable collection of his papers has been deposited by his grandson, the present (3rd) Baron Ashbourne, in the House of Lords Record Office (ref. H.L.R.O. Historical Collections, Ashbourne Papers). Most of the papers are in bundles whose contents are occasionally indicated on the outside. As well as personal and legal papers, there are papers referring to Gibson's election campaigns, including letters of support and Gibson's election address for Waterford in 1874. The bulk of the papers is composed of correspondence from

EDWARD GIBSON (cont.)

Gibson's terms of office. His correspondents included Salisbury 1884-1907, Hartington, A.J. Balfour 1887-1902, and the various viceroys of Ireland.

There are some printed Cabinet memoranda and draft bills and also a few fragments of notes on Cabinet meetings. There are volumes of press cuttings, photographs, and speeches; and notes and correspondence concerning Gibson's biography of Pitt.

Three volumes of diaries cover the years 1884, 1890-1891, 1894, 1898, 1902 and 1912 but most of the entries are disjointed jottings mainly written in 1912, and one volume concerns journeys abroad in 1872. There are also ten notebooks whose subjects range from the establishment of a life peerage to quotations from politicians on various questions.

A calendar of the papers is to be published jointly by the House of Lords Record Office and the Public Record Office of Northern Ireland.

SIR HARDINGE STANLEY GIFFARD, 1st EARL OF HALSBURY (1823-1921)

Hardinge Stanley Giffard was Conservative M.P. for Launceston 1877-1885. He was Solicitor-General November 1875-April 1880 and Lord Chancellor June 1885-February 1886, August 1886-August 1892 and June 1895-December 1905. He was knighted in 1875, created Baron Halsbury in 1885 and Earl of Halsbury in 1898.

Eight volumes of Giffard's papers were given to the British Library by his grandson, the present (3rd) Lord Halsbury, in 1970 (ref. Add. MSS. 56370-56377). These papers had previously been described in report 579 of the National Register of Archives. There are three volumes of general correspondence 1867-1921 and three volumes of special correspondence, including letters from the 3rd Marquess of Salisbury 1885-1903, the 4th Marquess of Salisbury 1904-1917, W.H. Smith 1886-1891, the 8th Duke of Devonshire 1894-1902, Joseph Chamberlain 1895-1914, the 5th Marquess of Lansdowne 1896-1915, and Lord James of Hereford 1897-1906. In addition, there are two volumes of drafts and notes for speeches and memoranda on Giffard's career. Amongst the topics covered by these papers is the 1911 Parliament Act — Giffard was a leader of the Tory 'Die-hard' peers — as well as some of Giffard's more famous legal cases.

Alice Wilson Fox, *The Earl of Halsbury, Lord High Chancellor (1823-1921)* (1929), quotes from many of these papers.

SIR JOHN GILMOUR, 2nd Bt (1876-1940)

John Gilmour was Conservative M.P. for Renfrewshire (East) 1910-1918 and Glasgow (Pollok) 1918-1940. He was Secretary of State for Scotland November 1924-June 1929, Minister of Agriculture and Fisheries August 1931-September 1932, Secretary of State for Home Affairs 1932-June 1935, and Minister of Shipping October 1939-March 1940. He succeeded his father as 2nd baronet in 1920, and was created G.C.V.O. in 1935.

Gilmour's papers are in the possession of his son, the Rt. Hon. Col. Sir John Gilmour, Bt, D.S.O., M.P. We have not been able to examine them, but Sir John informs us that eventually he intends to deposit the papers in the Scottish Record Office.

HERBERT JOHN GLADSTONE, VISCOUNT GLADSTONE (1854-1930)

Herbert Gladstone was Liberal M.P. for Leeds 1880-1885 and for Leeds (West) 1885-1910. He was Financial Secretary to the War Office February-July 1886, Under-Secretary of State for Home Affairs August 1892-March 1894, 1st Commissioner of Works 1894-June 1895, Secretary of State for Home Affairs December 1905-February 1910, and Governor-General of South Africa 1910-1914. He was created G.C.M.G. and Viscount Gladstone in 1910.

The greater part of Gladstone's papers — 134 volumes — was deposited by his widow in 1935 in the British Library (ref. Add. MSS. 45985-46118). They have been divided into eight main divisions: royal correspondence; special correspondence; family correspondence; general correspondence; official papers; notes; diaries; literary papers. An index of correspondents has been compiled.

HERBERT JOHN GLADSTONE (cont.)

There is one volume of correspondence with successive sovereigns and their secretaries. There are 57 volumes of special correspondence including two volumes of correspondence with Sir Henry Campbell-Bannerman 1886-1908, one volume with H.H. Asquith 1892-1922, one volume with Lord Crewe 1886-1928, six volumes with Lewis Harcourt 1894-1920 (mainly for the period when Harcourt was Colonial Secretary and Gladstone Governor-General of South Africa), two volumes with General Botha 1910-1914, one volume with J.C. Smuts 1910-1928, and one volume with Lord Buxton (Gladstone's successor in South Africa). There is considerable correspondence with more of Gladstone's political contemporaries and with Liberal Whips (Gladstone was Liberal Chief Whip 1899-1905). There is also correspondence with his constituents, including three volumes 1880-1923 with Joseph Henry, Lord Mayor of Leeds in 1918. There are only three volumes of family correspondence including correspondence with his father 1881-1884. There are 39 volumes of general correspondence 1880-1930.

Gladstone's official papers have been sub-divided by his various terms of office. There are three volumes of papers as 1st Commissioner of Works and two volumes as Under-Secretary at the Home Office. The five volumes for Gladstone's period as Secretary of State at the Home Office cover some of the most difficult problems of his department: the 1906-1908 Licensing Bill; the passage of the 1908 Coal Mines (Eight Hours) Act; and the 1907-1908 Prevention of Crime Act. There are four volumes of papers as Governor-General of South Africa. An additional three books of press cuttings mainly for this period are available in the Printed Books department of the British Library (ref. 1899.b.11). There are five volumes of Gladstone's papers as Liberal Chief Whip, including two notebooks of lists of possible Liberal candidates. Gladstone's later activities are also represented, for example, his work for Belgian war refugees.

There are two volumes of notes for speeches 1881-1929. The diary in this collection is for 1910-1913. Gladstone's literary manuscripts include his Oxford lecture notes and the typescript of an unpublished autobiography.

A further thirteen volumes of Gladstone's papers were opened for research in 1960 (ref. Add. MSS. 46474-46486). They are arranged on the same principles as the preceding collection. They include Gladstone's diaries — mainly notes of interviews — for 1899-1905 and 1922-1924. An original name index for these diaries survives. There are more papers concerning Parliamentary constituencies and candidates, including papers on the administration of the Liberal Party and two volumes of correspondence with Sir Donald Maclean 1921-1929.

Most of the Gladstone family's personal papers have been deposited in St Deiniol's Library, Hawarden (ref. Glynne-Gladstone papers). Access to these papers is granted by the Flintshire County Record Office, to which all applications should be addressed. Researchers wishing to see these papers are advised to give several days' notice of their visits so that the papers may be transferred to the record office. Lists of the papers are in preparation. There are a few fragments of Gladstone's papers in this collection, including his political diary 1880-1885. There is some correspondence with various members of his family and with political contemporaries 1882-1928. Of considerable interest for any study of Gladstone is his correspondence with his brother H.N. Gladstone, Baron Gladstone 1865-1930. There are over 2000 letters in this series including many written when Gladstone was at the Home Office and in South Africa.

Sir Charles Mallet, *Herbert Gladstone. A Memoir* (1932) is based on Gladstone's papers and quotes from the draft autobiography.

WILLIAM GEORGE ARTHUR ORMSBY-GORE, 4th BARON HARLECH (1885-1964)

William George Arthur Ormsby-Gore was Conservative M.P. for Denbigh 1910-1918, and for Staffordshire (Stafford) 1918-1938. He was Under-Secretary of State for the Colonies October 1922-January 1924 and November 1924-June 1929, Postmaster-General September-November 1931, 1st Commissioner of Works 1931-June 1936, and Secretary of State for the Colonies 1936-May 1938. He was created G.C.M.G. in 1938 and K.G. in 1948. He succeeded his father as the 4th Baron Harlech in 1938.

WILLIAM GEORGE ARTHUR ORMSBY-GORE (cont.)

His son, the present (5th) Lord Harlech, informs us that a thorough search has not revealed any private papers and that it is to be feared that his father destroyed his papers before he died.

GEORGE JOACHIM GOSCHEN, 1st VISCOUNT GOSCHEN (1831-1907)

George Goschen was Liberal M.P. for the City of London 1863-1880, Ripon 1880-1885, and Edinburgh (East) 1885-1886. He became Liberal Unionist M.P. for St George's, Hanover Square 1887-1900. He was Paymaster-General November 1865-March 1866, Chancellor of the Duchy of Lancaster January-July 1866, President of the Poor Law Board (and in the Cabinet) December 1868-March 1871, 1st Lord of the Admiralty 1871-February 1874 and June 1895-November 1900, Chancellor of the Exchequer January 1887-August 1892. He was created Viscount Goschen in 1900.

A small collection of Goschen's papers was deposited in the Bodleian Library, Oxford (ref. Dep.c.182, 183) by his grand-daughter, the Hon. Mrs F. Balfour. There are 33 letters from A.J. Balfour 1887-1895, mainly about Ireland. There are sixteen typed copies of letters to Queen Victoria 1885-1886; the originals are in the Royal Archives. There are also three packets of letters from Goschen, writing in his capacity as Chancellor of Oxford University, to Percy Matheson 1904-1907. The Bodleian Library has also acquired several miscellaneous letters including a register of some of Goschen's letters as 1st Lord of the Admiralty (ref. MS. Eng.hist.c.286, 101 ff).

The small size of this collection is something of a mystery since the Hon. Arthur D. Elliot, in his biography *The Life of George Joachim Goschen, 1st Viscount Goschen 1831-1907* (2 vols., 1911), quoted from diaries, letters, and an autobiographical fragment concerning Goschen's childhood and early years. These papers seem to have been used as late as 1946 by Percy Colson in his *Lord Goschen and his friends: The Goschen Letters* (1946). But when the 2nd Viscount died in 1952 his daughter, Mrs Balfour, found only those papers which she has deposited in the Bodleian. Mrs Balfour inquired at that time amongst other members of her family but discovered no other papers. It is possible that the 2nd Viscount destroyed them when he moved from his old house. The present (3rd) Viscount Goschen knows of no papers other than those in the Bodleian. The Hon. Arthur Elliot's papers have now been deposited in the National Library of Scotland but there are no Goschen papers among them nor is there any indication there of what became of them. (See also *Addenda*, p. 167.)

HARRY GOSLING (1861-1930)

Harry Gosling was Labour M.P. for Stepney, Whitechapel, and St George's 1923-1930. He was Minister of Transport and Paymaster-General January-November 1924.

Gosling's adopted daughter, Mrs Christina Mann, informs us that she believes that her father's papers were all destroyed. She has only press cuttings of his obituary notices. Gosling's autobiography, *Up and Down Stream* (1927), does not appear to quote from any papers.

GEORGE GRANVILLE SUTHERLAND-LEVESON-GOWER, 5th DUKE OF SUTHERLAND (1888-1963)

George Granville Sutherland-Leveson-Gower, Earl Gower 1888-1892, and Marquess of Stafford from 1892 till he succeeded his father as 5th Duke of Sutherland in 1913, was Under-Secretary of State for Air October 1922-January 1924, Paymaster-General June 1925-December 1928, and Parliamentary Under-Secretary of State for War 1928-June 1929. He was created K.T. in 1929.

Neither his widow, Clare, Duchess of Sutherland, nor his kinsman, the present (6th) Duke of Sutherland, nor his niece, the present (24th) Countess of Sutherland, knows what became of Sutherland-Leveson-Gower's papers. There are none in the Muniment Room at Dunrobin Castle, nor are there any in the Sutherland Papers in the Staffordshire Record Office.

Sutherland-Leveson-Gower's memoirs, *Looking Back* (1958), do not appear to quote from any papers.

64

WILLIAM GRAHAM (1887-1932)

William Graham was Labour M.P. for Edinburgh (Central) 1918-1931. He was Financial Secretary to the Treasury January-November 1924, and President of the Board of Trade June 1929-August 1931.

We have been unable to trace any Graham papers. There was no issue of his marriage. His wife, Ethel Margaret, to whom he left all his property, died in 1947. The solicitors who acted for her executrixes were unable to put us in touch with them and we have been unable to trace them.

Graham's brother, Thomas Newton Graham, wrote a biography *Willie Graham* (1948). He quoted from several articles by Graham and a few letters. T.N. Graham died in 1965 but his sister, Lady Mathers, informs us that the papers on which the book was based were returned to Graham's widow when the book was finished and that no one in the family knows what became of these papers.

ARTHUR GREENWOOD (1880-1954)

Arthur Greenwood was Labour M.P. for Nelson and Colne 1922-1931, and Wakefield 1932-1954. He was Parliamentary Secretary to the Ministry of Health January-November 1924, Minister of Health June 1929-August 1931, Minister without Portfolio in charge of economic affairs May 1940-February 1942, Lord Privy Seal July 1945-April 1947, Paymaster-General July 1946-March 1947, and Minister without Portfolio April-September 1947.

Greenwood's son, Lord Greenwood of Rossendale, informs us that Mr Geoffrey McDermott is writing a study of his father's work based on Greenwood's papers and, at least until that work is completed, the papers will not be available for research. The collection includes 35 files and parcels formerly available at Transport House. The ultimate resting place of the collection has not yet been decided.

SIR (THOMAS) HAMAR GREENWOOD, 1st Bt, 1st VISCOUNT GREENWOOD (1870-1948)

Hamar Greenwood (he was christened Thomas Hubbard) was Liberal M.P. for York 1906-1910, Sunderland 1910-1922, and Conservative M.P. for Walthamstow (East) 1924-1929. He was Under-Secretary of State for Home Affairs January-April 1919, Secretary for Overseas Trade 1919-April 1920, and Chief Secretary for Ireland 1920-October 1922. He was created a baronet in 1915, Baron Greenwood in 1929, and Viscount Greenwood in 1937.

Greenwood's daughter, the Hon. Mrs D.R. de Lazlo, informs us that her father's papers were stored in a cellar in a part of Gray's Inn which was destroyed by an incendiary bomb in the last war. Mr Richard Miller, who was asked by the present (2nd) Lord Greenwood to write a biography of his father, was unable to find any papers, and has, therefore, abandoned the project.

SIR EDWARD GREY, 3rd Bt, VISCOUNT GREY OF FALLODON (1862-1933)

Sir Edward Grey was Liberal M.P. for Northumberland (Berwick-on-Tweed) 1885-1916. He was Parliamentary Under-Secretary of State for Foreign Affairs August 1892-June 1895 and Secretary of State for Foreign Affairs December 1905-December 1916. He succeeded his grandfather as 3rd baronet in 1882, and was created K.G. in 1912, and Viscount Grey of Fallodon in 1916.

In his memoirs, *Twenty-Five Years* (2 vols., 1925), Grey said that all his private papers, with two unspecified exceptions, were at the Foreign Office. These papers are now available at the Public Record Office (ref. F.O. 800/35-113). There are five volumes of general papers from his period as Under-Secretary; the remaining papers derive from his term as Secretary of State. They include 46 boxes of papers arranged by country — for example, three boxes about Egypt 1905-1916, twelve about France, and two about Germany. There are also sixteen boxes of correspondence with other departments of state, and correspondence with King Edward VII, King George V, and Queen Alexandra. The remaining eight boxes are miscellaneous papers, including some concerning Sir Roger Casement. An original index survives.

SIR EDWARD GREY (cont.)

Grey himself quoted extensively from these papers in his memoirs, though they were selected for him from the Foreign Office archives by J.A. Spender because of Grey's failing eyesight. Other official papers are cited in G.P. Gooch and H.W.V. Temperley, *British Documents on the Origins of the War 1898-1914* (11 vols., 1926-38). Some personal papers, for example, Grey's correspondence with his first wife, are quoted in G.M. Trevelyan, *Grey of Fallodon* (1937); Trevelyan also quoted from an unpublished autobiography, but the fate of these private papers is not known for certain, and they cannot now be found.

Grey had no children. His two wives died before him and their families have no knowledge of the existence of any papers other than those in the Public Record Office. Grey's will contains no reference to his papers, nor did he appoint literary executors. For his biography, *Sir Edward Grey* (1971), Professor Keith Robbins pursued the two possible sources of information: the Grey family and the Trevelyan family. Grey's estate was inherited by his nephew, Captain (later Sir) Cecil Graves. Sir Cecil is now dead but neither his widow, Lady Graves, 77 Swanston Avenue, Edinburgh 10, who owns the copyright of Grey's letters, nor his son knows of the existence of any papers. It is of course likely that not many papers survived the two house fires suffered by Grey. The present owners of Fallodon have no knowledge of any papers and a personal inspection by Professor Robbins failed to discover them. Trevelyan's family and friends were unable to give any positive information but all assume that he would have returned the papers to the family. Professor Robbins would be happy to give more detailed information about his searches to interested scholars.

JAMES GRIFFITHS (1890-   )

James Griffiths was Labour M.P. for Carmarthenshire (Llanelli) 1936-1970. He was Minister of National Insurance August 1945-February 1950, Secretary of State for the Colonies 1950-October 1951, and Secretary of State for Wales October 1964-April 1966.

Mr Griffiths has recently deposited three suitcases of papers in the Library of Coleg Harlech (ref. James Griffiths papers). The papers are not yet listed but they are available for research.

The bulk of the papers refer to Mr Griffiths's Welsh activities. From 1925 till 1936 he was Miners' Agent to the Anthracite Miners' Association. His 1925 election address for this position survives, as do press cuttings on the coal industry, notes of meetings with officials of the Mines Department, and many papers on compensation for accidents in general and for silicosis in particular. Mr Griffiths's work on behalf of the miners he represented is reflected by correspondence on particular cases and copies of the major legal judgements of the period. No papers relating to Mr Griffiths's work as President of the South Wales Miners Federation are included in this collection.

Many papers have survived from Mr Griffiths's parliamentary election campaigns, including all his election addresses 1936-1964, as well as press cuttings, posters, and typescripts of the many election broadcasts Mr Griffiths made. In addition, for the 1936 by-election, when Mr Griffiths first stood for Llanelli, there are many letters encouraging him to stand and wishing him well. They include a letter from Sir Stafford Cripps (10 February 1936) saying '. . . it is so important to have real Socialists in the House of Commons now, there are so many reformists'.

Mr Griffiths's constituency work is represented by correspondence on particular cases and on matters of general interest to Llanelli, especially economic matters such as the location of new strip mills and the suggested closure of the ordnance factory at Penby. There are also papers dealing with a suggested new town for mid Wales.

Mr Griffiths's parliamentary activities are represented by the manuscript of his maiden speech (delivered 23 April 1936 on the effects of the tariff on the Welsh economy), a note of congratulation for the speech from Clement Attlee, and papers relating to an attempt in 1969 to amend the Workmens' Compensation and Benefit Act by a private member's bill. There are also a few Parliamentary Labour Party papers: the report of a questionnaire on House of Commons' services conducted in 1968; a declaration on how the party would elect a prime minister if similar circumstances to those arising on the resignation of Sir Anthony

JAMES GRIFFITHS (cont.)

Eden occurred while the Labour Party was in office; and the party's code of conduct adopted in 1968.

There are drafts and press cuttings of articles by or about Mr Griffiths, including biographical articles, articles about the Ammanford White House Society in 1925, Mr Griffiths's 'Westminster Commentary' written for the *Llanelly Mercury* 1959-1960, and many press cuttings on Welsh nationalism. There is a manuscript draft of Mr Griffiths's *Glo* (Liverpool, 1945) and the type-script of his memoirs, *Pages from Memory* (1969). The latter includes some of the original typed notes described by Mr Griffiths in his memoirs as his substitute for a diary.

A few papers survive relating to Mr Griffiths's work as a Governor of the B.B.C. in Wales. There are also manuscript notes for speeches, for example nominating the then Dr H. King as Speaker (1966) and commemorative addresses on David Lloyd George and V. Hartshorn.

Mr Griffiths has still more papers relating to his many and varied activities at his home, 32 Combemartin Road, London SW18 5PR. They include, for example, material used by Mr Griffiths in drawing up articles published in *The Western Mail* 17 and 18 May 1972 on how strip-mills came to Wales. Unfortunately Mr Griffiths destroyed most of the contemporary notes or diaries he kept because at that time he felt they would be of no future interest. Mr Griffiths says that he would be happy to help researchers.

SIR EDWARD WILLIAM MACLEAY GRIGG, 1st BARON ALTRINCHAM (1879-1955)

Sir Edward Grigg was Liberal M.P. for Oldham 1922-1925 and National Conservative M.P. for Cheshire (Altrincham) 1933-1945. He was Parliamentary Secretary to the Ministry of Information September 1939-April 1940, Financial Secretary to the War Office April-May 1940, Joint-Under-Secretary to the War Office 1940-March 1942 and Minister Resident in the Middle East November 1944-May 1945. He was created K.C.V.O. in 1920, K.C.M.G. in 1928, and Baron Altrincham in 1945.

His papers are in the possession of his son, Mr John Grigg, 32 Dartmouth Row, London S.E.10. A microfilm of the greater part of the papers was made by the Douglas Library, Queen's University, Kingston, Ontario, Canada; a copy is now available in the Bodleian Library (ref. MSS. film 999-1013).

Except for a few miscellaneous letters and press cuttings, no papers appear to have survived from Grigg's terms of office. However, much has survived which relates to his other activities: military secretary to the Prince of Wales 1919-1920; private secretary to Lloyd George 1920-1922; Governor of Kenya 1925-1930; and Chairman of the Milk Reorganization Committee 1932. These papers, which cover the years 1919-1946, and fill 30 boxes, have been divided into six main sections: General Correspondence; Subject Files; Printed Material; Speeches and Publications; Personal; Duplicates.

The General Correspondence series consists of private correspondence and official correspondence which has no subject file. The series is arranged chronologically by year and within each year alphabetically by correspondent. An index has been compiled for this section; it too is arranged chronologically by year and then by correspondent. Each entry for a particular individual gives the number of letters, their outside dates and sometimes an indication of the content of the letter(s).

The subject files have been arranged into twelve main divisions: World War I schemes 1916-1918; the Prince of Wales' tours 1919-1920; Foreign Affairs 1919-1922; Imperial Relations 1918-1922; India 1920-1922 — which has a considerable amount of material on the resignation of E.S. Montagu; Ireland 1920-1921; (these last four sub-sections relate to Grigg's years as secretary to Lloyd George); East Africa 1925-1930; Lady Grigg's Welfare League; Milk Reorganization Commission; Election material 1923 and 1933: many letters which would have been put in this category have been destroyed; Defence 1932-1945 (many letters which for the most part expressed agreement with the National Register proposals or suggested alternatives have been destroyed); *The Observer* tribunal 1941-1942: Grigg was a member of the tribunal appointed to settle the differences between J.L. Garvin and W. Astor when the former resigned.

SIR EDWARD WILLIAM MACLEAY GRIGG (cont.)

The printed material is divided into seven sections: press cuttings 1919-1925: these were arranged by Grigg's secretary and cross-referenced (not microfilmed); a scrapbook for the 1933 Altrincham by-election; press cuttings for 1940-1945 (not microfilmed); reviews of *Faith of an Englishman* (1936), *The British Commonwealth* (1943), *British Foreign Policy* (1944); and various pamphlets.

Grigg's speeches have been divided into speeches and broadcasts. The section including his articles does not include his letters to *The Times:* they are to be found in the General Correspondence series.

The personal papers consist of family correspondence arranged alphabetically and miscellaneous items — bills, statements, etc., which were not microfilmed. The final section of duplicates was also not microfilmed.

SIR PERCY JAMES GRIGG (1890-1964)

Sir James Grigg, after a long career as a senior civil servant (he was Principal Private Secretary to successive Chancellors of the Exchequer 1921-1930), was National M.P. for Cardiff (East) 1942-1945. He was Secretary of State for War February 1942-August 1945. He was created K.C.B. in 1932.

Grigg's papers have been deposited by his executors in Churchill College, Cambridge. A list is available but the post-1945 papers are closed to research. Grigg wrote in the preface to his autobiography *Prejudice and Judgment* (1948): 'From none of my jobs have I brought away more than a handful of papers and at no time have I ever kept a diary' (p. 8); nevertheless some interesting papers have survived.

The only material relating to Grigg's early life came from his father's papers; it includes a speech day address by his headmaster, Grigg's school-certificate, the order of service for his wedding and an early photograph. Only a few letters from the various Chancellors he served have survived.

Most of the papers derive from Grigg's Indian service: he was Financial Member of the Government of India 1934-1939. Correspondence with Neville Chamberlain, Winston Churchill, Montagu Norman, Lords Linlithgow and Lothian and others has survived. It includes several long and blunt letters from Philip Snowden 1935-1936 (3/12). There are files on Indian Federation, the Indian political situation, on the Reserve Bank, and on a financial enquiry. There are also ten albums compiled by Lady Grigg which include not only programmes, photographs and souvenirs, but also her letters to her husband 1934-1936, and to Thomas Jones 1934-1939. Grigg's own attitude to Indian affairs and later events is revealed in his letters to his father 1937-1953.

Only a few papers have survived from Grigg's term of office as Secretary of State and as an M.P. They include congratulations, correspondence about the loss of his pension, and correspondence inviting Grigg to stand as National M.P. for Cambridge University in April 1945. The miscellaneous correspondence includes many letters from soldiers, including Sir Bernard Paget and especially from Field Marshal Lord Montgomery. The latter seems to have sent Grigg drafts of speeches for comment as well as frequently corresponding with him, particularly in 1949-1958 and 1962-1963.

There is a good deal of material concerned with the publication of Grigg's memoirs; it includes permissions to quote from letters, and reviews by Winston Churchill and others. There are also cuttings of reviews by Grigg and related correspondence, correspondence with Sir James Butler on the official history of the second world war, and several draft obituaries of Winston Churchill, Lord Montgomery, Lord Alanbrooke, Sir John Dill, Sir Bernard Paget, and Lord Wavell. A few papers have survived from Grigg's other postwar activities, in particular a file of correspondence relating to his chairmanship of the Commission of Inquiry into the preservation of departmental records, and the proposal in 1957 that he be Chairman of the Independent Television Authority.

FREDERICK EDWARD GUEST (1875-1937)

'Freddie' Guest was Liberal M.P. for Dorset (East) 1910-1922, Gloucestershire (Stroud) 1923-1924 and Bristol (North) 1924-1929. In 1930 he became a Conservative and was M.P. for Plymouth (Drake) 1931-1937. He was Secretary of State for Air April 1921-October 1922.

Neither Guest's son, Raymond R. Guest, nor his great nephew, the present (3rd) Lord Wimborne, knows of any papers.

IVOR CHURCHILL GUEST, 1st BARON ASHBY ST LEDGERS, 2nd BARON WIMBORNE, 1st VISCOUNT WIMBORNE (1873-1939)

Ivor Churchill Guest was Conservative M.P. for Plymouth 1900-1904. He became a Liberal in 1904 and sat for Plymouth until 1906 when he became Liberal M.P. for Cardiff 1906-1910. He was Paymaster-General February 1910-May 1912. He was created Baron Ashby St Ledgers in 1910, succeeded his father as 3rd baronet and 2nd Baron Wimborne in 1914, and was created Viscount Wimborne in 1918.

His grandson, the present (3rd) Viscount Wimborne, knows of no papers relating to Guest's career.

Mr David Satinoff, Melcote, Broadway, Hall, Cheshire, has a collection of sixteen letters, spanning the years 1898-1912, from Winston Churchill to Guest.

WALTER EDWARD GUINNESS, 1st BARON MOYNE (1880-1944)

Walter Edward Guinness was Conservative M.P. for Bury St Edmunds (Suffolk West, Bury St Edmunds from 1918) 1907-1931. He was Under-Secretary of State for War October 1922-October 1923, Financial Secretary to the Treasury 1923-January 1924 and November 1924-November 1925, Minister of Agriculture and Fisheries 1925-June 1929, Joint Parliamentary Secretary to the Ministry of Agriculture May 1940-February 1941, Secretary of State for the Colonies and Leader of the House of Lords 1941-February 1942, Deputy Minister of State, Middle East August 1942-January 1944, and Minister Resident in the Middle East January-November 1944. He was created Baron Moyne in 1932.

His son, the present (2nd) Lord Moyne, knows of no surviving papers relating to his father's career.

RICHARD BURDON HALDANE, VISCOUNT HALDANE (1856-1928)

Richard Haldane was Liberal M.P. for Haddingtonshire or Lothian (East) 1885-1911. He was Secretary of State for War December 1905-June 1912, and Lord Chancellor 1912-May 1915 and January-November 1924. He was created K.T. in 1913 and Viscount Haldane in 1911.

Haldane's papers form the greater part of a large deposit of Haldane family papers in the National Library of Scotland (ref. MS. Acc. 5901-6108). As well as a considerable body of correspondence 1882-1928, there are several drafts and memoranda, for example, on Haldane's role in Anglo-German negotiations before 1914, and his impressions of several of his contemporaries — Asquith, Grey, Rosebery, A.J. Balfour, and John Morley. Though not strictly a part of Haldane's own papers, his almost daily letters to his mother 1866-1924 are a vital source for historians (MS. Acc. 5927-6007). Haldane himself seems to have regarded these letters as his diary. His letters to his sister Elizabeth 1874-1928 (MS. Acc. 6010-6013) are also an important source because they are often more detailed though less frequent than the letters to his mother. Elizabeth Haldane's diary (MS. Acc. 5594) has recently been added to the collection.

It is clear from Haldane's posthumously published *An Autobiography* (1929) that he himself sorted through and destroyed a large part of his papers. What survives has been used and is frequently quoted in Sir Frederick Maurice K.C.M.G., *Haldane* (2 vols., 1937-39), Dudley Sommer, *Haldane of Cloan* (1960), and Stephen Koss, *Lord Haldane: Scapegoat for Liberalism* (New York and London, 1969).

GEORGE HENRY HALL, 1st VISCOUNT HALL (1881-1965)

George Henry Hall was Labour M.P. for Merthyr Tydfil (Aberdare) 1922-1946. He was Civil Lord of the Admiralty June 1929-August 1931, Parliamentary Under-Secretary of State for the Colonies May 1940-February 1942, Financial Secretary to the Admiralty 1942-September 1943, Parliamentary Under-Secretary of State for Foreign Affairs 1943-May 1945, Secretary of State for the Colonies August 1945-October 1946, and 1st Lord of the Admiralty 1946-May 1951. He was created Viscount Hall in 1946.

A small collection of his papers is in the possession of his son, the present (2nd) Viscount Hall, Belgrave Cottage, Upper Belgrave Street, London S.W.1. The papers have not been arranged but numbers have been assigned to the various packets and these are given below in brackets.

Hall's local political activities are mainly represented by printed papers and press cuttings. There is a cuttings book 1916-1956 (9), copies of the *Aberdare Division Labour News* 1922 (38), and the 1929 election issue of the *Aberdare Leader* (2). There are also copies of the I.L.P.'s 'Notes for Speakers' March 1929 (38), mainly concerned with Lloyd George's promises and performance, and 'Bullets for Baldwinism' n.d. (38). There is a stencilled copy of voting in the various miners' lodges for a miners' parliamentary candidate 12 July 1920 (36). There is a copy of Hall's 1929 election address. There are also photographs and press cuttings of a visit to Aberdare of the then Duchess of York (15).

Hall's parliamentary activities are, again, mainly covered by press cuttings — one book covers 1929-1956 and includes some of Hall's campaign literature (34). Hall seems to have particularly interested himself in the 1924 Miners' Bill (there is a letter from Thomas Richards congratulating him on a speech, 30 May 1924) (38), in *nystagmus*, the miners' disease (14, 20), and the 1934 Unemployment Bill (36). There is a typescript entitled *The Coordination of the Social Services* (n.d.) (12). A file marked 'letters important' (13) includes letters from Churchill, the Attlees, and Eden but they are mainly concerned with Hall's appointment to office or his retirement.

A very small number of papers has survived from Hall's terms of office. His first and last acts as Civil Lord to the Admiralty were to write to his son, the present Viscount. In his last letter, 24 August 1931, he described the cabinet held before J.R. MacDonald went to Buckingham Palace to hand in his resignation (34). There is also a typed letter from MacDonald explaining the need for a National Government (13). Apart from press cuttings, only fragments survive from his wartime positions, for example a page in Hall's writing recording the war cabinet's approval of his discussions with the American Ambassador 16 August 1944 — no subject is mentioned (13). Hall's tenure of the Colonial Office is represented by a file on the Brooke family of Sarawak — their tax liabilities and their administration in 1946 (36). There is also a 'Diary of Negotiations with the Jewish Agency on Jewish Participation in the Conference' 27 July-30 September 1946 (36). Hall's tenure of the Admiralty is covered by press cuttings, photographs of a visit to the Fleet by the Royal Family (15), and of the Admiralty Board in session, as well as letters from naval personnel on his retirement.

There are various miscellaneous papers from the last period in Hall's political life: memoranda on free trade in Europe 1957 and 1959 (35); notes and diaries from trips abroad — to Northern Rhodesia in 1954 (28), Australia 1956 (26, 35), and the U.S.A. and Canada 1958 (24, 25); notes for a speech in the House of Lords on (?) Wales (n.d.) (22); a collection of press cuttings about political leaders, including reviews of Attlee's memoirs. There are several copies of *Punch* 19 September 1947 with Illingworth's cartoon featuring Hall (6, 15, 30).

A small collection of more personal papers has survived. There are address books and pocket diaries for 1930, 1941, 1944, 1947-1961. Several copies of Hall's will survive (14), as well as letters of condolence to his son (2). There are also cuttings of obituaries in the local and national press (4, 14, 31).

LORD GEORGE FRANCIS HAMILTON (1854-1927)

Lord George Hamilton was Conservative M.P. for Middlesex 1868-1885 and for Middlesex (Ealing) 1885-1906. He was Under-Secretary of State for India February 1874-April 1878, Vice-President of the Council (responsible for education) 1878-April 1880, 1st Lord of the Admiralty June 1885-February 1886 and August 1886-August 1892, and Secretary of State for India July 1895-October 1903. He was created G.C.S.I. in 1903.

Hamilton's son, Ronald Hamilton, O.B.E., presented 34 volumes of his papers relating to India to the India Office Library in 1951 (ref. MSS. Eur. D. 508-510 and C. 125-126). The papers consist of fifteen volumes of correspondence and papers 1895-1898 between Hamilton and the then Viceroy, Lord Elgin, and eighteen volumes of correspondence 1899-1903 between Hamilton and Lord Curzon, Elgin's successor. There is also one volume of printed telegrams 1895-1898. Hamilton left behind him in the India Office his correspondence with members of the Royal family and governors, as well as files on special cases. These are also available for research at the India Office Library (ref. MSS. Eur. F. 123). Two volumes of printed correspondence 1896-1898 between Hamilton and Lord Sandhurst, Governor of Bombay, were purchased by the Indian Institute, part of the Bodleian Library, in 1940 (ref. 98 C 69, 70).

We have been unable to contact Hamilton's only surviving descendant, his grand-daughter, the Countess Czernin. In his two volumes of memoirs, *Parliamentary Reminiscences and Reflections 1868-1885*, and *1886-1906* (1917, 1922), Hamilton quoted from a few letters and papers.

ROBERT WILLIAM HANBURY (1845-1903)

Robert Hanbury was Conservative M.P. for Tamworth 1872-1878, Staffordshire (North) 1878-1880, and Preston 1885-1903. He was Financial Secretary to the Treasury June 1895-November 1900, and President of the Board of Agriculture and Fisheries 1900-May 1903.

We have been unable to trace Hanbury's papers. Hanbury was twice married but had no children. His second wife remarried; there was no issue of this marriage. She died in 1931, her second husband in 1944; his executor did not know of the existence of any papers. In his will, Hanbury had particularly mentioned his eight nieces, the daughters of his sister. We have been able to trace one of his nieces, Mrs Margaret Harriet Swann-Mason. She died in 1955 but her daughter, Hanbury's great-niece, informs us that his sister destroyed practically all the papers she had before her death and certainly nothing now survives with either Miss Swann-Mason or her cousins relating to Hanbury.

Hanbury lived and was buried at Ilam Hall, Ashbourne, then in Derbyshire, but now in Staffordshire. Neither of the two county record offices knows of any papers. The house is now owned by the National Trust but the Trust has no records concerning Hanbury.

SIR MAURICE PASCAL ALERS HANKEY, 1st BARON HANKEY (1877-1963)

Maurice Hankey was created K.C.B. in 1916, G.C.B. in 1919, and Baron Hankey in 1939. He was Minister without Portfolio September 1939-May 1940, Chancellor of the Duchy of Lancaster 1940-July 1941, and Paymaster-General 1941-March 1942.

Five hundred and thirty eight files of Hankey's papers have been deposited in the Library, Churchill College, Cambridge, where Captain Stephen Roskill is engaged on Hankey's biography. To date Captain Roskill has published two volumes: *Hankey, Man of Secrets vol. i. 1877-1918, vol. ii. 1919-1931* (1970-72); the third and final volume will be published in April 1974. The diaries and general correspondence for these periods are now open to research after the permission of the present Lord Hankey or Captain Roskill has been obtained. Applications should be made through the Keeper of the Archives, Churchill College. Hankey's personal papers are closed to research except by special permission of Captain Roskill. Captain Roskill has quoted extensively from Hankey's diary (begun in March 1915) and from Hankey's many letters to his wife. Hankey himself quoted from his diary and papers in his *The Supreme Command* (2 vols., 1961) and *The Supreme Control* (1963).

SIR MAURICE PASCAL ALERS HANKEY (cont.)

A further collection of Hankey's papers has recently been opened in the Public Record Office (ref. Cab. 63). The collection includes what Hankey called his 'Magnum Opus' files which may possibly have been used by him in writing *The Supreme Command*. They include memoranda prepared by Hankey for the Prime Minister and the War Cabinet, notes, and correspondence. In particular there is much material about the Gallipoli campaign and the Dardanelles Commission, including correspondence January-May 1915 between Winston Churchill and Admiral Fisher about the Dardanelles, Hankey's own letters from Gallipoli July-August 1915, and the memoranda he submitted as evidence to the Dardanelles Commission. There are also pre-war memoranda on the organization of the expeditionary force, and appreciations of the war situation. But most of this collection is concerned with Hankey's role between the wars and in the second world war. There are papers relating to his visits abroad, from the 1921-1922 Washington Conference (Hankey was British Secretary) which include letters from Tom Jones describing negotiations with the Sinn Fein leaders, some personal correspondence which includes requests for help, congratulations for various honours and appointments, and papers concerning the Suez Canal Company (Hankey was a director 1938-1939 and 1945-1958). Cab. 63/83-119 are second world war papers and some are closed for 50 years, particularly those on the conduct of the war. As Hankey was Government Spokesman in the House of Lords on Economic Warfare there are many papers from this department, especially on oil. There are also papers concerning refugees, and contingencies for the invasion of Britain. There is correspondence with W. Beveridge in February 1940 on the composition of the 1916 War Cabinet.

LEWIS HARCOURT, 1st VISCOUNT HARCOURT (1863-1922)

Lewis Harcourt was Liberal M.P. for North-East Lancashire (Rossendale) 1904-1916. He was 1st Commissioner of Works December 1905-November 1910, and May 1915-December 1916, and Secretary of State for the Colonies November 1910-May 1915. He was created Viscount Harcourt in 1916.

A large collection of papers was deposited in the Bodleian Library in 1972 by his son, the present (2nd) Viscount Harcourt (ref. Harcourt Papers). This collection contains the papers of both Lewis Harcourt and of his father, Sir William Harcourt, as well as many family papers relating to both men. The papers of father and son are inextricably related, as Lewis was for many years his father's private secretary. An extensive political correspondence, in which Lewis Harcourt was engaged on his father's behalf, and both sides of the correspondence between father and son, are to be found as part of the papers of Sir William Harcourt. The whole collection is at present (March 1974) undergoing extensive reorganization, and a catalogue and index are being prepared.

Nonetheless, one part of the collection can be said to consist of Lewis Harcourt's own papers, as distinct from those relating to his father's affairs. This section consists of about 87 boxes, the major part of which are printed government papers. The amount of correspondence surviving in this part of the collection is relatively slight, and what there is relates almost solely to Lewis Harcourt's affairs and his political career after his father's death in 1904. It includes correspondence with his wife, and with his step-mother, and political correspondence with Asquith, Lloyd George, Sir Edward Grey, and other prominent politicians.

The diaries kept by Lewis Harcourt, mainly while his father was in office, are among the more interesting items in his papers. They cover the years 1880-1887 and 1892-1895. There are typed copies of these diaries, although they have been edited and slightly altered. These diaries are available for research. There is also a manuscript diary for the years 1905-1915 in the possession of Lord Harcourt, but this is not available for research.

There are two boxes of papers relating to Harcourt's term of office as 1st Commissioner of Works. They include printed estimates, 1906-1911, and files on various matters in which the Office of Works was involved, including the allocation of rooms in the Palace of Westminster, extensions to the Tate Gallery, and alternatives for the Latin inscription above Admiralty Arch.

Twenty-two boxes, neatly sorted and labelled in 1916 under the supervision of Harcourt's assistant private secretary, J.C.C. Davidson, later 1st Viscount Davidson, represent much of Harcourt's activity as Colonial Secretary. There are files of correspondence with

LEWIS HARCOURT (cont.)

various governors, such as Lords Gladstone, Liverpool, Islington, and Buxton. The latter reported secret interviews with Botha and Smuts October 1914-May 1915. There are also four volumes of official correspondence 1911-1916, and two volumes of private correspondence for the same dates. These volumes are arranged alphabetically by correspondent; lists at the front of each volume give the names of the correspondents and the dates and subjects of their letters. Similar lists are to be found in the correspondence files. Scattered throughout both series are Colonial Office memoranda and correspondence with Davidson 1915-1916 on 'office news'.

There is one box of papers 1915-1916 when Harcourt was Acting President of the Board of Trade. The papers cover such problems as the supply of petrol, the quantity of beef available from South America, and the wages of South Wales' miners. Harcourt received several deputations at this time. To one, from the miners, on 19 June 1916, which demanded the nationalization of the mines, Harcourt replied: 'This is not the time, but they can at least show that nationalization would be a success. From this point of view, now is their chance'.

Harcourt's membership of the Cabinet is represented by printed Cabinet memoranda and Foreign Office telegrams (some annotated) 1908-1916. There are also some pages of pencilled notes taken at Cabinet meetings. Two issues stand out as being of special interest to Harcourt: the 1909-1910 Budget and the negotiations with Germany. In the budget, Harcourt was mainly concerned with Lloyd George's proposals for a succession duty; he used information from his Oxfordshire estates in several memoranda written for the Cabinet. Distrust for Lloyd George is demonstrated in his correspondence with Sir A. Thring, the First Parliamentary Counsel. Harcourt was deeply involved in the negotiations with Germany 1911-1914. As Colonial Secretary he took part in the attempts to revise the secret treaty of 1898, especially in reference to Portuguese Africa. He was also concerned in the attempts to reach a more general understanding with the Germans, as his interviews and correspondence with von Kühlmann, Admiral Eisendecher, and Sir Edward Grey demonstrate.

WILLIAM FRANCIS HARE, 5th EARL OF LISTOWEL (1906-   )

William Francis Hare, known as Viscount Ennismore from 1924 till he succeeded his father as 5th Earl of Listowel in 1931, was Parliamentary Under-Secretary of State for India October 1944-May 1945, Postmaster-General August 1945-April 1947, Secretary of State for India and Burma 1947-January 1948, Minister of State for the Colonies 1948-February 1950, Parliamentary Secretary to the Ministry for Agriculture and Fisheries November 1950-October 1951, and Governor-General of Ghana 1957-1960. He was created G.C.M.G. in 1957.

Lord Listowel, The House of Lords, London S.W.1, has only a very small collection of papers relating to his political career. Most of these papers concern his appointment as Governor-General of Ghana. They include correspondence with President Nkrumah and with the Queen's secretaries, as well as correspondence with the Foreign and Commonwealth Office on domestic arrangements. There are also some letters concerning Mr Harold Macmillan's visit to Ghana in January 1960, and some notes of Mr Macmillan's conversations with Ghanaian leaders.

Only a few fragments survive from Lord Listowel's earlier periods in office. The most important is a volume of weekly letters between Lord Listowel and Lord Mountbatten 25 April-9 August 1947 about the transfer of power from Britain to India and Pakistan. Lord Mountbatten's permission, as well as Lord Listowel's, is needed in order to read these letters. There is also a postcard from George Bernard Shaw advocating a return to the penny post, a copy of a long letter from General Wavell to Winston Churchill 24 October 1944, giving Wavell's views on the situation in India, some letters from the Governor of Burma 1947, a long letter from John Freeman on the negotiations with Burma in 1947, a letter of thanks for his work at the India and Burma Office from C.R. Attlee, and some papers concerning the work of the Molson committee in 1961 on the boundary dispute between the Buganda and the Bunyoro.

SIR HAROLD SIDNEY HARMSWORTH, 1st Bt, 1st VISCOUNT ROTHERMERE (1868-1940)

Harold Harmsworth was Secretary of State for Air November 1917-April 1918. He was created a baronet in 1910, Baron Rothermere in 1914 and Viscount Rothermere in 1919.

Harmsworth bequeathed all his papers to William Collin Brooks. Brooks died in 1959 and his widow died in 1972. Shortly before Mrs Brooks's death, she returned Harmsworth's papers to his son, the present (2nd) Viscount Rothermere. Lord Rothermere informs us that there are only a very small number of papers; most of Harmsworth's papers were destroyed during his lifetime. The few papers which do survive are of a purely personal and family nature. They are not available for research.

VERNON HARTSHORN (1872-1931)

Vernon Hartshorn was Labour M.P. for Glamorganshire (Ogmore) 1918-1931. He was Postmaster-General January-November 1924, and Lord Privy Seal, with special responsibility for unemployment, June 1930-March 1931.

Hartshorn's son, Mr V.I. Hartshorn, 36 Windsor Avenue, Radyr, Cardiff, had until recently a large collection of press cuttings 1910-1930 relating to his father's political career, but these were sent for salvage. Only one volume of press cuttings now survives. It includes some letters of sympathy sent to Mrs Hartshorn after her husband's death, including one from J.R. MacDonald. The volume formed the basis of an article by Peter Stead, 'Vernon Hartshorn: Miners' Agent and Cabinet Minister', *Glamorgan Historian*, vi (1969), pp. 83-94.

SIR PATRICK GARDINER HASTINGS (1880-1952)

Patrick Hastings was Labour M.P. for Wallsend 1922-1926. He was Attorney-General January-November 1924. He was knighted in 1924.

Neither of his daughters, Mrs Patricia Hastings and Mrs N. Bentley, has any papers relating to their father's political career. Hastings's widow told Mr H. Montgomery Hyde, when he was writing his biography, that Hastings used to throw everything away.

None of the various books on Hastings's life appears to quote from unpublished material: *The Autobiography of Sir Patrick Hastings* (1948); Patricia Hastings, *The Life of Patrick Hastings* (1959); H. Montgomery Hyde, *Sir Patrick Hastings. His Life and Cases* (1960).

ARTHUR HENDERSON (1863-1935)

Arthur Henderson was Labour M.P. for Durham (Barnard Castle) 1903-1918, Lancashire (Widnes) 1919-1922, Newcastle (East) 1923, Burnley 1924-1931 and Derbyshire (Clay Cross) 1933-1935. He was President of the Board of Education May 1915-August 1916, Paymaster-General with special responsibility for labour August-December 1916, Minister without Portfolio and Member of the War Cabinet December 1916-August 1917, Home Secretary January-November 1924, and Secretary of State for Foreign Affairs June 1929-August 1931. He presided over the world disarmament conference 1932-1935 and was awarded the Nobel Prize for Peace in 1934.

Mary A. Hamilton, in the preface to her biography *Arthur Henderson* (1938) said that once Henderson had answered a letter or finished with a document, he put it into the waste-paper basket and that only a small amount of written material survived him. Nonetheless, she occasionally quoted from letters by Henderson. According to Raymond Postgate, *The Life of George Lansbury* (1951), 'a long and intimate' correspondence between Henderson and Lansbury existed when Miss Hamilton was writing her book but it has since been 'wantonly destroyed' (p. 279).

Henderson's sons do not have any of their father's papers. But, although it seems that many of Henderson's personal papers have been destroyed, much of his political correspondence has survived. Most of the letters, files, reports, and memoranda that he wrote and received in his capacity as Secretary of the Labour Party are preserved in the archives of the National Executive of the Labour Party at Transport House. Application to see these papers should be made to the librarian.

ARTHUR HENDERSON (cont.)

The Transport House records can be divided into two broad categories. There are, first, the minutes of the National Executive Committee; they include not only formal minutes of meetings, but also appended reports, memoranda, and circulated correspondence. As Henderson was secretary of the Party from 1911 to 1934, much of this material was written by him. Secondly, the correspondence files of the Party are also preserved at Transport House. Again, in his secretarial capacity, much of this is Henderson's work, and for the period 1911-1924 the files are very extensive. At the moment, most of the correspondence is not catalogued and individual items can only be found with difficulty. Until 1907 correspondence is filed by year; after then (loosely) by subject or by individual. The biggest single classification is correspondence boxed under the name of the assistant secretary, J.S. Middleton. Cataloguing of these papers is now being undertaken by the Historical Manuscripts Commission.

There are several lacunae. The period 1915-1917 is not well covered and correspondence becomes thin after 1924. On the other hand, more material is constantly appearing and these gaps may be filled slowly.

Separate from the archives of the National Executive are four boxes of papers catalogued as 'Henderson Papers'. They are very miscellaneous and patchy. There is some political correspondence for the years 1917 and 1929-1931. There is a box of Cabinet papers 1915-1917. There are also some press cuttings and private letters.

A further small collection of Henderson papers has been deposited in the Public Record Office (ref. F.O. 800/280-284). It consists of miscellaneous correspondence for June 1929-August 1931.

ARTHUR HENDERSON, BARON ROWLEY (1893-1968)

Arthur Henderson was Labour M.P. for Cardiff (South) 1923-1924 and 1929-1931, Staffordshire (Kingswinford) 1935-1950, and Rowley Regis and Tipton 1950-1966. He was Joint Parliamentary Under-Secretary of State for War March-December 1942, Financial Secretary to the War Office February 1943-May 1945, Under-Secretary of State for India and Burma August 1945-August 1947, Minister of State for Commonwealth Relations August-October 1947, and Secretary of State for Air 1947-October 1951. He was created Baron Rowley (a life peerage) in 1966.

His brother, Lord Henderson, informs us that Arthur Henderson did not keep official papers in his private files and that, unfortunately, the latter were all destroyed after Arthur Henderson's death by his secretary.

AUBERON THOMAS HERBERT, 8th BARON LUCAS, 11th BARON DINGWALL (1876-1916)

Auberon Herbert succeeded his uncle as 8th Baron Lucas and 11th Baron Dingwall in 1905. He was Under-Secretary of State for War April 1908-March 1911, Under-Secretary of State for the Colonies March-October 1911, Parliamentary Secretary to the Board of Agriculture and Fisheries 1911-August 1914, and President of the Board of Agriculture and Fisheries 1914-May 1915.

A small collection of Herbert's papers is in the possession of his niece, the present (10th) Baroness Lucas and (13th) Baroness Dingwall, The Old House, Wonston, Winchester, Hants.

There are several papers connected with Herbert's taking his seat in the House of Lords and with his maiden speech, 24 and 25 June 1907. At that time Herbert was private secretary to R.B. Haldane and his speech was in support of the Territorial Army Bill. As well as the *Hansard* reports and letters of congratulation, there is a letter written by Herbert describing his own feelings and reactions. There are also press cuttings on the King's speech to Lord Lieutenants about the bill October 1907, and a memorandum of August 1906 on the formation of territorial associations.

Some correspondence and a pamphlet 1907-1908 demonstrate Herbert's interest in the New Forest Ponies. His interest in agriculture is represented by correspondence on the formation of a Southern Counties Agricultural Cooperative September-November 1910.

AUBERON THOMAS HERBERT (cont.)

There are no papers referring to Herbert's terms of office. When he resigned in 1915, he joined the Royal Flying Corps. There is a photograph of him in uniform. Among other contributions to the war effort, he offered land for a land settlement scheme for servicemen. Correspondence July 1916 explains that the land was geologically unsuited for small-holdings. There are also obituary notices and extracts from the *Dictionary of National Biography* and the *Balliol War Memorial Book*. He was posted missing, presumed dead, in November 1916.

SIR GORDON HEWART, 1st VISCOUNT HEWART (1870-1943)

Gordon Hewart was Liberal M.P. for Leicester (Leicester East from 1918) 1913-1922. He was Solicitor-General December 1916-January 1919, and Attorney-General 1919-March 1922. He was Lord Chief Justice 1922-1940. He was knighted in 1916, and created Baron Hewart in 1922, and Viscount Hewart in 1940.

Hewart's widow, Lady Hewart, informs us that no papers have survived. Some years ago her flat was burgled and a deed box was stolen, presumably in the hope that it contained jewellery; in fact it contained Lord Hewart's private and official papers. The box has not been recovered. Robert Jackson, *The Chief. The Biography of Gordon Hewart, Lord Chief Justice of England 1922-1940* (1959) was based on Hewart's papers, and quotes extensively from a memorandum Hewart wrote about his appointment as Lord Chief Justice.

SIR WILLIAM JOYNSON-HICKS, 1st Bt, 1st VISCOUNT BRENTFORD (1865-1932)

William Joynson-Hicks (he assumed the additional surname Joynson in 1895 on his marriage) was Conservative M.P. for Manchester (North-West) 1908-1910, Middlesex (Brentford) 1911-1918, and Middlesex (Twickenham) 1918-1929. He was Parliamentary Secretary to the Overseas Trade Department October 1922-March 1923, Postmaster- and Paymaster-General March-May 1923, Financial Secretary to the Treasury (with a seat in the Cabinet) May-October 1923, Minister of Health August 1923-January 1924, and Secretary of State for Home Affairs November 1924-June 1929. He was created a baronet in 1919 and Viscount Brentford in 1929.

The present (3rd) Viscount Brentford informs us that he has the very few papers left by his father but they are not available for research. They were used in the biography by H.A. Taylor, *Jix: Viscount Brentford* (1933). According to Mr Taylor's preface, Joynson-Hicks had prepared both memoranda and draft chapters for a volume of memoirs. These are quoted in the book, for example, Joynson-Hicks's feelings at being 'Minister in attendance'. Taylor also quoted from a diary.

SIR SAMUEL JOHN GURNEY HOARE, 2nd Bt, VISCOUNT TEMPLEWOOD (1880-1959)

Samuel Hoare was Conservative M.P. for Chelsea 1910-1944. He was Secretary of State for Air October 1922-January 1924, November 1924-June 1929, and April-May 1940, Secretary of State for India August 1931-June 1935, Secretary of State for Foreign Affairs June-December 1935, 1st Lord of the Admiralty June 1936-May 1937, Secretary of State for Home Affairs 1937-September 1939, and Lord Privy Seal and a Member of the War Cabinet September 1939-April 1940. Hoare succeeded his father as 2nd baronet in 1915; he was created G.B.E. in 1927, G.C.S.I. in 1934, and Viscount Templewood in 1944.

One hundred and fifteen boxes of his papers were deposited by his executors (his widow and his nephew) in the Cambridge University Library (ref. Templewood papers). The papers are generally available, but exceptions include official papers less than 30 years old, some first world war files (for example, papers of the British Intelligence Mission to Petrograd 1915-1917), confidential or personal papers, and some royal correspondence. A detailed list of the papers has been made with subject and correspondents' indices.

There are very few official papers, most of them presumably having been left in his respective ministries. Nevertheless there are 28 boxes of general political papers. In addition

SIR SAMUEL JOHN GURNEY HOARE (cont.)

there are volumes of cabinet ministers' and other papers, press cuttings, and scrapbooks. There is also an extensive collection of correspondence and other material concerning his early life: his letters from school and college, and various notes and reports from 1905, when Hoare was assistant private secretary to Alfred Lyttelton, then Colonial Secretary. There are many drafts and notes relating to Hoare's various publications including his study, *Empire of the Air: The Advent of the Air Age 1922-1929* (1957), and his memoirs for the years 1931-1940, *Nine Troubled Years* (1954). Hoare wrote that the latter book was based on his own contemporary notes and papers; he also acknowledged the help of Mrs Neville Chamberlain and Miss Hilda Chamberlain. Copies of Neville Chamberlain's letters to his sisters 1938-1939 have been deposited with this collection but they are closed till 1 February 1975.

Hoare deposited some of his India Office papers with the India Office Library in 1958 (ref. MSS. Eur. E. 240); a list is available. They include 32 volumes, 55 files, sixteen pamphlets, and an album compiled to commemorate his visit to India in 1927. These papers include eight volumes of correspondence with Freeman Freeman-Thomas, 1st Marquess of Willingdon, Sir John Anderson, Viscount Waverley, E.F.L. Wood, 1st Earl of Halifax, J.F. Ashley, Lord Erskine, W. Malcolm, 1st Baron Hailey, Gandhi, and others, as well as speeches by Hoare and Freeman-Thomas, and selections from *Hansard*.

One volume of miscellaneous general correspondence relating to his tenure of the Foreign Office has been deposited in the Public Record Office (ref. F.O. 800/295).

SIR CHARLES EDWARD HENRY HOBHOUSE, 4th Bt (1862-1941)

Charles Hobhouse was Liberal M.P. for Wiltshire (East or Devizes) 1892-1895 and Bristol (East) 1900-1918. He was Under-Secretary of State for India January 1907-April 1908, Financial Secretary to the Treasury 1908-October 1911, Chancellor of the Duchy of Lancaster 1911-February 1914, and Postmaster-General 1914-May 1915. He succeeded his father as 4th baronet in 1916.

As there were no children of his marriages, Hobhouse was succeeded by his half-brother, the father of the present (6th) baronet, Sir Charles Hobhouse. Sir Charles has been unable to discover any of his uncle's papers. The family home was used by a school and by the army during the last war and much seems to have disappeared at that time. Moreover some papers were pulped in salvage drives. The present baronet's father deposited some family papers in the Wiltshire County Record Office but these deposits do not include any of Hobhouse's papers. Mrs W.D.C. Trotter, Hobhouse's step-daughter, knows of the existence of no papers.

JOHN HODGE (1855-1937)

John Hodge was Labour M.P. for South-East Lancashire (Gorton; Manchester Gorton from 1918) 1906-1923. He was Minister of Labour December 1916-August 1917, and Minister of Pensions 1917-January 1919.

No papers have survived in the possession of his family, except for a photograph album owned by his daughter, Miss Wilhelmina Hodge, 30 Molyneux Park Road, Tunbridge Wells, Kent. As well as photographs of Hodge during the period in which he held office, there are four press cuttings. Two of these report a visit paid by Hodge to the Hepworth Studios where a scheme for retraining and employing disabled soldiers was being organised by Cecil Harmsworth. While there Hodge acted as Minister of Pensions in a film about the problems of the wounded soldier. There is a typed copy of a poem (anon.) entitled 'The Staying of Arthur' which condemned Arthur Henderson for remaining in office after the introduction of conscription (January 1916).

Hodge's *Workman's Cottage to Windsor Castle* (1931) quotes from a few letters but appears to be mainly based on Hodge's reminiscences.

SIR DOUGLAS McGAREL HOGG, 1st VISCOUNT HAILSHAM (1872-1950)

Douglas Hogg was Conservative M.P. for St Marylebone 1922-1928. He was Attorney-General October 1922-January 1924 and November 1924-March 1928, Lord Chancellor 1928-June 1929 and June 1935-March 1938, Secretary of State for War November 1931-June 1935, and Lord President of the Council March-October 1938. He was knighted in 1922, created Baron Hailsham in 1928, and Viscount Hailsham in 1929.

His son, Lord Hailsham of Marylebone, informs us that his father systematically destroyed his papers. All that survives are his fee books and letters of congratulation and condolence, sometimes with his replies. As these papers are in store they are not readily available. They were used and are frequently quoted in R.F.V. Heuston, *Lives of the Lord Chancellors 1885-1940* (Oxford, 1964).

JOHN ADRIAN LOUIS HOPE, 1st MARQUESS OF LINLITHGOW (1860-1908)

John Adrian Louis Hope, known as Lord Hope until he succeeded his father as the 7th Earl of Hopetoun in 1873, was created G.C.M.G. in 1889, K.T. in 1900, and Marquess of Linlithgow in 1902. He was Governor of Victoria 1889-1895, Paymaster-General 1895-1898, Governor-General of Australia 1900-1902, and Secretary for Scotland February-December 1905.

Very few of Hope's papers appear to have survived; at present they are being listed by the National Register of Archives (Scotland) and are not available for research. The papers are controlled by the Hopetoun Papers Trust; enquiries should be directed to J.N. Douglas Menzies Esq., F.L.A.S., Hopetoun Estate Office, South Queensferry, West Lothian, Scotland.

Almost all of the papers which have survived relate to Hope's term of office as first Governor-General and Commander-in-Chief of Australia. There is a wooden chest of formal addresses of welcome and a dispatch case of official papers. The papers cover such topics as the various schemes for Australian federation, the defence of Australia, arrangements for the opening of the first Parliament, and proposals for the design of a Commonwealth of Australia flag. There is also some miscellaneous correspondence with Australian and British politicians, including the Secretary of State for the Colonies, Joseph Chamberlain, letters to Hope's Private Secretary, and the letter (30 January 1905) in which A.J. Balfour invited Hope to take over the Scottish Office. The collection also includes Australian account books, some from 1889-1895 when Hope was Governor of Victoria. This earlier period is also represented by two volumes of press cuttings 1888-1889 and 1892-1895. A further volume for 1881-1887 also survives. Apart from papers concerning various honours made to Hope — such as the Knighthood of the Thistle — the only other surviving papers appear to be printed order papers and bills from the House of Lords 1883.

SIR ROBERT STEVENSON HORNE, VISCOUNT HORNE OF SLAMANNAN (1871-1940)

Robert Horne was Conservative M.P. for Glasgow (Hillhead) 1918-1937. He was Minister of Labour January 1919-March 1920, President of the Board of Trade 1920-April 1921, and Chancellor of the Exchequer 1921-October 1922. He was created K.B.E. in 1918, G.B.E. in 1920, and Viscount Horne of Slamannan in 1937.

Horne died unmarried. His nephew, Mr J.R. Lamberton, was one of his executors, and he received all of Horne's chattels. Mr Lamberton informs us that he has only Horne's personal and family papers and that these papers are not available for research. Mr Lamberton has no knowledge of any political papers.

HENRY FITZALAN-HOWARD, 15th DUKE OF NORFOLK (1847-1917)

Henry Fitzalan-Howard, known as Lord Maltravers 1847-1856, and as the Earl of Arundel from 1856 till he succeeded his father as 15th Duke of Norfolk in 1860, was Postmaster-General July 1895-April 1900 when he resigned to go to South Africa on active service. He was created K.G. in 1886.

HENRY FITZALAN-HOWARD (cont.)

Fitzalan-Howard's papers are in the possession of his son, the present (16th) Duke of Norfolk, at Arundel Castle, Sussex. They are described in *Arundel Castle Archives: Interim Lists 1-12* ed. F.W. Steer (Chichester, 1968); a new edition is being prepared. Mr Steer is now archivist to the Duke of Norfolk and all applications to use the Arundel Castle papers should be addressed to him at 63 Orchard Street, Chichester, Sussex. The 15th Duke's papers are described in lists 9 and 11. They are very extensive, filling some 245 cubic feet. He seems to have kept all his correspondence, which is chronologically arranged; however, these papers are not available for research and no opening date is foreseen at the present time.

ROBERT SPEAR HUDSON, 1st VISCOUNT HUDSON (1886-1957)

Robert Hudson was Conservative M.P. for Cumberland (Whitehaven) 1924-1929, and Southport 1931-1952. He was Parliamentary Secretary to the Ministry of Labour November 1931-June 1935, Minister of Pensions 1935-July 1936, Parliamentary Secretary to the Ministry of Health 1936-May 1937, Parliamentary Secretary, Department of Overseas Trade, Board of Trade 1937-April 1940, Minister of Shipping April-May 1940, Minister of Agriculture and Fisheries 1940-July 1945. He was created Viscount Hudson in 1952.

Hudson left all his personal effects to his son, the second viscount, who died in 1963. The widow of the second viscount, now Mrs D. Sandys, has none of her father-in-law's papers and thinks that what papers there were went to Hudson's sister, Miss Violet Hudson. Hudson's widow died in 1969 and Mrs Maclean, a close friend of Lady Hudson, who helped to dispose of her effects, knows of no papers.

Miss Violet Hudson, Manor Farm, Marningford Bohune, Pewsey, Wiltshire, has a small collection of papers. Miss Hudson says that her brother kept very few papers and much of what he kept was destroyed during the bombing of the second world war. The papers Miss Hudson has include press cuttings 1929-1949, a few personal family letters, and correspondence on financial and legal matters. There is also a visitors' book for the 1930s and some photograph albums.

SIR ROBERT HUTCHISON, BARON HUTCHISON (1873-1950)

Major-General Robert Hutchison was Liberal M.P. for Kirkcaldy Burghs 1922-1923, and Montrose Burghs 1924-1932; he became a Liberal National in 1931. He was Paymaster-General December 1935-June 1938. He was created K.C.M.G. in 1919 and Baron Hutchison in 1932.

Hutchison's widow, Mrs I.L.W.D. Laurie, knows of no papers.

JOHN BURNS HYND (1902-1971)

John Hynd was Labour M.P. for Sheffield (Attercliffe) 1944-1970. He was Chancellor of the Duchy of Lancaster and Minister for Germany and Austria August 1945-April 1947, and Minister of Pensions April-October 1947.

Hynd's papers are in the possession of his widow, Mrs J.B. Hynd, 18 Lakeside, Enfield, Middlesex. The papers are in the same order as Hynd left them, and he was very methodical. The collection fills four filing cabinet drawers and about twenty box files.

Hynd did not keep a diary, nor has much correspondence survived. His constituency work is represented by two box-files and three files. They include correspondence with the National Union of Railwaymen about getting on their panel of prospective candidates, his selection for Sheffield in 1938, and later correspondence about election expenses. Hynd was an N.U.R. clerk 1924-1945 but there is little material about this early career. There is printed election material for all the general elections 1945-1966, including some of Hynd's opponents' material. There are some local party pamphlets from the 1920s, press cuttings about local politics, a small amount of correspondence with his agent, his monthly letters to his local party 1966-1968, lists of rules and members of the local party, and some correspondence on the grant of the freedom of Sheffield to Hynd in 1970.

JOHN BURNS HYND (cont.)

The chief source for Hynd's pre-parliamentary activities is a volume of press cuttings beginning in the nineteen-thirties. Hynd kept further cuttings but these were not arranged in a volume. There is also a volume of cuttings of articles by him for the earlier period as well as two box-files of later articles. There are two slim volumes of political cartoons which Hynd drew in the 1930s under the name 'Hynder'.

Very little material has survived from Hynd's period in office: he was a keen photographer and there are four albums containing photographs he took while in Germany; there is also volume one of the *British Zone Review* (1945).

The remaining boxes and files may be described as 'subject' files: leaflets, press cuttings, etc. on particular topics or geographical areas, for example housing, race, prices and incomes, Latin America, Central Africa. Hynd continued his interest in German affairs and there is a great deal of material about many aspects of Germany including Command Papers on the various treaties and the wider problems of disarmament. Hynd was a firm supporter of European Unity and the Common Market, an interest reflected by many files: for example he was a founder of the Anglo-Austrian Society, and of the Parliamentary Council of the European Movement. As well as these subject files, there are two boxes of speeches and a box-file of broadcasts made by Hynd. Many of the latter were on the overseas network of the B.B.C. or for foreign networks.

There is very little Labour Party material: a box of Parliamentary Labour Party standing orders, a file of speeches at various local meetings, and a box of various leaflets. Hynd's appointment diaries 1944-1971 (except 1945) have survived. Mrs Hynd also has an interesting file of letters of condolence, many of which describe him at work, particularly in Germany. Hynd wrote a biography of his friend *Willy Brandt* (1966); the typescript and correspondence concerning publication have survived.

There are also several tape recordings of speeches made by Hynd, including the speech he made on receiving the freedom of Sheffield and radio broadcasts made during a visit to Latin America in 1965.

We understand that a collection of Hynd's constituency papers is in the care of Alderman S.I. Dyson of Sheffield; but we have been unable to make contact with Alderman Dyson.

ALBERT HOLDEN ILLINGWORTH, BARON ILLINGWORTH (1865-1942)

Albert Illingworth was Coalition Liberal M.P. for Lancashire (Heywood) 1915-1918, and Lancashire (Heywood and Radcliffe) 1918-1921. He was Postmaster-General December 1916-April 1921. He was created Baron Illingworth in 1921.

His widow, Lady Illingworth, 2 York House, Kensington Church Street, London W.8, has his papers. Most of the papers are in store and inaccessible at present. We have only been able to see two files of correspondence. All the letters and memoranda date from the period 1916-1921; they deal with such diverse topics as National Service schemes in 1915, oil supplies in 1916, government policy on Irish Home Rule in November 1918, and the proposed Excess Profits Duty of 1921. There are several League of Nations Union papers 1921 about disarmament and the Hungarian Monarchy; several papers related to Illingworth's work on the War Office Committee advising the Director of Army Contracts; and several War Cabinet memoranda and agenda concerning rationing and the Whitley Council Civil Service reform proposals, and the Civil Service's pay rise in 1920.

PHILIP ALBERT INMAN, BARON INMAN (1892-   )

Philip Albert Inman was created Baron Inman in January 1946. He was Lord Privy Seal April-October 1947.

Lord Inman informs us that he has kept very few papers from the period when he was in office, a time when he was under great stress (his son was gravely ill and he himself was not well) and without much secretarial help. Moreover, Lord Inman has sorted much of his correspondence and destroyed a large number of letters. All that survives from that period is a collection of more than 500 letters of congratulation (including letters from Sir Stafford

PHILIP ALBERT INMAN (cont.)

Cripps and Lord Longford), a letter concerning his swearing in as a Privy Councillor, some correspondence about the appointment of Lord Inman's successor as Chairman of the B.B.C., and a list of the many Cabinet Committees on which Lord Inman served. There are also a large number of press cuttings including some dating from Lord Inman's entry and departure from office.

Lord Inman's autobiography, *No Going Back* (1952), quotes only from press cuttings. The correspondence mentioned there with George Lansbury has since been destroyed. Nor has Lord Inman systematically kept correspondence with such friends as Arthur Henderson and Ellen Wilkinson and other Labour figures, though odd letters may still survive.

Lord Inman does have three large boxes of papers, mostly press cuttings. They consist mainly of articles or reviews by Lord Inman or reviews of his many books. There are also papers related to Lord Inman's long connection with Charing Cross Hospital.

SIR THOMAS WALKER HOBART INSKIP, 1st VISCOUNT CALDECOTE (1876-1947)

Thomas Inskip was Conservative M.P. for Bristol (Central) 1918-1929 and Hampshire (Fareham) 1931-1939. He was Solicitor-General October 1922-January 1924, November 1924-March 1928, and September 1931-January 1932, Attorney-General 1928-June 1929, and January 1932-March 1936, Minister for the Coordination of Defence 1936-January 1939, Secretary of State for Dominion Affairs January-September 1939, and May-October 1940, Lord Chancellor September 1939-May 1940, and Lord Chief Justice 1940-1946. He was knighted in 1922, and created Viscount Caldecote in 1939.

Inskip's son, the present (2nd) Viscount Caldecote, informs us that his father kept very few papers and amongst these the only item of any importance is his diary. A copy of this diary for 26 August-19 September 1938 and 10 January 1939-20 April 1940 has been deposited at Churchill College, Cambridge (ref. Inkp 1,2) but it is not yet open to general inspection; Lord Caldecote's permission is required before access can be granted. R.F.V. Heuston in his *Lives of the Lord Chancellors 1885-1940* (Oxford, 1964) quoted extensively from these sections of Inskip's diary (pp. 590-602). Professor Heuston also quoted from earlier sections of Inskip's diary and from several letters, most of them letters of appreciation written after Inskip's death. Lord Caldecote thinks that these earlier diaries may survive amongst his mother's papers. If he finds them he will probably deposit them with the other diaries at Churchill.

GEORGE ALFRED ISAACS (1883-   )

George Isaacs was Labour M.P. for Kent (Gravesend) 1923-1924, Southwark (North) 1929-1931, and 1939-1950, and Southwark 1950-1959. He was Minister of Labour and National Service August 1945-January 1951, and Minister of Pensions January-October 1951.

Mr Isaacs states that he has no papers of any kind relating to his political career and that it was always his intention to ensure this state of affairs.

Southwark Public Library, in its Southwark Historical Collection, has a small collection of biographical press cuttings about Mr Isaacs, and a copy of the Order of Proceedings in 1957 when Mr Isaacs was made a Freeman of the Borough. The library also has the *South London Press* for 1900-1951 which has many references to Mr Isaacs's activities.

George Eastwood's biography, *George Isaacs* (1952), was partly based on information supplied by Mr Isaacs but it does not quote from any documents.

SIR RUFUS DANIEL ISAACS, 1st MARQUESS OF READING (1860-1935)

Rufus Isaacs was Liberal M.P. for Reading 1904-1913. He was Solicitor-General March-October 1910, Attorney-General 1910-October 1913, Lord Chief Justice 1913-1921, Viceroy of India 1921-1926, and Secretary of State for Foreign Affairs August-November 1931. He was knighted in 1910, and created G.C.B. in 1915, Baron Reading in 1914, Viscount Reading in 1916, Earl of Reading in 1917, and Marquess of Reading in 1926.

SIR RUFUS DANIEL ISAACS (cont.)

Isaacs's grandson, the present (3rd) Marquess of Reading, informs us that he has only a few of his grandfather's personal papers. These papers are not available for research but they are not thought to be of political significance.

A considerable collection of papers concerning Isaacs's term of office as Viceroy was deposited in the India Office Library by his widow. The collection was deposited in two parts (ref. MSS. Eur. E. 238 and MSS. Eur. F. 118). The first part contains Isaacs's official Indian papers, the second (which was only opened for research in January 1972) contains personal papers. In his biography, *Rufus Isaacs, 1st Marquess of Reading* (2 vols., 1943-45), Isaacs's son, the 2nd Marquess, said that his father wrote very few letters and kept even fewer.

MSS. Eur. E. 238 includes several volumes of printed correspondence, some of which were indexed. The Viceroy's correspondence was traditionally divided into letters and telegrams to the Sovereign, letters and telegrams to the Secretary of State, correspondence with persons in England, and correspondence with persons in India. There are also several volumes of speeches by Isaacs, the printed 'Summary' of his administration, and volumes of Legislative Assembly decisions. The collection includes many files related to Isaacs's membership of the Joint Committee for Indian Constitutional Reform (1933-1934) and his activities during the Round Table Conference and the Simon Commission. There are also several departmental files.

MSS. Eur. F. 118 comprises more personal correspondence though there are more papers on Indian affairs. There are 90 files of correspondence arranged alphabetically, generally covering the period 1910-1935 but with some earlier correspondence. There are also further correspondence files with prominent politicians such as D. Lloyd George 1919-1929, E.S. Montagu 1904-1923, the then Lord Irwin 1926-1930, and Sir John Simon 1916-1935. In addition there are Cabinet Papers 1913-1919, peace negotiations papers, papers concerning Isaacs's mission to the U.S.A. 1917, papers concerning Land Taxes 1909, correspondence with Lloyd George and Lord Grey of Fallodon about political funds 1929, correspondence about the 1931 political crisis, and press cuttings 1901-1923.

A small collection of papers has also been deposited in the Public Record Office (ref. F.O. 800/222-226). They include three indexed volumes of miscellaneous correspondence 1918-1919, and a volume of telegrams to and from Sir W. Wiseman, all concerned with Isaacs's special mission to the U.S.A. in 1918-1919, and one volume of miscellaneous correspondence from his tenure of the Foreign Office in 1931.

It is known that Isaacs sometimes made notes, in a personal code, relating to contemporary events. These notes do not appear to have survived.

SIR HENRY JAMES, BARON JAMES OF HEREFORD (1828-1911)

Henry James was Liberal M.P. for Taunton 1869-1885, and for Bury 1885-1895. He became a Liberal Unionist in 1886. He was Solicitor-General September-November 1873, Attorney-General 1873-February 1874 and May 1880-June 1885, and Chancellor of the Duchy of Lancaster July 1895-August 1902. He was knighted in 1873, and created Baron James of Hereford in 1895.

An important collection of his papers has been deposited by his nephew, Mr Philip Gwynne James, in the Hereford County Record Office (ref. M45). A calendar of the papers is being compiled; in the meantime restricted access to the papers is allowed. The collection consists of a trunk of correspondence for the years 1880-1909. It was used by Lord Askwith in *Lord James of Hereford* (1930); and there is some correspondence to Askwith from the families of James's contemporaries about the difficulties of finding James's letters in their own family papers.

The correspondence was originally arranged in bundles for each year, each bundle being further sub-divided into political, professional, social, and royal sections. Letters from prominent individuals have been put into separate bundles though this arrangement is not entirely consistent. As might be expected, the letters are an important source for a study of late Victorian politics. Askwith pointed out that the Marquess of Hartington, later 8th Duke of Devonshire, the Liberal Unionist leader, wrote frequently to James, sometimes twice a

SIR HENRY JAMES (cont.)

week; and Hartington's letters form a large part of this correspondence. There are also series of letters from Sir Charles Dilke, G.J. Goschen, Lord Salisbury, Lord Randolph Churchill, and W.E. Gladstone. A list of the contents of the trunk made in 1912 states that correspondence covered the years 1840-1911 and that an index and notes about their contents existed; these cannot now be found, and only the correspondence for 1880-1909 appears to have survived.

As well as the correspondence, there is a memoir for 1886-1909 (a typed copy fills 152 pages), which was possibly written by James with the aim of interesting someone in writing a biography. There is also a manuscript diary for 1894, notes on the framing of the Corrupt Practices Act 1883, unflattering press cuttings on James's role in the Parnell Commission (he acted for *The Times* with Sir Richard Webster), and a scrapbook of obituaries and tributes on James's death.

THOMAS JOHNSTON (1881-1965)

Thomas Johnston was Labour M.P. for Stirlingshire (West) 1922-1924, 1929-1931, 1935-1945, and for Dundee 1924-1929. He was Parliamentary Under-Secretary of State for Scotland June 1929-March 1931, Lord Privy Seal March-August 1931, and Secretary of State for Scotland February 1941-May 1945.

Johnston's widow does not know of the existence of any papers. In his *Memories* (1952) Johnston described much of his career but only quoted from published sources.

ARTHUR CREECH JONES (1891-1964)

Arthur Creech Jones was Labour M.P. for the West Riding of Yorkshire (Shipley) 1935-1950, and for Wakefield 1954-1964. He was Under-Secretary of State for the Colonies August 1945-October 1946, and Secretary of State for the Colonies 1946-February 1950.

Sixty-one boxes of Creech Jones's papers have been deposited by his widow in the library of Rhodes House (ref. MSS. Brit. Emp. S. 332). The papers have been catalogued in great detail and an index of names and subjects is being compiled. The papers have been divided into six main groups: biographical material; personal correspondence; speeches and writings; visits; Labour Party; Colonial work. Permission for access to Creech Jones's letters to his wife must be obtained from Mrs Creech Jones.

There are five boxes of biographical papers. They include personal correspondence 1904-1920, election pamphlets, papers relating to Creech Jones's conscientious objections (he was imprisoned 1916-1919), papers relating to the Workers' Travel Association 1929-1959, notes on Creech Jones's parliamentary work as Colonial Secretary, as well as cartoons, photographs, and honours.

The three boxes of personal correspondence include many letters from R.H. Tawney 1929-1962, as well as letters of congratulations for Creech Jones's various achievements, and letters of condolence to his widow. The miscellaneous correspondence 1913-1961 is arranged alphabetically.

There are two boxes of papers relating to Creech Jones's visits to British dependencies and four boxes of Labour Party material. The latter is almost entirely concerned with colonial policy and with the New Fabian Research Bureau.

The material relating to Creech Jones's Colonial work is the most extensive. It has been subdivided into five groups: papers concerning specific territories (there are, for example, four boxes of papers concerning Palestine); ten boxes of papers concerning the Colonial Office's Advisory Committee on Education in the Colonies (Creech Jones was a member of the committee 1936-1945); papers concerning Colonial Development and Welfare; printed material; and seven boxes of official papers. The latter have had to be closed under the thirty-year rule since they include Colonial Office internal reports and minutes, dispatches, correspondence, and a few Cabinet Papers. No papers relating to Creech Jones's work as Parliamentary Private Secretary to Ernest Bevin seem to have survived.

FREDERICK WILLIAM JOWETT (1864-1944)

Frederick Jowett was Labour M.P. for Bradford (West) 1906-1918, and Bradford (East) 1922-1924 and 1929-1931. He was 1st Commissioner of Works January-November 1924.

Jowett's papers are extensively quoted in A. Fenner Brockway, *Socialism over Sixty Years. The Life of Jowett of Bradford* (1946). This book was planned as an autobiography and the author attempted to let Jowett speak for himself wherever possible. Lord Brockway informs us that after using Jowett's papers he sent them for deposit in Bradford City Library. Unfortunately the papers were 'intercepted' by Jowett's literary executor, Alderman Brown, who kept them in his own home. Alderman Brown died in 1952 and, before anyone could intervene, his sister destroyed all the papers in his care — including the early minute books of the Bradford I.L.P. as well as Jowett's papers.

The only surviving Jowett papers in Bradford City Library are letters exchanged with Philip Snowden and Sir Rupert Haworth in September and October 1934 in which Jowett undertook to return Cabinet documents in his possession to the Cabinet Office.

SIR WILLIAM ALLEN JOWITT, EARL JOWITT (1885-1957)

William Allen Jowitt was Liberal M.P. for the Hartlepools 1922-1924 and Preston 1929. He resigned to become Labour M.P. for Preston 1929-1931 (National Labour M.P. August-October 1931), and Labour M.P. for Ashton-under-Lyne 1939-1945. He was Attorney-General June 1929-January 1932, Solicitor-General May 1940-March 1942, Paymaster-General March-December 1942, Minister without Portfolio 1942-October 1944, Minister of Social Insurance (renamed National Insurance November 1944) 1944-May 1945, and Lord Chancellor July 1945-October 1951. He was knighted in 1929, created Baron Jowitt in 1945, Viscount Jowitt in 1947, and Earl Jowitt in 1951.

Jowitt's papers are in the possession of his only child, Lady Penelope Wynn-Williams, but we have not been able to see them. The collection includes over 50 volumes of press cuttings covering most of Jowitt's life, and some letters and files.

SIR HUDSON EWBANKE KEARLEY, 1st Bt,
1st VISCOUNT DEVONPORT (1856-1934)

Hudson Ewbanke Kearley was Liberal M.P. for Devonport 1892-1910. He was Parliamentary Secretary to the President of the Board of Trade December 1905-January 1909, and Food Controller December 1916-June 1917. He was created a baronet in 1908, Baron Devonport in 1910, and Viscount Devonport in 1917.

Kearley's son, the late (2nd) Viscount Devonport, informed us that no papers have survived relating to his father's life or political career.

Kearley's *The Travelled Road — Some Memories of a Busy Life* (1934) does not quote from any papers.

FREDERICK GEORGE KELLAWAY (1870-1933)

Frederick Kellaway was Liberal M.P. for Bedford (Bedfordshire, Bedford from 1918) 1910-1922. He was Parliamentary Secretary to the Ministry of Munitions December 1916-April 1921, Deputy Minister of Munitions January 1919-April 1921, Secretary of the Department of Overseas Trade, an Additional Under-Secretary of State for Foreign Affairs, and an Additional Parliamentary Secretary to the Board of Trade April 1920-April 1921, and Postmaster-General April 1921-October 1922.

Kellaway's two daughters each have a small collection of his papers — his son has none. His elder daughter, Mrs King, of Hunts Green, Bradford Road, Sherborne, Dorset, has a small collection of press cuttings. They include Kellaway's election addresses for the 1907 London County Council elections as well as for the January 1910, 1918, and 1922 Parliamentary elections. There are reports of Kellaway's withdrawal as Liberal candidate for South Northamptonshire, and of his victory in Bedford. There are also reports of a speech he made in 1919 defending the work of the Munitions Ministry, and reports of his activities as Postmaster-General.

FREDERICK GEORGE KELLAWAY (cont.)

Kellaway's younger daughter, Mrs Beckley of Withermere, Burwash, Etchingham, Sussex, has a small collection of letters and press cuttings. Most of the letters are collected in an album; they are mainly letters of congratulation and appreciation; but there is also, for example, a letter 20 July 1908 from J.A. Pease, then Liberal Chief Whip, asking Kellaway to stand as Liberal candidate for Northamptonshire (South), and a letter from Viscount Althorp commiserating with Kellaway on his defeat in that constituency in 1910. The letters of congratulation include several from D. Lloyd George and Winston Churchill.

Possibly the most interesting part of this collection are six letters 1914-1917 from Kellaway to his wife, mostly describing his work at the Ministry of Munitions under Lloyd George and how Lloyd George conducted the Ministry: Kellaway quotes Lloyd George's welcome to him at Munitions: 'another Pacifist come to make shells. . .'.

The collection also includes a few press cuttings, the *Bedford Liberal Searchlight* for November 1921, some cartoons of Kellaway as Postmaster-General, and Kellaway's 1922 election manifesto.

PHILIP HENRY KERR, 11th MARQUESS OF LOTHIAN (1882-1940)

Philip Kerr succeeded his cousin as 11th Marquess of Lothian in 1930. He was created K.T. in 1940. He was Chancellor of the Duchy of Lancaster August-November 1931, and Parliamentary Under-Secretary of State for India 1931-September 1932.

A large collection of Kerr's papers has been deposited by his cousin, the present (12th) Lord Lothian, in the Scottish Record Office (ref. Lothian papers). The papers are currently being listed (an additional deposit was made in 1971) and the resulting list will be the first in a new series to be published by the Scottish Record Office, entitled 'Scottish Record Office Lists'. It is hoped to publish the Lothian list in Spring, 1975. The papers are open for research on the condition that any proposed publication based on the papers must be submitted to Lord Lothian for his approval.

The original deposit was divided into six main groups: Round Table papers; papers as private secretary to Lloyd George; subject files; general correspondence; papers as Ambassador to the U.S.A.; and articles and speeches.

There are 879 pages of papers concerning the Round Table 1897-1931, including pamphlets, articles, memoranda, and correspondence. The 55 files of papers as private secretary to Lloyd George 1917-1921 range from Russia, India, the Middle East, the Peace Negotiations, Reparations, European Frontiers, Germany and Ireland. There are 125 subject files 1921-1939. They include Kerr's correspondence as editor of the *Daily Chronicle* 1921-1922, papers on East Africa 1927-1930, the control of naval armaments 1927-1930, and the formation of the National Government 1931 (including letters from J.R. MacDonald and Herbert Samuel). There are many papers on India 1931-1937, particularly concerning constitutional reforms. Files on Germany 1935-1938 include memoranda of a visit there, and of conversations with Hitler and Goering. The 192 volumes of general correspondence 1918-1939 are arranged by year and then alphabetically. There are thirteen volumes of Kerr's private correspondence as Ambassador to the U.S.A. 1939-1940. They are arranged alphabetically by writer or by subject. There are 34 volumes of articles and speeches.

The second deposit in 1971 included 600 letters from Kerr to his family 1903-1940, press cuttings, articles, two notebooks concerning the Indian Franchise Committee 1932, and material collected by Sir James Butler for his biography of Kerr (see below). The bulk of this deposit concerns Kerr's work as private secretary to Lloyd George. There are letters, memoranda and minutes on India, economic affairs, conscientious objectors, the Dardanelles 1916-1917, Kerr's mission to Switzerland 1918, war aims, reparations, Ireland, Russia and Turkey. There are also correspondence files of letters between the two men, reporting on the Peace Conferences, reparations, and European relations.

Sir James R.M. Butler, *Lord Lothian, Philip Kerr 1882-1940* (1960), was based on the papers and quotes from a large number of letters, memoranda, and press cuttings. *The American Speeches of Lord Lothian July 1939 to December 1940* (1941) includes a memoir of Kerr by Sir Edward Grigg.

CHARLES WILLIAM KEY (1883-1964)

Charles Key was Labour M.P. for Poplar, Bow and Bromley 1940-1950, and for Poplar 1950-1964. He was Parliamentary Secretary to the Ministry of Health August 1945-February 1947, and Minister of Works 1947-February 1950.

Key had no children and on the death of his widow in 1965 a small suitcase of papers and photographs was inherited by his cousin, Mr W.A. Ankerson, who deposited the collection in the Bodleian Library in 1972 (ref. Dep. a.51, c.475-476, d.369-373, e.172).

The greater part of the collection consists of photographs. Perhaps most interesting of these is an album of photographs of the Poplar rate strike presented to Key on 9 November 1922. There are photographs of the council passing its resolution, of the march to answer the High Court summons, and of the arrest and release of the councillors. Most of the photographs are identified. Key's own version of the rates strike is to be found in his pamphlet *Red Poplar* (1925). Another album has photographs of Key at various functions as Minister of Works: from lighting the Christmas tree in Trafalgar Square 1947, to laying the foundation stone of the new House of Commons in May 1948. There is also a collection of photographs showing Key's work during the second world war as Regional Commissioner for the London Civil Defence Region.

A slim volume of press cuttings has survived for the period 1940-1941. It covers Key's election; there are copies of his electoral address and photographs of him arriving at Westminster to take his seat. There are also reports of his maiden speech, and other speeches in which he was particularly concerned about the supply of milk for mothers and infants. There are some press cuttings about Key's work for the provision of air-raid shelters (Poplar, partly through his efforts, had the lowest death rate in London from the raids) and the script of a broadcast he made on the same subject. There is also a copy of Cmd. 7616, *The Report of the Tribunal appointed to inquire into Allegations reflecting on the Official Conduct of Ministers of the Crown and other Public Servants, 1948-49:* the report of the Lynskey Tribunal, to which Key gave evidence and from which he emerged completely cleared of any misconduct. The collection includes some letters of condolence to Key's widow, including a tribute from C.R. Attlee, obituary notices, and Key's birth certificate. There is also a meticulously arranged notebook on a wide range of subjects, from agriculture to war pensions.

SIR HORATIO HERBERT KITCHENER,
1st EARL KITCHENER OF KHARTOUM (1850-1916)

Horatio Herbert Kitchener was Secretary of State for War August 1914-June 1916. He was created K.G.M.G. in 1894, K.G. in 1915, Baron Kitchener in 1898, Viscount Kitchener in 1902, and Earl Kitchener of Khartoum in 1914.

Sir Philip Magnus, in the introduction to his biography, *Kitchener. Portrait of an Imperialist* (1958), said that from the age of 34 Kitchener diligently kept what he regarded as important papers, including copies of telegrams and reports sent, as well as those received, and that while Kitchener was at the War Office he removed papers which would now be regarded as official papers. Sir Philip went on to say that with regard to his personal papers Kitchener was very chaotic and that chance played a large part in determining what survived and what did not. Sir Philip frequently quoted from Kitchener's papers, as did Sir George Arthur in his *Life of Lord Kitchener* (3 vols., 1920).

Kitchener's great-nephew, the present (3rd) Earl, has deposited the collection Sir Philip used in the Public Record Office (ref. P.R.O. 30/57). The papers have been divided into four sections: papers up to 1914; 1914-1916 papers; personal and estate papers; and papers collected by Sir George Arthur for his biography.

The papers up to 1914 reflect Kitchener's military career: there are papers connected with the Palestine and Cyprus Surveys 1874-1878; the 1884-1885 Sudan Expedition (including Kitchener's own notes); the conquest of the Sudan (including telegrams, intelligence reports, and Kitchener's correspondence with Lord Cromer 1897-1899); the Boer War (including Kitchener's correspondence with Queen Victoria 1899-1901, with Lord Roberts 1901-1902, and with Lord Midleton); Kitchener's term of office as Commander-in-Chief in India 1902-1909 (including correspondence with Lord Curzon 1900-1905 especially on their dispute

86

SIR HORATIO HERBERT KITCHENER (cont.)

about control of the Indian army); and his term as Minister Plenipotentiary in Egypt 1911-1914.

The first world war papers include a complete series of dispatches from Sir John French and Sir Douglas Haig in France, Sir Ian Hamilton and General Birdwood in Gallipoli, and Sir John Hanbury Williams in Moscow. There is also Kitchener's correspondence with his Cabinet colleagues, correspondence about munitions, and about his fateful journey to Russia.

The personal and estate papers are very disconnected and miscellaneous but they do include some royal letters, letters from Margot Asquith, and an engagement diary for 1913-1914.

The papers collected by Sir George Arthur include letters of condolence sent on Kitchener's death and Sir George's own correspondence with people who knew Kitchener, arranged alphabetically.

A small collection (23 pieces) of Kitchener's War Office Private Office papers 1914-1916 is also available at the Public Record Office (ref. W.O. 159). W.O. 159/1 is an index to the collection and was contemporaneously described as a general catalogue of 'The Creedy (Kitchener) Papers'. Sir Herbert Creedy (1878-1973) was Private Secretary to successive Secretaries of State at the War Office including Kitchener. The collection has been divided into three sections: strategical and political papers; miscellaneous papers; and letters from Colonel (later Brigadier-General) the Hon. Sir H. Yarde Buller 1914-1916, the British Military Attaché to the French Army Headquarters 1914-1917.

The strategic and political papers include Cabinet memoranda and drafts of Cabinet memoranda. There are also four letters from Sir Edward Grey 24-26 September 1914 warning Kitchener about indiscreet articles on the war in *The Times.* The miscellaneous papers include notes by Sir Henry Wilson and an undated paper on the risk of a gas scandal which describes Lloyd George as not having a grasp of the seriousness of the situation.

A further collection of Kitchener's papers is available at the India Office Library among a collection of the papers of his Military Secretary in India, W.R. Birdwood, 1st Baron Birdwood (ref. MSS. Eur. D. 686/1-53). As well as correspondence with Lords Curzon and Roberts on the dual military control dispute, there are official documents on the defence of India, and relations with Afghanistan and Persia.

Another small collection was purchased by the British Library at Sotheby's in 1963 (ref. Add. MSS. 52276-52278). The collection consists of three volumes of the papers of Kitchener's A.D.C. in India, Lt.-Col. R.J. Marker, but some of Kitchener's own papers are included, for instance in the correspondence between Kitchener and Marker 1902-1911. As well as some general correspondence, there are letters from H.O. Arnold-Forster 1905-1909, and Lt Col. C. à Court Repington 1904-1911.

SIR ERNEST HENRY LAMB, 1st BARON ROCHESTER (1876-1955)

Ernest Henry Lamb was Liberal M.P. for Rochester 1906-January 1910 and December 1910-1918. He was Paymaster-General November 1931-December 1935. He was knighted in 1914, and created Baron Rochester in 1931.

Lamb's elder son, the present (2nd) Baron Rochester, informs us that he has no papers relating to his father's political and official career.

GEORGE LANSBURY (1859-1940)

George Lansbury was Labour M.P. for Tower Hamlets (Bow and Bromley) 1910-1912 and for Poplar, Bow and Bromley 1922-1940. He was 1st Commissioner of Works June 1929-August 1931. He led the Labour Party 1931-1935.

Twenty-six bound volumes of Lansbury's papers were deposited by Raymond Postgate (his son-in-law) in the British Library of Political and Economic Science (ref. Lansbury papers). These are all that remain after 30 boxes of both official and personal papers were removed by the Cabinet Office in 1944 (see Postgate's Foreword to *The Life of George Lansbury* [1951]). According to the Cabinet Office, only Cabinet papers were removed from the collection and the 'few items of correspondence' were returned to Postgate. The Cabinet papers were 'not

GEORGE LANSBURY (cont.)

retained' by the Cabinet Office. A list and index of the papers at the London School of Economics is available.

The papers were divided by Postgate into five main divisions when he was writing the biography: seventeen volumes of correspondence and papers arranged chronologically 1877-1940; Postgate's own correspondence about Lansbury arranged alphabetically 1940-1950; memoranda, correspondence and pamphlets arranged by subject — for example, voluntary schools 1928-1931, unemployment and the means test, India, the Labour Party manifesto and programme of 1929, and a memorandum by Lansbury on 'The Cabinet Crisis of 1931'; photographs; and press cuttings of books by Lansbury.

Lansbury wrote several volumes of memoirs including *My Life* (1928) and *Looking Backwards and Forwards* (1935). Lansbury's son Edgar wrote a biography entitled *George Lansbury My Father* (1934) which quotes from private correspondence as well as public speeches and articles.

Three box files of press cuttings about George Lansbury are available at the Tower Hamlets Central Library (ref. 100). There are over 2000 cuttings 1894-1940 including cartoons 1920-1936. The collection includes a few letters.

ANDREW BONAR LAW (1858-1923)

Andrew Bonar Law was Conservative M.P. for Glasgow (Blackfriars) 1900-1906, Camberwell (Dulwich) 1906-1910, Lancashire (Bootle) 1911-1918, and Glasgow (Central) 1918-1923. He was Parliamentary Secretary to the Board of Trade August 1902-December 1905, Secretary of State for Colonial Affairs May 1915-December 1916, Chancellor of the Exchequer 1916-January 1919, member of the War Cabinet December 1916-October 1919, Lord Privy Seal 1919-March 1921, and Prime Minister October 1922-May 1923. He was Leader of the Conservative Party 1911-1921 and 1922-1923.

One hundred and seventeen boxes of his papers were bequeathed to his close friend, Lord Beaverbrook, and are now in the Beaverbrook Library; they have been listed and thoroughly indexed. Only seventeen boxes concern his personal and business life, the rest reflect his political and ministerial career; they have been arranged under the following headings: papers as an M.P.; as Parliamentary Secretary to the Board of Trade; leader of the Conservative Party; Colonial Secretary; Chancellor; Leader of the House of Commons; Lord Privy Seal; 1921-1922 papers; and papers as Prime Minister.

Bonar Law's papers as an M.P. have been divided into correspondence 1900-1911 (one box), general papers (including press cuttings, papers on the 1908 Licensing Bill, trade unionism, and tariff reform), and constituency correspondence (one box). There is a single box of papers as Parliamentary Secretary to the Board of Trade. Boxes 24-37 are filled with his correspondence as Leader of the Conservative Party. Boxes 38-49 contain other papers — memoranda and press cuttings — on such topics as elections, finance, foreign affairs, Ireland, House of Lords' reform, and the Marconi inquiry. There are also some papers from the Committee of Imperial Defence's Subcommittee on Invasion (1907-1914) and papers of the Diverted Cargoes Committee (August 1914-January 1915). Boxes 50-84 cover Bonar Law's term of office as Secretary of State for the Colonies. As well as Cabinet papers, correspondence, and memoranda (including political as well as official), arranged chronologically, there are press cuttings, suggestions for honours, papers on Ireland, and post-war reconstruction. There is also some political correspondence and Bonar Law's own account of the events of December 1916. Boxes 65-76 contain Law's papers as Chancellor of the Exchequer, including his warrant to act as Chancellor. The many official papers include draft Cabinet minutes for 5 April 1917-15 August 1919 which were so secret that they were not printed. Boxes 77-80, his papers as Leader of the House, include a box of letters to the King (22 March 1916-21 November 1918) describing the House's proceedings. There is also an index to Bonar Law's speeches in the House. His papers as Lord Privy Seal include papers on the peace conference as well as papers on Cabinet conclusions and ministerial conferences. There are letters to the King (4 February 1919-23 December 1920), notes for debates, and correspondence. Boxes 95 and 96 contain his papers as Leader of the Party 1918-1921 and are mostly memo-

ANDREW BONAR LAW (cont.)

randa and correspondence about the Coalition. One box of correspondence covers the period in 1921-1922 after he resigned all his offices because of ill-health. Boxes 108-117 contain his papers as Prime Minister. There are both general and special correspondence series including papers on appointments and the November 1922 general election. There are also many subject files.

Lord Blake's biography, *The Unknown Prime Minister. The Life and Times of Andrew Bonar Law 1858-1923* (1955), quotes substantially from these papers.

There is evidence that some of Bonar Law's papers were returned to official keeping: for example in the Public Record Office (ref. F.O. 899), a miscellaneous collection of printed Cabinet papers 1900-1918, there are two volumes of papers for 1915-1916 which were returned by Bonar Law's secretary in May 1923.

It should be noted that the papers of J.C.C. Davidson (q.v.) contain a number of files of Bonar Law's correspondence and official documents which were evidently kept by Davidson when he served as Law's private secretary at the Colonial Office.

RICHARD KIDSTON LAW, BARON COLERAINE (1901-   )

Richard Kidston Law was Conservative M.P. for Kingston-upon-Hull (South-West) 1931-1945, for Kensington (South) 1945-1950, and for Kingston-on-Hull (Haltemprice) 1950-1954. He was Financial Secretary to the War Office May 1940-July 1941, Parliamentary Under-Secretary of State for Foreign Affairs 1941-September 1943, Minister of State at the Foreign Office 1943-May 1945, and Minister of Education May-July 1945. He was created Baron Coleraine in 1954.

Lord Coleraine informs us that he has never systematically kept papers though some do survive, not arranged in any way or accessible. He never kept a diary nor subscribed to a press cuttings agency. Lord Coleraine adds that the most important papers concerning his period as Minister of State will be in the public records since he personally drafted most of the Cabinet papers circulated in his name.

FREDERICK WILLIAM PETHICK-LAWRENCE, BARON PETHICK-LAWRENCE (1871-1961)

Frederick William Pethick-Lawrence (he assumed the additional surname Pethick in 1912 on his mother's second marriage) was Labour M.P. for Leicester (West) 1923-1931, and Edinburgh (East) 1935-1945. He was Financial Secretary to the Treasury June 1929-August 1931, and Secretary of State for India and Burma August 1945-April 1947. He was created Baron Pethick-Lawrence in 1945.

Pethick-Lawrence's literary executrixes are his two secretaries, Miss Esther Knowles and Mrs Gladys Groom-Smith. Miss Knowles informs us that, when she has been able to sort the papers, she will present them to the library of Pethick-Lawrence's old college, Trinity College, Cambridge, but so far she has been unable to do this. In the meantime, Pethick-Lawrence's papers are closed to research.

Pethick-Lawrence himself presented a small collection of papers concerning India and Burma to the India Office Library in 1958 (ref. MSS. Eur. D. 540). They include correspondence and memoranda between the Financial Secretary and the Secretary of State for India on the 'Financial Safeguards' 1931, and press cuttings, cartoons, and photographs from the British and Indian press on the 1946 British Cabinet Mission to India.

Pethick-Lawrence's autobiography *Fate has been kind* (1943) quotes from only a few papers but Vera Brittain, *Pethick-Lawrence* (1963), was based on all of the papers and quotes frequently from them, particularly Pethick-Lawrence's letters to his first wife Emmeline, which Emmeline Lady Pethick-Lawrence left to Miss Knowles.

JOHN JAMES LAWSON, BARON LAWSON (1881-1965)

'Jack' Lawson was Labour M.P. for Durham (Chester-le-Street) 1919-1949. He was Financial Secretary to the War Office January-November 1924, Parliamentary Secretary to the Ministry of Labour June 1929-August 1931, and Secretary of State for War August 1945-October 1946. He was created Baron Lawson in 1950.

JOHN JAMES LAWSON (cont.)

Lawson's daughter, the Hon. Mrs C.F.C. Lawson, 24 Park Road North, Chester-le-Street, Co. Durham, has a small collection of her father's papers.

Very little appears to have survived from Lawson's term of office at the War Office; all that has been found is a draft letter of resignation (26 November 1945) when doctors were being released from military service out of turn. No contemporary document survives from Lawson's time as Financial Secretary to the War Office but there is an article by Lawson published about 1950 describing that government. Lawson was appointed Lord Lieutenant of Durham in 1949. Some correspondence about a visit by the Queen Mother in 1956 survives. The bulk of the papers relates to Lawson's interests in mining and his constituency and also to his various books, articles, and radio programmes.

There are many surviving papers which relate to Lawson's activities on behalf of the miners amongst whom he began his life. There are pit agreements (including one dated 1897), arbitration agreements, and notes on conditions in the mines culled from Royal Commissions and other sources. There are also photographs of the mines, press cuttings largely concerned with accidents, and a fourteen-page mansucript, entitled 'The Monster', about accidents underground.

Lawson published several books and many articles during his lifetime, for example, his own autobiography *A Man's Life* (1932). Some correspondence and other papers concerning these publications survive. The autobiography does not appear to quote from any papers. There is also a typescript and some correspondence concerning a radio broadcast entitled 'Something of My Philosophy' (28 March 1954). There are notes or memoirs of several of his colleagues, including George Lansbury and C.R. Attlee, an eight-page memorandum of Lawson's visit to Spain in 1936, and a 62-page memorandum on his visit to the Near East in 1937.

A considerable amount of miscellaneous correspondence survives especially from the late 1950s and early 1960s; and there are also three letters (1915) from Lawson's brother William, who was killed later in the first world war. There is a letter from Hore-Belisha (15 March 1938) congratulating Lawson on a speech. Congratulations on his peerage have also survived. There are many notes for speeches and sermons. Fourteen pocket diaries for the years 1933-1959 have addresses and appointments.

One file of constituency correspondence has survived, mainly dating from 1926, and this relates to unemployment and the general strike. The file contains Lawson's notes to ministers and civil servants as well as the original complaints and his replies.

FREDERICK JAMES LEATHERS, 1st VISCOUNT LEATHERS (1883-1965)

Frederick James Leathers was Minister of War Transport May 1941-July 1945, and Secretary of State for the Coordination of Transport, Fuel, and Power October 1951-September 1953. He was created Baron Leathers in 1941 and Viscount Leathers in 1954.

His son, the present (2nd) Viscount Leathers, informs us that he has no papers of consequence relating to his father's political or ministerial career.

Some of Leather's Private Office papers from the Ministry of War Transport are now available in the Public Record Office (ref. M.T. 62/3-95). As well as papers concerning various conferences, there are copies of telegrams between Winston Churchill and F.D. Roosevelt about American assistance. There are many papers on shipping, including files of meetings with the seamen's trade union leaders and the ship owners.

SIR ARTHUR HAMILTON LEE, VISCOUNT LEE OF FAREHAM (1868-1947)

Arthur Lee was Conservative M.P. for Hampshire (Fareham) 1900-1918. He was a Civil Lord of the Admiralty October 1903-December 1905, Parliamentary Secretary to the Ministry of Munitions November 1915-July 1916, Minister of Agriculture and Fisheries August 1919-February 1921, and 1st Lord of the Admiralty 1921-October 1922. He was created K.C.B. in 1916, G.C.B. in 1929, Baron Lee of Fareham in 1918 and Viscount Lee of Fareham in 1922.

SIR ARTHUR HAMILTON LEE (cont.)

A very small miscellaneous collection of Lee's papers is in the Beaverbrook Library (ref. Lee of Fareham papers); it is not yet listed. Most of the papers (including four cartons of catalogues) refer to Lee's art collection. There is an attaché case of letters from Theodore Roosevelt and his family, speech notes, miscellaneous correspondence and press cuttings about Lee's gift of the Chequers estate to the nation, including letters of appreciation from Neville Chamberlain and other prime ministers, and the pen used in signing the 1921 Naval Treaty in Washington. There is a collection of biographical press cuttings and a 'summary' of Lee's public services. There is a letter from David Lloyd George (1 November 1922) about Lee's viscountcy, a letter from H.L. French (18 February 1919) about the second anniversary of Lee's taking charge of Food Production, a copy of a letter from Lee to Lloyd George (15 February 1917) on means to stimulate food production, and a copy of Lee's 1918 report on Food Control. There are also a few papers from Lee's military career — a lecture on the battle of Waterloo, the 1893 report on the examination for admission to the Staff College, and notes by Lee on the defences of Vladivostok (1889). There is also a copy of *Letters that Remain (friendly or otherwise) from the Postbag of Arthur and Ruth Lee 1891-1941*, which Lee published privately in 1941. In 1939 he published privately *A Good Innings and a Great Partnership*, three volumes of memoirs which frequently quote from his correspondence and his wife's diaries, none of which appear to have survived. An edition of these memoirs is being prepared for publication by Mr Alan Clark.

THOMAS WODEHOUSE LEGH, 2nd BARON NEWTON (1857-1942)

Thomas Wodehouse Legh was Conservative M.P. for South-West Lancashire (Newton) 1886-1899, till he succeeded his father as second baron. He was Paymaster-General June 1915-August 1916, and Assistant Under-Secretary of State for Foreign Affairs 1916-January 1919.

His grandson, the present (4th) Lord Newton, informs us that Legh left only voluminous diaries, beginning in 1883, but these are not generally available for research. The diaries are extensively quoted and paraphrased in Lord Newton's *Retrospection* (1941).

FREDERICK ALEXANDER LINDEMANN, VISCOUNT CHERWELL (1886-1957)

Frederick Alexander Lindemann was Paymaster-General December 1942-August 1945 and October 1951-November 1953. He was created Baron Cherwell in 1941, and Viscount Cherwell in 1956.

A large collection of his papers has been deposited in the Library, Nuffield College, Oxford (ref. Cherwell papers). They have been divided into four classes on the basis of security: class A is closed; classes B and C are open only with the prior permission of the Cabinet Office; class D is open to *bona fide* researchers. A list of classes B, C, and D is available both at Nuffield and at the National Register of Archives. Researchers wishing to read papers in classes B and C should complete the application forms available in the library; the forms will then be sent by the library to the Cabinet Office for approval, a process taking some ten days.

The papers in classes B and C relate to Lindemann's official career: they include seven boxes of minutes to the Prime Minister and subject files covering large areas of the war effort including air defence and offence, manpower problems, coal production, postwar research and reconstruction, reparations policy, refugees, and atomic energy.

The papers in class D are Lindemann's personal papers. They include private correspondence from 1895 as well as 'special' correspondence with Winston Churchill 1923-1957, and the 1st Lord Birkenhead. In the first world war Lindemann worked at R.A.F. Farnborough where, amongst other successes, he worked out the theory of aircraft spinning and how to prevent it; a box of aeronautical papers survives. In 1919 he was appointed Dr Lee's Professor of Experimental Philosophy at Oxford University and many papers have survived from his scientific and university career. They include administrative papers concerning the Clarendon Laboratory, as well as correspondence with distinguished scientists, lecture notes, and manuscripts of articles. Lindemann's life within the university is represented by eight boxes of

FREDERICK ALEXANDER LINDEMANN (cont.)

papers including some on his unsuccessful candidature in the Oxford University by-election of 1937, and on the many proposals for an Oxford relief road. There are also papers from Lindemann's activities in the House of Lords, and files of letters to the press.

These papers are extensively quoted in Lord Birkenhead's biography *The Prof in Two Worlds* (1961). Sir Roy Harrod, *The Prof* (1959) is a personal memoir not based on these papers.

DAVID ALEXANDER EDWARD LINDSAY, 27th EARL OF CRAWFORD, 10th EARL OF BALCARRES (1871-1940)

David Alexander Edward Lindsay, known as Lord Balcarres 1880-1913, succeeded his father as 27th Earl of Crawford in 1913. He was created K.T. in 1921. He was Conservative M.P. for North Lancashire (Chorley) 1895-1913. He was President of the Board of Agriculture and Fisheries July-December 1916, Lord Privy Seal 1916-January 1919, Chancellor of the Duchy of Lancaster 1919-April 1921, and 1st Commissioner of Works 1921-October 1922.

Lindsay's papers are in the possession of his son, the present (28th) Earl of Crawford. Lindsay kept a diary which covers general, social, political, and artistic matters. He also kept some papers relating to his period as Chief Whip and as 1st Commissioner of Works. Limited access to the papers may be allowed to senior researchers.

SIR PHILIP CUNLIFFE-LISTER, 1st EARL OF SWINTON (1884-1972)

Philip Cunliffe-Lister (he changed his name from Lloyd-Greame in 1924) was Conservative M.P. for Middlesex (Hendon) 1918-1935. He was Parliamentary Secretary to the Board of Trade August 1920-April 1921, Secretary to the Overseas Trade Department and Additional Parliamentary Secretary to the Board of Trade 1921-October 1922, President of the Board of Trade 1922-January 1924, November 1924-June 1929, and August-November 1931, Secretary of State for the Colonies 1931-June 1935, Secretary of State for Air 1935-May 1938, Cabinet Minister Resident in West Africa June 1942-November 1944, Minister of Civil Aviation 1944-July 1945, Chancellor of the Duchy of Lancaster and Minister of Materials October 1951-November 1952, and Secretary of State for Commonwealth Relations 1952-April 1955. He was created K.B.E. in 1920, G.B.E. in 1929, Viscount Swinton in 1935, and Earl of Swinton in 1955.

Cunliffe-Lister bequeathed his papers to the library of Churchill College, Cambridge (ref. Swinton papers), but they will not be available for research until a biography by Mr Robert Rhodes James has been completed. The papers will be subject to the 30-year rule operated by Churchill College.

Cunliffe-Lister's memoirs, *I Remember* (1948), quote frequently from his correspondence and in his further volume, *Sixty Years of Power: Some Memories of the Men who Wielded it* (1966), he gave his views on the prime ministers he had known and on the working of the Cabinet system. A Manchester University M.A. thesis by Alan Earl (September 1960) on Cunliffe-Lister's early political career was written with Cunliffe-Lister's help and quotes from many letters, mainly before 1932.

A small collection of Cunliffe-Lister's Air Ministry papers is available at the Public Record Office (ref. Air 19/23, 24, 522). The collection includes documents on the Inskip enquiry into the relationship between the Fleet Air Arm and shore-based aircraft 1936-1939, papers on the state of air preparedness 1937-1938, and minutes and reports of the Nursing Service Committee.

JOHN JESTYN LLEWELLIN, BARON LLEWELLIN (1893-1957)

'Jay' Llewellin was Conservative M.P. for Middlesex (Uxbridge) 1929-1945. He was a Civil Lord of the Admiralty May 1937-July 1939, Parliamentary Secretary to the Ministry of Supply July 1939-May 1940, Parliamentary Secretary to the Ministry of Aircraft Production 1940-May 1941, Parliamentary Secretary to the Ministry of Transport (later War Transport) 1941-February 1942, President of the Board of Trade February 1942, Minister of Aircraft Production February-November 1942, Minister for Supply Resident in Washington

JOHN JESTYN LLEWELLIN (cont.)

D.C. 1942-November 1943, Minister of Food 1943-August 1945, and Governor-General of the Federation of Rhodesia and Nyasaland 1953-1957. He was created G.B.E. in 1953, and Baron Llewellin in 1945.

Llewellin's sister, Miss M.M. Llewellin of White Lovington, Bere Regis, near Wareham, Dorset, has a small collection of her brother's papers.

Possibly of greatest interest is a long (47 pages) note by Llewellin on his work at the Ministry of Aircraft Production under Lord Beaverbrook and at the Board of Trade. The note describes Llewellin's first meeting with Beaverbrook and the formation of the Ministry. Llewellin gives Beaverbrook warm praise for his work: 'It was his drive and initiative which did the trick. . .' There is also a file of speech notes and carbon copies of letters written to Miss Llewellin in 1943 when Llewellin was Minister Resident in Washington.

The remainder of the collection consists of fifteen volumes of press cuttings and photographs. The first, covering the years 1889-1919, includes cuttings of his parents' wedding, his days at Eton, rowing at Oxford, and fighting in the first world war (his commission as second lieutenant in 1916 has also survived). Other volumes cover his election campaigns and public activities. A very full volume of cuttings survives from Llewellin's tenure of the Ministry of Food; it includes reports of the first experiments with frozen and dehydrated food as well as the resumption of the distilling of whisky (August 1944). The bulk of the volumes cover Llewellin's term of office as first Governor-General of the Federation of Rhodesia and Nyasaland, the formation of the federation, Llewellin's arrival, and his varied activities. Llewellin died suddenly, while still in office, and a number of obituaries and tributes from both England and Rhodesia have survived.

In addition to these papers, Miss Llewellin has a large collection of her brother's letters to herself and to their elder brother William. Although these letters mainly concern family matters, there is also some political content. Gilbert Thomas, *Llewellin* (1961), frequently quotes from these letters. Thomas also gave long quotations from Llewellin's diaries; these can no longer be found, and indeed Miss Llewellin has no recollection of diaries being kept.

SIR GEORGE AMBROSE LLOYD, 1st BARON LLOYD (1879-1941)

George Ambrose Lloyd was Conservative M.P. for Staffordshire (West) 1910-1918 and for East Sussex (Eastbourne) 1924-1925. He was Governor of Bombay 1918-1923, High Commissioner for Egypt and the Sudan 1925-1929, and Secretary of State for the Colonies and Leader of the House of Lords May 1940-February 1941. He was created G.C.I.E. in 1918, G.C.S.I. in 1924, and Baron Lloyd in 1925.

The present (2nd) Lord Lloyd has deposited most of his father's papers in the library of Churchill College, Cambridge. The papers have been listed, but they are not generally available. Applications should be made to the Keeper of the Archives. The papers have been divided into seven main groups: Personal; Eastern Affairs; India; Egypt; Public and Political; Literary; Business. This arrangement was largely Lloyd's own, his main interest being to use the papers for reference for speeches and articles. This has led to the letters not being arranged in chronological order and to there being some overlapping between divisions.

The personal papers include Lloyd's birth certificate, school reports, passports, car and aeroplane log books, as well as a large collection of press cuttings and photographs, correspondence concerning his various appointments, letters from his father and other members of his family, and several letters (1929-1936) from T.E. Lawrence. The section includes copies of letters from Lloyd to his wife (4/1) written in 1939. Lady Lloyd has kept her own diaries and letters from her husband; they were used and are quoted in Colin Forbes Adam, *Life of Lord Lloyd* (1948). They may be deposited with the other papers at a later date but they are not at present available for research.

The Eastern Affairs papers include correspondence and reports compiled by Lloyd when he was attaché in Constantinople (1905-1907) and special commissioner for British Trade to the area 1907-1908. They include 62 volumes of telegrams between the Porte and its ambassadors 1889-1908 which Lloyd acquired in 1908. There is also war correspondence concerning this area, Lloyd's diary for Gallipoli (March-October 1915), and for a journey with T.E. Lawrence probably made in 1917.

SIR GEORGE AMBROSE LLOYD (cont.)

The Indian papers derive from Lloyd's governorship of the Bombay Presidency and from his later continued interest in the area. They include papers concerning his arrival and departure, various administrative problems, and correspondence with princes and chiefs. Lloyd's Egyptian papers (he was High Commissioner for Egypt and the Sudan 1925-1929) are of the same type but include a considerable correspondence with Sir Austen Chamberlain and Sir William Tyrrell, as well as copies of official telegrams and Cabinet papers on the Middle East.

Lloyd's political papers include about 130 subject files on the domestic, colonial, and foreign problems of his day. There are also papers concerning his West Staffordshire constituency, including receipts and general correspondence. There are no papers relating to Eastbourne. Lloyd's political correspondence is mainly for 1930-1940, arranged alphabetically within each year. There is a great deal of material concerning Lloyd's work for the British Council, including correspondence, and papers from Lloyd's many tours on the Council's behalf. There are also six files from the Colonial Office in this section — two files of 1940 correspondence and four subject files.

Lloyd's literary papers are mainly typed notes for speeches and articles written after 1921 though a few notes from 1909-1911 have survived. There are eighteen files on Lloyd's personal financial affairs.

Lloyd himself described his Egyptian career in *Egypt since Cromer* (2 vols., 1933-34).

WALTER HUME LONG, 1st VISCOUNT LONG (1854-1924)

Walter Long was Conservative M.P. for Wiltshire (North) 1880-1885, Wiltshire (East or Devizes) 1885-1892, Liverpool (West Derby) 1893-1900, Bristol (South) 1900-1906, County Dublin (South) 1906-1910, Strand 1910-1918, and Westminster (St. George's) 1918-1921. He was Parliamentary Secretary to the Local Government Board 1886-1892, President of the Board of Agriculture July 1895-November 1900, President of the Local Government Board 1900-March 1905, and May 1915-December 1916, Chief Secretary for Ireland March-December 1905, Secretary of State for Colonial Affairs December 1916-January 1919, and 1st Lord of the Admiralty 1919-February 1921. He was created Viscount Long in 1921.

According to Long's own *Memories* (1923), he 'faithfully kept' records though he did not, for instance, record conversations in his diaries. His book is based only on his recollections. Sir Charles Petrie, Bt, in *Walter Long and His Times* (1936) said that shortly before his death Long destroyed many of his papers. There are letters from Long's grandson in Austen Chamberlain's papers which also mention specifically that Long seems to have destroyed papers concerning the formation of the 1916 coalition.

Thus only a small collection of Long's papers has been deposited in the Wiltshire Record Office (ref. WRO 947). A list of the papers has been drafted; the papers have been arranged as far as possible according to the offices Long held.

Long's work as Parliamentary Secretary to the Local Government Board is reflected by copies of bills with civil servants' memoranda 1889-1892, papers concerning the administration of the poor law 1887-1892, and papers concerning the Labourers' Allotments Bill 1886-1887. Long's work at the Board of Agriculture is represented by papers, including correspondence with the Treasury, on grants for agricultural training centres 1896-1897, papers on the salaries and rank of the Board's staff 1897-1898, papers concerning the appointment of the Director-General of the Ordnance Survey 1898, and delays to the survey's work because of lack of accommodation 1899. There are no papers concerning Long's unpopular attempts to eradicate rabies. Long's Irish Office papers cover education, nationalist societies 1903-1905, recruitment to the Royal Irish Constabulary 1904-1906, the working of the 1903 Land Act, land congestion, the state of the west and south-west of the country 1905, and the position of Sir A. MacDonnell, the Permanent Under-Secretary 1905. In addition there are a large number of draft bills and Cabinet memoranda on a variety of subjects 1895-1905.

A gap occurs in the papers and the later (1915-1924) papers are more miscellaneous. As well as Cabinet papers on the war and on peace negotiations, and a report by Sir Basil Thompson on communist activities in Britain 1921, there is a memorandum of the discussions leading up to the formation of the 1916 coalition and letters from political contemporaries

WALTER HUME LONG (cont.)

1915-1916. There are a few memoranda on Admiralty business, on Ireland, and the Turko-Greek war. In addition, there is material on Conservative party affairs 1922-1924. This includes a memorandum by Long on the break up of the Coalition, which gives details of some of the various meetings and interviews which occurred. There is also a letter from Long to Sir George Younger 22 October 1922 on the end of the Coalition.

Long's grandson, the present (3rd) Viscount Long, has just (June 1973) discovered some more of Long's papers. They will be added to the collection in the Wiltshire Record Office. They fill a tin trunk and five dispatch boxes and appear to have been sent to Long by his civil servants when he finally left office in 1921.

One dispatch box contains papers relating to Long's term of office at the Irish Office in 1905. Most of the papers relate to the dispute with Sir A.P. MacDonnell. We were unable to look at the contents of one dispatch box as it was locked. A third dispatch box contained files on various parliamentary measures 1910-1912, including reform of the House of Lords, land policy, and poor law reform. A fourth dispatch box contained papers on the Unionist party's reorganization 1910-1911, with memoranda from local parties on how they were organized and how they selected their candidates. The final dispatch box contained a great deal of genealogical material, a file on Colonial Office administration, and a file of correspondence with Lord Derby January 1917-July 1918. The later letters in this file are particularly interesting as they were written when Derby was at the Paris Embassy and Long was describing the political situation to him. The large tin trunk contains a great number of papers from the Irish Office, the Colonial Office, and the Admiralty, as well as some personal investment papers, and reports and memoranda of the Unionist reorganization committee. There are files of correspondence with Sir John French, A.J. Balfour, D. Lloyd George, A. Bonar Law, Hamar Greenwood, and others concerning the various attempts to settle the Irish problem 1916-1922. Most of the files contain copies of Long's letters; there are very few replies.

An additional volume of Long's papers is available for research in the Public Record Office (ref. ADM. 116/3623). The contents are rather miscellaneous and range from correspondence found when Bloemfontein was captured in 1901, and Long's trusteeship of the Wiltshire Yeomanry, to minutes of the War Cabinet's Raw Materials Board. There is also some correspondence with M.P.A. Hankey 6 December 1920 on leaks to the press of Cabinet discussions, and correspondence with F.E. Smith on the Sex Disqualification Bill 1919-1920.

WILLIAM LYGON, 7th EARL BEAUCHAMP (1872-1938)

William Lygon, known as Viscount Elmley till he succeeded his father as 7th Earl Beauchamp in 1891, was Lord President of the Council June-November 1910 and August 1914-May 1915, and 1st Commissioner of Works November 1910-August 1914. He was created K.C.M.G. in 1899, and K.G. in 1914.

His son, the present (8th) Earl Beauchamp, of Madresfield Court, Malvern, Worcestershire, knows of no letters or papers and informs us that his father did not keep a diary. The only papers he has are some twenty scrapbooks for the years 1891-1938 which cover his father's career. As well as mementos, such as menus, programmes, and photographs, the scrapbooks include press cuttings which, in particular, illustrate Lygon's strong support for free trade.

THE HON. ALFRED LYTTELTON (1857-1913)

Alfred Lyttelton was Liberal Unionist M.P. for Warwick and Leamington 1895-1905, and Conservative M.P. for St George's, Hanover Square 1906-1913. He was Secretary of State for the Colonies September 1903-December 1905.

Lyttelton's own papers, with those of other members of his family, including his wife, were deposited in 1970 by their son, Lord Chandos, in the library of Churchill College, Cambridge (ref. Lyttelton Papers). The papers have been listed. Applications for access should be made to the Keeper of the Archives. The whole collection comprises 70 boxes of papers, of which about a third are Alfred Lyttelton's papers. The collection has been divided into the papers of the several individuals represented; each division is arranged in alphabetical order of correspondents. Lyttelton's papers are to be found in Sections 2 and 3. Most of the papers are family letters. The only political papers are several boxes of correspondence with governors and others when

ALFRED LYTTELTON (cont.)

Lyttelton was Colonial Secretary. For example, there are several letters from Joseph Chamberlain 1899-1909, Lord Grey 1903-1911, Lord Milner 1903-1905, and Lord Selborne 1905-1909. There are also a few miscellaneous Colonial Office files, speech notes, and press cuttings.

Many of Lyttelton's letters to his wife are quoted in her biography, *Alfred Lyttelton. An Account of his Life* (1917). His brother, the Hon. Edward Lyttelton, published privately an account of Lyttelton's early background: *Alfred Lyttelton, His Home-Training and Earlier Life* (1915).

OLIVER LYTTELTON, 1st VISCOUNT CHANDOS (1893-1972)

Oliver Lyttelton was Conservative M.P. for Hampshire (Aldershot) 1940-1954. He was President of the Board of Trade October 1940-June 1941, and May-August 1945, Minister of State June 1941-March 1942, Minister of State Resident in the Middle East February-March 1942, Minister of Production March 1942, Minister of Production March 1942-August 1945, and Secretary of State for the Colonies October 1951-July 1954. He was created K.G. in 1970 and Viscount Chandos in 1954.

Lyttelton deposited his family's papers, including his own, in the library of Churchill College, Cambridge (ref. Lyttelton Papers). The papers have been listed; applications for access should be made to the Keeper of the Archives. Lyttelton's own papers are very few in number. They consist almost entirely of his letters to his mother from the front 1915-1918. He himself informed us that he had never kept a diary or copies of his own letters.

The Memoirs of Lord Chandos (1962) appear to be based on the author's reminiscences and do not quote from any papers. In *From Peace to War: A Study in Contrast 1857-1918* (1965) Lyttelton quoted from his family papers, and included selections from his own letters from the front.

A small collection of papers relating to Lyttelton's work at the Board of Trade is available for research at the Public Record Office (ref. B.T. 87). It includes papers relating to Lyttelton's visit to the U.S.A. in 1942, and notes for speeches and broadcasts.

CHARLES ALBERT McCURDY (1870-1941)

Charles McCurdy was Liberal M.P. for Northampton 1910-1923. He was Parliamentary Secretary to the Ministry of Food January 1919-April 1920, Food Controller 1920-March 1921, and Joint Parliamentary Secretary to the Treasury and Coalition Liberal Chief Whip 1921-October 1922.

Because McCurdy's chambers were bombed, only a small collection of papers has survived in the possession of the son of McCurdy's late secretary, Mr C.J.Brook, 44 Bathgate Road, London SW19 5PJ. Apart from obituary notices and a letter of condolence sent to Miss Brook, the collection includes a press cutting on the end of the *Daily Chronicle* with a note by McCurdy giving his version of events, a letter from Lord Beaverbrook (1941) thanking McCurdy for his support for the Empire Crusade, and a carbon copy of a letter to *The Times* on the duty of citizens to intervene in crimes of violence. The collection also includes a note by Miss Brook that (in 1958) she had 'no papers at all'.

McCurdy's niece, Mrs G.G. Wingfield, 10 Dover Park Drive, Rockhampton, London S.W.15, has only a copy of McCurdy's 1910 election address.

SIR GORDON MACDONALD, 1st BARON MACDONALD OF GWAENYSGOR (1888-1966)

Gordon Macdonald was Labour M.P. for Lancashire (Ince) 1929-1942. He was Paymaster-General April 1949-October 1951. He was created K.C.M.G. in 1946 and Baron Macdonald of Gwaenysgor in 1949.

His son, the present (2nd) Lord Macdonald of Gwaenysgor, knows of no papers. His younger daughter, the Hon. Mrs Fullard, has some papers but they are not at present available for research as they include some personal papers. We have not been able to contact Macdonald's other children.

Macdonald published *Atgofion Seneddol [Parliamentary Reminiscences]* (1949).

JAMES RAMSAY MacDONALD (1866-1937)

James Ramsay MacDonald was Labour M.P. for Leicester 1906-1918, Glamorganshire (Aberavon) 1922-1929, Durham (Seaham) 1929-1931; National Labour M.P. for Durham (Seaham) 1931-1935, and the Scottish Universities 1936-1937. He was Prime Minister and Secretary of State for Foreign Affairs January-November 1924, Prime Minister June 1929-June 1935, and Lord President of the Council 1935-May 1937.

His papers have been deposited at the Public Record Office (ref. P.R.O. 30/69) but they will not be open to researchers until a biography by David Marquand M.P. is completed. The collection contains 1669 'pieces', some of which contain several files. It includes the papers of MacDonald, his wife, Margaret Ethel Gladstone (d. 1911), and papers given by MacDonald to his secretary, Mrs Rosenberg (Rose Hoenig). The latter are only on loan to the Public Record Office and are designated by the letter 'R' throughout the list. The papers have been listed under three main headings: Personal; Political; and Official.

Both MacDonald and his wife appear to have been very methodical in keeping their papers: Mrs MacDonald made an index to her personal correspondence. But their original order was disturbed, partly by MacDonald himself (possibly with a view of writing an auto-biography), by Sir Frank Markham, by Ishbel MacDonald, by a thief, and by a fire! Nevertheless, there are no obvious gaps in the papers, apart from the possible destruction of 'crank' letters after 1931. There are, however, very few letters for the period 1916-1923, possibly because MacDonald had no private secretary at that time.

MacDonald's personal papers include 45 files of correspondence from 1890 onwards, as well as earlier papers relating to his mother, aunt, and maternal grandparents. There is correspondence between MacDonald and his wife, and with their children. There is a school diary, five pages of a diary for 1912, and two larger bound volumes of diary from 1910 to 1937. There is also an engagement diary for 1911, an appointments diary for 1917, and MacDonald's official diary as Lord President. There are several notebooks: on his South African tour (1902); and on the labour unrest of 1911 and the part MacDonald played in this. His wife's papers include some twenty volumes of diary and notebooks for 1883-1906, as well as a considerable amount of correspondence and papers concerning her own family. There are 132 files of papers concerning MacDonald's literary activities.

MacDonald's political papers cover a wide range in both time and scope. They include his activities in the Fabian Society, the Independent Labour Party, the Social Democratic Federation, the Labour Party, and the National Labour Party, as well as his pacifist activities, and his work for the Fellowship of the New Life. They include long runs of socialist newspapers 1892-1937 and a large number of pamphlets. There are over 100 boxes of general correspondence as well as subject files. There are also notes for speeches, interviews with the press, and press cuttings. There are a few memoranda by MacDonald on, for example, Labour-Liberal relations (1906-1907), and on the possibility of socialists joining the Coalition Government, both in May 1915 and December 1916. For the period of MacDonald's term of office as Secretary to the Labour Representation Committee (L.R.C.) 1900-1906, the papers are not very revealing, but for the period 1906-1914, when MacDonald was Chairman of the L.R.C. 1906-1909 and was struggling to become Leader of the Parliamentary Labour Party (P.L.P.), the papers illuminate the internal struggles of the P.L.P., and MacDonald's increasingly close relationship with the Liberal Party. The papers for 1914 are of great value; but thereafter their volume and interest declines sharply. There are 66 files of constituency papers. There are also a few, very interesting, papers related to MacDonald's candidature at Dover and Southampton in the 1890s.

The last but greatest part of the collection (nearly 700 files) relates to MacDonald's terms in office. The main series of Cabinet Papers have been returned to the Cabinet Office. The private office files of the 1924 government were found to be in great chaos and it appears that no successful filing system was devised at the time. For example, a collection of correspondence to be filed by Miss Cracknell was filed under the heading 'Miss Cracknell'. Some attempt at subject division has been made, as well as separating purely Foreign Office papers from the Prime Minister's own. By 1929 a proper system had been devised and this has been reconstructed. Running parallel to these papers are some 50 files of more private correspondence on official matters, particularly on such problems as honours and appointments.

JAMES RAMSAY MacDONALD (cont.)

The papers of Rose Rosenberg, MacDonald's private secretary, form the basis of this group. These papers are very full and throw a good deal of light on MacDonald himself, the Labour Party, national and international politics.

A small collection (two pieces) of Foreign Office general correspondence 1923-1924 arranged alphabetically by country is also available at the Public Record Office (ref. F.O. 800/218, 219).

A further eight volumes of MacDonald papers are deposited in the British Library of Political and Economic Science (ref. MacDonald papers). Five of the volumes contain Mrs MacDonald's papers 1895-1912 on various social issues such as the employment of women, factory and shop legislation, the 1901-1902 Licensing bill, and housing. The three volumes of MacDonald's papers 1896-1923 have been arranged chronologically. They include much printed material, press cuttings and some correspondence. The papers have been indexed.

MALCOLM JOHN MacDONALD (1901-   )

Malcolm MacDonald was Labour M.P. for Nottinghamshire (Bassetlaw) 1929-1935 and National M.P. for Inverness-shire, Ross and Cromarty 1936-1945. He was Parliamentary Under-Secretary of State for Dominion Affairs September 1931-June 1935, Secretary of State for Colonial Affairs June-November 1935, and May 1938-May 1940, Secretary of State for Dominion Affairs November 1935-May 1938, and October 1938-January 1939, and Minister of Health May 1940-February 1941.

Mr MacDonald informs us that he has not yet been able to sort through his papers and that they are therefore not available for research. In the introduction to *People and Places: Random Reminiscences* (1969), Mr MacDonald states that he has never kept a diary or notes or reflections on current events for his own use. In *Titans and Others* (1972) Mr MacDonald gives his impressions of political figures he has known.

REGINALD McKENNA (1863-1943)

Reginald McKenna was Liberal M.P. for Monmouthshire (North) 1895-1918. He was Financial Secretary to the Treasury December 1905-January 1907, President of the Board of Education 1907-April 1908, 1st Lord of the Admiralty 1908-October 1911, Secretary of State for Home Affairs 1911-May 1915, and Chancellor of the Exchequer 1915-December 1916.

A small collection of McKenna's papers was deposited by his son in the library of Churchill College in 1966 (ref. McKenna papers). A list of the papers is available. The description of the papers as very large and 'very nearly complete' by McKenna's nephew, Stephen McKenna, in the preface of his *Reginald McKenna* (1948) appears to have been exaggerated, although it is possible that some of the papers used by Stephen McKenna have not survived.

The collection deposited at Churchill College, Cambridge, contains a few miscellaneous personal letters 1908-1911, and some miscellaneous Board of Education correspondence 1906-1908. The major part of the collection derives from McKenna's term of office at the Admiralty. In 1913 some of these papers were listed, probably by the Admiralty Historical Section. McKenna's correspondents include the King, the Prime Minister, members of the Cabinet, especially D. Lloyd George and Winston Churchill, members of the Admiralty Board, naval officers, and M.P.s. Particularly outstanding is the correspondence of both McKenna and his wife with Lord Fisher 1908-1920. There are, in addition, some printed papers and press cuttings.

McKenna's tenure of the Home Office is represented by correspondence with Asquith about the move from the Admiralty September-October 1911, notes of a conversation with Asquith 20 October 1911, correspondence with Winston Churchill 1911-1912, and miscellaneous correspondence.

McKenna's Letters Patent for the Exchequer have survived, as well as his budget speech notes for 1915 and 1916, correspondence about the mission to the United States August-September 1915, correspondence with the Prime Minister 1915-1916, and miscellaneous correspondence.

SIR WILLIAM WARRENDER MACKENZIE, 1st BARON AMULREE (1860-1942)

William Warrender Mackenzie was created K.B.E. in 1918, G.B.E. in 1926, and Baron Amulree in 1929. He was Secretary of State for Air October 1930-November 1931.

His son, the present (2nd) Lord Amulree, deposited a small collection of Mackenzie's papers in the Bodleian Library in 1970 (ref. Dep. c. 384-391, d. 307). The collection comprises four boxes of miscellaneous correspondence 1925-1937, and papers relating to the 1933 Royal Commission on the future of Newfoundland.

Mackenzie's correspondents include the leading Labour politicians of his day – J.R. MacDonald, J.H. Thomas, Margaret Bondfield, Lord Parmoor, and William Graham. There are also a few drafts of letters by Mackenzie and memoranda by him on industrial rationalization 1928, colonial development 1929, and notes of the conclusions of a Cabinet meeting 24 August 1931.

The papers on Newfoundland include correspondence, telegrams to the Dominions Office, and memoranda. There is also a desk diary containing notes of evidence and interviews, and some conclusions by Mackenzie.

SIR JOHN PATON MACLAY, 1st Bt, 1st BARON MACLAY (1857-1951)

John Paton Maclay was Minister of Shipping December 1916-March 1921. He was created a baronet in 1914 and Baron Maclay in 1922.

His grandson, the present (3rd) Lord Maclay, tells us that all his papers were destroyed.

SIR DONALD MACLEAN (1864-1932)

Donald Maclean was Liberal M.P. for Bath 1906-1910, Selkirkshire and Peebles-shire (Midlothian and Peebles-shire, Peebles and Southern from 1918) 1910-1922 and Cornwall (North) 1929-1932. He was President of the Board of Education August 1931-June 1932. He was created K.B.E. in 1917.

A small collection of Maclean's papers was deposited by his family in the Bodleian Library in 1972 (ref. Dep. a.49-50, c.465-471, 473, e.171). The papers have been listed. There are two boxes of correspondence which have been arranged in two chronological series: early letters to his wife 1905-1907, and general papers 1906-1931. There are also appointment diaries for 1909-1913, 1916, 1920-1921, 1923-1924, and 1926-1930.

The general papers mostly concern Liberal party affairs. There is correspondence on the financing of the *Westminster Gazette* 1912-1916; letters and memoranda on the organization of the Asquithian Liberals 1918-1919; several memoranda of meetings with Lloyd George 1919-1924, and notes on Liberal reunion 1924; and notes on the position of the party at the various general elections. There are a few papers about Maclean's appointment as President of the Board of Education. Maclean's letters to his wife are full of accounts of his political activities and comments on current issues.

HUGH PATTISON MACMILLAN, BARON MACMILLAN (1873-1952)

Hugh Pattison Macmillan was Lord Advocate February-November 1924, and Minister of Information September 1939-January 1940. He was a Lord of Appeal in Ordinary 1930-1939 and 1941-1947, and a Lord of Appeal 1947-1952. He was created G.C.V.O. in 1937, and Baron Macmillan (a judicial life peerage) in 1930.

About 400 miscellaneous letters were deposited by Macmillan's niece, Mrs H.P. Dyson, in the National Library of Scotland (ref. Acc. 4849). Most of the letters are 'ceremonial', that is letters on his entering or leaving office. However, there are about 100 letters from J.R. MacDonald with copies of Macmillan's letters to MacDonald. This correspondence covers the period 1924-1937 and includes such topics as Scottish legal business, the Royal Commission on lunacy, Macmillan's appointment to the Honours Committee, and the Oscar Slater appeal. Oscar Slater had been convicted of murder in 1909 but in 1928, after nineteen years of imprisonment and much agitation on his behalf, the conviction was quashed and he was released

HUGH PATTISON MACMILLAN (cont.)

(see William Roughhead, *The Trial of Oscar Slater*, 3rd edn., 1929). The Library also has a box of papers presented by Macmillan himself concerning the foundation of the National Library, in which he was closely involved (ref. Acc. 2390).

Mrs Dyson deposited four additional boxes of her uncle's papers in the British Library (ref. Add. MSS. 54575-54578). These papers cover the years 1934-1949 and largely relate to Macmillan's work as a Trustee of the British Museum.

Macmillan's *A Man of Law's Tale* (1952) quotes from a few letters, for example his letter of resignation as Minister of Information in 1940.

(MAURICE) HAROLD MACMILLAN (1894-   )

Harold Macmillan was Conservative M.P. for Stockton-on-Tees 1924-1929 and 1931-1945, and for Bromley 1945-1964. He was Parliamentary Secretary to the Ministry of Supply May 1940-February 1942, Parliamentary Under-Secretary of State for the Colonies February 1942-January 1943, Minister Resident in North West Africa December 1942-May 1945, Secretary of State for Air May-August 1945, Minister for Housing and Local Government October 1951-October 1954, Minister of Defence 1954-April 1955, Secretary of State for Foreign Affairs April-December 1955, Chancellor of the Exchequer December 1955-January 1957, and Prime Minister 1957-October 1963.

Mr Macmillan informs us that he does not wish his papers to be examined during his lifetime. After his death the future of his papers will be determined by his trustees. Mr Macmillan quoted extensively from his papers in his memoirs: *Winds of Change 1919-1939* (1966); *The Blast of War 1939-1945* (1967); *Tides of Fortune 1945-1955* (1969); *Riding the Storm 1956-1959* (1971); *Pointing the Way 1959-1961* (1972); and *The End of the Day 1961-1963* (1973).

A collection of papers relating to the work of the various Ministers Resident has been opened in the Public Record Office (ref. F.O. 660). It includes papers derived from Mr Macmillan's work as Minister Resident in North West Africa 1943-1944 (F.O. 660/12-105 and 200-343). There are memoranda on the political situation in the Mediterranean and in North West Africa, and on General de Gaulle and the Free French. There are also many press cuttings.

THOMAS JAMES MACNAMARA (1861-1931)

Thomas James Macnamara was Liberal M.P. for Camberwell (North) 1900-1924 (the division became North-West Camberwell in 1918 when he became a Coalition Liberal). He was Parliamentary Secretary to the Local Government Board January 1907-April 1908, Parliamentary and Financial Secretary to the Admiralty 1908-April 1920, and Minister of Labour March 1920-October 1922.

We have been unable to trace Macnamara's papers. His widow died in 1955. They had three sons and one daughter. The eldest son, Neil Cameron Macnamara, died in 1967; his widow had never heard him mention anything about his father's papers and did not know of the existence of any papers. We have been unable to trace the second son. The youngest son, Terence Macnamara, has no idea of what may have happened to his father's papers but thought that as his only sister was very interested in politics she may have had them. Macnamara's only daughter, Mrs Elsie Cameron Scott, died in 1965; her husband knows of no papers.

HECTOR McNEIL (1907-1955)

Hector McNeil was Labour M.P. for Greenock 1941-1955. He was Parliamentary Under-Secretary of State for Foreign Affairs August 1945-October 1946, Minister of State for Foreign Affairs 1946-February 1950, and Secretary of State for Scotland 1950-October 1951.

His widow informs us that McNeil kept no personal papers and that apart from film and tape recordings of three speeches he made at the United Nations, she has only his letters to her, and an incomplete rough draft of a biography she began writing. None of these papers is available for research.

RONALD JOHN McNEILL, BARON CUSHENDUN (1861-1934)

Ronald John McNeill was Conservative M.P. for Kent (St. Augustine's; Canterbury from 1918) 1911-1927. He was Parliamentary Under-Secretary of State for Foreign Affairs October 1922-January 1924 and November 1924-November 1925, Financial Secretary to the Treasury 1925-October 1927, and Chancellor of the Duchy of Lancaster 1927-June 1929. He was created Baron Cushendun in 1927.

A selection was copied from McNeill's papers by the Public Record Office of Northern Ireland in 1961 (ref. T. 1829 and Mic. 63). A description of this selection may be seen in Public Record Office of Northern Ireland, *The Report of the Deputy Keeper of the Records for the years 1960-1965*, Cmd. 521 (Belfast, 1968), p. 134. Most of the papers copied concern McNeill's earlier life. There are letters to him as editor of the *St. James's Gazette* 1900-1904, including one from Lord Milner on the labour question in the Transvaal November 1903. There are also some autobiographical notes, compiled about 1910. There are several letters about McNeill's unsuccessful attempts to enter Parliament, and letters of congratulation on his Privy Councillorship (1924), and on his entry to the Cabinet (1927). There is a particularly interesting letter from McNeill to his family August 1928 explaining the circumstances of his being Acting Secretary of State for Foreign Affairs August-December 1928, when Sir Austen Chamberlain was ill. A small file of estate papers for Cushendun, Co. Antrim, has also been deposited in the record office (ref. D. 971).

The original papers from which the selection was made were in the possession of McNeill's elder daughter, the Hon. Mrs Esther McNeill-Moss. She died in 1968 and we have not been able to contact her son, Mr G.M. McNeill-Moss, to ascertain whether he now has the papers, and whether they are available for research.

A further collection of McNeill's papers is available at the Public Record Office (London) (ref. F.O. 800/227-228). It consists of two volumes of miscellaneous correspondence 1922-1923 and 1927-1929.

SIR JAMES IAN MACPHERSON, 1st Bt, 1st BARON STRATHCARRON (1880-1937)

James Ian Macpherson was Liberal M.P. for Ross and Cromarty (Inverness-shire, Ross and Cromarty from 1918) 1911-1935. He was Under-Secretary of State for War December 1916-January 1919, Chief Secretary for Ireland 1919-April 1920, and Minister of Pensions 1920-October 1922. He was created a baronet in 1933, and Baron Strathcarron in 1936.

Most of Macpherson's papers were destroyed by bombing during the second world war. He had written his autobiography but while going to deliver the manuscript to his publishers, he lost it by leaving it on the seat of a taxi. The manuscript was never recovered; it was the only copy. Until 1970 Macpherson's family believed that no papers had survived but a small suitcase of papers was then discovered and these have now been given by Macpherson's son, the present (2nd) Lord Strathcarron, and his daughter, Lady Runge, to the Bodleian Library (ref. MSS. Eng. hist. c.490-492, d.309).

Almost all of the papers refer to Ireland. As well as the printed *Intelligence Reports* for 1913 and 1914, and Horace Plunkett's printed *Report to the King on the Irish Convention* (1918), there is a stencilled *Report of Censorship December 1918* by Lord Decies, the Irish Press Censor, and a file on the effect of demobilisation on Irish unemployment. This includes memoranda by E. Shortt and Sir S. Kent, as well as suggestions for remedies. There is also a draft Administration of Justice (Ireland) Bill, November 1919, with a stencilled memorandum by the Home Secretary on the imprisonment of Sinn Fein prisoners in England and drafts of the Government of Ireland Bill with a commentary by 'F.F.L.', September 1918. There are also a number of letters to Macpherson from Lord French, then Lord Lieutenant of Ireland. The letters are full of the problems French had to face: whether or not to use discharged servicemen to fill the ranks of the R.I.C. (25 May 1919); the problems of martial law and of a curfew (20 October 1919); the number of troops needed (8 November 1919); and the infiltration of spies into Dublin Castle (11 December 1919). There are several memoranda: on the possibility of enlisting ex-servicemen as special constables August 1919; on the difficulties of the Three Judges Bill (by Walter Long) December 1919; on the raising

SIR JAMES IAN MACPHERSON (cont.)

of a loan by Sinn Fein; on the activities of such prominent individuals as Michael Collins; and (by Macpherson) describing Lloyd George's reactions to Irish events 20-22 December 1919.

The only papers relating to Macpherson's tenure of the Ministry of Pensions are a press cutting and a pamphlet by Macpherson entitled *The Nation's Debt to the Disabled, Widowed and Fatherless. How it has been met* (June 1922).

There are a few constituency papers for the period 1920-1922 including agents' letters and reports, as well as constituents' problems. The agents reported on the opinions of 'Important People' and their views on Coalition Liberals. There are also a few press cuttings and several anti-Asquith leaflets. A few miscellaneous letters have survived, for example, R.S. Horne to Mrs Macpherson approving Macpherson's planned transfer to the Scottish Office 28 September 1922.

SIR ARTHUR HERBERT DRUMMOND RAMSAY-STEEL-MAITLAND, 1st Bt (1876-1935)

Arthur Steel-Maitland (he changed his name from Steel on his marriage in 1901) was Conservative M.P. for Birmingham (East; Birmingham, Erdington from 1918) 1910-1929, and for Warwickshire (Tamworth) 1929-1935. He was Parliamentary Under-Secretary of State for the Colonies May 1915-September 1917, Joint Parliamentary Under-Secretary of State for Foreign Affairs and Parliamentary Secretary to the Board of Trade as Secretary to the Overseas Trade Department 1917-April 1919, and Minister of Labour November 1924-June 1929. He was created a baronet in 1917.

A very large collection of Steel-Maitland family papers, including Sir Arthur's papers, was deposited in the Scottish Record Office (ref. GD 193) by Mrs R.M. Stafford, Steel-Maitland's grand-daughter. The papers are available for research on the condition that any proposed publication based on them is submitted for Mrs Stafford's approval prior to publication. A list of the papers has been compiled. As well as a large number of domestic papers, correspondence, and some university notebooks, most aspects of Steel-Maitland's career are represented in his papers. He was Private Secretary to C.T. Ritchie and Austen Chamberlain 1902-1905 when they were successive Chancellors of the Exchequer. Treasury papers, for example on the budget, and on Chamberlain's 1905 Financial Statement, have survived. Steel-Maitland seems to have maintained a close relationship with Chamberlain, to which the large number of letters from Chamberlain in the collection bear witness. Steel-Maitland served as special commissioner on the Royal Commission on the Poor Law 1906-1907: memoranda and correspondence concerning this work have survived. By that time he was prospective candidate for Rugby and a considerable number of papers have survived 1904-1908. A large amount of Birmingham constituency material has survived 1910-1929: correspondence with constituents, with his agent, and arrangements for meetings. Steel-Maitland's work as Chairman of the Conservative Party is reflected by papers on party organization and correspondence, for example, on the need in 1912 to purchase the *Daily Express* in order to preserve it for the Conservative cause. There are many papers on party organization and administration 1923-1935. There are also papers on contemporary political issues: Ireland; tariff reform; land taxation; women's suffrage; national insurance; reform of the House of Lords; and the empire.

Steel-Maitland's official career is well represented. There are papers concerning the work of the Colonial Office, including correspondence with Winston Churchill, L.S. Amery, and A. Chamberlain. The Department of Overseas Trade is represented by papers on the organization of the department, on the problems of inter-departmental rivalry, and on the reasons for Steel-Maitland's resignation — a disagreement with Sir Auckland Geddes. Steel-Maitland was also interested in the League of Nations' Union, an interest represented by pamphlets, minutes of meetings, correspondence, and a diary for the 1922 Geneva Assembly. Apart from travel diaries and a few fragments, this is the only diary in the collection, though there are notes and memoranda relating to other international conferences. The Ministry of Labour papers include a considerable amount of material on the General Strike. There are Cabinet papers, memoranda on the origins of the 1926 coal strike, suggestions for settlement

SIR ARTHUR HERBERT DRUMMOND RAMSAY-STEEL-MAITLAND (cont.)
terms, notes of the course of negotiations, and notes concerning the cabinet committee on
the report of the Royal Commission on the coal industry. Correspondence for the 1920s
includes a letter (1922) from Steel-Maitland to Austen Chamberlain expressing his doubts
about the coalition and a reply rebuking him for splitting the Conservative party over Ireland.
There are several boxes of papers on Russia, and on the reform of trade union legislation.
There are 30 boxes of speech notes 1906-1929.

(HENRY) DAVID (REGINALD) MARGESSON, 1st VISCOUNT MARGESSON (1890-1965)

David Margesson was Conservative M.P. for West Ham (Upton) 1922-1923, and for
Warwickshire (Rugby) 1924-1942. He was Government Chief Whip and Parliamentary Secre-
tary to the Treasury November 1931-December 1940, and Secretary of State for War 1940-
February 1942. He was created Viscount Margesson in 1942.

A small collection of Margesson's papers was deposited in the library of Churchill College,
Cambridge, by his daughter in March 1967 (ref. Margesson papers). They consist almost
entirely of letters which have been arranged in chronological order 1924-1950. The only
exception to this arrangement is a ten-page 'candid portrait' of Neville Chamberlain written
in 1939. This document is unsigned and its author is unknown. These papers are not generally
available; applications to see them should be made to the Keeper of the Archives at Churchill
College.

None of Margesson's papers as Chief Whip is known to exist in the possession of the
Conservative party.

EDWARD MARJORIBANKS, 2nd BARON TWEEDMOUTH (1849-1909)

Edward Marjoribanks was Liberal M.P. for Berwickshire 1880-1894. He was Parliamentary
Secretary to the Treasury and Chief Liberal Whip August 1892-March 1894, Lord Privy Seal
and Chancellor of the Duchy of Lancaster 1894-July 1895, 1st Lord of the Admiralty
December 1905-April 1908, and Lord President of the Council April-October 1908. He suc-
ceeded his father as 2nd Baron Tweedmouth and second baronet in 1894. He was created
K.T. in 1908.

According to his sister, Lady Aberdeen, Marjoribanks '. . . made it a rule never to keep any
notes or journal of any kind, and he made it a point of honour to destroy all confidential
communications between himself and Mr Gladstone and the many other politicians and public
men with whom he corresponded' (*Edward Marjoribanks, Lord Tweedmouth K.T. Notes and
Recollections 1849-1909*, [1909], pp. v-vi).

Nonetheless a small collection of Marjoribanks's papers is held by the Ministry of Defence
Library (Navy). There are eight volumes of printed or typed memoranda, and letters (three
volumes for 1906, four for 1907, one for 1908), some of which are annotated. These volumes
have been indexed. There are also three boxes of correspondence with members of the
Cabinet, M.P.s, Admiralty officials, naval officers and others. These include files on the 1907-
1908 and 1908-1909 naval estimates, as well as routine business such as requests for help
and for influence with appointments. The authors of this correspondence have been indexed.

HILARY ADAIR MARQUAND (1901-1972)

Hilary Marquand was Labour M.P. for Cardiff (East) 1945-1950, and Middlesbrough
(East) 1950-1961. He was Secretary of the Department of Overseas Trade August 1945-
March 1947, Paymaster-General 1947-July 1948, Minister of Pensions 1948-January 1951,
and Minister of Health January-October 1951.

Marquand's son, Mr David Marquand M.P., informs us that he thinks his father's papers
contain little of interest for his life or political career. They are not available for research.

SIR FREDERICK JAMES MARQUIS, 1st EARL OF WOOLTON (1883-1964)

Frederick Marquis was knighted in 1935 and created Baron Woolton in 1939, Viscount Woolton in 1953, and Earl of Woolton in 1956. He was Minister of Food April 1940-November 1943, Minister of Reconstruction 1943-May 1945, Lord President of the Council May-August 1945 and October 1951-November 1952, Chancellor of the Duchy of Lancaster 1952-December 1955, and Minister of Materials September 1953-July 1954.

Three four-drawer filing cabinets of his papers were given by his daughter-in-law, Lady Forres, to the Bodleian Library in 1973 (ref. Woolton Papers). Some of Marquis's papers, mainly receipts and documents concerning family trusts and houses, but also including personal papers such as correspondence between Marquis and his first wife, have not survived. The remainder have been very well arranged by Marquis's secretary and an outline list of contents compiled. Conditions of access to the collection will be decided when the papers have been listed. Until then the papers are not available for research.

A considerable number of papers survive from Marquis's tenure of the Ministry of Food, including many speech and broadcasting notes such as 'The Kitchen in Wartime' December 1940. There are, for example, memoranda on the organization of the ministry 1940, on agricultural prices, and aspects of rationing. There are also minutes to and from the Prime Minister, and diary notes September 1940-January 1944. A note on the envelope containing these says that a gap occurs from then till 1952 and then the notes were kept only spasmodically.

Marquis made notes on his feelings at becoming Minister of Reconstruction in November 1943. Several memoranda and some correspondence have survived including a note of a conversation with Erskine Hill in November 1943 on the future of the Conservative party, and memoranda on the Beveridge report, on postwar Conservative policy, and on the position of 'political' and 'technical' ministers in the Cabinet.

From 1945 till 1955 Marquis was Chairman of the Conservative party and some papers have survived from this work. They include correspondence with Churchill, particularly on party organization, a reply by Conservative Central Office to allegations of inefficiency (December 1946), a file of papers on negotiations with the National Liberals in 1950 and much printed material including press cuttings and cartoons.

Apart from congratulations on his return to office, no papers seem to have survived from Marquis's terms of office as Lord President. Only a list of Duchy officials, Duchy accounts 1951-1952, and papers concerning a visit by the Queen to her Lancashire estates in 1955 survive from his term as Chancellor of the Duchy. No papers seem to have survived from the Ministry of Materials.

In 1959 Marquis published his *Memoirs*. Drafts and correspondence relating to the publication of this and other books and articles survive. There are also various memoranda, for example, on the machinery of government and cabinet-making, on his first meeting with Winston Churchill, and Marquis's assessment of Churchill. Fragments of correspondence survive, for example, with Sir Anthony Eden, now Lord Avon, on Marquis's surprise at the admission by Sir Arthur Steel-Maitland, published in Lord Blake's biography of Bonar Law, that some peerages had resulted from contributions to party funds and the strong denial by Marquis that this had ever happened while he was in charge of the Conservative party.

From 1908 to 1914 Marquis worked for the Liverpool University Settlement. A few photographs, some letters and some reflections on the significance of the work there are all that survive, apart from a draft obituary for C.R. Attlee in which Marquis contrasts the similarity of their early work with the dissimilarity of their later viewpoints. Many of Marquis's business papers have been destroyed, and all that remain from the earlier part of his life are papers from the various committees on which he served, such as the 1938 Cadman Committee on Civil Aviation.

CHARLES FREDERICK GURNEY MASTERMAN (1874-1927)

Charles Masterman was Liberal M.P. for West Ham (North) 1906-1911, Bethnal Green (South-West) 1911-1914, and Manchester (Rusholme) 1923-1924. He was Parliamentary Secretary to the Local Government Board April 1908-July 1909, Under-Secretary of State for Home Affairs 1909-February 1912, Financial Secretary to the Treasury 1912-February 1914, and Chancellor of the Duchy of Lancaster 1914-February 1915 (throughout his period in the Cabinet Masterman had no seat in the House of Commons and for this reason had to resign in 1915).

Masterman's papers are in the possession of his widow, Mrs Lucy Masterman; but her son, Mr Neville Masterman, Department of History, University College of Swansea, University of Wales, Singleton Park, Swansea, informs us that his father's papers are not available for research. Mr Masterman himself hopes to write something about his father and in the meantime the papers are unsorted, and personal papers are mixed up with official papers. For these reasons Mr Masterman does not want the papers to be used for research.

Lucy Masterman, *C.F.G. Masterman. A Biography* (1939, reprinted 1968), quotes fully from many letters and from her own contemporary diaries and notes.

SIR FREDERIC HERBERT MAUGHAM, 1st VISCOUNT MAUGHAM (1866-1958)

Frederic Herbert Maugham was a Judge of the High Court, Chancery Division 1928-1934, Lord Justice of Appeal 1934-1935, Lord of Appeal in Ordinary 1935-1938 and 1939-1941, and Lord Chancellor March 1938-September 1939. He was knighted in 1928, and created Baron Maugham (a judicial life peerage) in 1935, and Viscount Maugham in 1939.

His son, the present (2nd) Viscount Maugham, has only a very small collection of personal papers which are not open for research. Most of the papers have been published in his (Robin Maugham's) book, *Somerset and all the Maughams* (1966), and in the chapter on Maugham in R.F.V. Heuston, *Lives of the Lord Chancellors 1885-1940* (Oxford, 1964). Lord Maugham's book quotes from a sketch of his father in an unpublished book by his sister, Kate Mary Bruce, entitled *Family Group*. Maugham himself published his memoirs, *At the End of the Day* (1954), but these contain almost no documentary material.

SIR ALFRED MILNER, VISCOUNT MILNER (1854-1925)

Alfred Milner was High Commissioner for South Africa 1897-1905, member of the War Cabinet December 1916-April 1918, Secretary of State for War 1918-December 1919, and Secretary of State for the Colonies 1919-February 1921. He was created K.C.B. in 1895, K.G. in 1921, Baron Milner in 1901, and Viscount Milner in 1902.

Six hundred boxes of Milner's papers were bequeathed to New College, Oxford, but the papers are now housed in the Bodleian Library (ref. Milner papers). Applications to see the papers should be made to the Librarian, New College, Oxford, giving the reasons for wishing to read them. A list of the papers is available. They have been arranged under the following main headings: South Africa; Rhodes Trust; Miscellaneous pre-war; World War I; Post-War; Personal Correspondence and Papers; Notebooks; Diaries; Biographical Material; Press Cuttings; and Printed Material.

Not unexpectedly, the South African papers form the largest division of Milner's papers (boxes 1-92). They include 61 volumes of bound official correspondence with the Secretary of State (Joseph Chamberlain), with the governors of the African colonies and, during the Boer War, with the military leaders. There is also a great deal of private correspondence (which includes some up to 1921) including private correspondence with Chamberlain. The correspondence includes copies of outgoing as well as incoming letters. Some of Milner's journals compiled during his various African journeys are included in this section. There are papers from the 1899 Bloemfontein Conference, from the peace negotiations, and even 'loot' from Bloemfontein — papers of Cape Ministers and telegrams found there. There are also papers concerning the offer to Milner of the Colonial Secretaryship in 1903, and some early papers concerning the Rhodes Trust.

SIR ALFRED MILNER (cont.)

The Rhodes Trust papers are mainly financial and fill only five boxes. The miscellaneous pre-war papers fill eight boxes and include papers on the various topics which interested Milner: Canada; Ireland; the Army; land policy.

The first world war papers (boxes 107-151) contain both private and official documents which reflect Milner's active role in the war. There are many official papers, particularly on Russia, Siberia, and Persia 1917-1918, minutes of the Eastern Committee of the War Cabinet March 1918-January 1919, papers on man-power and recruiting (including some on National Service 1915-1916), naval and military strategy, and on peace overtures. There are also seven boxes of private correspondence and two boxes of miscellaneous War Office papers.

Milner's postwar papers (boxes 152-177) cover the peace negotiations and reconstruction as well as his Colonial Office work and his mission to Egypt.

His personal correspondence and papers (boxes 178-223) cover the period 1863-1925 and include many copies of outgoing letters as well as his own letters from Oxford to his mother. There are also financial and domestic papers, some of Lady Milner's papers, papers of Cecil Headlam relating to the publication of *The Milner Papers* (see below), including the typescript of an unfinished book on Milner, and papers concerning his election as Chancellor of Oxford University, as well as condolences on his death.

Milner's notebooks (boxes 224-249) cover a wide range of subjects from French and Arabic grammar, bimetallism, and economics. They include his lecture notes on political economy and on socialism, and notes about South Africa and Egypt. His diaries (boxes 250-295) cover the years 1881-1925. There are also special diaries for Egypt 1919-1920, Palestine 1922, and South Africa 1924-1925.

The biographical material (boxes 296-302) includes notes on his early life by a Mr Blount or Blunt, notes by Lady Milner, and the diary of his private secretary, Sir Hugh Thornton, for 11 December 1916-29 December 1917.

The newspaper cuttings (boxes 303-338) cover all aspects of his career, as their bulk indicates. The printed papers (boxes 339-601) are largely official papers, in particular command papers.

A further collection of Milner's papers has been deposited in the Public Record Office (ref. P.R.O. 30/30). It contains 25 boxes of papers for the period 1915-1920 and includes papers on the 1915 military agreement between the allies and Italy, papers in defence of General Sir Hugh Gough, papers on the conflicting claims of the French and Arabs in Syria, on the 1919 campaign in Russia, papers of the Liquor Restrictions Committee 1919, the 1919 India Reform Committee, and the 1920 Indian Disorders Committee. The collection also includes the agreement made between France and Britain which gave General Foch supreme command of the allied forces in France and Milner's diary for 23-26 March 1918. This 1918 material was published in *The Times* 22 and 23 May 1928. The class list for these papers has been published by the List and Index Society, *Public Record Office, Gifts and Deposits. Supplementary Lists.* vol. 70 (1971).

A further 27 volumes of papers concerning Milner's mission to Egypt 1919-1920 are also available at the Public Record Office (ref. F.O. 848). The aim of the mission was to decide on future British policy in Egypt. The collection includes not only correspondence, memoranda, and minutes but also records of conversations in Egypt, notes of evidence taken, the Commissioner's reference books and press cuttings.

A large number of Milner's papers have been published, in accordance with his own wishes; these only relate to South Africa: *The Milner Papers*, ed. Cecil Headlam (2 vols., 1931-33). Alfred M. Gollin, *Proconsul in Politics* (1964) quotes from the later papers.

A further collection of Milner's papers — two tin trunks and some box files — was given to the Bodleian Library in 1973 by Mr Jan Milner (ref. MSS. Eng. hist. c.686-709; d.362; e.305-307). The papers have not yet been listed. Application to read them should be made to the Bodleian Library. These papers include much material from the 1890s but they are mainly from the last seven years of Milner's life and include War Office and Colonial Office files.

SIR ALFRED MILNER (cont.)

Some of Lady Milner's papers were deposited by her daughter, Lady Hardinge of Penshurst, in the Kent Archives Office (ref. U 1599) in 1973. As the collection has not yet been listed it is not available for research; but an initial sorting appears to indicate that it does not include any of Lord Milner's papers.

ROBERT OFFLEY ASHBURTON CREWE-MILNES, 2nd BARON HOUGHTON, MARQUESS OF CREWE (1858-1945)

Robert Offley Ashburton Crewe-Milnes (he adopted the additional surname of Crewe in 1894 when he succeeded to his uncle's estates) succeeded his father as 2nd Baron Houghton in 1885; he was created K.G. in 1908, Earl of Crewe in 1895, and Marquess of Crewe in 1911. He was Lord President of the Council December 1905-April 1908 and May 1915-December 1916, Secretary of State for Colonial Affairs April 1908-November 1910, Lord Privy Seal October 1908-October 1911 and February 1912-May 1915, Secretary of State for India November 1910-March 1911 and May 1911-May 1915, President of the Board of Education August-December 1916, Ambassador to Paris 1922-1928, and Secretary of State for War August-November 1931.

Many of Crewe-Milnes's papers were accidentally destroyed during his lifetime in fires at his homes. Nevertheless, a very large collection — 150 boxes — of his papers was deposited in the Cambridge University Library by his widow in 1958 (ref. Crewe Papers). In 1970 all except some letters exchanged with various members of the royal family were opened to research. The collection has been divided into five main groups: 'C' — 61 boxes of General Correspondence; 'P' — four boxes of personal papers; 'S' — three boxes of speeches; 'M' — 21 boxes of miscellaneous papers; and 'I' — 21 boxes of India Office papers. A card index of correspondents has been compiled for most of the collection.

The General Correspondence has been arranged alphabetically by name of correspondent; where more than one letter exists from an individual, the letters are in chronological order. Copies or drafts of Crewe-Milnes's outgoing letters have been placed under their recipient's name. Amongst the longer series of correspondence are four volumes of letters from Lord Hardinge to Crewe-Milnes 1910-1915 and two volumes of Crewe-Milnes's replies, a box of correspondence with H.H. Asquith 1908-1927, two boxes of letters from Lord Curzon (mainly 1908-1925), and a box of letters from J.R. MacDonald 1924. This section of the papers includes Crewe-Milnes's letters to the various Indian governors.

The personal papers include drafts, notes, and final versions of Crewe-Milnes's writings — letters to the press, articles, book reviews. There are letters of congratulation and of regret (for example, on his resignation as Secretary of State for India). In addition there is some family correspondence — letters to his sisters and to his elder son.

The speeches include notes and correspondence for speeches 1908-1939. The miscellaneous section includes papers concerning various funds, such as the Florence Nightingale Memorial Fund 1910-1916, political dinners for fellow peers, and the Imperial College of Science and Technology. It also includes papers concerning his term as Lord Lieutenant of Ireland 1892-1895: there are papers concerning the Irish Land Commission and the Board of National Education. There are papers of the 1916 Reconstruction Committee, the Dardanelles Commission and various Cabinet Committees.

The India Office papers consist of a large number of subject files ranging from the Durbar, the appointment of various governors, the visit to India in 1912-1913 of the Under-Secretary of State, E.S. Montagu, and the problems of Indians in South Africa, to correspondence about the need in the British Museum for a stuffed elephant.

The rest of the collection (some 40 boxes) consists of printed material: confidential prints, parliamentary bills, debates etc. A card index to this part of the collection, arranged in chronological order, has been compiled.

A further small collection of papers is available in the Public Record Office (ref. F.O. 800/300). It consists of reports from the Press Attaché to Crewe-Milnes when he was Ambassador to Paris.

ROBERT OFFLEY ASHBURTON CREWE-MILNES (cont.)

James Pope-Hennessy, *Lord Crewe 1858-1945. The Likeness of a Liberal* (1955), is based on Crewe-Milnes's papers and frequently quotes from them.

SIR ALFRED MORITZ MOND, 1st Bt, 1st BARON MELCHETT (1868-1930)

Alfred Mond was Liberal M.P. for Chester 1906-1910, Swansea (Swansea, West from 1918) 1910-1923, and Carmarthenshire (Carmarthen) 1924-1928. He joined the Conservative Party in 1926. He was 1st Commissioner of Works December 1916-April 1921, and Minister of Health 1921-October 1922. He was created a baronet in 1910 and Baron Melchett in 1928.

His papers were used by Hector Bolitho for his biography, *Alfred Mond, First Lord Melchett* (1933). Bolitho said in his foreword that Mond inherited a desk full of family papers from his father but never looked at them, either because he was too busy or because he was not interested. He also says that Mond never kept a diary or any souvenirs of his childhood. According to Bolitho anything of interest was used in the biography and the papers were returned to the family. Unfortunately these papers were destroyed by a fire during the second world war.

The only papers in the possession of the present (4th) Lord Melchett are contained in 29 manilla folders. They are available to researchers, if his permission is obtained, at Courtyard Farm, Ringstead, Hunstanton, Norfolk. The number in brackets ( ) refer to the numbers of the folders. They include several folders of biographical details: pedigrees; the Royal Licence to bear supporters to arms; and typed portions of Bolitho's biography (1, 4, 7). There appear to be no papers surviving which relate to Mond's early career as a barrister, to his work as an M.P., either in his constituency or in Parliament, apart from his 1910 Swansea election address (21), or to his term as 1st Commissioner of Works. Only a few papers survive from his period at the Ministry of Health, and those few are mainly Cabinet memoranda. Several of these are by Mond: on disability pensions and outdoor relief November 1921, on the Economy Bill May 1922, on the Increase of Rent Act, on the Local Authorities (Financial Provisions) Bill October 1921, on National Health Insurance May 1921-March 1922, and on Housing August 1922 (5, 6, 11, 19, 22, 23, 25). There is some political correspondence with Asquith, Baldwin, and Birkenhead, amongst others (24). There is some 1914 correspondence with Lloyd George, marked 'Letters used in Frank Owen biography', on financial policy and trade prospects (28).

One folder (10) is entitled 'Palestine and Zionism'. It includes correspondence with Lloyd George on the delay in settling the future of Palestine 1920, with Herbert Samuel on the need to lessen military expenditure so that the British taxpayer would be less concerned about the burden of Palestine 1921, and about the desirability of increasing Jewish immigration 1923, and with Lord Beaverbrook about the British presence in Palestine 1929. There are also addresses presented to Mond in Palestine.

There are several folders relating to Mond's political activities during the 1920s: a letter to Beaverbrook offering help to the Empire Crusade 1929 (7), and several speeches (12); on unemployment, 1922-1929 (14, 21); on his departure from the Liberal party in 1926, including letters from Churchill and Lord Oxford amongst others (27); and on land policy (29).

There are several folders of speeches and press cuttings (2, 3, 12, 16, 18, 20) as well as photographs and miscellanea such as his birth certificate (15), and a definition of the word 'rationalization' as supplied to Nuttall's Standard Dictionary.

Papers relating to Mond's business interests survive among the archives of Imperial Chemicals Industries. W.J. Reader in *Imperial Chemicals Industries. A History vol. 1. The Forerunners 1870-1926* (1970), was given free access to all the documents available but he stated, in his bibliography: 'These archives are part of the working records of the business, and the Company does not provide for general public access' (p. 524).

G.M. Bayliss, *The Outsider: Aspects of the Political Career of Alfred Mond, 1st Lord Melchett (1868-1930)* (Ph.D. thesis, University of Wales, 1969), incorporates material from a wide range of sources; but it does not draw on the family papers or I.C.I. archives.

SIR BOLTON MEREDITH EYRES-MONSELL, 1st VISCOUNT MONSELL (1881-1969)

Bolton Meredith Eyres-Monsell was Conservative M.P. for Worcestershire (South or Evesham) 1910-1935. He was Civil Lord of the Admiralty April 1921-October 1922, Parliamentary and Financial Secretary to the Admiralty 1922-May 1923, Parliamentary Secretary to the Treasury July 1923-January 1924, November 1924-June 1929, and September-November 1931, and 1st Lord of the Admiralty 1931-June 1936. He was created G.B.E. in 1929, and Viscount Monsell in 1935.

Seven boxes of Eyres-Monsell's papers are in the possession of his widow, Lady Monsell. We have not been able to examine these papers as they are kept in Lady Monsell's bank while she lives in Italy.

THE HON. EDWIN SAMUEL MONTAGU (1879-1924)

Edwin Montagu was Liberal M.P. for Cambridgeshire (Chesterton; Cambridgeshire from 1918) 1906-1922. He was Parliamentary Under-Secretary of State for India February 1910-February 1914, Financial Secretary to the Treasury 1914-February 1915, and May 1915-July 1916, Chancellor of the Duchy of Lancaster February-May 1915, and January-July 1916, Minister of Munitions July-December 1916, and Secretary of State for India June 1917-March 1922.

Six boxes of Montagu's papers have been deposited in the Library, Trinity College, Cambridge (ref. Montagu papers). The papers are not catalogued and are not at present available for research.

Most of the papers in Trinity College relate to Montagu's work at the India Office 1910-1914 and 1917-1922. There is correspondence with the various governors of India 1913-1914, with the Viceroy 1913, and with Lord Crewe 1913-1914, and also about the organization of the Secretary of State's Council 1911-1913. Montagu made a tour of India in 1912-1913 and a typed copy of the diary he kept then has survived. Extracts from this diary and a memoir were published by his nephew, Sir David Waley, in *Edwin Montagu* (1964). From his term of office as Secretary of State several files have survived, especially on the post-war settlement with Turkey 1918-1922. There is a file on the Amritsar massacre and on the problem of the Indians in Africa (including some correspondence with Winston Churchill). There is correspondence with Lord Curzon 1917-1922 and Austen Chamberlain 1917-1920. A file of correspondence and press cuttings on Montagu's resignation has also survived. In 1917-1918, after his announcement that the ultimate aim of British policy in India was the 'progressive realization of responsible government', Montagu made a second tour of India and again kept a diary which he dictated and sent to D. Lloyd George to give him some understanding of Indian problems. This diary has also survived; it was published by Montagu's widow: *An Indian Diary*, ed. Hon. Venetia Montagu (1930).

Some of Montagu's interest in non-Indian events is represented in this collection: there are papers from the Cabinet Committee on Food Supplies 1914-1916, on Ireland 1914-1921 (including a note by Montagu on the secret negotiations of June-July 1914), the problems of reconstruction March-July 1917, and correspondence with Lewis Harcourt and F.E. Smith on ministerial salaries 1915-1916. There are memoranda and copies of letters sent to Lloyd George 1917-1922 and a note by Montagu written 9 December 1916 on the fall of Asquith's government. Montagu was Asquith's parliamentary private secretary from 1906 to 1910 and there is some correspondence with Asquith 1904-1917, and notes for Asquith's 1908 Budget speech and various 1909 speeches. Montagu's own notes for the 1912 and 1913 Budgets have also survived.

The collection also includes miscellaneous correspondence 1904-1922 arranged alphabetically, including correspondence with Lord Crewe 1911-1919, and Edward Grey 1909-1916. There are eight files of letters from Montagu to his parents, mainly to his mother 1890s-1918. The minute book of the Cambridge University Liberal Club November 1886-December 1896 is to be found in the collection. There are also some of Montagu's wife's papers: a diary kept on a tour of Russia and the Middle East, miscellaneous letters, and letters of condolence on Montagu's death.

EDWIN SAMUEL MONTAGU (cont.)

The long series of letters 1910-1915 between Asquith and Mrs Montagu, then the Hon. Venetia Stanley, are in the possession of the widower of Montagu's daughter, Mr Milton Gendel, Piazza Mattei, 10, Rome, Italy. As a description both of Cabinet meetings and private discussions between Asquith and his colleagues (many of them were actually written during Cabinet meetings), they are an invaluable historical source. Mr Gendel is hoping to arrange the publication of an edition of these letters. They are quoted frequently in Roy Jenkins, *Asquith* (1964).

A further collection of Montagu's papers — 44 volumes of correspondence during his period as Secretary of State for India — was deposited by his sister in 1955 in the India Office Library (ref. MSS. Eur. D. 523). There are eleven volumes of correspondence 1917-1921 between Montagu and Lord Chelmsford, the Viceroy from 1916 to 1921, and three volumes 1921-1922 between Montagu and Lord Reading, Chelmsford's successor. There are six volumes of correspondence 1917-1922 between Montagu and Lord Willingdon, then Governor of Bombay and later of Madras, five volumes of correspondence 1918-1922 with Lord Lloyd, Governor of Bombay, and six volumes of correspondence 1917-1922 with the then Earl of Ronaldshay (later 2nd Marquess of Zetland), Governor of Bengal. In addition the collection includes various addresses presented in India, three volumes of Montagu's diary for his 1912-1913 visit to India, appendices to the diary for his 1918 visit, two scrapbooks from the 1918 visit, and a signed copy of the Montagu-Chelmsford Report.

JOHN MORLEY, VISCOUNT MORLEY OF BLACKBURN (1838-1923)

John Morley was Liberal M.P. for Newcastle-upon-Tyne 1883-1895, and Montrose Burghs 1896-1908. He was Chief Secretary for Ireland February-August 1886, and August 1892-July 1895, Secretary of State for India December 1905-November 1910, and March-May 1911, and Lord President of the Council November 1910-August 1914. He was created Viscount Morley of Blackburn in 1908.

Sixty-seven volumes of Morley's papers were presented to the India Office Library (ref. MSS. Eur. D. 573.) by his biographer F.W. Hirst at various dates between 1933 and 1947. They are almost entirely related to Morley's tenure of the India Office. They also include papers found at the National Liberal Club which were possibly left there by Hirst or Sir Gilbert Jackson, and which were added to the India Office collection in 1960.

MSS. Eur. D. 573 mainly consists of bound volumes of correspondence between Morley and Lord Minto, then Viceroy. There are five volumes of letters from Morley to Minto 1905-1910, and nineteen volumes of letters from Minto to Morley for the same period. There are two volumes of correspondence March-May 1911 between Morley and Lord Hardinge, who succeeded Lord Minto. As well as correspondence, these volumes include notes of conversations and meetings, as well as various memoranda which were originally enclosed with the letters. In addition there are five volumes of telegrams exchanged between the Secretaries of State and the Viceroys 1903-1910. There are many subject files on various topics of Morley's administration: for example, three files about reforms of the Indian Council 1907-1909; a file on Mohammedan representation 1906-1909; files on army administration; and files on the Kitchener-Curzon controversy. There is a file of papers relating to Lord Curzon, ranging from his views on Tibet, a 1906-1909 Everest expedition, and on the Clive Memorial. There are eight volumes of correspondence between Morley and the Governor of Bombay, Sir George Clarke, later Lord Sydenham.

In addition to this Indian material, the collection contains a small amount of Morley's private correspondence. There are eighteen letters from Lord Rosebery 1905-1909, and copies of several letters from Andrew Carnegie (the originals were returned by Hirst to Mrs Carnegie in 1927; they are now in the Library of Congress, Washington, D.C.; a microfilm of the Carnegie-Morley correspondence 1883-1919 is available in the Bodleian Library [ref.MS. FILM 569]). The collection also includes a few of Hirst's own papers — lectures on Morley, and letters collected by Hirst for his unfinished biography. There are also lists of speeches and correspondence that are no longer included in this collection.

JOHN MORLEY (cont.)

It is known that Morley destroyed many of his papers. He told Edwin Montagu in 1910: 'I have not a large collection of papers. Everything gets torn up in its turn' (Memorandum by Montagu, 3 November 1910, *Montagu MSS*). Other papers may have been burnt immediately after his death in 1923. Those which survived were left to 'the full discretion' of his nephew, Guy Morley, with the proviso that his executors should neither help nor encourage any memoir, nor allow the papers to be used for any biography of Morley or his friends. Nonetheless, Morley expected that this proviso would be ignored, and was favourably disposed to the declared intention of F.W. Hirst to write a biography. Encouraged by the rest of his family, including Lady Morley, Guy Morley passed the papers on to Hirst, a close friend of Morley in his later years. Apart from the collection referred to above, the papers remained in Hirst's hands until his death in 1953. Thereafter it was decided, in accordance with Hirst's wishes, that they should eventually be deposited at Wadham College, Oxford, in the custody of Mr A.F. Thompson. It proved difficult to locate some of this material, but Mr Thompson believes that the final stages in the transfer of the remaining papers were completed by 1971.

The collection at Wadham mainly consists of miscellaneous memoranda and correspondence relating to Morley's political and literary activities between the 1870s and the end of the century. There are many gaps, and it appears that few of Morley's twentieth-century papers were in Hirst's possession at the time of his death. This collection is not yet available for examination, but Mr Thompson, who is preparing a study of Morley, is empowered to deal with enquiries.

Many of Morley's papers were published both by Morley himself and later historians. His *Recollections* (2 vols., 1917) include much of his correspondence with Lord Minto. Morley also arranged to publish posthumously his *Memorandum on Resignation* (1928). F.W. Hirst, *Early Life and Letters of John Morley* (2 vols., 1927) is based largely on Morley's papers. Morley was a prolific correspondent and many of his letters can be found in other collections. A useful guide to their whereabouts is given in the bibliography of D.A. Hamer, *John Morley: Liberal Intellectual in Politics* (Oxford, 1968).

HERBERT STANLEY MORRISON, BARON MORRISON OF LAMBETH (1888-1965)

Herbert Morrison was Labour M.P. for Hackney (South) 1923-1924, 1929-1931, 1935-1945, for Lewisham (East) 1945-1950, and for Lewisham (South) 1950-1959. He was Minister of Transport June 1929-August 1931, Minister of Supply May-October 1940, Secretary of State for Home Affairs and Home Security 1940-May 1945, Lord President of the Council August 1945-March 1951, and Secretary of State for Foreign Affairs March-October 1951. He was created Baron Morrison of Lambeth (a life peerage) in 1959.

A small suitcase of papers is in the possession of Sir Norman Chester, Warden of Nuffield College, Oxford, and Morrison's joint literary executor. Lady Morrison, 14 Colepits Wood Road, Eltham, London S.E.9, is the other literary executor. The suitcase contains several typed draft chapters of Morrison's autobiography, *Herbert Morrison: an Autobiography* (1960), some of which contain manuscript amendments and all of which seem to contain much that was not used in the published autobiography. The drafts are entitled 'Personalities in Churchill's War Cabinet' (84 typed pages), 'The Chamberlain Government' (24 typed pages), 'On the Way to World War Again' (41 typed pages), 'Ministry of Transport' (92 typed pages), 'J.R. MacDonald' (93 typed pages), and 'The General Strike' (54 typed pages). There are two files of press cuttings on reactions to the memoirs as well as other miscellaneous press cuttings and a file of cartoons collected 1949-1950. The few pamphlets include Morrison's election addresses for the 1920 London County Council by-election (he was a member of the L.C.C. 1922-1945) and for the 1945 general election. There is also a transcript of an interview given to Derek Cooper in 1962 in which Morrison was asked biographical and political questions.

In addition there is a small collection of correspondence including letters of congratulation for various speeches etc. from Winston Churchill 1940-1945. There is a memorandum of a discussion with C.R. Attlee, H. Dalton, and E. Bevin on the post-war reorganization of industry. There is correspondence with Attlee in 1947 on Morrison's illness and the resulting transfer of

HERBERT STANLEY MORRISON (cont.)

responsibility for economic affairs to Sir Stafford Cripps. There is also correspondence with Cripps on the desirability of Attlee's continuing as Prime Minister (summer 1947). There is a memorandum of a meeting with Attlee in April 1951 on Aneurin Bevan's resignation, and some correspondence on the timing of the 1951 general election. There is very little material for the period 1951-1965. All of this material was used for *Herbert Morrison: Portrait of a Politician* (1973) by Bernard Donoughue and G.W. Jones.

WILLIAM SHEPHERD MORRISON, 1st VISCOUNT DUNROSSIL (1893-1961)

William Shepherd Morrison was Conservative M.P. for Gloucestershire (Cirencester and Tewkesbury) 1929-1959. He was Financial Secretary to the Treasury November 1935-October 1936, Minister of Agriculture and Fisheries 1936-January 1939, Chancellor of the Duchy of Lancaster 1939-April 1940, Minister of Food September 1939-April 1940, Post-master-General 1940-December 1942, and Minister of Town and Country Planning 1942-August 1945. He was Speaker of the House of Commons 1951-1959, and Governor-General of Australia 1960-1961. He was created G.C.M.G. in 1959, and Viscount Dunrossil in 1959.

Morrison's son, the present (2nd) Viscount Dunrossil, informs us that his father did not keep records for posterity, and that only personal or private papers, which are not available to researchers, have survived.

SIR OSWALD ERNALD MOSLEY, 6th Bt (1896-   )

Sir Oswald Mosley was Conservative M.P. for Middlesex (Harrow) 1918-1922, Independent M.P. for Middlesex (Harrow) 1922-1924, and Labour M.P. for Smethwick 1926-1931. He was Chancellor of the Duchy of Lancaster June 1929-May 1930. He succeeded his father as 6th baronet in 1928.

Sir Oswald is making arrangements for the future disposition of his papers, but at present they are not available for research. In *My Life* (1968-70) Sir Oswald says that most of his earlier papers were lost during the second world war and that he wrote the book mostly from memory.

ROBERT MUNRO, BARON ALNESS (1868-1955)

Robert Munro was Liberal M.P. for the Wick Burghs 1910-1918 and Coalition Liberal M.P. for Roxburghshire and Selkirkshire 1918-1922. He was Secretary for Scotland December 1916-October 1922. He took the judicial title of Lord Alness in 1922 and was created G.B.E. in 1946, and Baron Alness in 1934.

His widow knows of no papers relating to her husband's political career. His book, *Looking Back: Fugitive Writings and Sayings* (1930), contains some articles previously printed elsewhere, his non-political speeches as Secretary for Scotland, and some of his speeches after he became a judge.

ANDREW GRAHAM MURRAY, VISCOUNT DUNEDIN (1849-1942)

Andrew Graham Murray was Conservative M.P. for Bute 1891-1905. He was Solicitor-General for Scotland October 1891-August 1892 and July 1895-May 1896, Lord Advocate of Scotland 1896-October 1903, and Secretary for Scotland 1903-February 1905. He was Lord Justice-General and Lord President of the Scottish Court of Session 1905-1913 and a Lord of Appeal in Ordinary 1913-1932. He was created K.C.V.O. in 1908, G.C.V.O. in 1923, Baron Dunedin in 1905, and Viscount Dunedin in 1926.

The bulk of Murray's estate was left by his second wife to his grand-daughter, Mrs G.R. Shaw, but she does not know of the existence of any papers. Mrs Shaw informs us that her grandfather was writing his memoirs but these cannot be found. Murray's family had close ties with the Edinburgh law firm of Tods, Murray, and Jamieson but they do not have any of his papers.

ANDREW GRAHAM MURRAY (cont.)

Twenty-two volumes of Murray's papers as Chairman of the Irish Free State Compensation Committee 1925-1926 are available in the Public Record Office (ref. C.O. 905/17, 18). The papers include registers of claims for compensation as well as the committee's correspondence.

HARRY LOUIS NATHAN, 1st BARON NATHAN (1889-1963)

Colonel Harry Nathan was Liberal M.P. for Bethnal Green (North-East) 1929-1935; he was Labour M.P. for Wandsworth (Central) 1937-1940. He was Parliamentary Under-Secretary of State for War August 1945-October 1946, and Minister of Civil Aviation 1946-May 1948. He was created Baron Nathan in 1940.

Nathan's papers are in the possession of his son, the present (2nd) Lord Nathan, but they are not available for research. The papers include several boxes of press cuttings 1924-1939 and 1945-1957, an album of Nathan's speeches and articles, a box of letters 1914-1917 between Nathan and his parents, and seven boxes of correspondence. The papers were used by H. Montgomery Hyde in his biography of Nathan, *Strong for Service* (1968).

SIR SYDNEY HALDANE OLIVIER, BARON OLIVIER (1859-1943)

Sydney Olivier was Secretary of State for India January-November 1924. He was created K.C.M.G. in 1907 and Baron Olivier in 1924.

A small collection of Olivier's papers is in the possession of his grandson, Dr R.B.O. Richards, but these are not at present available for research.

The only papers to have survived concerning Olivier's official career, both as a civil servant and as Secretary of State for India, are the official letters of appointment and commission, some letters 1930-1938 on trade unionism and the fixing of a minimum wage in the Colonies, and some printed official reports. However, the collection does reflect some of Olivier's activities in the Fabian Society (he was honorary secretary 1886-1889, a very active member and a friend of George Bernard Shaw, Graham Wallas, and Sidney Webb). There is a note by Olivier on the origin and early history of the Society (written in 1889) and correspondence 1906-1907 with Edward R. Pease, one of the founders of the society and secretary for fifteen years. There are also copies of Fabian articles and pamphlets with which Olivier was concerned, and draft chapter headings 1939 for *The Dual Ethic in Empire*, a book which Olivier never completed. The collection also includes Olivier's account books 1909-1938, some letters to his wife 1894-1898, his wife's diaries and note-books 1908-1913, 1929, 1931-1933, 1935-1939, and 1940-1948, miscellaneous correspondence 1935-1945 including letters from Graham Wallas and Leonard and Virginia Woolf, various photographs, press cuttings, and some speech notes. Lady Olivier's diaries and her husband's letters to her have many observations on Olivier's civil service career, especially in British Honduras and the West Indies.

There are also several papers connected with the publication of Lady Olivier's memoir: Margaret Olivier, *Sydney Olivier: Letters and Selected Writings* (1948). The book includes a twenty-page autobiographical fragment by Olivier covering his life to 1907, several articles by him, a short biography by his widow, and recollections by George Bernard Shaw. Lady Olivier's biography quotes from many letters, both from and to her husband. The manuscript collection includes these original letters or photocopies of them, the typescript of various sections of the book, and the proofs and correspondence about its publication.

RICHARD WILLIAM ALAN ONSLOW, 5th EARL OF ONSLOW (1876-1945)

Richard William Alan Onslow, Viscount Cranley from 1876 till he succeeded his father as 5th Earl of Onslow and 10th baronet in 1911, was Civil Lord of the Admiralty October 1920-April 1921, Parliamentary Secretary to the Ministry of Agriculture April 1921, Parliamentary Secretary to the Ministry of Health April 1921-May 1923, Parliamentary Secretary to the Board of Education 1923-January 1924, Under-Secretary of State for War November 1924-December 1928, and Paymaster-General 1928-June 1929. He was created G.B.E. in 1938.

RICHARD WILLIAM ALAN ONSLOW (cont.)

A small collection of Onslow's papers was deposited by Jo, Dowager Countess of Onslow, widow of the 6th Earl, in 1972 in the Guildford Muniment Room (ref. 173). There are six bound volumes of 'Private Papers' 1899-1913, twelve volumes of press cuttings, and a nine-volume typed history of the family. A further volume of reminiscences is still in the possession of the family but it is not available for research.

The 'Private Papers' are almost all from the period when Onslow was in the diplomatic service 1901-1911, and when he was Permanent Private Secretary to Sir Edward Grey and to Sir Arthur Nicolson in the Foreign Office 1911-1913. Possibly of greatest interest for the earlier period are Onslow's letters from his father February 1904-March 1906 describing the British political situation. From the Foreign Office period there are letters from British diplomats abroad and copies of Onslow's memoranda to Sir Arthur Nicolson on Foreign Office organization. There are also several memoranda on whether Onslow should be allowed to vote in the House of Lords and still continue to work as a civil servant (he was allowed to vote but not to speak in debates).

The press cuttings, which are arranged chronologically, are very full; they cover national and local political activities as well as social and personal events. There are two volumes of cuttings on the Boer War and one volume on Onslow's death and funeral.

The nine volumes of family history were completed by Onslow with the help of several researchers in 1925. In the introduction he says that 'it embodies every scrap of information I can find relating to any member of the Onslow family'. It includes an unfinished biography of Onslow's father by Reginald Lucas. Three volumes describe in great detail Onslow's own life up to when he became a Civil Lord.

Some of these papers are quoted in Onslow's memoirs, *63 years* (1944).

WILLIAM HILLIER ONSLOW, 4th EARL OF ONSLOW (1853-1911)

William Hillier Onslow succeeded his great-uncle as 4th Earl of Onslow and 9th baronet in 1870. He was created K.C.M.G. in 1887, and G.C.M.G. in 1889. He was Under-Secretary of State for the Colonies February 1887-February 1888, and November 1900-May 1903, Parliamentary Secretary to the Board of Trade February-December 1888, Under-Secretary of State for India July 1895-November 1900, and President of the Board of Agriculture and Fisheries May 1903-March 1905.

Jo, Dowager Countess of Onslow, widow of the 6th Earl, deposited in 1972 a small collection of Onslow's papers in the Guildford Muniment Room (ref. 173). A preliminary list of the papers has been drawn up. There are fifteen bound volumes entitled 'Private Papers' 1887-1911, thirteen volumes of diaries, some travel journals, and three volumes of press cuttings 1889-1911. The latter, arranged chronologically, are very full; they range from political speeches to kennel records. The diaries cover the years 1869-1892 (volumes for 1875-1877, 1880-1882, 1886-1888, and 1890-1891 are missing). They mainly record details of Onslow's travels and hunting; in some volumes there are only a few entries. The travel journals mainly date from the 1880s and cover Onslow's journies in America, India, Switzerland, and elsewhere.

The volumes of 'Private Papers' include a large number of letters, as well as copies of bills, a few Cabinet memoranda, and some departmental papers. Onslow's early work at the Colonial Office is represented by papers on the Sugar Bounties Conference, and on proposals for an Australian federation. There is a gap in the papers between 1888-1892, when Onslow was Governor of New Zealand. Only a copy of Onslow's letter to Queen Victoria on his return 14 August 1892 has survived. Throughout the volumes there is a great deal of material about smallholdings. There are several letters from Lord Salisbury, including some 1895-1896 on Onslow's leadership of the Moderate Party on the London County Council. There are also many letters from Joseph Chamberlain both on Colonial Office business and on political affairs. At the time of the 1903 Cabinet split over Chamberlain's tariff reform proposals there are a good many letters from members of the Cabinet, including one from Lord George Hamilton giving the reasons for his resignation. A small locked volume contains more letters from Cabinet colleagues but we were not able to examine its contents. There are many

WILLIAM HILLIER ONSLOW (cont.)

departmental papers from Agriculture and Fisheries, e.g. on the North Sea fisheries. There is also a fifteen page memorandum by Onslow on the political situation in St Petersburg and Berlin, written in December 1904, after a visit there. Onslow was Chairman of Committees in the House of Lords 1905-1910 and there are a number of papers on House of Lords' business, mainly of a routine and administrative nature, e.g. on the allocation of committee rooms. The three volumes for 1908-1911 are particularly interesting for Onslow's part in the opposition to Lloyd George's 1909 Budget and to the 1911 Parliament Act. There are a great number of memoranda, minutes, drafts, and notes on reform of the House of Lords, including some papers of the House's own Select Committee (February-March 1908).

FRANCIS AUNGIER PAKENHAM, 7th EARL OF LONGFORD (1905-   )

Francis Aungier Pakenham was created K.G. in 1971, and Baron Pakenham in 1945; he succeeded his brother as 7th Earl of Longford in 1961. He was Parliamentary Under-Secretary of State for War October 1946-April 1947, Chancellor of the Duchy of Lancaster and Minister in Charge of the Administration of the British zone of Germany 1947-May 1948, Minister of Civil Aviation 1948-May 1951, 1st Lord of the Admiralty May-October 1951, Lord Privy Seal October 1964-December 1965 and April 1966-January 1968, and Secretary of State for the Colonies 1965-April 1966.

Lord Longford informs us that the only papers he keeps are his wife's letters to him; Lady Longford keeps her husband's letters to her. But none of these letters is available for research. According to Lord Longford, his three volumes of autobiography, *Born to Believe* (1953), *Five Lives* (1964), and *The Grain of Wheat* (1974), were written 'out of the top of my head' with no reference to any papers.

WILFRED PALING (1883-1971)

Wilfred Paling was Labour M.P. for the West Riding of Yorkshire (Doncaster) 1922-1931, the West Riding of Yorkshire (Wentworth) 1933-1950, and the West Riding of Yorkshire (Dearne Valley) 1950-1959. He was Parliamentary Secretary to the Ministry of Pensions February 1941-May 1945, Minister of Pensions August 1945-April 1947, and Postmaster-General 1947-February 1950.

Paling's brother, Mr W.T. Paling, informs us that shortly after Paling's death his family moved house and burnt what papers they found.

ROUNDELL CECIL PALMER, 3rd EARL OF SELBORNE (1887-1971)

Roundell Cecil Palmer, known as Viscount Wolmer 1895-1941, was Conservative M.P. for South-West Lancashire (Newton) 1910-1918, and for Hampshire (Aldershot) 1918-1940. He was Parliamentary Secretary to the Board of Trade October 1922-January 1924, Assistant Postmaster-General November 1924-June 1929, and Minister of Economic Warfare February 1942-May 1945. Palmer was summoned to the House of Lords in 1941 in his father's barony of Selborne and succeeded his father as 3rd Earl of Selborne in 1942.

Palmer's grandson, the present (4th) Lord Selborne, informs us (March 1974) that he will deposit Palmer's political and ecclesiastical papers in the Bodleian Library in the near future. Papers relating to Palmer's work at the Ministry of Economic Warfare, which are deposited with the Foreign and Commonwealth Office, form an integral part of the records of the Special Operations Executive and as such are closed indefinitely for research.

WILLIAM WALDEGRAVE PALMER, 2nd EARL OF SELBORNE (1859-1942)

William Waldegrave Palmer was Liberal M.P. for Hampshire (East) 1885-1886; in 1886 he became a Liberal Unionist and held the seat till 1892. He was Liberal Unionist M.P. for Edinburgh (West) 1892-1895. He was Under-Secretary of State for the Colonies June 1895-November 1900, 1st Lord of the Admiralty 1900-March 1905, High Commissioner for South Africa 1905-1910, and President of the Board of Agriculture and Fisheries May 1915-July 1916. Palmer, who was known as Viscount Wolmer 1882-1895, succeeded his father as 2nd Earl of Selborne in 1895. He was created G.C.M.G. in 1905 and K.G. in 1909.

WILLIAM WALDEGRAVE PALMER (cont.)

Palmer's great-grandson, the present (4th) Earl of Selborne, gave his papers to the Bodleian Library in 1971 (ref. MSS. Selborne 1-222). The collection has been listed and indexed. Palmer's papers have been divided into nine main groups: special correspondence, correspondence and memoranda arranged by subject; general correspondence; family and personal correspondence; printed Government papers; official papers arranged by subject; official papers arranged chronologically; non-official printed material; and miscellaneous papers.

Palmer's special correspondence fills twelve volumes and includes letters from A.J. Balfour, Lord Midleton, the Duke of Devonshire, the Marquess of Salisbury, Lord Curzon, Lord Milner, and Joseph Chamberlain, under whom Palmer worked at the Colonial Office.

The correspondence arranged by subject has been subdivided by Palmer's main interests. His political correspondence 1885-1895 (MSS. Selborne 13 and 13*) includes the correspondence relating to his work as Liberal Unionist Chief Whip and his forecast of the results of the 1892 General Election. There are two volumes of Colonial Office papers (MSS. Selborne 14-15). They include notes of a conversation with Cecil Rhodes in 1897. The Admiralty correspondence (MSS. Selborne 16-47) includes correspondence with the Royal Family, the Cabinet, and the Admiralty Board, as well as with various commanders. MSS. Selborne 48-72 are papers related to Palmer's term of office as High Commissioner for South Africa. They contain a good deal of correspondence with successive Colonial Secretaries, as well as with the Royal Family, other governors, and South African politicians, Palmer's correspondence on domestic politics 1900-1914 (MSS. Selborne 73-79) ranges over tariff reform, the 1910-1912 constitutional crisis (including papers concerning the Halsbury Club and minutes of some of its meetings), as well as Irish Home Rule. MSS. Selborne 80-87 contain the papers related to Palmer's work as a member of the War Cabinet and his later political activities 1915-1942. They include 'pen portraits' by Palmer of his cabinet colleagues after his resignation. MSS. Selborne 88-91, Palmer's correspondence on ecclesiastical topics, ranges from Welsh Disestablishment, and divorce reform, to the 1927-1929 Prayer Book controversy.

The general correspondence (MSS. Selborne 92-95), which covers the period 1883-1941, has been arranged in chronological order. Palmer's family and personal correspondence (MSS. Selborne 96-116) includes letters from his parents and family as well as letters to his parents about him. There are also nine volumes of correspondence with his wife 1900-1939.

The printed official papers (MSS. Selborne 117-129) include White Papers, Bills, Cabinet Memoranda, etc. and cover the years 1899-1905, and 1915-1916. The official papers arranged by subject include a large number of Admiralty papers (MSS. Selborne 130-161) and papers on South Africa, particularly on the Union of South Africa Act (MSS. Selborne 162-177). There are four volumes of official papers, chronologically arranged, relating to measures in which Palmer was particularly interested. The non-official papers, arranged by subject, fill ten volumes and include two volumes of press-cuttings. The miscellaneous papers (MSS. Selborne 191-222) include three volumes of reminiscences written by Palmer in 1937.

A further small collection of papers has been deposited by Palmer's sister, Lady Laura Ridding, in the Hampshire Record Office (ref. 9M68/95-1052). The collection includes letters from Palmer to his son Jocelyn in 1909, letters from Palmer's wife to Jocelyn 1908-1909 and to their daughter 1906-1917, 1917-1939. Possibly of greatest interest in the collection is a memorandum dated by Palmer 30 June 1916 giving his reasons for resigning from the Cabinet.

SIR WEETMAN DICKINSON PEARSON, 1st Bt, 1st VISCOUNT COWDRAY (1856-1927)

Weetman Pearson was created G.C.V.O. in 1925, a baronet in 1894, Baron Cowdray in 1910, and Viscount Cowdray in 1917. He was President of the Air Board January November 1917.

A small collection of Pearson's papers was deposited by his grandson, the present (3rd) Lord Cowdray, in the Science Museum in 1972 (ref. Pearson papers). The collection has not yet been listed. Apart from diaries of foreign tours and family financial papers, the collection includes a file of papers connected with Pearson's tenure of the Air Board; there is a letter from Lloyd George 2 January 1917, saying that Pearson's claim on behalf of the Mexican

SIR WEETMAN DICKINSON PEARSON (cont.)

Eagle Oil Company against the Admiralty could stand over while Pearson was a Minister; there is a file of papers concerning Pearson's resignation, including a cutting of Lord Northcliffe's letter to *The Times*, stencils of Pearson's letters to Lloyd George and his replies, letters of regret at his resignation, and a letter from Northcliffe 25 January 1918 saying that he thought Pearson was resigning because of affairs in Mexico. The collection also includes a bundle of Pearson's letters to his wife 1895-1927, though they are mainly for the period 1908-1910. There are various personal financial papers and also some press cuttings from 1922 when Pearson proposed collaboration between Asquithian Liberals and Labour.

The present (3rd) Lord Cowdray does not know of any other papers. The short biography by R.K. Middlemas in *The Master-Builders* (1963), J.A. Spender, *Weetman Pearson, First Viscount Cowdray* (1930), and Desmond Young, *Member for Mexico* (1966), are all based on and quote from Pearson's papers.

JOSEPH ALBERT PEASE, 1st BARON GAINFORD (1860-1943)

'Jack' Pease was Liberal M.P. for Northumberland (Tyneside) 1892-1900, Essex (Saffron Walden) 1901-1910, and the West Riding of Yorkshire (Rotherham) 1910-1916. He was Chancellor of the Duchy of Lancaster February 1910-October 1911, President of the Board of Education 1911-May 1915, and Postmaster-General January-December 1916. He was created Baron Gainford in 1917.

Pease's grandson, the present (3rd) Lord Gainford, has deposited a large collection (three bays) of his papers in the library of Nuffield College, Oxford (ref. Pease papers). The papers have been sorted but only a preliminary list has been made. Pease's papers have been divided into the following sections: diaries and scrap books; press cuttings; correspondence; business papers; domestic papers; political papers; official papers; claims commission papers; and B.B.C. papers.

The main volumes of Pease's diary cover the period March 1908-May 1915. They are closed to research while an edition of them is prepared by Dr Cameron Hazlehurst and Mrs Christine Woodland. Pease recorded in the diaries the course of discussions in Cabinet. Long selections from the diaries, as well as from the rest of his papers, are quoted in 23 draft chapters, entitled *War Reminiscences*, included in this division of the papers. There is also a diary of 10-11 December 1905, when Pease was offered a Junior Lordship of the Treasury. This section also includes scrap-book diaries 1892-1908 which Pease called his 'Political Diaries'. They mostly contain press cuttings of political events but they also include Pease's voting records and some comments by him on events.

There are sixteen volumes of press cuttings 1881-1938, several of which overlap. They cover most aspects of Pease's life: his election campaigns, his official activities, as well as his social activities. There are 40 boxes of correspondence 1886-1943, arranged in a single chronological series. Pease's business papers cover a wide range of industries. There is a great deal of material about his family's ironstone collieries, and about the collapse of the family bank, J. & J.W. Pease, in 1902. After the first world war Pease was active in the electricity industry, as well as maintaining his mining interests. The domestic papers include the sale and purchase of various houses, domestic arrangements, insurance, etc.

The first part of Pease's political papers covers his election campaigns. There are press cuttings, posters, buttons, receipts, and election addresses for the various constituencies he held. There are drafts for several speeches and a collection of pamphlets and leaflets on the political interests of his day. For brief periods in 1906 and 1907 Pease reported to the King on the daily proceedings of the House of Commons. Copies of the telegrams he sent have survived.

Pease's official papers have been divided by the offices he held, with an additional section of miscellaneous Cabinet memoranda. As Chancellor of the Duchy, Pease was in charge of formulating various changes in the franchise and election laws. There are volumes of papers (memoranda, letters, notes of deputations, press cuttings, etc.) on this work, which aimed at the abolition of plural voting, and having general elections on the same day. There are also many papers on various aspects of women's suffrage. There are more bound volumes from

JOSEPH ALBERT PEASE (cont.)

Pease's tenure of the Education Office. These concern proposals for a new Education Bill 1912-1914. The Post Office papers are mainly routine but they include Pease's papers on his inspection of the Dublin Post Office in 1916, with a collection of photographs of the damage done during the rebellion.

After his exclusion from office in May 1915 Pease worked for the Claims Commission in France and Italy. His job was to assess damage done by the Allied troops and to arrange compensation. A few papers have survived for this period.

Pease was chairman of the British Broadcasting Company (before it became the Corporation) 1922-1926. His papers include the company's first two minute books. There are many letters from John Reith and Mrs Snowden in the correspondence series. The papers were used by Asa Briggs in *The History of Broadcasting in the United Kingdom* vol. 1, *The Birth of Broadcasting* vol. 2, *The Golden Age of Broadcasting* (1961-65), and Andrew Boyle, *Only the Wind Will Listen, Reith of the BBC* (1972).

The collection includes not only Pease's own papers, but some of his father's, and of other members of his family. The most important of these are the papers of his wife, Elsie. They include nine boxes of letters from Pease 1882-1941, many of which include important comments on the political situation. For example, in the summer of 1914, when the Cabinet was discussing the imminent outbreak of war, Elsie was at the Peases' Darlington home and Pease wrote long and frequent letters describing the course of the discussions.

WILLIAM ROBERT WELLESLEY PEEL, 2nd VISCOUNT PEEL, 1st EARL PEEL (1867-1937)

William Robert Wellesley Peel was Conservative M.P. for Manchester (South) 1900-1906, and Taunton 1909-1912. He was Joint Parliamentary Secretary to the Ministry of National Service April-December 1918, Under-Secretary of State for War and Air January 1919-April 1921, Chancellor of the Duchy of Lancaster 1921-April 1922, Minister of Transport November 1921-April 1922, Secretary of State for India 1922-January 1924 and October 1928-June 1929, 1st Commissioner of Works November 1924-October 1928, and Lord Privy Seal September-November 1931. He succeeded his father as 2nd Viscount Peel in 1912 and was created G.B.E in 1919, G.C.S.I. in 1932, and Earl Peel in 1929.

Peel's son, the present (3rd) Earl Peel, informs us that when his mother moved to Scotland she destroyed all the papers concerning his father's political career.

A small (22 ff.) collection of letters from Peel's terms as Secretary of State for India is in the India Office Library (ref. MSS. Eur. D. 528). No list of these papers is available.

EUSTACE SUTHERLAND CAMPBELL PERCY, BARON PERCY OF NEWCASTLE (1887-1958)

Eustace Percy (he became Lord Eustace Percy in 1899 when his father became 7th Duke of Northumberland) was Conservative M.P. for Hastings 1921-1937. He was Parliamentary Secretary to the Board of Education March-May 1923, Parliamentary Secretary to the Ministry of Health 1923-January 1924, President of the Board of Education November 1924-June 1929, and Minister without Portfolio June 1935-March 1936. He was created Baron Percy of Newcastle in 1953.

His widow, Lady Percy, informs us that he never kept either correspondence or a diary and nothing now remains. This is also stated in the preface to his own memoirs, *Some Memories* (1958). The book includes a chapter on his ministerial and political career but it does not quote from any letters.

SIR ERNEST MURRAY POLLOCK, 1st Bt, 1st VISCOUNT HANWORTH (1861-1936)

Ernest Pollock was Unionist M.P. for Warwick and Leamington (Warwickshire, Warwick and Leamington from 1918) 1910-1923. He was Solicitor-General January 1919-March 1922,

SIR ERNEST MURRAY POLLOCK (cont.)

and Attorney-General March-October 1922. He was created K.B.E. in 1917, a baronet in 1922, Baron Hanworth in 1926, and Viscount Hanworth in 1936.

Only a small quantity of his papers has survived, but these papers throw an important light on the end of the Coalition Government in 1922. They have been given to the Bodleian Library (ref. Pollock Papers) by his daughter, the Hon. Lady Farrer.

The papers concerning the fall of the Coalition consist of some correspondence and a memorandum by Pollock entitled 'The Fall of the Coalition Government under Lloyd George in October 1922' (69 MS. pages). It is not clear when this was written but a typed copy is marked 'Corrected by H. 14 Sept. 1931'. This memorandum is extensively quoted in R.F.V. Heuston, *Lives of the Lord Chancellors 1885-1940* (Oxford, 1964), pp. 387-391, 424-427, 460-462. It describes how Pollock and some Conservative junior ministers were so appalled by the honours scandal that they brought their own and the alleged feelings of the constituency parties before Austen Chamberlain at a meeting in June 1922. It goes on to describe a further meeting between Conservative Cabinet Ministers and M.P.s on 3 August 1922, when Lord Birkenhead contemptuously dismissed the M.P.s' concern. Despite what Pollock calls misinterpretation and mishandling of the M.P.s' doubts, he voted to stay in the Coalition at the Carlton Club meeting. Having done so, he then felt obliged to refuse office in the new administration, despite a pressing offer by Bonar Law of the Lord Chancellorship, and great efforts in persuasion by Lord Beaverbrook through Pollock's cousin Guy Pollock. Some of the correspondence relating to these events survives with the memorandum.

There appear to be no surviving papers which relate either to Pollock's work as an M.P. or to his terms in office: only letters of congratulation on becoming Solicitor-General, Attorney-General, Master of the Rolls, and on being created a peer. There are, however, six volumes of press cuttings 1894-1935, though the major part of these is concerned with protection 1902-1909. There are also seven volumes of miscellaneous letters 1881-1932. There do not seem to be any surviving papers relating to his work as Chairman of the Contraband Committee 1915-1917, or as Controller of the Foreign Trade Department of the Foreign Office 1917-1919. There is, however, a bundle of papers relating to his activities at the Peace Conference 1919, and a bundle concerning German War Trials 1921-1922. Of Pollock's later activities as Master of the Rolls 1923-1935, and his concern for the preservation of historical documents, there remains only a bundle of notes, and correspondence on a proposed bill to allow the British Museum to make loans to other museums 1931. The collection includes nineteenth century Pollock family papers, some of which were used by Pollock in his biography of his grandfather, *Chief Justice Baron Pollock* (1929).

ARTHUR AUGUSTUS WILLIAM HARRY PONSONBY, 1st BARON PONSONBY OF SHULBREDE (1871-1946)

Arthur Ponsonby was Liberal M.P. for Stirling Burghs 1908-1918, and Labour M.P. for Sheffield (Brightside) 1922-1930. He was Under-Secretary of State for Foreign Affairs January-November 1924, Under-Secretary of State for Dominion Affairs June-December 1929, Parliamentary Secretary to the Ministry of Transport December 1929-March 1931, and Chancellor of the Duchy of Lancaster March-August 1931. He was created Baron Ponsonby of Shulbrede in 1930.

An important collection of his papers has been given to the Bodleian Library (ref. MSS. Eng. hist. a.20; c.651-685; d.363) by his son, the present (2nd) Baron Ponsonby of Shulbrede. They do not include family papers or Ponsonby's diaries; the latter cover mainly personal affairs and for this reason they are closed to researchers. The papers which are available in the Bodleian are mainly correspondence and press cuttings, with a few notes for speeches and memoranda.

The letters begin in the 1890s while Ponsonby was in the Diplomatic Service. It is clear that by 1898 he was disillusioned with that service and by the lack of work to be done. His memorandum written in 1900 entitled 'Suggestions for reform in the Diplomatic Service' survives. In the same year he wrote to John Hare describing the 'hopelessly unsatisfactory' situation in which he found himself and proposing to join an acting company. In August 1902 he actually resigned and there are many letters to him, and drafts of his own letters

ARTHUR AUGUSTUS WILLIAM HARRY PONSONBY (cont.)

which explain the circumstances. He wrote to Herbert Gladstone, the Liberal Chief Whip: 'I am a more faithful follower than ever of the Liberalism of which yourself & John Morley are the exponents . . .' and was offered a job working in the Liberal party organization.

In 1906 he stood for Taunton but was defeated; a number of letters of sympathy from Taunton Liberals, an election poster, and an election address survive. He then became private secretary to Sir Henry Campbell-Bannerman, the new Prime Minister. There is a considerable amount of correspondence from this period: letters from Sir Henry; his Cabinet; the King's secretaries; letters from Taylor and Vaughan Nash — a long series from the latter describes Sir Henry's last illness; and, equally important, a long series of letters from his brother Frederick (Fritz), Assistant Private Secretary to the King. These cover a wide range of political topics, for example, a letter dated 26 March 1906 discusses Ireland, Old Age Pensions, the Milner Debate, and Army Reforms. There is also an exchange of letters in June 1908 when Ponsonby spoke against the King's intended visit to the Tsar. As well as correspondence related to his post as secretary to the Prime Minister, there is Ponsonby's own correspondence with leading Liberals and Radicals — Morley, C.F.G. Masterman, the Hammonds, and C.P. Trevelyan. The correspondence with Trevelyan and the Hammonds continued throughout Ponsonby's life and is an important source on their activities. There are also 'Leaves of a Diary begun in Downing St. Jan '06 but owing to pressure of work never gone on with' (January 1907). (See also *Addenda*, p. 167.)

When Sir Henry died, Ponsonby became Liberal M.P. for Stirling Burghs, Sir Henry's constituency. Apart from a printed election address and letters of congratulation on being elected, the only constituency papers to survive are in a bundle entitled '1914-1917 Full correspondence with regard to the breach with the Officers and Executives of the Stirling Burghs Liberal Associations'. There is some correspondence on the defeat of Ponsonby and others in the peace movement in the 1918 general election. No correspondence for his term of office as M.P. for Sheffield seems to have survived.

Ponsonby's parliamentary career is vividly represented by his correspondence. There are letters about his exclusion from a Palace garden party in 1908, about the Liberal Foreign Affairs Committee 1910-1914, about his publications and speeches, his stand against the war, and his activities with members of the Union of Democratic Control. There is a great deal of material on his activities in the 1920s and 1930s: his vote against the 1926 service estimates; the 1927 Peace Letter Campaign; the various peace movements of the 1930s — the No More War Movement, the War Resisters International, the British Anti-War Movement, and the Peace Pledge Union. Ponsonby's correspondents for this period include Bertrand Russell, Albert Einstein, Aldous Huxley, George Lansbury, and Laurence Housman.

Little remains of his official activities. From the 1924 government there are only letters of congratulation on the conclusion of the Russian treaties and a few letters from J.R. MacDonald. On his decision to become a peer there is an exchange of letters from friends giving advice, and a letter from his brother Fritz 2 January 1929:

> The King spoke very strongly about your peerage. . . How could anyone place any reliance on what labour politicians said when you and Sidney Webb had to eat your words and tamely became Peers.
> I explained the whole thing to him and he then came round completely and finally ended by saying he saw your point of view and that no doubt you were quite right in accepting a peerage!

There is nothing from his periods of office at the Dominions Office and Transport; but a letter from Lord Passfield 4 January 1931 relates how MacDonald '. . . broke out into an admission that we were "too old a lot. . ." '. For the Duchy there are only congratulations on entering office and a few papers connected with a scheme to obtain portraits of all previous holders of the office. There is some correspondence in August 1931 on the end of the Labour Government and an undated 'appreciation' of J.R. MacDonald expressing great disillusionment.

There is some correspondence on Ponsonby's activities in the Lords though little for his period as Leader of the Opposition. There is correspondence and press cuttings on his resignation as Leader. There is correspondence, and press cuttings referring to his numerous broadcasts, some of which were non-political, for example, on keeping a diary. There are no papers on his literary activities apart from reactions from friends in their letters.

SIR WYNDHAM RAYMOND PORTAL, 3rd Bt, VISCOUNT PORTAL (1885-1949)

Wyndham Portal succeeded his father as third baronet in 1931; he was created G.C.M.G. in 1949, Baron Portal in 1935, and Viscount Portal in 1945. He was Additional Parliamentary Secretary to the Ministry of Supply September 1940-March 1942, Minister of Works and Planning and 1st Commissioner of Works 1942-November 1944.

There was no issue of Portal's marriage and he was succeeded as fourth baronet by his uncle. His cousin, the present (5th) baronet, does not know of the existence of any papers, and adds that his cousin avoided putting pen to paper whenever possible.

ALBERT EDWARD HARRY MAYER ARCHIBALD PRIMROSE, 6th EARL OF ROSEBERY (1882-)

Albert Edward Harry Mayer Archibald Primrose, known as Lord Dalmeny from his birth till he succeeded his father as 6th Earl of Rosebery in 1929, was Liberal M.P. for Edinburghshire 1906-1910. He was Secretary of State for Scotland May-July 1945. He was created K.T. in 1947.

Lord Rosebery informs us that he never kept any papers because they did not seem of sufficient importance.

ROWLAND EDMUND PROTHERO, BARON ERNLE (1851-1937)

Rowland Prothero was Conservative M.P. for Oxford University 1914-1919. He was President of the Board of Agriculture and Fisheries December 1916-August 1919. He was created Baron Ernle in 1919.

Prothero left '. . . all my manuscripts letters and papers and the copyright in all my books . . .' to his daughter Beatrice Hope, Mrs Victor Gilpin. She died in 1958 and left all her chattels to her two sons. The elder son, Mr T.E. Gilpin, informs us that all he has of his grandfather's papers are some scrapbooks of cuttings from Prothero's electoral campaigns in North Bedford and some letters from eminent people 1919-1937 which are 'of little consequence'. He knows nothing of the fate of any other papers which may have survived. Prothero's *Whippingham to Westminster* (1938) contains his reminiscences but gives few quotations from documents.

SIR (PERCY) JOHN PYBUS, Bt (1880-1935)

John Pybus was Liberal M.P. for Essex (Harwich) 1929-1931 and Liberal National M.P. 1931-1935. He was Minister of Transport September 1931-February 1933. He was created a baronet in 1934.

His brother, Mr S.J. Pybus, informs us that he kept his brother's papers for many years but eventually destroyed them as no one had wanted to use them.

HERWALD RAMSBOTHAM, 1st VISCOUNT SOULBURY (1887-1971)

Herwald Ramsbotham was Conservative M.P. for Lancashire (Lancaster) 1929-1941. He was Parliamentary Secretary to the Board of Education November 1931-November 1935, Parliamentary Secretary to the Ministry of Agriculture and Fisheries 1935-July 1936, Minister of Pensions 1936-June 1939, 1st Commissioner of Works 1939-April 1940, and President of the Board of Education 1940-July 1941. He was created G.C.M.G. in 1949, Baron Soulbury in 1941, and Viscount Soulbury in 1954.

Only a very small collection of Ramsbotham's papers survives in the possession of his younger son, the Hon. Sir Peter Ramsbotham, K.C.M.G. This collection is currently in the care of Mr Nigel Middleton, Ulster College, The Northern Ireland Polytechnic, Jordanstown, Newtownabbey, Co. Antrim, Northern Ireland. He is gathering material for a biography of Ramsbotham.

The surviving papers consist of five volumes of speeches made while Ramsbotham was at the Board of Education, two volumes of press cuttings, mainly covering Ramsbotham's 1920s election campaigns, and a small collection of miscellaneous papers.

SIR ROBERT THRESHIE REID, EARL LOREBURN (1846-1923)

Robert Reid was Liberal M.P. for Hereford 1880-1885, and for Dumfries 1886-1905. He was Solicitor-General May-October 1894, Attorney-General 1894-June 1895, and Lord Chancellor December 1905-June 1912. He was knighted in 1894, created G.C.M.G. in 1899, Baron Loreburn in 1906, and Earl Loreburn in 1911.

We have been unable to find any of Reid's papers. He died without leaving any issue. Reid's nephew, Dr R.C. Reid, who has since died, had a few early letters to his parents and family, but his widow can no longer find them. Reid's second wife, Violet Elizabeth Hicks Beach, was a niece of the 1st Earl St Aldwyn but her family know of no surviving papers. Mr G.W. Monger informs us that he enquired without success of Reid's widow's executor (The Public Trustee), the solicitors acting for the estate (Messrs Trower, Still & Keeling), and Major W.W. Hicks Beach, Reid's widow's nephew. It may well be that Reid kept very few papers; he wrote to Arthur Ponsonby 23 April 1920: 'I have no papers. I never keep them . . .' (Ponsonby MSS.).

SIR JOHN CHARLES WALSHAM REITH, 1st BARON REITH (1889-1971)

John Reith was knighted in 1927 and created K.T. in 1969, and Baron Reith in 1940. He was Minister of Information January-May 1940, Minister of Transport May-October 1940, and Minister of Works (later Works and Planning) 1940-February 1942.

Reith's papers, including a voluminous diary kept from 1911 till his death, are not available for research while Mr C.H. Stuart prepares an edition of the diaries for publication. Mr Stuart hopes that his edition will be published in 1974 by Collins. No decision has yet been taken on access to the papers after Mr Stuart's work has been completed. Applications to read the papers should be addressed to Reith's literary executor, Mr J.F. Burrell, of Messrs Farrer & Co., 66 Lincoln's Inn Fields, London W.C.2.

Reith himself quoted frequently from the diaries in his memoirs, *Into the Wind* (1949), and extensive selections from his first world war diary were published as *Wearing Spurs* (1966). The first two volumes of the history of the B.B.C. by Asa Briggs also drew on the diaries for the 1920s and 1930s: *The History of Broadcasting in the United Kingdom*, vol. 1, *The Birth of Broadcasting*, vol. 2, *The Golden Age of Broadcasting* (1961-65). Andrew Boyle's biography of Reith, *Only the Wind Will Listen* (1972), makes no use of Reith's papers; but it quotes from a report on the diaries made for Lord Beaverbrook when he was considering buying them a few years before Reith's death.

SIR JOSEPH COMPTON-RICKETT (1847-1919)

Joseph Compton-Rickett (he assumed the additional surname of Compton in 1908) was Liberal M.P. for Scarborough 1895-1906 and for the West Riding of Yorkshire (Osgoldcross; Pontefract from 1918) 1906-1919. He was Paymaster-General December 1916-October 1919. He was knighted in 1907.

We have been unable to trace any of Compton-Rickett's heirs. His executors and trustees, to whom he left his copyright and his papers, were the Public Trustee, his son Arthur, Reginald Neale Spiers, and the Rev. John Scott Lidgett. Compton-Rickett's widow died in 1933; her executors were R.N. Spiers and her son Arthur. Arthur Compton-Rickett died in 1937. His executors were R.N. Spiers and Reginald Denham. We have been unable to trace Mr Spiers; Mr Denham could tell us nothing of Sir Joseph's papers; he lost contact with the Compton-Rickett family in 1941 but believes that they have all died (Sir Joseph had four sons and four daughters). Arthur Compton-Rickett published several books, including *Joseph Compton-Rickett. A memoir* (1922), but his several publishers have been taken over and their successors were unable to put us into contact with the Compton-Rickett family. Arthur Compton-Rickett left the copyright of his plays and some of his papers to Ella Mary Cressee, who died in 1959. She left Arthur Compton-Rickett's manuscripts to Miss Pamela Richardson. Miss Richardson, in her turn, passed the manuscripts to her nephew but she informs us that they consisted solely of Arthur Compton-Rickett's essays and short plays.

SIR MATTHEW WHITE RIDLEY, 5th Bt, 1st VISCOUNT RIDLEY (1842-1904)

Matthew Ridley was Conservative M.P. for Northumberland (North) 1868-1885, and North Lancashire (Blackpool) 1886-1900. He was Under-Secretary of State for Home Affairs April 1878-April 1880, Financial Secretary to the Treasury September 1885-January 1886, and Secretary of State for Home Affairs July 1895-November 1900. He succeeded his father as 5th baronet in 1877 and was created Viscount Ridley in 1900.

A large collection of Ridley family papers, which includes a small number of Ridley's own papers, was deposited by the present (4th) Viscount Ridley in the Northumberland Record Office (ref. Ridley [Blagdon] MSS.). A list and index of the papers are available.

The collection contains 100 letters to Ridley from politicians 1875-1903 arranged chronologically (ref. ZRI.25.97). There are a few letters from Benjamin Disraeli, Sir Stafford Northcote, and Queen Victoria. The only other political papers are notes of Ridley's election expenses in 1868, 1880 and 1886, and his letter of appointment as a privy councillor in 1892. The other papers include a diary of a French tour 1873-1874, letters from Harrow and Oxford about Ridley's scholarship, bank account books 1884-1901, game books 1864-1914, letters about his house and furniture, a copy of his will, and an album of letters of condolence to Lady Ridley in 1904.

CHARLES THOMSON RITCHIE, 1st BARON RITCHIE OF DUNDEE (1838-1906)

Charles Thomson Ritchie was Conservative M.P. for Tower Hamlets 1874-1885, Tower Hamlets (St George's) 1885-1892, and Croydon 1895-1905. He was Financial Secretary to the Admiralty 1885-1886, President of the Local Government Board August 1886-August 1892, President of the Board of Trade June 1895-November 1900, Secretary of State for Home Affairs 1900-August 1902, and Chancellor of the Exchequer 1902-October 1903. He was created Baron Ritchie of Dundee in 1905.

One volume of Ritchie's papers, all that appears to have survived, was given to the British Library by his grandson, the present (3rd) Lord Ritchie, in 1966 (ref. Add. MSS. 53780). The letters and papers all concern Ritchie's resignation in 1903 on the tariff reform issue.

ALFRED ROBENS, BARON ROBENS OF WOLDINGHAM (1910-   )

Alfred Robens was Labour M.P. for Northumberland (Wansbeck) 1945-1950, and for Blyth 1950-1960. He was Parliamentary Secretary to the Ministry of Fuel and Power October 1947-April 1951, and Minister of Labour and National Service April-October 1951. He was created Baron Robens of Woldingham (a life peerage) in 1961.

Lord Robens informs us that he never brought papers away from his various ministries, nor has he systematically kept papers; he adds that the only diaries he kept were appointment diaries. Lord Robens has described his years as Chairman of the National Coal Board 1961-1971 in *Ten Year Stint* (1972).

FREDERICK OWEN ROBERTS (1876-1941)

Frederick Owen Roberts was Labour M.P. for West Bromwich 1918-1931 and 1935-1941. He was Minister of Pensions January-November 1924 and June 1929-August 1931.

Roberts's son, Mr Reuben V. Roberts, Rectory Cottage, Depden, Bury St Edmunds, Suffolk, informs us that his mother destroyed most of his father's papers after his death, including a large volume of press cuttings and letters arranged in chronological order. All that remains in Mr Roberts's possession is a splendidly illuminated address of appreciation, presented to Roberts by the townspeople of Northampton in 1920, a file containing ballots for notices of motions, a lengthy correspondence about conditions in China in 1928, miscellaneous press cuttings including *Hansard*'s record of the announcement of the death of George V, a souvenir of the first airmail post between England and India, and the first minute

FREDERICK OWEN ROBERTS (cont.)

book of the Group of Midland Branches of the Typographical Association 28 July 1917-27 August 1918. The minute book is particularly interesting because it traces the formulation of the Group's constitution and also contains press cuttings of the Group's activities and rough drafts of wages agreements.

GEORGE HENRY ROBERTS (1869-1928)

George Henry Roberts was Labour M.P. for Norwich 1906-1918 and Independent M.P. for the same seat 1918-1923. He joined the Conservative party in 1923. He was Parliamentary Secretary to the Board of Trade December 1916-August 1917, Minister of Labour 1917-January 1919, and Food Controller 1919-February 1920.

Roberts's daughter, Miss V.A. Roberts, 235 College Road, Norwich NOR5 4F, has a small collection of her father's papers. It includes a note from Charles Bathurst 18 April 1914 congratulating Roberts on a speech about social reform: ' . . . If you make many more of the same kind I shall feel bound to come across and sit on your benches'; a note from Lloyd George congratulating him on a speech 25 April 1917; the official notification of Roberts's being sworn as a Privy Councillor 22 August 1917; and a letter from John Wheatley in August 1924 asking Roberts to continue as chairman of an advisory committee on the welfare of the blind. There are also a few press cuttings, for example on Roberts's speech about Indian support for the British war effort September 1914, and on his work as Food Controller.

GEORGE FREDERICK SAMUEL ROBINSON, 1st MARQUESS OF RIPON (1827-1909)

George Frederick Samuel Robinson was Liberal M.P. for Hull 1852-1853, Huddersfield 1853-1857 and for the West Riding of Yorkshire 1857-1859. He was known as Viscount Goderich from 1833 till he succeeded his father as 2nd Earl of Ripon in 1859; he was created K.G. in 1869, and Marquess of Ripon in 1871. He was Under-Secretary of State for War June 1859-January 1861 and July 1861-April 1863, Under-Secretary of State for India January-July 1861, Secretary of State for War April 1863-February 1866, Secretary of State for India February-June 1866, Lord President of the Council December 1868-August 1873, Viceroy of India 1880-1884, 1st Lord of the Admiralty February-August 1886, Secretary of State for the Colonies August 1892-June 1895, Lord Privy Seal and Liberal Leader in the House of Lords December 1905-April 1908.

One hundred and thirty-five volumes of his papers were presented to the British Library in 1923 (ref. Add. MSS. 43510-43644). The papers have been arranged under the following headings: Royal Correspondence, Special Correspondence, Correspondence about India, Family Correspondence, General Correspondence, Diaries, and Miscellaneous.

Robinson's royal correspondence (two volumes) is arranged by individuals and includes letters from Queen Victoria and her secretaries 1869-1895, and from King Edward VII 1864-1901. Robinson's special correspondents (53 volumes) — i.e. those from whom a considerable body of letters survive — include the 1st Earl Russell 1863-1867, the 3rd Viscount Palmerston 1859-1863, W.E. Gladstone (three volumes) 1863-1896, Lord Rosebery (one volume) 1886-1908, Sir H. Campbell-Bannerman 1888-1908, H.H. Asquith 1894-1908, John Morley (one volume) 1886-1909, and the 1st Earl of Kimberley (six volumes) 1864-1901. This series also includes six volumes of correspondence with colonial governors arranged by colony.

There are 55 volumes of correspondence concerning India. They include five volumes of correspondence 1859-1904 with the 8th Duke of Devonshire, mainly when he was Secretary of State for India, four volumes with Robinson's predecessor as Viceroy, the 1st Earl of Northbrook, volumes of correspondence with various Indian governors and Indian government officials and fourteen volumes of printed official correspondence and papers with manuscript additions and corrections. Other copies of some of these printed volumes are available in the printed books department of the British Library.

There are twenty volumes of general correspondence 1849-1909 and three volumes of diary for 1878-1880. The miscellaneous section includes notes for speeches and lectures

GEORGE FREDERICK SAMUEL ROBINSON (cont.)

and two political memoranda. Robinson's family correspondence consists of one volume of letters to his wife in 1880. His father's papers form a separate collection in the British Library.

Lucien Wolf, *Life of the 1st Marquess of Ripon* (2 vols., 1921), quotes from these papers including a political memorandum by Ripon and his diary.

SIR WILLIAM SNOWDON ROBSON, BARON ROBSON (1852-1918)

William Snowdon Robson was Liberal M.P. for Tower Hamlets (Bow and Bromley) 1885-1886 and South Shields 1895-1910. He was Solicitor-General December 1905-January 1908, Attorney-General 1908-October 1910, and a Lord of Appeal in Ordinary 1910-1912. He was knighted in 1905, and created G.C.M.G. in 1911, and Baron Robson (a judicial life peerage) in 1910.

Robson's daughter-in-law, the Hon. Mrs I. Robson, Pinewood Hill, Wormley, Godalming, Surrey, has only a few papers, including a 1906 election leaflet, a memorandum by Earl Grey on the Newfoundland Fisheries case (Robson presented the British Government's case to the International Court at the Hague 1910-1911), a letter from Lewis Harcourt offering the G.C.M.G. as a reward for his efforts in that case, December 1910, and correspondence relating to his resignation as a law lord in 1912.

Professor George W. Keeton, in his biography of Robson, *A Liberal Attorney-General* (1949), quoted from this collection, but added that Robson 'refused to keep any adequate record of his career and he had a distrust of "letters written for posterity" '. The privately published religious treatise referred to by Professor Keeton for 'many important clues to the depths of Robson's character' (p. 233) was part of this collection but appears to have since been lost.

A further collection of some 300 letters and miscellaneous papers was found by Mr P. Audley-Miller, 48 High Street, Oxford, in an old desk. They seem to be an autograph collection; many of the letters were in envelopes headed 'signatures'. The letters are mainly from barristers, judges, civil servants and politicians, written when Robson was Solicitor-General and Attorney-General. They are in chronological order with undated letters at the end. There are seventeen from the period 1891-1905 and 250 from 1906-1920. There are eleven letters to Flood, Robson's clerk 1888-1910, and six letters to Sir Ryland Adkins 1913-1919. There are also two writs summoning Robson to attend Parliament 1906 and 1910, and admission tickets to the Members' Gallery, the Official Gallery, and the Strangers' Gallery, and other miscellaneous papers.

WALTER RUNCIMAN, 1st VISCOUNT RUNCIMAN OF DOXFORD (1870-1949)

Walter Runciman was Liberal M.P. for Oldham 1899-1900, Dewsbury 1902-1918, Swansea (West) 1924-1929, Cornwall (St Ives) 1929-1937. He was a Liberal National from 1931. He was Parliamentary Secretary to the Local Government Board December 1905-January 1907, Financial Secretary to the Treasury 1907-April 1908, President of the Board of Education 1908-October 1911, President of the Board of Agriculture and Fisheries 1911-August 1914, President of the Board of Trade 1914-December 1916 and November 1931-May 1937, and Lord President of the Council October 1938-September 1939. He was created Viscount Runciman of Doxford in 1937.

Six tin trunks and thirteen dispatch-boxes filled with Runciman's papers were deposited in the library of the University of Newcastle upon Tyne in 1969 (ref. Runciman of Doxford papers). The papers are not yet catalogued but a brief preliminary list has been compiled; they are available to researchers but application should be made in advance to the University Librarian.

A large number of Cabinet papers from most of Runciman's offices appear to have survived in this collection. There are two volumes of Board of Education papers (bills, notes and correspondence) on the 1908 Education Bill; there is a complete set of memoranda circulated by Runciman as President of the Board of Trade August 1914-September 1915;

WALTER RUNCIMAN (cont.)

and papers on the major problems of the day: the Committee of Imperial Defence; Ulster; Germany; the 1912 Coal Strike; the problems of blockade 1914-1916. As well as these more formal papers, there is a collection of miscellaneous notes by Runciman, including some taken at Cabinet on the reform of the House of Lords.

There are many political papers: papers concerning Runciman's various elections; constituency matters; the Liberal party — including files on the party's attitude to the General Strike, the party's financial problems 1926, and correspondence with Herbert Samuel. There is also a large amount of correspondence, including letters of congratulation, letters from Winston Churchill 1906-1915, and letters from Cabinet colleagues 1931-1937. There are a few papers on Runciman's mission to Czechoslovakia in 1938, and on his shipping and banking concerns.

In addition there is a large collection of press cuttings and copies of, or notes for, speeches.

A further small collection (five volumes) relating to the mission to Czechoslovakia is available in the Public Record Office (ref. F.O. 800/304-308).

HERBRAND EDWARD DUNDONALD BRASSEY SACKVILLE, 9th EARL DE LA WARR (1900-   )

Herbrand Edward Dundonald Brassey Sackville succeeded his father as 9th Earl De La Warr in 1915; till then he was known as Lord Buckhurst. He was created G.B.E. in 1956. He was Parliamentary Under-Secretary of State for War June 1929-June 1930, Parliamentary Secretary to the Ministry of Agriculture and Fisheries 1930-November 1935, Parliamentary Under-Secretary to the Board of Education 1935-July 1936, Parliamentary Under-Secretary of State for the Colonies 1936-May 1937, Lord Privy Seal 1937-October 1938, President of the Board of Education 1938-May 1940, 1st Commissioner of Works April-May 1940, and Postmaster-General November 1951-April 1955.

Lord De La Warr informs us that he has no papers; some years ago he went through what papers he had and destroyed them because he did not think they would be of any interest.

SIR (JAMES) ARTHUR SALTER, BARON SALTER OF KIDLINGTON (1881-   )

Arthur Salter was Independent M.P. for Oxford University 1937-1950, and Conservative M.P. for Lancashire (Ormskirk) 1951-1953. He was Parliamentary Secretary to the Ministry of Shipping (War Transport from May 1941) November 1939-February 1942, Chancellor of the Duchy of Lancaster May-July 1945, Minister for Economic Affairs October 1951-November 1952, and Minister of Materials 1952-September 1953. He was created K.C.B. in 1922, G.B.E. in 1944, and Baron Salter in 1953.

Lord Salter informs us that his papers are not available for research: at the moment his biography is being written by Dr Sidney Aster; when that is completed Lord Salter will consider further the ultimate disposition of his papers.

Lord Salter's papers fill two four-drawer filing cabinets. There are no papers before 1917 when he was a civil servant. A diary for 28 November-1 December 1917, notes and memoranda, have survived from the International Conference on Shipping concerning convoys. The papers are particularly good for the period 1919-1931 when Lord Salter worked for the League of Nations. There are memoranda by Lord Salter for the Reparations Commission 1919-1930, notes on the organization and administration of the League, correspondence with Lord Robert Cecil, for example on the entrance to the League of Germany in 1925, speeches, broadcast notes, and papers on particular topics such as the 1928 Kellogg Pact, and various proposals for a United States of Europe 1925-1930.

Lord Salter's papers reflect his diverse interests after his departure from the League in 1931. They cover his trips to India and China in 1931, and to China again in 1933, his work on economic problems, and his activities on such bodies as the B.B.C.'s Advisory Council and the All Souls' Foreign Affairs Group 1938-1939. Correspondence about his nomination, election material, and press cuttings survive from his entry into Parliament in 1937. Lord Salter was Gladstone Professor of Political Theory and Institutions at Oxford University

SIR ARTHUR SALTER (cont.)

1934-1944; his lifelong interest in Oxford is fully represented by his papers: agenda, minutes, and notes on college policy from All Souls, lecture notes, papers on the Oxford Preservation Trust and other Oxford bodies, including papers on various road schemes 1957-1962. There are also papers relating to Lord Salter's campaign 1937-1939 for the storage of food and raw materials.

Lord Salter's work at the Ministry of Shipping (later the Ministry of War Transport) is represented by both correspondence and memoranda. From October 1941 till 1943 Lord Salter was Head of the British Merchant Shipping Mission to Washington D.C. A large number of memoranda and correspondence has survived from this period including the official diary (that is, copies of all correspondence and telegrams) October 1941-June 1943. In 1944 Lord Salter was Senior Deputy Director-General of the United Nations' Relief and Rehabilitation Administration; papers concerning his appointment and his work have survived, including papers relating to his visit to Germany in 1945. Only papers relating to his appointment and to the resignation of the government survive from Lord Salter's tenure of the Duchy of Lancaster. There is some printed election material and lists of supporters from the 1945 general election. Election material and some correspondence with Churchill have survived from Lord Salter's election for Ormskirk in 1951.

A considerable amount of material has survived from Lord Salter's tenure of the Ministry for Economic Affairs and the Ministry of Materials. It includes correspondence, minutes, and memoranda largely on such economic issues as the balance of payments, inflation, and the Council of Europe. Lord Salter's correspondents include Winston Churchill and L.S. Amery.

Several files of correspondence, draft speeches, memoranda, and extracts from *Hansard* reflect Lord Salter's activities in the House of Lords. Subjects covered include the United Nations, Defence, Atomic Energy, and Rhodesia. In 1954 Lord Salter was asked for economic advice by the government of Iraq. His resulting visits led to a considerable amount of correspondence, press cuttings, and a published report. A coup in Iraq prevented the implementation of his suggested reforms.

Lord Salter has published three volumes of memoirs: *Personality in Politics* (1947), *Memoirs of a Public Servant* (1961) and *Slave of the Lamp* (1967). Drafts, correspondence, and reviews of these and Lord Salter's other publications are included in his papers.

Some of Lord Salter's Private Office papers from the Ministry of War Transport are now available in the Public Record Office (ref. M.T. 62/95-123). The papers comprise correspondence files alphabetically arranged, with an original index. Lord Salter's earlier career as a civil servant may also be traced in the surviving files of the ministries with which he was associated.

SIR HERBERT LOUIS SAMUEL, 1st VISCOUNT SAMUEL (1870-1963)

Herbert Samuel was Liberal M.P. for the North Riding of Yorkshire (Cleveland) 1902-1918 and Lancashire (Darwen) 1929-1935. He was Parliamentary Under-Secretary of State for Home Affairs December 1905-July 1909, Chancellor of the Duchy of Lancaster 1909-February 1910 and November 1915-January 1916, Postmaster-General 1910-February 1914 and May 1915-January 1916, President of the Local Government Board 1914-May 1915, Secretary of State for Home Affairs January-December 1916, and August 1931-September 1932, and High Commissioner for Palestine 1920-1925. He was created G.B.E. in 1920, G.C.B. in 1926, and Viscount Samuel in 1937.

In his *Memoirs* (1945) Samuel wrote that although he had never kept a diary, he did keep notes of interesting conversations, in addition to a large collection of letters and political papers. Most of these papers were deposited in 1963 by his son, the present (2nd) Viscount Samuel, in the House of Lords Record Office (ref. Samuel Papers). The papers are available for research, though most post-1946 papers will not be opened till they are thirty years old; permission to quote from the papers must be obtained from Samuel's executors and from the Clerk of the Records, House of Lords Record Office.

Samuel's family still have some personal papers. Papers concerning Samuel's work in Palestine have beem deposited in the Israel State Archives, Jerusalem. They are described

SIR HERBERT LOUIS SAMUEL (cont.)

in *Herbert Louis, First Viscount Samuel. A Register of His Papers at the State Archives,* by Elie Mizrachi (Jerusalem, 1965). Most of this list is in Hebrew. Microfilm and other photographic copies of these papers are available at the House of Lords Record Office. They include sixteen volumes of correspondence 1915-1962, one volume of memoranda and minutes 1919-1939, one volume of official papers 1920-1944, and two volumes of press cuttings 1917-1962.

The papers deposited in the House of Lords Record Office are described briefly in M.F. Bond, *Guide to the Records of Parliament* (1971) pp. 283-284. Very detailed lists of the papers are contained in the House of Lords Record Office, *Memoranda nos. 35* (1966) and *41* (1969).

The papers in the House of Lords Record Office have been divided into six main groups: political papers (A); personal papers (B); photographs (C); press cuttings (D); literary, philosophical and scientific papers (E); formal and ceremonial papers (F).

The political papers fill over 170 boxes; most of them are arranged in subject files. The earliest papers concern the conditions of employment of match box makers 1890-1892. There are papers on Samuel's candidature for South Oxfordshire 1893-1900 and on his Cleveland constituency. There are a large number of papers concerning the Liberal party's organization and administration. Samuel returned most of his Cabinet papers to the Cabinet Office but there are papers on some of the major political problems of Samuel's career: Ireland; reform of the House of Lords; the formation of the 1915 and 1916 Coalition governments and the 1931 National Government; India; Germany — including correspondence and notes of conversations with N. Chamberlain, Lord Halifax, and others. There are also a few departmental papers including papers on the Marconi crisis (Samuel was then Postmaster-General), and the trial of Roger Casement (Samuel was at the Home Office). There are papers concerning the 1926 general strike and draft settlement terms by Samuel. Some of these papers were deposited in the record office in 1968 by Mr Frank Singleton who had borrowed them in 1939 for a projected biography of Samuel. Also included in the political papers are Samuel's letters to his mother 1881-1918, his wife 1898-1933, and his brother-in-law 1902-1938, which include a great deal of political material. There are thirteen volumes of general correspondence and papers 1888-1962.

Samuel's personal papers include his school papers, family correspondence and some press cuttings. They also include some 50 letters from his wife 1925-1952. His literary papers include drafts of his articles, pamphlets, and books and correspondence arising from them.

John Bowle, *Viscount Samuel* (1957), was based on the papers and quotes extensively from them.

SIR ROBERT ARTHUR SANDERS, Bt, BARON BAYFORD (1867-1940)

Robert Arthur Sanders was Conservative M.P. for Somerset (Bridgwater) 1910-1923 and Somerset (Wells) 1924-1929. He was Under-Secretary of State for War April 1921-October 1922 and Minister of Agriculture and Fisheries 1922-January 1924. He was created a baronet in 1920 and Baron Bayford in 1929.

Two notebooks (some 75,000 words) containing Sanders's diary for February 1910-1921, and 1921-April 1935, have been deposited in the Conservative Research Department. Written applications should be made to Mr G.D.M. Block, O.B.E. An edition is being prepared for publication by Mr John Ramsden. It will include all that is known to survive from Sanders's correspondence (letters of 1911, 1914-1918, 1920-1921) in the possession of his daughter, the Hon. Mrs Vera Butler, Kentisbeare House, Cullompton, Devon, EX15 2DR. Permission to quote from the diaries must be obtained from Mrs Butler.

DUNCAN EDWIN SANDYS (1908-   )

Duncan Sandys was Conservative M.P. for Lambeth (Norwood) 1935-1945, and Wandsworth (Streatham) 1950-1974. He was Financial Secretary to the War Office July 1941-February 1943, Parliamentary Secretary to the Ministry of Supply December 1942-November 1944, Minister of Works 1944-August 1945, Minister of Supply

DUNCAN EDWIN SANDYS (cont.)

October 1951-October 1954, Minister of Housing and Local Government 1954-January 1957, Minister of Defence 1957-October 1959, Minister of Aviation 1959-July 1960, Secretary of State for Commonwealth Relations 1960-October 1964, and Secretary of State for the Colonies July 1962-October 1964.

Mr Sandys informs us that although he has a large collection of papers they are largely unsorted and therefore not available for research.

SIR JOHN SANKEY, VISCOUNT SANKEY (1886-1948)

John Sankey was Lord Chancellor June 1929-June 1935. Until 1929 his career had been confined to the law. He was knighted in 1914, and created G.B.E. in 1917, Baron Sankey in 1929, and Viscount Sankey in 1932.

Sankey's papers have now been given to the Bodleian Library (ref. MSS. Eng. hist. a.19; c. 502-556, 558; d.313-340; e.242-303; f.21, 25), having been kept in solicitor's offices since the death of Sankey's sister in 1959. Some of the papers were destroyed in an effort to gain space, but it is thought that these were only press cuttings. Even so, some of the papers seen by Professor R.F.V. Heuston for his *Lives of the Lord Chancellors 1885-1940* (Oxford, 1964) do not appear to have survived — for example, bar examination papers, and barrister's fee book. It should be pointed out that most of the papers now in the Bodleian were not produced for Professor Heuston because their existence had been forgotten.

More than two trunks of papers have survived. They seem to have been sorted by Sankey himself in 1940 and by his sister in 1948. The most important section of these papers is Sankey's diary covering the years 1888, 1891-1947. The diary was written in small desk diaries and many of the entries are simply brief notes of appointments or activities. For example, while the Coal Commission of 1919 was sitting, the most informative entry about Sankey's attitude is for 13 March 1919: 'Owners' evidence. They are hopeless!' However, the diary is often kept in some detail, particularly after 1929, and is, for instance, very informative on the events leading up to the formation of the National Government. Sankey himself described it as 'fairly copious'.

The bulk of the papers is in the form of miscellaneous correspondence. This includes many letters of congratulation on Sankey's various appointments and honours: K.C. 1909, judge 1914, justice of appeal 1928, Lord Chancellor 1929, Viscount 1932, as well as more general correspondence for the 1930s and 1940s. There are also a great many press cuttings.

Sankey himself arranged his large collection of notes for speeches into what he described as 'volumes' or large bundles. The thirteen 'volumes' are indexed, giving the date, the occasion, and the place of each speech; each 'volume' has a list of contents.

Apart from the diaries, general correspondence, and press cuttings, Sankey's career is well represented by his papers. There is a minute book of the Home Office Advisory Committee on Enemy Aliens (16 April 1916-11 December 1918) of which Sankey was chairman and which usually records who was present or absent and occasionally gives details of the cases heard. There are some press cuttings, a small amount of correspondence, and minutes of evidence for 16 June 1919 of the 1919 Coal Commission.

There are also three seals and many papers derived from Sankey's tenure of the Woolsack. Papers concerning the Indian Round Table Conference predominate. For December 1930 there are drafts of the proposed Indian Constitution and comments by MacDonald and the former Viceroy, Lord Reading. For 1931 there are several printed reports and memoranda, often annotated by Sankey. There is also some correspondence: a nine page typed letter from Sir Malcolm Hailey, Governor of the United Provinces 18 July 1931, and a seven page letter from Lord Reading 28 November 1931, both on the state of affairs and future policy. There are notes by both Sankey 15 September 1931 (ten typed pages), and Lord Irwin (later Earl of Halifax) 25 September 1931 of their conversations with Gandhi. There is also a fifteen page note by Sankey on the proceedings of the Federal Structure Committee. For 1932 there is a bundle of miscellaneous letters about the Round Table Conference, notes on a meeting of the Cabinet's Indian Committee 26 May 1932 which give the opinions of the various speakers, and notes for Sankey's speech at the close of the conference 24 December 1932.

SIR JOHN SANKEY (cont.)

There are many memoranda and minutes of the Cabinet's Committee 1934-1935; including what Sankey describes as the 'key document' — a 23 page memorandum by the Secretary of State for India, Sir Samuel Hoare, 27 October 1934 — and the report of the Committee to the Cabinet 29 January 1935.

As well as these papers on India there are many pages of notes by Sankey on Cabinet meetings: 22 July 1930; 15 June 1931; 21 and 22 January 1932; 26 May 1932; 28 and 30 September 1932. They cover various topics including agricultural policy, tariffs, the Ottawa Conference, and the resignation of Snowden, Samuel and Sinclair. Sankey wrote a 26-page memorandum on the 1930 Imperial Conference, its proceedings, and its participants. There is also an exchange of correspondence with MacDonald 13 May 1931 on a speech by the Prince of Wales concerning protection, and whether it was an incursion into politics. Perhaps most interesting of all is a twelve-page memorandum written by Sankey in June 1935 on the events leading up to his resignation. In it he says that MacDonald offered him the Lord Chancellorship in 1924 if Haldane would take Education. He goes on to claim that he nearly prevented the Government's collapse in August 1931; he says that Arthur Henderson, the leader of the revolt against MacDonald, got cold feet at the last minute and that a reconciliation was only prevented by the intervention of Arthur Greenwood.

There is also a photograph of a letter from Adolf Hitler to the 1st Viscount Rothermere dated 20 December 1935 with an English translation. Rothermere appears to have asked Hitler for his views on the current international situation and this letter sets these views out in some detail (eight typed pages).

SIR PHILIP ALBERT GUSTAVE DAVID SASSOON, 3rd Bt (1888-1939)

Philip Sassoon was Conservative M.P. for Hythe 1912-1939. He was Under-Secretary of State for Air November 1924-June 1929 and September 1931-May 1937, and 1st Commissioner of Works May 1937-June 1939. He succeeded his father as 3rd baronet in 1912. He was created G.B.E. in 1922.

Sassoon's sister, Sybil, Marchioness of Cholmondeley, informs us that several boxes of his papers were lost during the second world war when his former house, Trent Park, was occupied by the War Office. Lady Cholmondeley adds that her brother did not keep copies of letters or memoranda which he wrote. All that Lady Cholmondeley has is a small collection of approximately 40 letters. A large number of these are from Lord Esher during the period 1916-1922 in which Lord Esher discusses the political situation. Sassoon's replies to these letters are to be found in Lord Esher's own papers, which have been deposited in the library of Churchill College, Cambridge.

JOHN EDWARD BERNARD SEELY, 1st BARON MOTTISTONE (1868-1947)

'Jack' Seely was Conservative M.P. for the Isle of Wight 1900-1904 and Liberal M.P. for the same place 1904-1906 and 1923-1924, for Liverpool (Abercromby) 1906-1910, and for Derbyshire (Ilkeston) 1910-1922. He was Under-Secretary of State for the Colonies April 1908-March 1911, Under-Secretary of State for War 1911-June 1912, Secretary of State for War 1912-March 1914, Parliamentary Under-Secretary of State to the Ministry of Munitions June 1918-January 1919, and Under-Secretary of State for Air January-December 1919. He was created Baron Mottistone in 1933.

Seely's son, the present (4th) Lord Mottistone, has deposited a small collection (26 boxes) of his papers in the Library, Nuffield College, Oxford (ref. Mottistone papers). The collection was weeded by Seely's second wife. The papers have been divided into five main groups: general correspondence; political papers; official papers; military papers; and literary papers and miscellaneous.

There are seven boxes of correspondence 1876-1947. The political papers include speeches, notes, correspondence, and press cuttings concerning Seely's non-official political life. There are many papers on the 1903-1904 fiscal question, and on Chinese labour in South Africa, both controversies which contributed to Seely's becoming a Liberal in 1904. Seely's official papers are divided by his various terms of office at the Colonial Office, the War Office, and

JOHN EDWARD BERNARD SEELY (cont.)

Munitions and Air. In addition there are two boxes of Committee of Imperial Defence papers, 1910-1914. These papers include many papers of the subcommittee on the transportation and distribution of food supplies in time of war 1910-1911. Seely's War Office papers (six boxes) include notes and correspondence concerning his audiences with the King, and his 'Plot' dossier concerning the Curragh mutiny. There are also three boxes of Cabinet memoranda 1912-1914. The military papers concern the administration of the Canadian Cavalry Brigade and include battle reports, reports on individual officers, speeches, and souvenirs of post-war reunions. Seely's literary papers consist of drafts or cuttings of his numerous newspaper articles. A personal name index of the collection has been compiled.

Seely related some of the more adventurous exploits of his life and quoted from a few of his papers in *Adventure* (1930).

THOMAS SHAW (1872-1938)

Tom Shaw was Labour M.P. for Preston 1918-1931. He was Minister of Labour January-November 1924, and Secretary of State for War June 1929-August 1931.

Shaw's only surviving daughter, Mrs M.E. Halliwell, informs us that she has none of her father's papers, and that they were probably destroyed during the bombing of the second world war. Shaw's widow had put most of her belongings into Harrods' furniture store and the store received a direct hit. Mrs Halliwell adds that, in any case, her father never kept speech notes or press cuttings.

SIR HARTLEY WILLIAM SHAWCROSS, BARON SHAWCROSS (1902-   )

Hartley Shawcross was Labour M.P. for St Helens 1945-1958. He was Attorney-General August 1945-April 1951, and President of the Board of Trade April-October 1951. He was knighted in 1945, and created Baron Shawcross (a life peerage) in 1959.

Lord Shawcross informs us that he has kept some press cuttings, copies of speeches, and a few personal letters; but none of these papers is at present available for research.

EMANUEL SHINWELL, BARON SHINWELL (1884-   )

Emanuel Shinwell was Labour M.P. for Linlithgowshire 1922-1924 and 1928-1931, Durham (Seaham) 1935-1950, and Durham (Easington) 1950-1970. He was Financial Secretary to the War Office June 1929-June 1930, Parliamentary Secretary, Department of Mines at the Board of Trade, January-November 1924 and June 1930-August 1931, Minister of Fuel and Power August 1945-October 1947, Secretary of State for War 1947-February 1950, and Minister of Defence 1950-October 1951. He was created Baron Shinwell (a life peerage) in 1970.

Lord Shinwell informs us that although his papers are not at present available for research he hopes to make them available shortly by depositing them in a suitable library, but he has not yet decided which. Lord Wigg is to be Lord Shinwell's literary executor, and Lord Shinwell's papers are to be kept with Lord Wigg's.

Many of Lord Shinwell's papers were thrown away as he went along but he has tried to keep letters which he felt would be of historical interest. He has a large collection of files of articles for the press. Although he never subscribed to a press cutting agency, a large number of press cuttings collected by himself, his family, and friends, has survived, particularly for the 1930s, especially reports of his numerous meetings. There is also material concerning Lord Shinwell's elections — election addresses, leaflets, posters, roneoed news-sheets. Lord Shinwell has kept some papers relating to his Cabinet career, in particular drafts and notes for Cabinet memoranda which he circulated.

EDWARD SHORTT (1862-1935)

Edward Shortt was Liberal M.P. for Newcastle-upon-Tyne (Newcastle-upon-Tyne, West from 1918) 1910-1922. He was Chief Secretary for Ireland May 1918-January 1919, and Secretary of State for Home Affairs 1919-October 1922.

A very small collection of his papers is in the possession of his daughter, Mrs A.D. Ingrams, Bewley Down, nr. Axminster, Devon. Mrs Ingrams informs us that her father kept no diary and that she does not know of the existence of any other papers. Transcripts of almost all the letters in this collection have been deposited in the Library, Nuffield College, Oxford (ref. Shortt Papers).

The collection consists of two books of press cuttings and a few letters. The press cuttings are mainly of a biographical nature, but they cover the 1908 Newcastle by-election which Shortt fought and lost, as well as the December 1910 and the 1918 general elections. Shortt's election campaigns are also represented by photographs, a letter of support from Asquith in 1908, and his election address in 1918. Nothing survives relating to his activities in support of the 1912 Home Rule Bill. A letter from Lloyd George 25 November 1915 thanks Shortt for his work in selecting munition workers to be withdrawn from military units. A very small number of letters survives from Shortt's tenure of the Irish Office including some very hostile letters to Mrs Shortt, as well as letters of regret when Shortt was transferred to the Home Office. Nothing survives from Shortt's tenure of the Home Office apart from letters of regret on his departure, including one from a policeman praising Shortt's handling of the police strikes. An illuminated scroll was presented to Shortt from the Police Federation on 21 November 1922 as an appreciation of his work. There are several photographs and letters of thanks from the Royal Family. The press cuttings include material on Shortt's activities as film censor from 1929 to 1935.

LEWIS SILKIN, 1st BARON SILKIN (1889-1972)

Lewis Silkin was Labour M.P. for Camberwell (Peckham) 1936-1950. He was Minister of Town and Country Planning August 1945-February 1950. He was created Baron Silkin in 1950.

Lord Silkin told us, shortly before his death, that he had made it a practice never to keep any documents. His eldest son, the Hon. Arthur Silkin, confirms that no papers have survived.

SIR JOHN ALLSEBROOK SIMON, 1st VISCOUNT SIMON (1873-1954)

John Simon was Liberal M.P. for Essex (South-West or Walthamstow) 1906-1918 and for the West Riding of Yorkshire (Spen Valley) 1922-1940; he was a Liberal National from 1931. He was Solicitor-General October 1910-October 1913, Attorney-General 1913-May 1915, Secretary of State for Home Affairs 1915-January 1916 and June 1935-May 1937, Secretary of State for Foreign Affairs November 1931-June 1935, Chancellor of the Exchequer 1937-May 1940, and Lord Chancellor 1940-August 1945. He was knighted in 1910, and created G.C.S.I. in 1930, and Viscount Simon in 1940.

Simon's papers are in the possession of his son, the present (2nd) Lord Simon. They are not available for research but long quotations from them are made in Simon's own memoirs *Retrospect* (1952) and in a University of California, Berkeley, Ph.D. thesis by Edward B. Segal, 'Sir John Simon and British Foreign Policy: the Diplomacy of Disarmament in the Early 1930s'. Dr Segal's thesis is available through University Microfilms Ltd (ref. 70-6219). Dr Segal says in his thesis that the biography of Simon by C.E. Bechhofer Roberts ('Ephesian'), *Sir John Simon* (1938), is based to a large extent on memoranda provided by Simon, particularly on his period at the Foreign and Home Offices, and that Simon himself corrected and edited Roberts's manuscript.

Simon's papers fill a large trunk, two tea chests, a suitcase and sixteen box files. The latter contain correspondence roughly sorted in chronological order 1890s-1930. There are 21 volumes of diary or notebooks. The earlier volumes appear to have been kept to help Simon with his speeches, and to keep him informed on particular subjects: there are notes and press cuttings on free trade and licensing. But the later volumes (1938-1940) contain a fairly full narrative of events. Volume eight contains many notes on Liberal Party organization 1922.

SIR JOHN ALLSEBROOK SIMON (cont.)

There is a volume on the 1930-1931 split of the Liberal Party, including a long report of a meeting of leading Liberals 20 November 1930 on proposals for 'a definite understanding with Labour'. The great bulk of the papers is formed by press cuttings 1903-1921, and 1931-1945. Some of the cuttings are arranged by subject, for example, India, successive general election campaigns, the 1938 Czechoslovakia crisis. There are some papers on the General Strike, the 1926-1927 Liberal Party split, the 1931-1932 activities of the Liberal Nationals, and India, particularly the work of the Statutory Commission 1927-1930. The post-1940 papers mainly relate to Simon's legal judgements and opinions, for example, on capital punishment.

Forty-three boxes of Simon's papers as Chairman of the Indian Statutory Commission 1927-1930 — correspondence and evidence — are in the India Office Library (ref. MSS. Eur. F. 77). A list of the papers is being prepared.

Seven volumes of miscellaneous Foreign Office correspondence 1931-1935 are available in the Public Record Office (ref. F.O. 800/285-291).

SIR ARCHIBALD HENRY MACDONALD SINCLAIR, 4th Bt, 1st VISCOUNT THURSO (1890-1970)

Sir Archibald Sinclair was Liberal M.P. for Caithness and Sutherland 1922-1945. He was Secretary of State for Scotland August 1931-September 1932, and Secretary of State for Air May 1940-May 1945. He succeeded his grandfather as fourth baronet in 1912, and was created K.T. in 1941, and Viscount Thurso in 1952.

Many of Sinclair's papers were destroyed during the bombing of the second world war and in a fire at his Caithness home but a large collection of papers has been deposited by his son, the present (2nd) Viscount, in the library of Churchill College, Cambridge. The papers were deposited in several stages, and in varying states of repair. Some of the papers have been listed and are available for research.

The largest section of the collection is Sinclair's general political correspondence 1922-1938. The correspondence is arranged alphabetically within each year. There are several boxes of speeches 1925-1951, and five boxes of the correspondence 1928-1937 of Captain Keith, Sinclair's constituency and estate agent. Sinclair was Liberal Chief Whip 1930-1931 and Leader of the Parliamentary Liberal Party 1935-1945. Thirteen boxes of Liberal organization papers 1932-1939 and six boxes of Scottish Liberal organization papers 1932-1938 are included in this collection. There are also several boxes of League of Nations Union Papers 1936-1939, boxes of papers on the 1929 Electoral Reform Conference and the 1932 Ottawa Conference, and two boxes of personal papers 1942-1952. There are a large number of constituency papers. A second deposit of political correspondence was very badly charred and will not be available for research until it has been repaired and listed. A further deposit of 23 boxes of papers covers politics 1945-1951. These papers are not yet available for research. Eight boxes of private correspondence 1915-1922 include letters from Winston Churchill, Edward Marsh, and Jack Seely. These papers have been listed and are available.

Sinclair's constituency papers, which were deposited with the National Register of Archives (Scotland), have now been added to the collection at Churchill College. There are 23 files, almost all of them correspondence 1923-1937 with the Scottish Office on particular cases arising in Sinclair's constituency though some issues of more general Scottish interest arise. There are two files from Sinclair's tenure of the Scottish Office, largely concerned with departmental work, but they include comments on cabinet conclusions. There is also a file of correspondence 1934-1936 between Sinclair and the Duke of Montrose on the possibility of co-operation between the Liberal party and the Scottish Nationalist party. This correspondence includes much material about the votes and policies of the two parties.

Some — though not all — of Sinclair's papers as Secretary of State for Air are now available at the Public Record Office (ref. AIR 19/73-557). There are a great many departmental files on technical matters such as bomb sights and the defence of factories from aerial attack, but there are also many files of policy papers: correspondence with the Ministries of Aircraft Production and Economic Warfare on the division of responsibilities and cooperation between the three departments; papers on bombing policy over occupied countries and on German crops

SIR ARCHIBALD HENRY MACDONALD SINCLAIR (cont.)

and forests. There are also drafts of some of the Prime Minister's speeches with Sinclair's comments, and Sinclair's own speeches.

A twenty-page memorandum by Sinclair is available in the Gladstone Library (ref. Sinclair Memorandum). It records a number of meetings between Sinclair and Neville Chamberlain 28 August, 2 and 3 September 1939, and meetings of Liberal leaders to consider those meetings. The document, a typed top copy, has manuscript amendments by Sinclair and is initialled by him. It is annotated 'Notes dictated to me by Sir Archibald Sinclair for sending to members of the Liberal Party Committee, T.D. Nudds 1939 August'. Nudds gave the document to the late Sydney Hope, whose executors gave it to the Gladstone Library.

JOHN SINCLAIR, 1st BARON PENTLAND (1860-1925)

John Sinclair was Liberal M.P. for Dumbartonshire 1892-1895 and Forfarshire 1897-1909. He was Secretary for Scotland December 1905-February 1912. He was created G.C.I.E. in 1912, G.C.S.I. in 1918, and Baron Pentland in 1909.

Marjorie, Lady Pentland, Sinclair's wife, wrote *The Right Honourable John Sinclair, Lord Pentland, G.C.S.I. A Memoir* (1928) and quoted from many letters and a diary. She said that the section of the book devoted to his governorship of Madras 1912-1919 was longer than other sections because more material was available, partly because her husband had contemplated writing his memoirs of that period. Unfortunately, after she had published the memoir, Lady Pentland disposed of her husband's papers, and if they still survive, they can no longer be found. Her son, the present (2nd) Lord Pentland, and daughter thought that she might have given papers to the Scottish Record Office, the British Library, or the Hawarden Library, but none of these institutions has any of Sinclair's papers. Sinclair was Sir Henry Campbell-Bannerman's executor, and the last two volumes of the latter's papers, deposited in the British Library (ref. Add. MSS. 52520, 52521), contain letters, copies, and memoirs sent to Sinclair in response to his appeal for letters from Campbell-Bannerman.

SIR BEN SMITH (1879-1964)

Ben Smith was Labour M.P. for Bermondsey (Rotherhithe) 1923-1931, and 1935-1946. He was Parliamentary Secretary to the Ministry of Aircraft Production March 1942-November 1943, Minister Resident in Washington for Supply 1943-May 1945, and Minister of Food August 1945-May 1946. He was created K.B.E. in 1945.

Lady Smith, his widow, has only a very small collection of papers which are not generally available. She informs us that many papers, including diaries, were destroyed in the bombing of the second world war. All that she now has are two volumes of press cuttings on Smith's work as Chairman of the West Midland district of the National Coal Board 1948-1949 and 1946-1950, and a volume of cuttings mostly about Smith's work at the Ministry of Food. The latter volume also includes a collection of obituary notices. In addition to these volumes, Lady Smith has Smith's letter of appointment as a Privy Councillor 1944, a few social notes from Lord Beaverbrook, press cuttings on Smith's appointment to Washington, notes for a lecture on trade unionism given to Camberley Staff College 1934, and telegrams concerning the request of the Australian government for an official visit by Smith in 1945 (he was unable to go because of the 1945 general election).

SIR FREDERICK EDWIN SMITH, 1st Bt, 1st EARL OF BIRKENHEAD (1872-1930)

F.E. Smith was Conservative M.P. for Liverpool (Walton) 1906-1918 and Liverpool (West Derby) 1918-1919. He was Solicitor-General June-November 1915, Attorney General 1915-January 1919, Lord Chancellor 1919-October 1922, and Secretary of State for India November 1924-October 1928. He was knighted in 1915, created G.C.S.I. in 1928, a baronet in 1918, Baron Birkenhead in 1919, Viscount Birkenhead in 1921, and Earl of Birkenhead in 1922.

SIR FREDERICK EDWIN SMITH (cont.)

His papers as Secretary of State for India are in the India Office Library (ref. MSS. Eur. D. 703). These papers have been divided into bound volumes of correspondence with the viceroy and governors, telegrams exchanged with the viceroy, twelve files of departmental papers, miscellaneous files, and miscellaneous files on English political questions. This last section includes papers on the 1926 General Strike, the 1927 Poor Law Amendment Act, and the 1928 parliamentary debates on the case of Major G. Bell Murray.

Only a small collection of papers now exists in the possession of his son, the present (2nd) Earl of Birkenhead, who states that his father never kept a diary nor, on leaving office, did he take away any departmental papers. Of the few which now survive, many have either been quoted or paraphrased in the 2nd Earl's biography, the second edition of which includes additional material: *F.E. The Life of F.E. Smith First Earl of Birkenhead* by his son, the 2nd Earl of Birkenhead (1959).

The surviving papers, which are not generally available for research, comprise fourteen files or envelopes. Several of these are of a miscellaneous nature but some are restricted to a particular subject with a note of their contents on the outside of the file.

The earliest papers are letters, including one from H. Hensley Henson, referring to Smith's appearance before Oxford magistrates following a demonstration during a visit to Oxford by the Prince of Wales in May 1897. Smith's commission in the Oxfordshire Imperial Yeomanry is dated 9 August 1907. There is a small file of early personal letters. Correspondents include Edward Carson 1913, Winston Churchill 1908, 1911, 1913, Lord Fisher 1908, and Andrew Bonar Law 1912. There are a few letters relating to the 1906 election and some election addresses for January 1910.

A large portion of this collection covers Smith's wartime activities. There is correspondence concerning a dispute in 1916 over the calling-up of W.A. Pursey, the Attorney-General's second clerk, who was fit only for garrison duties. There is a letter from Lord Finlay 17 January 1917 in which he states his intention to adhere to Lord Buckmaster's decision not to create any silks for the duration of the war. There is correspondence concerning the organization of a committee by J.H. Morgan to report on the 'breaches of the laws and customs of the war' by the Germans and their allies and on the degree of responsibility of the German General Staff or 'other highly placed individuals'. There is an Imperial War Cabinet Paper on 'Our Attitude towards the Ex-Kaiser' 28 November 1918.

At the end of 1917 Smith undertook a tour of Canada and the U.S.A. to encourage their war efforts. Correspondence concerning this tour and another made in 1923 survive. There is also a file dealing with allegations made by Ellis Powell in November 1918 concerning the Marconi case. There is a six page typed introduction for the second edition of his book (written with J.W.B. Merewether), *The Indian Corps in France* (1917).

There are files of congratulations on his becoming Lord Chancellor and on becoming Secretary of State for India. There is a file of letters from friends and colleagues throughout the twenties, including letters on his resignation in October 1928. There are letters and press cuttings referring to the 1921 Irish Treaty, and letters from successive Viceroys of India, Lord Reading and Lord Irwin. There is also a series of letters from Lord Rothermere March-April 1923 on the need for a new Conservative leader.

There are several files concerning the second Earl's biography including letters giving information about his father's life, as well as the contract and correspondence relating to the publication of the book and two files of reviews. There are press cuttings and photographs of the unveiling of a bust of Lord Birkenhead at the Oxford Union on 4 November 1932.

HASTINGS BERTRAND LEES-SMITH (1878-1941)

Hastings Bertrand Lees-Smith was Liberal M.P. for Northampton 1910-1918, and Labour M.P. for the West Riding of Yorkshire (Keighley) 1922-1923, 1924-1931, and 1935-1941. He was Postmaster-General June 1929-March 1931, and President of the Board of Education March-August 1931.

HASTINGS BERTRAND LEES-SMITH (cont.)

We have not been able to trace any of Lees-Smith's papers. He left most of his estate to his wife for her benefit and, after her death, for their two sons; but we have been unable to trace either Lees-Smith's widow or his children. His widow does not appear in the registers at Somerset House, which either means that she is still alive or that she remarried and died under a different name. Their sons were not named in the probate papers. Lees-Smith was Professor of Public Administration at Bristol University but the university authorities were unable to give us any information about his family — they have no records extant from before the second world war. Another executor named in Lees-Smith's earliest will was the Rev. William Major Scott. Mr Scott, a Congregationalist minister, died before Lees-Smith in 1932. Mr Scott's solicitors were unable to help us to trace his widow though they thought that she was probably now dead and that there were no children of the marriage. There are too many Lees-Smiths in the various telephone directories to write to them all, but we did write to Mr A. Lees-Smith in London and Mr B.I. Lees-Smith in Malmesbury: neither of these two gentlemen is related to H.B. Lees-Smith, nor were they able to help us in any way. Neither the Keighley Labour Party nor the Keighley Public Library was able to give us any help.

SIR REGINALD HUGH DORMAN-SMITH (1899-)

Colonel Reginald Dorman-Smith was Conservative M.P. for Hampshire (Petersfield) 1935-1941. He was Minister of Agriculture and Fisheries January 1939-May 1940, and Governor of Burma 1941-1946. He was knighted in 1937, and created G.B.E. in 1941.

Sir Reginald informs us that, apart from what he has deposited in the India Office Library, he has kept no papers. He says that he left very little in the Ministry of Agriculture since he wrote his own speeches and did much of his own typing. What papers he accumulated in Burma had to be destroyed before the Japanese could capture them though the Japanese did capture his red dispatch box which contained some papers. Enquiries to both the Japanese and American governments have failed to produce any trace of the dispatch box or its contents.

There are eight boxes of papers in the India Office Library (ref. MSS. Eur. E. 215) deposited in 1955 and 1966 and almost entirely concerning Sir Reginald's governorship of Burma. These papers will not be available for research until 1 January 1977. The collection includes the letters patent confirming his appointment, press cuttings, a draft chapter of memoirs on his appointment, daily reports 1941-1942, letters and telegrams 1943-1945, and personal letters and telegrams to the Secretary of State 1945-1946. There is also some correspondence with the Burma and India Office 1946, correspondence with Burmese ministers, and a few official notes and drafts. Several papers concerning the invasion of Burma survive, including a report by Sir Reginald on the Burma campaign 1941-1942 (written in 1943), correspondence and minutes on the return to civil administration in 1945, and an article written by Sir Reginald: 'Civil Government under Invasion Conditions'. There is some correspondence with L.S. Amery. In addition the collection includes Lady Dorman-Smith's diaries for 1941-1946, Sir Reginald's letters to her 1943-1945, and hers to him 1941-1946. There is some miscellaneous personal correspondence 1942-1944 and press cuttings.

JAN CHRISTIAN SMUTS (1870-1950)

Jan Christian Smuts was Minister without Portfolio and a member of the War Cabinet June 1917-January 1919. He was Prime Minister of South Africa 1919-1924 and 1939-1948.

An account of the papers found after Smuts's death, his wishes, and how they were interpreted, is to be found in the 1955 Creighton Lecture by Sir Keith Hancock, *The Smuts Papers* (1956). The greater part of Smuts's early papers was destroyed during the Boer War but what survives includes some of Smuts's student notes, secret telegrams from President Kruger, some letters received by Smuts while on commando, letters from Boer generals and copies of Smuts's replies, some daily jottings, and Smuts's notes on the surrender, including notes of a meeting with General Lord Kitchener. An enormous collection of papers has survived from the post-Boer War period. Rather than break up this collection by returning official papers to the South African and British Governments, it was decided to deposit

JAN CHRISTIAN SMUTS (cont.)

the whole collection in the South African Government Archives, Pretoria (ref. A. 1), after it had been catalogued by the Smuts Archive Trustees. This was done in 1971.

The papers have been divided into Public and Private Papers. The Public Papers were sub-divided into British Government papers (95 volumes) and South African papers (89 volumes). The British papers include 78 volumes 1916-1919 and seventeen volumes 1940-1946. The South African papers have been subdivided as follows: six volumes of South African Republic papers 1897-1902; four volumes of Transvaal papers 1906-1910; three volumes of National Convention papers 1908-1909; and 73 volumes of Union of South Africa papers 1910-1948. This division also includes a volume of Anglo-Boer telgrams 1899-1900, and eight volumes of United Nations papers 1945-1946. Under the South African Archives Act (1962), papers dating from 1926 onwards are not yet open for research. Access to these later papers can only be granted after ministerial permission has been obtained. They will be progressively opened for research at five-year intervals.

The Private Papers have been subdivided into minor and major papers. There are 50 volumes of minor papers; these are mainly routine letters from secretaries, invitations, greetings, and so forth, but there are also parliamentary papers, the papers of the South African National Party 1912-1934 and the papers of the United Party. The major papers, which mainly comprise Smuts's private correspondence, include 'out' letters copied from other collections. There are 102 volumes arranged chronologically, and alphabetically within each volume. A card index has been compiled. Microfilm copies of these papers and of the card index have been given to the University of Cape Town and the Cambridge University Library (ref. Microfilm 666-766, and 832-854). The major papers also include Smuts's law notes, his philosophical writings, speeches and broadcasts 1902-1950, political notes 1899-1950, and one box of papers concerning the South African National Party 1905-1934. There is also a large collection of press cuttings made by Smuts's wife. In 1962 five boxes of the papers of Mr and Mrs Arthur C. Gillett were added to the collection. They include letters from Smuts 1906-1950 and the Gilletts' replies 1917-1919. Typed copies of some of these letters had been put into the correspondence volumes. The original letters are closed till 1 January 1987. Nine reels of microfilm copies of these letters have been deposited in the Cambridge University Library; they are closed till 1985 (ref. Microfilm 773-782).

A large number of the papers have been published, edited by Sir W. Keith Hancock and Jean Van der Poel, *Selection from the Smuts Papers, 1886-1950* (7 vols., Cambridge, 1966-1973). The entire collection was used for Sir W. Keith Hancock's biography: *Smuts: I. The Sanguine Years 1870-1919; II. The Fields of Force 1919-1950* (2 vols., Cambridge, 1962-68). The biography by Smuts's son, Jan Christian Smuts Jnr, *Jan Christian Smuts* (1952) is meant to be only a memoir of his father but it does quote from Smuts's papers. *I Lived in his Shadow*, by Kathleen Mincher, his adopted daughter (1965), is based only on her reminiscences.

PHILIP SNOWDEN, VISCOUNT SNOWDEN (1864-1937)

Philip Snowden was Labour M.P. for Blackburn 1906-1918 and for West Riding of Yorkshire (Colne Valley) 1922-1931. He was Chancellor of the Exchequer January-November 1924 and June 1929-November 1931, and Lord Privy Seal 1931-September 1932. He was created Viscount Snowden in 1931.

In the introduction to *An Autobiography* (2 vols., 1934) Snowden wrote that he never kept a diary but he did have full contemporaneous notes of various important events such as the formation of the first Labour government and the 1931 financial crisis. In the autobiography itself he appears to quote only from published speeches. After writing the autobiography he destroyed many of his papers. Snowden's most recent biographer, Mr Colin Cross, discovered from a family source that what remained was destroyed after the death of Lady Snowden: see his *Philip Snowden* (1966). Snowden's library and a collection of press cuttings and cartoons were given to the Keighley Public Library.

SIR DONALD BRADLEY SOMERVELL, BARON SOMERVELL OF HARROW (1889-1960)

Donald Bradley Somervell was Conservative M.P. for Cheshire (Crewe) 1931-1945. He was Solicitor-General September 1933-March 1936, Attorney-General March 1936-May 1945, and Home Secretary May-August 1945. He was a Lord Justice of Appeal 1946-1954, and a Lord of Appeal in Ordinary 1954-1960. He was knighted in 1933, and created Baron Somervell of Harrow (a judicial life peerage) in 1954.

Somervell had no children and bequeathed his estate including a small collection of papers to his nephew, Mr Robert Somervell. Mr Somervell has given these papers or xerox copies of them to the Bodleian Library (ref. Somervell Papers). The papers include a short political memoir, a journal for 1933-1937, typed copies of letters sent to the King's Proctor concerning the divorce of Mrs Simpson, a memorandum written by the Parliamentary Counsel on the legislation needed if the King were to abdicate, two pages of diary for October 1945, and a transcript of a speech given by J.C. Smuts to the Other Club c. 1942.

The political memoir consists of 84 typed pages which cover Somervell's political and official career. As well as comments on the role of the Attorney-General, it also contains recollections of the legal issues and political personalities of the day.

The journal begins with Somervell's reminiscences of his appointment as Solicitor-General; it is 88ff. long and has a short summary of contents. It also contains details about the abdication of King Edward VIII and for this reason parts of the journal, and the file of copied letters, are closed for research until the death of the Duchess of Windsor. Long extracts from the journal are published in H. Montgomery Hyde, *Baldwin. The Unexpected Prime Minister* (1973).

SIR FRANK SOSKICE, BARON STOW HILL (1902-   )

Frank Soskice was Labour M.P. for Birkenhead (East) 1945-1950, Sheffield (Neepsend) 1950-1955, and Newport 1956-1966. He was Solicitor-General August 1945-April 1951, Attorney-General April-October 1951, Secretary of State for Home Affairs October 1964-December 1965, and Lord Privy Seal 1965-April 1966. He was knighted in 1945 and created Baron Stow Hill (a life peerage) in 1966.

Lord Stow Hill's papers are being listed by the Royal Commission on Historical Manuscripts and they will not be open to research at least until this work has been completed. Lord Stow Hill has destroyed many of his constituency and legal papers but a few fragments survive which reflect his political career. There are a few constituency papers 1960-1963, largely routine, dealing with local issues. There are miscellaneous papers and letters, mostly from M.P.s and trade union officials asking for legal advice, but including a small amount of private social correspondence with parliamentary colleagues such as Clement Attlee and Hugh Gaitskell. There are in addition a few papers concerning Lord Stow Hill's work as a Q.C., particularly his appearance before the International Court at the Hague on behalf of the Indian and Thai governments.

JAMES RICHARD STANHOPE, 7th EARL STANHOPE, 13th EARL OF CHESTERFIELD (1880-1967)

James Richard Stanhope, known as Viscount Mahon from 1875 until he succeeded his father as 7th Earl Stanhope in 1905, was Parliamentary Secretary to the War Office May 1918-January 1919, Civil Lord of the Admiralty November 1924-June 1929, Parliamentary and Financial Secretary to the Admiralty September-November 1931, Parliamentary Under-Secretary of State for War 1931-January 1934, Under-Secretary of State for Foreign Affairs 1934-June 1936, 1st Commissioner of Works 1936-May 1937, President of the Board of Education 1937-October 1938, 1st Lord of the Admiralty 1938-September 1939, and Lord President of the Council 1939-May 1940. He was created K.G. in 1934. He succeeded his kinsman as 13th Earl of Chesterfield in 1952.

Most of the Stanhope family archives, known as the Chevening papers, and covering three centuries of the family's history, have been transferred to the Kent Archives Office. They include some of the 7th Earl's papers but the entire collection is vast — 300 linear feet — and

JAMES RICHARD STANHOPE (cont.)

uncatalogued. Parts of it were listed by the Royal Commission on Historical Manuscripts ten years ago and those papers may at the present time be used; the list may be seen at the National Register of Archives and the Kent Archives Office. However, once the Archives Office begins to catalogue the collection — a task which is envisaged as taking several years — access to all of the papers will be increasingly restricted. Applications for access to the papers should be made to the Kent Archives Office. The numbers in brackets below refer to the Royal Commission on Historical Manuscripts' list.

Stanhope's papers now at the Kent Archives Office include his school reports, some papers concerning his military career including mentions in dispatches, pocket diaries 1902, 1912-1914, and 1918-1958, and journals of foreign tours. There is also some of his correspondence: general correspondence arranged alphabetically 1893-1960 (775-781), which includes some congratulations on achieving his various offices, two letters about his appointment as 1st Lord from Winston Churchill and Sir Andrew Cunningham (1268, 1269), a few papers on his appointment as Lord President (1266), and many letters from his mother 1905-1922. His mother's papers include many letters from him, particularly concerning his foreign tours and his first world war experiences (1101, 1102, 1190, 1211-1218). There is also a typed memoir 'The War of 1914-1918' (784B). No papers concerning Stanhope's official career are mentioned in the Royal Commission on Historical Manuscripts' list.

Aubrey N. Newman, *The Stanhopes of Chevening* (1969) includes a short biography of Stanhope. The book was based on the family archives and the chapter on Stanhope quotes frequently from memoirs compiled between 1945 and 1965.

SIR ALBERT (HENRY) STANLEY, BARON ASHFIELD (1874-1948)

Albert Stanley was Conservative M.P. for Ashton-under-Lyne 1916-1920. He was President of the Board of Trade December 1916-May 1919. He was knighted in 1914 and created Baron Ashfield in 1920.

Neither of Stanley's two daughters has any papers relating to their father's life or career. They think this may well be because he himself was very averse to publicity and so kept nothing.

From 1919 till 1933 Stanley was Chairman of what is now London Transport (he was largely responsible for the passage of the 1933 London Passenger Transport Act). None of Stanley's papers appear to have survived amongst London Transport's papers.

EDWARD GEORGE VILLIERS STANLEY, 17th EARL OF DERBY (1865-1948)

Edward Stanley, Lord Stanley from 1893 until he succeeded his father as the 17th Earl of Derby in 1908, was Conservative M.P. for South-East Lancashire (Westhoughton) 1892-1906. He was Financial Secretary to the War Office November 1900-October 1903, Postmaster-General with a seat in the Cabinet 1903-December 1905, Under Secretary of State for War July-December 1916, Secretary of State for War 1916-April 1918 and October 1922-January 1924, and Ambassador in Paris 1918-1920. He was created K.C.V.O. in 1905, and K.G. in 1919.

A very large collection of his papers has been deposited on loan by his grandson, the present (18th) Earl of Derby, in the Liverpool City Library (ref. 920 (DER) 17). The library already has deposits of nineteenth-century Derby family papers. The papers have been given a preliminary sorting and an outline list of the papers is available; a complete list of the papers will not be available for some time. Lord Derby's permission to read the papers must be obtained by writing to the City Librarian in advance of a visit to the library. The papers were used for, and are extensively quoted in, Randolph S. Churchill, *Lord Derby, King of Lancashire* (1959). Unfortunately, when this biography was being written, many of the letters were moved from the original files and not replaced; in some instances new subject files were created. Stanley's diaries, frequently quoted in this biography, and also used in Robert Blake, *The Unknown Prime Minister: The Life and Times of Andrew Bonar Law 1858-1923* (1955), cannot now be found.

EDWARD GEORGE VILLIERS STANLEY (cont.)

Stanley is said to have written 40 letters a day and certainly this collection comprises an enormous correspondence of both in- and out-letters. There is only a small amount of pre-1918 material; Randolph Churchill stated that the papers for 1900-1908 were missing when he was writing his biography. The papers have been divided into five main divisions: (1) Liverpool papers; (2) Lancashire papers; (3) Government offices; (4) Public Life; and (5) Domestic.

The Liverpool and Lancashire papers reflect Stanley's strong local ties and influence. There is correspondence on royal visits, with and about successive Lord Mayors, with Liverpool University, the Liverpool Chamber of Commerce, and with local politicians, including five files of correspondence with Sir Archibald Salvidge 1911-1928 (1/29-33).

The papers arising from Stanley's terms of public office have been divided by office. Only printed telegrams and reports by Lord Kitchener seem to have survived from his period as Financial Secretary to the War Office, and only draft bills and printed papers from the Post Office. Some correspondence from Stanley's term as Director-General of Recruiting 1916 has survived. Stanley's papers as Under-Secretary and later Secretary of State for War include much correspondence as well as Cabinet papers and official reports. For example there are files of correspondence with Lloyd George September 1916-April 1918, with Sir Douglas Haig and Sir Philip Sassoon August 1916-April 1918, and concerning the Supreme War Council 1918. Some correspondence has survived from Stanley's second tenure of the War Office. Many papers have survived from Stanley's term as British Ambassador in Paris. As well as various subject files, memoranda and minutes, there are correspondence files with specific individuals such as Austen Chamberlain, Lord Robert Cecil, Winston Churchill, and Sir Philip Sassoon.

The 'Public Life' division of papers (4) covers a wide range of topics. There is correspondence with Americans or about America 1930-1947, correspondence concerning various charities and other organizations, correspondence and papers connected with the Royal Commissions and Committees on which Stanley served, such as the Royal Commissions on Divorce and Matrimonial Clauses 1911, on Railways 1914, and on Indian Constitutional Reforms 1933-1934. There is also Stanley's correspondence with the War Office 1926-1944 and with the Paris Embassy 1928-1945. This division also includes Stanley's correspondence with such politicians as Stanley Baldwin 1924-1945, A.J. Balfour 1922, Lord Beaverbrook 1921-1928, Lord Crewe 1923-1928, Lord Curzon 1920-1924, and with the King's successive secretaries 1914-1915, 1924-1941. There is also a file of correspondence about Stanley's visit to Ireland 1921, and a file of memoranda on House of Lords' Reform 1911.

The 'Domestic' division of papers (5) includes family letters and a few typed extracts from Stanley's diary, December 1923, February 1924, and November 1924, as well as papers concerning his houses, his furniture, his finance, and his various clubs.

A further collection of Stanley's War Office papers 1922-1924 is available for research at the Public Record Office (ref. W.O. 137). A wide range of subjects is represented — reparations, Egypt, India, and Ireland — as well as correspondence with the King's private secretaries and with the Prime Minister.

THE HON. OLIVER FREDERICK GEORGE STANLEY (1896-1950)

Oliver Stanley was Conservative M.P. for Westmorland 1924-1945 and Bristol (West) 1945-1950. He was Parliamentary Under-Secretary of State for Home Affairs September 1931-February 1933, Minister of Transport 1933-June 1934, Minister of Labour 1934-June 1935, President of the Board of Education 1935-May 1937, President of the Board of Trade 1937-January 1940, Secretary of State for War January-May 1940, and Secretary of State for Colonial Affairs November 1942-August 1945.

Neither his son nor his daughter knows of the existence of any papers.

CHARLES STEWART VANE-TEMPEST-STEWART, 6th MARQUESS OF LONDONDERRY (1852-1915)

Charles Stewart Vane-Tempest-Stewart, Viscount Castlereagh from 1872 till he succeeded his father as 6th Marquess of Londonderry in 1884, was Conservative M.P. for Down 1878-1884. He was Viceroy of Ireland 1886-1889, Postmaster-General November 1900-August 1902, President of the Board of Education 1902-December 1905, and Lord President of the Council October 1903-December 1905. He was created K.G. in 1888.

Vane-Tempest-Stewart's great-grandson, the present (9th) Marquess of Londonderry, has deposited his family archives in the Durham Record Office (ref. D/LO). The handlist of the papers has been published: S.C. Newton, *The Londonderry Papers* (Durham, 1969). The collection includes only a small number of Vane-Tempest-Stewart's papers (ref. D/LO/F 517-575). The most important part of these papers is probably the extensive series of press cuttings 1886-1915 covering his political career. There are a few personal letters and invitations, some personal receipts and bills, and election expenses for the 1874 South Durham election. There are no personal papers — only estate papers — in the Londonderry Papers at the Public Record Office of Northern Ireland (ref. D. 654).

CHARLES STEWART HENRY VANE-TEMPEST-STEWART, 7th MARQUESS OF LONDONDERRY (1878-1949)

Charles Stewart Henry Vane-Tempest-Stewart, Viscount Castlereagh from 1884 till he succeeded his father as 7th Marquess of Londonderry in 1915, was Conservative M.P. for Maidstone 1906-1915. He was Under-Secretary of State for Air April 1920-July 1921, 1st Commissioner of Works October 1928-June 1929 and August-October 1931, Secretary of State for Air 1931-June 1935, and Lord Privy Seal June-November 1935. He was created K.G. in 1919.

Vane-Tempest-Stewart's grandson, the present (9th) Marquess of Londonderry, has deposited his family archives in the Durham Record Office (ref. D/LO). The handlist of the papers has been published: S.C. Newton, *The Londonderry Papers* (Durham, 1969). The collection includes a small number of Vane-Tempest-Stewart's papers (ref. D/LO/F 585-613 and D/LO/C 236-237). There are four files of parliamentary speeches 1910 and 1921, and a file on his 1906 Maidstone election expenses and the petition to unseat him. There are ten files on the opening in 1921 of the Northern Ireland Parliament (Vane-Tempest-Stewart was Minister of Education and Leader of the Senate in the Government of Northern Ireland 1921-1926). There are some personal accounts and miscellaneous sporting and social papers. There are some files of correspondence 1922-1927 and 1932-1938 arranged alphabetically, including correspondence with Sir Neville Henderson, L.S. Amery, C.R. Attlee, and Herbert Morrison.

Most of Vane-Tempest-Stewart's personal papers are in the possession of his youngest daughter, Lady Mairi Bury, but they are not available for research. Researchers should contact the Public Record Office of Northern Ireland for information about any change in the availability of these papers.

In his autobiography, *Wings of Destiny* (1943), Vane-Tempest-Stewart quoted from his papers, especially letters from J.R. MacDonald and Winston Churchill.

RICHARD RAPIER STOKES (1897-1957)

Richard Stokes was Labour M.P. for Ipswich 1938-1957. He was Minister of Works February 1950-April 1951, Lord Privy Seal April-October 1951, and Minister of Materials July-October 1951.

Approximately 42 boxes of Stokes's papers have been deposited by his family in the Bodleian Library (ref. Stokes Papers). Permission to read the papers must be obtained from Mr J. Hull, 33 Edwardes Square, London W.8. They have not yet been listed.

Stokes's political and official careers are very sparsely represented in this collection; there are files on the 1935 election at Glasgow (Central) — including Stokes's election address, press cuttings, and a campaign diary — and on the 1938, 1945, 1950, and 1955 elections at Ipswich. There is a file of invitation cards and a list of letters of congratulations on his appointment as Minister of Works, a file of congratulations on his appointment as Lord Privy Seal, and a file

RICHARD RAPIER STOKES (cont.)

of press cuttings on his attempt to settle the Persian Oil dispute in 1951. Nonetheless, the collection does enable the researcher to build up a picture of Stokes's career, particularly by the many volumes of press cuttings 1938-1957, and his secretary's engagement diaries 1926-1956. There is also an index of Stokes's speeches 1938-1957 and many speech notes 1950-1955.

One of Stokes's main interests was the Middle East. His interest began in the 1920s when he began to travel on behalf of his family firm, Ransomes and Rapiers. He kept a 'running diary' or 'running notes' of each of his tours, which were sent to his fellow-directors. Stokes continued the habit in politics and in office; for example, he sent notes to Lord Halifax of a conversation he had had with Von Papen in Turkey in 1940, and memoranda and notes of conversations made during a tour of the Middle East in 1947 to Clement Attlee and Ernest Bevin. Stokes's correspondence with Herbert Morrison 1952-1957 and Hugh Gaitskell 1950-1957 includes many assessments by Stokes of the political situation in the Near and Middle East. As well as his 'running notes' there are several files about Palestine 1938-1947, and the Near East, including press cuttings, pamphlets, general correspondence, memoranda, correspondence about parliamentary questions, and letters by Stokes to the press.

Stokes seems to have arranged his correspondence alphabetically; but apart from the correspondence already noted, and some correspondence with Winston Churchill, only the 'A's' seem to have survived: correspondence with Clement Attlee 1938-1954, with the Aga Khan, and with the Ministry of Agriculture and Fisheries.

Stokes's activities during the second world war are represented by files on the loss of H.M.S. *Glorious* (July 1940) including parliamentary questions, some press cuttings and publications of the Parliamentary Peace Aims Group 1939-1941, and several files on the application of regulation 18B which allowed the detention of suspected persons during war time.

Shortly before his death Stokes had begun to read through his papers with a view to writing his memoirs. His notes, for example on Stalin, and on his own Roman Catholicism, have survived.

About 100 letters from Stokes to various members of his family, mostly to his parents, June 1916-March 1919, have been deposited in the Department of Printed Books at the Imperial War Museum (ref. 323.1). They were all written when Stokes was an officer on the Western Front.

A further three boxes of papers demonstrating Stokes's great interest in a Land Values tax is in the possession of Mr V.H. Blundell, Secretary, The United Committee for the Taxation of Land Values Ltd, 177 Vauxhall Bridge Road, London S.W.1. There are three box-files, almost all relating to the activities of the Land Values Group within the Parliamentary Labour Party, of which Stokes was secretary. The Group's activities are well represented; there are notices of meetings, extracts from speeches and articles, information sent to marginal constituencies 1953-1954, distribution lists, and some correspondence files including A.W. Madsen 1950-1951 and 1955-1957, H.G. McGhee, M.P. 1951-1952, and a file of correspondence with Ministers about a rate on land values in 1948.

SIR EDWARD STRACHEY, 4th Bt, 1st BARON STRACHIE (1858-1936)

Edward Strachey was Liberal M.P. for Somersetshire (South) 1892-1911. He was Parliamentary Secretary to the Board of Agriculture and Fisheries December 1909-October 1911 (he had been spokesman for the Board from 1905), and Paymaster-General May 1912-May 1915. He succeeded his father as 4th baronet in 1901, and was created Baron Strachie in 1911.

His only son, the late (2nd) Baron Strachie, informed us that no papers have survived.

(EVELYN) JOHN ST LOE STRACHEY (1901-1963)

John Strachey was Labour M.P. for Birmingham (Aston) 1929-1931, Dundee 1945-1950, and Dundee (West) 1950-1963. He was Under-Secretary of State for Air August 1945-May 1946, Minister of Food 1946-February 1950, and Secretary of State for War 1950-October 1951.

142

JOHN ST LOE STRACHEY (cont.)

Strachey's papers are in the possession of his widow, Mrs Celia Strachey. Mrs Strachey has not yet decided on the ultimate disposition of the papers and they are not generally available. The papers have been used by Hugh Thomas in his biography, *John Strachey* (1973).

The papers consist of 30 box-files covering the period 1920-1963. The bulk of the papers come from the period after 1945 but there are a few earlier papers of considerable interest. There are no papers relating to Strachey's period at the Ministry of Food and very few relating to the War Office.

Possibly of greatest interest are the papers relating to the years 1931-1940, when Strachey was one of the most prominent and possibly the most articulate exponent in Britain of Communism. There are letters from R. Palme Dutt, Harry Pollitt, and other communist leaders on questions of party practice and policy. There is also an interesting collection of papers relating to the Left Book Club (Victor Gollancz, with Strachey and Harold Laski, organized the club and selected the books).

Strachey's later papers chiefly relate to his political writings. He was reconciled with the Labour Party and there are several letters from Hugh Gaitskell, Douglas Jay, and others.

GEORGE RUSSELL STRAUSS (1901-   )

George Russell Strauss was Labour M.P. for Lambeth (North) 1929-1931 and 1934-1950; he has been Labour M.P. for Lambeth (Vauxhall) since 1950. He was Parliamentary Secretary to the Ministry of Transport August 1945-October 1947, and Minister of Supply 1947-October 1951.

Mr Strauss informs us that he has kept very few papers concerning his political career and those few are closed for his lifetime. Mr Strauss has said that what papers he leaves may be deposited in the British Library of Political and Economic Science.

The papers of the North Lambeth Constituency Labour Party, recently deposited in the British Library of Political and Economic Science, include one box of Mr Strauss's constituency papers. The collection is not yet listed but papers can be made available.

The transcript of the interview which Mr Strauss gave to the Nuffield Oral History Project (see Robert Skidelsky, *Politicians and the Slump. The Labour Government of 1929-1931* [1967], p. 186) is not available for research.

SIR WILLIAM SUTHERLAND (1880-1949)

William Sutherland was Liberal M.P. for Argyll 1918-1924. He was Chancellor of the Duchy of Lancaster April-December 1922. He was created K.C.B. in 1919.

Sutherland had no children and the sole executrix and beneficiary of his will was his wife. She died two months before he did, having appointed him sole executor and main beneficiary of her own will. Their estate was divided between their respective families. We have been unable to trace any of Sutherland's wife's brothers and sisters. The children of Sutherland's own sisters know of no papers, nor does the solicitor who acted for them. Enquiries made by the Barnsley Local History Library to the area headquarters of the National Coal Board (who took over George Fountain & Co., which Lady Sutherland partly owned), to the local Liberal Party, and at the Sutherlands' house, Birthwaite Hall, have produced no clues to the whereabouts or fate of Sutherland's papers.

HAROLD JOHN TENNANT (1865-1935)

Harold John Tennant was Liberal M.P. for Berwickshire 1894-1918. He was Parliamentary Secretary to the Board of Trade January 1909-October 1911, Financial Secretary to the War Office 1911-June 1912, Under-Secretary of State for War 1912-July 1916, and Secretary for Scotland July-December 1916.

His daughter, Miss Alison Tennant, informs us that no papers have survived. Miss Tennant thinks that many papers were destroyed early in the second world war when her mother moved house. This is confirmed by her mother's former secretary, Mrs Hayesmore.

FREDERIC JOHN NAPIER THESIGER, 1st VISCOUNT CHELMSFORD (1868-1933)

Frederic John Napier Thesiger succeeded his father as 3rd Baron Chelmsford in 1905; he was created K.C.M.G. in 1906, G.C.S.I. in 1916 and Viscount Chelmsford in 1921. He was Viceroy of India 1916-1921, and 1st Lord of the Admiralty January-December 1924.

Thesiger's grandson, the present (3rd) Lord Chelmsford, has not yet come across any of Thesiger's papers. Thesiger's daughter, the late Anne, Lady Inchiquin, whose husband was Thesiger's A.D.C. when he was Viceroy of India, did not know of any papers. Her sister, the Hon. Mrs Monck, has only a volume of copied extracts from Thesiger's letters to his wife 1914-1915 (when he was on active service in India), and a collection of watercolours painted by her mother when she was vice-reine.

Thesiger's papers as Viceroy of India were deposited in 1962 by his son, the 2nd Viscount Chelmsford, in the India Office Library (ref. MSS. Eur. E. 264). Thesiger's papers were bound up by the India Office in the customary way: there is one volume of correspondence with the King 1916-1921; five volumes of correspondence with the Secretary of State; eight volumes of telegrams exchanged with the Secretary of State: two volumes of correspondence with persons in England and abroad; ten volumes of correspondence with persons in India; and two volumes of speeches. In addition, there are ten volumes of dispatches exchanged between the Secretary of State and the Viceroy as Governor-General in Council; a volume of letters, memoranda, and minutes on various proposals for Indian self-government 1916-1917; 25 volumes of reports on the Persian political situation 1916-1921, compiled by the Government of India's Foreign and Political Department; and sixteen volumes on the Afghan political situation 1916-1921, and Afghan claims to representation at the Peace Conference.

All Souls College, Oxford, of which Thesiger was Warden when he died, has none of his papers.

DAVID ALFRED THOMAS, VISCOUNT RHONDDA (1856-1918)

David Alfred Thomas was Liberal M.P. for Merthyr Tydfil 1888-1910, and Cardiff 1910. He was President of the Local Government Board December 1916-June 1917, and Minister of Food Control 1917-July 1918. He was created Baron Rhondda in 1916, and Viscount Rhondda in 1918.

A collection of 350 of Thomas's letters has been deposited by his daughter in the National Library of Wales (ref. D.A. Thomas Papers). The collection has been sorted but not catalogued. Most of the letters date from 1891-1895 and concern Thomas's political and industrial activities. His correspondents include constituents, Welsh leaders, and leading members of the Liberal Party. Subjects covered include Disestablishment of the Church in Wales, Thomas's revolt with D. Lloyd George, Herbert Lewis, and Frank Edwards against the Government in 1894, the eight-hour day in the mines, and women's suffrage. The collection also includes some genealogical material, press cuttings, copies of the *Journals* published by the Food Ministry whilst Thomas was there, and political pamphlets and tracts.

D.A. Thomas: Viscount Rhondda by his daughter and others (1921) quotes from some of Thomas's letters and includes reminiscences of him by his daughter, by J.R. Clynes, and by the then Sir William Beveridge. J. Vyrnwy Morgan, *Life of Viscount Rhondda* (1919), does not quote from unpublished material but was written with the help of Thomas's brother.

JAMES HENRY THOMAS (1874-1949)

James Henry Thomas was Labour M.P. for Derby 1910-1936; he became a National Labour M.P. in 1931. He was Secretary of State for Colonial Affairs January-November 1924 and November 1935-May 1936, Lord Privy Seal June 1929-June 1930, and Secretary of State for the Dominions 1930-November 1935.

A collection of Thomas's papers, formerly in the possession of his sons, has been deposited in the Kent Archives Office (ref. no. U 1625). A list of the papers is available.

JAMES HENRY THOMAS (cont.)

Thomas's *My Story* (1937) quotes from a few letters, including correspondence with J.R. MacDonald in February 1930 when Thomas offered to resign. But, according to W.G. Blaxland, in *J.H. Thomas: A Life for Unity* (1964), Thomas never kept a diary and wrote few letters. This seems to be borne out by the collection, of which a predominant feature is the very useful collection of press cuttings filling 33 volumes and covering the period 1919-1934. Some 200 miscellaneous letters have survived. Thomas's correspondents include Raymond Asquith, the Prime Minister's eldest son, who was killed in 1916 and who was a prospective Liberal candidate in Derby (five letters). There are six letters from Lord Beaverbrook 1918-1936, twelve from Lord Rothermere 1933-1934, and twenty from J.R. MacDonald 1923-1937. There are sixteen drafts or notes for speeches.

A few fragments survive from Thomas's official career, including an offer (declined) from Lloyd George in December 1916 of the Ministry of Labour. From Thomas's periods in both the Colonial and Dominions Offices, correspondence with governors survive. There is also a copy of a declaration made by Violet Digby in 1924 relating to the publication of the Zinoviev letter. A circular letter to governors dated 7 February 1936 sets out the economic position and prospects for the colonies. As Lord Privy Seal Thomas had special responsibility for unemployment and a few papers concerning this survive, including papers connected with his dispute with Sir Oswald Mosley, during which Thomas offered to resign.

Very few papers in the collection relate to Thomas's trade union activities: a few letters concerning job applications, letters and memoranda on the refusal of the Irish railway men to carry troops because of intimidation in 1920, and papers connected with the National Union of Railwaymen's refusal to give Thomas a pension. There is also a report of the British Labour delegation to the U.S.A. 4 May-2 June 1917.

CHRISTOPHER BIRDWOOD THOMSON, BARON THOMSON OF CARDINGTON (1875-1930)

Christopher Thomson was created Baron Thomson of Cardington in 1924. He was Secretary of State for Air January-November 1924 and June 1929-October 1930.

Thomson, who was unmarried, died in the R101 disaster. His brother, Col. R.G. Thomson, does not know of the existence of any of his brother's papers. The late Sir Christopher Bullock, Thomson's Principal Private Secretary at the time of his death, did not know of any papers; nor does the present (2nd) Lord Amwell, whose father was Under-Secretary of State for Air 1929-1931 and a great friend of Thomson. The Public Record Office has no more than the usual accumulation of private office material.

The late Princess Marthe Bibesco, in *Lord Thomson of Cardington: A memoir and some letters* (1932), quoted from her own long correspondence with Thomson and informed us that Thomson's mother permitted her to look at his correspondence. Some of these letters were quoted in Princess Bibesco's memoir but the fate of the originals is unknown.

Thomson's book, *Smaranda* (1926), includes an account in diary form of his wartime service from March 1915 mainly in England, Romania, Russia, and the Middle East; and a few entries on his post-war work at the Paris Peace Conference and his earliest election campaigns. In the 'Compiler's Preface' Thomson wrote that 'General Y' (himself) 'was aa profuse, discursive scribbler and notoriously indiscreet. Many entries in the diary have been entirely omitted and others rigorously expurgated. . .' Maie Casey (Lady Casey) in her memoirs, *Tides and Eddies* (1966), p. 51, records that she was a neighbour and friend of Thomson at the time he was writing *Smaranda*. The book, she writes, was in 'diary form', and Thomson 'read to me from this material, altering passages as he read, ironing them out and polishing. . .' Lady Casey informs us that the diary section of *Smaranda* 'was based on his diaries and was certainly *authentic* . . . Any alterations he made through reading part one to me were not substantial, but only the minor revisions that any writer makes when he hears the sounds and rhythms of his written words'.

The second and third parts of *Smaranda* are semi-autobiographical stories based on Thomson's personal observation and experience.

CHRISTOPHER BIRDWOOD THOMSON (cont.)

Thomson's *Old Europe's Suicide* (1920) is a narrative, partly in autobiographical form, of British policy in the Balkans 1912-1919. It contains no quotations from contemporary documents.

SIR WILLIAM LOWSON MITCHELL-THOMSON, 2nd Bt, 1st BARON SELSDON (1877-1938)

William Lowson Mitchell-Thomson was Conservative M.P. for Lanarkshire (North-West) 1906-1910, Down (North) 1910-1918, Glasgow (Maryhill) 1918-1922, and Croydon (South) 1923-1932. He was Parliamentary Secretary to the Ministry of Food April 1920-March 1921, Parliamentary Secretary to the Board of Trade 1921-October 1922, and Postmaster-General November 1924-June 1929. He succeeded his father as second baronet in 1918, and was created K.B.E. in 1918, and Baron Selsdon in 1932.

Mitchell-Thomson's grandson, the present (3rd) Lord Selsdon, informs us that he has little of interest relating to his grandfather's career: only letters of appointment; orders, certificates, and decorations; and cuttings of obituaries have survived.

GEORGE TOMLINSON (1890-1952)

George Tomlinson was Labour M.P. for Lancashire (Farnworth) 1938-1952. He was Joint Parliamentary Secretary to the Ministry of Labour and National Service February 1941-May 1945, Minister of Works August 1945-February 1947, and Minister of Education 1947-October 1951.

Tomlinson's only daughter, Mrs D. Hardman, does not know of the existence of any papers. Fred Blackburn, *George Tomlinson* (1954) was based largely on talks Mr Blackburn had with Tomlinson before his death. Mr Blackburn has no Tomlinson papers.

SIR CHARLES PHILIPS TREVELYAN, 3rd Bt (1870-1958)

Charles Trevelyan was Liberal M.P. for the West Riding of Yorkshire (Elland) 1899-1918, and Labour M.P. for Newcastle-upon-Tyne (Central) 1922-1931. He was Parliamentary Secretary to the Board of Education October 1908-August 1914, and President of the Board of Education January-November 1924 and June 1929-March 1931. He succeeded his father as third baronet in 1928.

Trevelyan's papers (65 boxes — they form a part of a larger collection of family papers) were deposited by his family in the Library of the University of Newcastle-upon-Tyne in 1967 (ref. Trevelyan of Wallington MSS.). A preliminary sorting and listing of the papers has been carried out. Researchers wishing to read these papers should apply in advance to the University Librarian. The later sections of the papers (post 1932) are not yet open for research.

The papers include nineteen boxes of political correspondence 1900-1927. Evidence that 'Special Correspondence' series were kept lies in the existence of a box of correspondence with Herbert Samuel mainly before 1900. There are several boxes of political papers, though these are mainly speech notes; they include three boxes of papers concerning the Union of Democratic Control 1914-1919. There are four boxes of speeches 1899-1933, and eight boxes of press cuttings mainly 1894-1911, including one box on the 1910 elections and one on the 1924 elections. Papers have also survived from the 1922, 1929, and 1931 elections, and on the U.S.S.R. 1930. There seem to be no papers from Trevelyan's term of office apart from some 1924 Cabinet memoranda, and letters of congratulation on entering the Cabinet in 1924.

In *From Liberalism to Labour* (1921) Trevelyan explained how he made the transition between the two political parties. A biography based on all of the papers, including those not yet available for research, is being written by Mr A.J.A. Morris of the London School of Economics.

GEORGE CLEMENT TRYON, 1st BARON TRYON (1871-1940)

George Clement Tryon was Conservative M.P. for Brighton 1910-1940. He was Under-Secretary of State for Air December 1919-April 1920, Parliamentary Secretary to the Ministry of Pensions 1920-October 1922, and October 1940-February 1941, Minister of Pensions 1922-January 1924, November 1924-June 1929, September 1931-June 1935, Postmaster-General 1935-April 1940, Chancellor of the Duchy of Lancaster April-May 1940, and 1st Commissioner of Works May-October 1940. He was created Baron Tryon in 1940.

Neither of his two sons knows of the existence of any papers relating to their father's political career.

EDWARD TURNOUR, 6th EARL WINTERTON (1883-1962)

Edward Turnour, Viscount Winterton until he succeeded his father as 6th Earl Winterton (an Irish peerage, which did not disqualify him from sitting in the House of Commons) in 1907, was Conservative M.P. for Sussex (Horsham) 1904-1918, Sussex, West (Horsham and Worthing) 1918-1945, and for Sussex, West (Horsham) 1945-1951. He was Under-Secretary of State for India March 1922-January 1924, and November 1924-June 1929, Chancellor of the Duchy of Lancaster May 1937-January 1939, and Paymaster-General January-November 1939. He was created Baron Turnour (in the United Kingdom peerage) in 1952.

Turnour left all his papers to his literary executor, Mr Alan Houghton Brodrick. These are not at present available for research. There are quotations from the papers, including the copious diaries, in Turnour's *Pre-War* (1932), *Orders of the Day* (1953), and *50 Tumultuous Years* (1955), as well as in Mr Houghton Brodrick's *Near to Greatness. A Life of the 6th Earl Winterton* (1965).

PATRICK CHRESTIEN GORDON WALKER (1907-   )

Patrick Gordon Walker was Labour M.P. for Smethwick 1945-1964, and for Leyton 1966-1974. He was Parliamentary Under-Secretary of State for Commonwealth Relations October 1947-March 1950, Secretary of State for Commonwealth Relations 1950-October 1951, Secretary of State for Foreign Affairs October 1964-January 1965, Minister without Portfolio January 1966-August 1967, and Secretary of State for Education and Science 1967-April 1968.

Mr Gordon Walker informs us that his papers are not available for research. He quotes from his papers, particularly from his diaries, in *The Cabinet* (1970, revised edn. 1972).

(DAVID) EUAN WALLACE (1892-1941)

Captain Euan Wallace was Conservative M.P. for Warwickshire (Rugby) 1922-1923 and for Hornsey 1924-1941. He was Civil Lord of the Admiralty November 1931-June 1935, Under-Secretary of State for Home Affairs June-November 1935, Secretary for Overseas Trade at the Board of Trade 1935-May 1937, Parliamentary Secretary to the Board of Trade 1937-May 1938, Financial Secretary to the Treasury 1938-April 1939, and Minister of Transport 1939-May 1940.

Wallace's widow, Mrs Herbert Agar, has given his diary to the Bodleian Library (ref. MS. Eng. hist. c.495-498). The diary covers the period 22 August 1939 to 18 October 1940. It appears to have been dictated daily and contains a considerable amount of detail, for example, on the Cabinet meetings leading up to the declaration of war, and on the events leading up to the formation of Churchill's government in May 1940. At that time Wallace was offered the Office of Works on condition he took a peerage. He refused because he did not wish to preclude a further career in the House of Commons and instead accepted the post of Senior Regional Commissioner for Civil Defence in London, a post originally offered to, but refused by, Herbert Morrison. The diary stops in October 1940 when Wallace fell ill.

SIR WILLIAM HOOD WALROND, 2nd Bt, 1st BARON WALERAN (1849-1925)

William Walrond was Conservative M.P. for Devonshire (East) 1880-1885 and Devonshire (Tiverton) 1885-1906. He was Chancellor of the Duchy of Lancaster August 1902-December 1905. He succeeded his father as second baronet in 1889, and was created Baron Waleran in 1905.

Lady Waleran, widow of the second Baron Waleran, Walrond's grandson, informs us that all his papers were destroyed during the first world war.

The Walrond Papers (1913) by the Hon. Charlotte M.L. Walrond, Walrond's daughter-in-law, is a family history that prints many family documents but carries the story only as far as Walrond's father, the first baronet.

STEPHEN WALSH (1859-1929)

Stephen Walsh was Labour M.P. for South-West Lancashire (Ince; Lancashire, Ince from 1918) 1906-1929. He was Parliamentary Secretary to the Ministry of National Service March-June 1917, Parliamentary Secretary to the Local Government Board 1917-January 1919, and Secretary of State for War January-November 1924.

Neither of his two surviving sons nor his surviving daughter knows of the existence of any papers; they believe that any papers that might have been kept were destroyed.

SIR (JOHN) TUDOR WALTERS (1868-1933)

John Tudor Walters was Liberal M.P. for Sheffield (Brightside) 1906-1922 and for Cornwall (Penryn and Falmouth) 1929-1931. He was Paymaster-General October 1919-October 1922 and September-November 1931. He was knighted in 1912.

Walters's only son and his son's wife are now dead. His only daughter, Mrs H. Lucey, has nothing other than a copy of her father's book *The Building of 12,000 Houses* (1927), a history of the Industrial Housing Association. Walters's grand-daughter, Signora Ann Sangiovanni, Via della Mole 12, 00041 Albano, Rome, Italy, has a small collection of press cuttings. They include a volume of cuttings mainly for 1903-1909 covering Walters's parliamentary and constituency activities. There are also several articles by Walters from *John Bull, The Spectator,* and *The Listener,* about post-war housing problems, and several obituary notices.

SIR JOHN LAWSON WALTON (1852-1908)

John Lawson Walton was Liberal M.P. for Leeds (South) 1892-1908. He was Attorney-General December 1905-January 1908. He was knighted in 1905.

A small collection of press cuttings is in the possession of Walton's grandson, Mr I.D.M. Reid, Barton's Mead, 44 Harriotts Lane, Ashtead, Surrey. The collection consists of two albums of obituary notices and a small file of press cuttings from Walton's political career in the 1890s. In addition there are some election cards, leaflets, election addresses, and election posters (including one in Hebrew). There are also several reprints of speeches by Walton and other Liberals, for example a lecture by Walton on Parliament, and a speech by Sir Henry Fowler on the Indian Frontier problem in 1894.

No other members of the family have any papers relating to Walton's life and political career.

MAURICE WEBB (1904-1956)

Maurice Webb was Labour M.P. for Bradford (Central) 1945-1955. He was Minister of Food February 1950-October 1951.

Webb left all his chattels to his widow, Mabel. She died in 1963 leaving her estate to Miss D.A. Williams. Miss Williams informs us that she does not know of the existence of any papers, though Webb was thought to have been writing a memoir at the time of his death. We have been unable to contact Webb's brother, Harold.

SIDNEY JAMES WEBB, BARON PASSFIELD (1859-1947)

Sidney Webb was Labour M.P. for Durham (Seaham) 1922-1929. He was President of the Board of Trade January-November 1924, Secretary of State for both Dominion and Colonial Affairs June 1929-June 1930, and for Colonial Affairs alone June 1930-August 1931. He was created Baron Passfield in 1929.

A large collection of the papers of both Sidney and Beatrice Webb has been deposited in the British Library of Political and Economic Science (ref. Webb papers). Written application to read these papers should be made in advance; special permission is needed to read Beatrice Webb's diaries.

The Webb collection has been divided into public and private papers. The former include 350 volumes of material collected for the Webbs' history of English local government, two volumes of papers related to their Board of Trade activities 1911-1918, twenty volumes relating to *New Statesman* special supplements 1915-1917 (the Webbs founded the *New Statesman* in 1913), and six volumes of papers on East African politics 1929-1931. There are also nine boxes of papers from the reconstruction committee of the Ministry of Reconstruction 1916-1918, and five boxes on the relief of distress 1914-1915.

The most important section of the private papers is Beatrice Webb's diaries 1873-1943. The manuscript version fills 58 notebooks and includes some letters and photographs. Beatrice Webb herself typed out many of her diaries and began editing them for publication. The following were the result: Beatrice Webb, *My Apprenticeship* (1926), *Our Partnership* ed. Margaret I. Cole and Barbara Drake (1948), *Beatrice Webb's Diaries 1912-1924* and *1924-1932* ed. Margaret I. Cole (1952-56), *Beatrice Webb's American Diary 1898* ed. David A. Shannon (Madison, Wisc., 1963), and *The Webbs' Australian Diary 1898* ed. A.G. Austin (Melbourne, 1965). Margaret Cole has also written a memoir, *Beatrice Webb* (1945). *Sidney and Beatrice Webb* by Mary A. Hamilton (1933) is not based on any previously unpublished material. Kitty Muggeridge is Beatrice Webb's niece and her biography (co-author Ruth Adam), *Beatrice Webb: A Life* (1967), is based on Potter family papers as well as the Webb collection.

In addition to the diaries, the papers include Potter family letters, Sidney Webb's letters to Beatrice 1890-1940, and letters from the Webbs given to the library after an appeal in 1956. There are personal papers concerning the various honours and certificates granted to the Webbs, their personal finances and their houses, including a catalogue to the sale of contents in 1948. There are papers related to the Webbs' political and public work, including a collection of papers made by Sidney Webb concerning the 1931 crisis. There is material concerning their many publications, lecture notes, articles, broadcasts and speeches, their bibliographies on various subjects such as the poor law and syndicalism, six boxes of Fabian Society papers, particularly concerning resident summer schools, and papers concerning the foundation, history, and administration of the London School of Economics (apart from his role in founding the L.S.E., Sidney Webb was Professor of Public Administration there 1912-1927).

SIR RICHARD EVERARD WEBSTER, Bt, VISCOUNT ALVERSTONE (1842-1915)

Richard Everard Webster was Conservative M.P. for Launceston 1885, and for the Isle of Wight 1885-1900. He was Attorney-General June 1885-February 1886, August 1886-August 1892, and July 1895-May 1900. He was knighted in 1885, and created G.C.M.G. in 1893, a baronet in 1900, Baron Alverstone in 1900, and Viscount Alverstone in 1913.

Webster's only son died before his father; his widow, who became Mrs I. Ramsey, tells us that all his papers were burnt during the second world war. Webster's grand-children by his only daughter — Lady Durston and Miss Barbara Mellor — do not have any papers; they think that Webster's papers were either destroyed at his death or later when their parents moved house. Webster's solicitors do not have any papers. In *Recollections of Bar and Bench* (1914) Webster gave his reminiscences of his tenure of the Attorney General's office and his period as Lord Chief Justice (1900-1912), but quoted from no original documents.

JOSIAH CLEMENT WEDGWOOD, 1st BARON WEDGWOOD (1872-1943)

Josiah Wedgwood was Liberal M.P. for Newcastle-under-Lyme 1906-1919 and Labour M.P. for the same constituency 1919-1942. He was Chancellor of the Duchy of Lancaster January-November 1924. He was created Baron Wedgwood in 1942.

Wedgwood's eldest daughter and executrix, the Hon. Mrs H.B. Pease, 1 High Street, Girton, Cambridge, is currently gathering together his papers but she has not yet decided where to deposit them.

The papers, almost all of which are letters, fill approximately seventeen box files. They have been weeded, and then divided into family and non-family letters, and arranged chronologically. The family letters naturally contain mainly family news but there are occasional comments on the political situation, particularly in Wedgwood's later letters to his children, who were themselves politically active. The non-family letters cover a wide range of topics but particularly reflect Wedgwood's interest in land value taxation, and East Africa. Mrs Pease informs us that she thinks it probable that many papers relating to Wedgwood's support for Zionism and his work to help Jews fleeing Germany in the 1930s were destroyed in 1938-1939 when he feared that England might be invaded. Most of Wedgwood's papers concerning the History of Parliament Trust have been returned to that body, but they are not generally available.

Several papers survive from Wedgwood's activities in the first world war, in particular a five page carbon copy of a letter from Wedgwood to Winston Churchill 24 April 1915 describing the landings at Gallipoli. This is quoted in full in Wedgwood's *Memoirs of a Fighting Life* (1940). Copies of this book are rare because the warehouse containing them was bombed just before they were distributed. The letter is also quoted in C.V. Wedgwood's biography of Wedgwood, *The Last of the Radicals* (1951). There is a report by Wedgwood on his impression of the Western Front, including his assessment of various generals, and his views on conscription, a letter to Lloyd George 11 October 1916 expressing his horror at the fact that British losses in France were four times those of the French army, a memorandum January 1917 on the deplorable nature of British propaganda in the U.S.A., and a memorandum on the effect of possible peace terms on East Africa. Wedgwood went to East Africa in 1916; typed notes of his conversations with the Governor, officials, and settlers survive. Wedgwood was sent to Siberia in 1918 to encourage the Russians to continue fighting and to persuade them of the worthlessness of German offers. His instructions have survived. He went to Siberia via the U.S.A. and his manuscript notes about that part of his voyage survive. Wedgwood's advice to the War Office (that they were wasting their money by helping the White Russians) was not well received and he was quickly recalled. On the way home he began to write an account for his grand-children of what he had done in the war; he never completed this.

No papers have survived from Wedgwood's tenure of the Duchy of Lancaster but there are carbon copies of letters he wrote in 1924 to J.H. Thomas about East Africa and to Lord Olivier about India. There are several long letters from Lajpat Rai concerning the course of Indian nationalism and also letters from the Viceroy, Lord Irwin (later the Earl of Halifax). There is a letter from Philip Snowden 24 November? 1924 expressing strong disapproval of J.R. MacDonald's fitness to continue as Leader of the Labour Party. There are two files of miscellaneous letters from the 1930s and early 1940s. Wedgwood's correspondents included Anthony Eden, Neville Chamberlain, Stanley Baldwin, Lord Beaverbrook, and Winston Churchill; to the latter he sent frequent long letters on how to conduct the war. There are also letters about his memoirs and congratulations on his peerage.

There is a volume of press cuttings, mainly reviews of Wedgwood's various publications, and some leaflets on land reform.

Twenty-one volumes of press cuttings 1908-1943 concerning Wedgwood's political career are in the Local Studies Collection in the Horace Barks Reference Library, Stoke City Library. They appear to have been compiled by or for Wedgwood and include miscellaneous pamphlets and election manifestos.

ANDREW WEIR, 1st BARON INVERFORTH (1865-1955)

Andrew Weir was Minister of Munitions (later Minister of Supply) January 1919-March 1921. He was created Baron Inverforth in 1919.

Only two files of papers have survived in the possession of Weir's son, the present (2nd) Baron Inverforth, Baltic Exchange Buildings, 21 Bury Street, London E.C.3. One file contains obituaries from local, national, and the shipping trade press. The other file includes correspondence with Lloyd George 1919-1921 on Weir's wish to resign ('As you know I am not a politician. . .'). There is also a collection of letters of appreciation when Weir did resign.

Some of Weir's papers as Surveyor-General of the Army 1917-1918, and Private Office papers have survived in the records of the Ministry of Munitions at the Public Record Office (ref. MUN/4/6467-6644 and MUN/4/6651-6868). They include correspondence on the supplies of such different items as boots, clothing, and airship fabric, notes for material for a speech to be made by Lord Curzon on the contribution of the Dominions and Allies July 1918, and notes of meetings and interviews held March-April 1917. There are also replies to letters of appreciation February 1919-October 1920, correspondence with Lloyd George on the need to reduce expenditure August-September 1920, and also papers relating to Weir's coat of arms and pedigree.

SIR WILLIAM DOUGLAS WEIR, 1st VISCOUNT WEIR (1877-1959)

William Douglas Weir was President of the Air Board April 1918-January 1919. He was knighted in 1917, and created G.C.B. in 1934, Baron Weir in 1918 and Viscount Weir in 1938.

Forty-two box-files of papers have been deposited by his son, the present (2nd) Viscount Weir, in the library of Churchill College, Cambridge. A list of the papers is available. The papers were used extensively by W.J. Reader in *Architect of Air Power: the Life of the First Viscount Weir of Eastwood* (1968). Reader says that Weir broke up his own files and only kept documents he thought historically important. Very few changes from Weir's own arrangement of the papers have been made by Churchill College: the papers are organized by subjects chronologically arranged; they form 24 sections. Most of the papers date from after 1918; it is possible that earlier papers were damaged by water and so destroyed. There are reports, 'impressions', and 'thoughts' as well as correspondence. No private correspondence is included in the collection.

Six boxes of papers have survived from Weir's term of office at the Air Ministry. They include notes on Lord Trenchard and ten items about the dismissal of the Hon. Miss Violet Douglas-Pennant as Commandant of the W.R.A.F. Weir's continued interest in air power is reflected by papers from the Civil Aviation Committee of which he was Chairman, 1918-1920.

Papers also survive relating to his interest in the coal industry: correspondence, the evidence submitted by Weir to the Coal Industry Commission, press cuttings, memoranda, and pamphlets 1919-1921, 1925-1926, and 1930. Weir was a member of the Trade Boards Acts Committee 1921-1922: correspondence, evidence, memoranda about the operation of the various boards, draft reports, and parliamentary debates have survived. Minutes, sub-committee papers and Weir's own notes to the Cabinet Committee for the Amalgamation of the Forces' Common Services 1922-1923 have also survived. There are minutes (and draft minutes), evidence, Weir's notes, and draft reports for the Cabinet Committee on the Reduction of National Expenditure 1922-1923. There are also papers from the Committee of Imperial Defence's Fleet Air Arm Committee 1923-1924 including undated notes by Trenchard, papers concerning electricity supply 1923-1933, railway electrification 1929-1931, the merger of the Cunard and White Star Lines, the 1931 financial crisis (including a transcript of a meeting between the government and the National Confederation of Employers Organization, as well as Weir's own notes on the situation), papers about air disarmament 1932, the Ottawa Conference of 1932 (Weir was an industrial adviser), papers from the Cabinet Committee on Trade and Employment Panels 1932-1934, the C.I.D.'s Defence Policy Sub-Committee 1936-1937, the Air Ministry 1935-1938 (Weir was adviser to the Minister), and the Ministry of Supply 1939-1941 (Weir was Director-General of Explosives at the Ministry).

JOSEPH WESTWOOD (1884-1948)

Joseph Westwood was Labour M.P. for Midlothian and Peeblesshire (Peebles and Southern) 1922-1931, and Stirling and Falkirk Burghs 1935-1948. He was Parliamentary Under-Secretary of State for Scotland March-August 1931 and May 1940-May 1945, and Secretary of State for Scotland August 1945-October 1947.

His son, Councillor David Westwood, and other members of Westwood's family do not know of the existence of any surviving papers.

JOHN WHEATLEY (1869-1930)

John Wheatley was Labour M.P. for Glasgow (Shettleston) 1922-1930. He was Minister of Health January-November 1924.

Wheatley had a son and a daughter. Dr Elizabeth Wheatley has none of her father's papers. Her brother, Mr J.P. Wheatley, had a small collection of letters, ministerial papers, press cuttings, and pamphlets which were used by R.K. Middlemas in *The Clydesiders* (1965). We have been unable to contact Mr Wheatley to determine the fate of these papers.

ELLEN CICELY WILKINSON (1891-1947)

Ellen Wilkinson was Labour M.P. for Middlesbrough (East) 1924-1931 and Durham (Jarrow) 1935-1947. She was Parliamentary Secretary to the Ministry of Pensions May-October 1940, Parliamentary Secretary to the Ministry of Home Security 1940-May 1945, and Minister of Education August 1945-February 1947.

Miss Wilkinson left all her estate to her sister Annie, who died in 1963. After Miss Annie Wilkinson's death, all Ellen Wilkinson's personal letters, etc., were destroyed in accordance with her sister's wishes. Miss Wilkinson's two brothers now have no papers relating to their sister's life. A few newspaper cutting and scrapbooks have been deposited at Transport House.

A biography is being written by Martha R. McCulloch, 53 Gower St., London W.C.1.

DAVID REES REES-WILLIAMS, BARON OGMORE (1903-   )

David Rees-Williams was Labour M.P. for Croydon (South) 1945-1950. He was Parliamentary Under-Secretary of State for the Colonies October 1947-March 1950, United Kingdom Delegate to the United Nations Assembly 1950, Parliamentary Under-Secretary of State for Commonwealth Relations July 1950-June 1951, and Minister of Civil Aviation June-October 1951. He was created Baron Ogmore in 1950. He was President of the Liberal Party 1963-1964.

Lord Ogmore, 48 Cheyne Court, Royal Hospital Road, London SW3 5TS, informs us that he has preserved many papers concerning his personal, professional, and official life. These papers have been selected and arranged by subject or by particular locations; they fill one tin trunk, two deed boxes, five suitcases, and twelve foot of shelving. They include many volumes of press cuttings, Lord Ogmore's letters to his parents while he was practising as a solicitor in the Straits Settlement in the 1930s, and his diaries from 1939 to the present. Lord Ogmore is willing to grant some access to his papers to a few senior researchers.

SIR EDWARD JOHN WILLIAMS (1890-1963)

Edward John Williams was Labour M.P. for Glamorganshire (Ogmore) 1931-1946. He was Minister of Information August 1945-March 1946. He was British High Commissioner in Australia 1946-1952. He was created K.C.M.G. in 1952.

Lady Williams died in 1968. We have been unable to contact either of Williams's daughters.

THOMAS WILLIAMS, BARON WILLIAMS OF BARNBURGH (1888-1967)

Thomas Williams was Labour M.P. for the West Riding of Yorkshire (Don Valley) 1922-1959. He was Parliamentary Secretary to the Ministry of Agriculture and Fisheries May 1940-May 1945, and Minister of Agriculture and Fisheries August 1945-October 1951. He was created Baron Williams of Barnburgh (a life peerage) in 1961.

THOMAS WILLIAMS (cont.)

Williams's son, the Hon. H. Williams, 11 Lombardy Drive, Berkhamsted, Hertfordshire, has a very small collection of his father's papers. There are some notes for a speech on the fiftieth anniversary of the Parliamentary Labour Party in 1956, and outline notes on some of Williams's contemporaries: George Lansbury, Arthur Henderson, Ramsay MacDonald, James Maxton, Winston Churchill, Sir Austen Chamberlain, and Sir Anthony Eden. There are several letters from C.R. Attlee: thanking Williams for his wartime work, 26 May 1945; informing him that a general election is to be called, 19 September 1951; commiserating with Williams's ill-health; and discussing the Labour M.P.s first elected in 1922 — they produced ten Cabinet Ministers, four other ministers, seven under-secretaries, a chief whip, five junior whips, and one deputy chairman. There is a letter from B. Dais (14 June 1933) thanking Williams for his work for the release of political prisoners in India and for his work on behalf of the Congress party. There are also several letters on Williams's retirement from the House in 1959. The collection also includes a few press cuttings: there are several articles from 1933 on Williams's work for the much-reduced Labour Opposition, and several from 1959 on Williams's retirement.

Digging for Britain (1965) is a volume of Williams's reminiscences; it does not quote from unpublished sources.

SIR HENRY URMSTON WILLINK, 1st BT (1894-1973)

Henry Willink was National Conservative M.P. for Croydon (North) 1940-1948. He was Minister of Health November 1943-August 1945. He was created a baronet in 1957.

Willink retained only a small collection of papers; this was deposited in 1973 by his widow in the Library of Churchill College, Cambridge (ref. Willink papers). Applications for access should be made to the Keeper of the Archives. They mostly relate to Willink's family and university affairs, but there are a few papers relating to his political career: a draft election manifesto 1938; correspondence with W.S. Morrison about Czechoslovakia 1938; and his letter of appointment as Minister of Health 1943. The collection also includes a copy of an unpublished autobiography entitled 'As I Remember'.

JOHN WILMOT, BARON WILMOT OF SELMESTON (1895-1964)

John Wilmot was Labour M.P. for Fulham (East) 1933-1935, Lambeth (Kennington) 1939-1945, and Deptford 1945-1950. He was Joint Parliamentary Secretary to the Ministry of Supply November 1944-May 1945, and Minister of Supply August 1945-October 1947. He was created Baron Wilmot of Selmeston in 1950.

To save her executors the trouble of dealing with both her own and her husband's papers, Lady Wilmot has burnt what papers she had.

(JAMES) HAROLD WILSON (1916-   )

Harold Wilson was Labour M.P. for Lancashire (Ormskirk) 1945-1950 and has been Labour M.P. for Lancashire (Huyton) since 1950. He was Parliamentary Secretary to the Ministry of Works August 1945-March 1947, Secretary for the Overseas Trade Department in the Board of Trade March-October 1947, President of the Board of Trade 1947-April 1951, and Prime Minister October 1964-June 1970, and from March 1974.

Mr Wilson informs us that until 1956 he destroyed most of his papers as he went along, so that very little material has survived from his early political life. His papers are not available for research. Many letters and memoranda are cited in Mr Wilson's *The Labour Government 1964-1970. A Personal Record* (1971).

SIR WALTER JAMES WOMERSLEY, 1st Bt (1878-1961)

Walter James Womersley was Conservative M.P. for Grimsby 1924-1945. He was Assistant Postmaster-General December 1935-June 1939, and Minister of Pensions 1939-August 1945. He was knighted in 1934 and created a baronet in 1945.

SIR WALTER JAMES WOMERSLEY (cont.)

Womersley's daughter, Mrs C.H. Moseley, Westbrooke House, Market Harborough, Leicester-shire, has a small suitcase of papers. Most of these papers are photographs or press cuttings. There are many photographs of Womersley performing his various official duties. There are several articles by Womersley including a few of the weekly articles which he wrote for the *Grimsby Telegraph* on his Parliamentary activities. There are also several biographical articles, obituaries, and tributes. There are some miscellaneous letters from Neville Chamberlain and Stanley Baldwin thanking Womersley for his support. There is also a long and interesting letter from Womersley to his wife describing the interview in which Winston Churchill asked him to stay on as Minister of Pensions in May 1940. The only papers surviving from Womersley's political campaigns are his election address for the Grimsby municipal elections of 1911 (Womersley was a Town Councillor 1911-1923, Mayor 1922-1923, and Alderman 1923-1945), his election address for 1929, and a copy of the *Grimsby News* 8 June 1945 with the results of the 1945 general election. No ministerial papers have survived in this collection but there are a few letters of support from November 1942 when the cabinet decision not to increase pensions was attacked. The correspondents include Sir John Anderson and James Stuart. The incident is referred to in Lord Winterton, *Orders of the Day* (1953), pp. 296-297. Womersley wrote to Lord Winterton after the publication of the book giving his own version; Lord Winterton's reply (23 April 1954), hoping that Womersley has not taken the criticism personally, survives.

Despite his defeat in 1945 Womersley remained politically active; this is demonstrated by a large bundle of notes for speeches given during the late forties and the 1950 and 1951 general elections. There is also a letter from Lord Woolton 2 November 1951 thanking him for his work and another from Lord Derby 28 October 1951 on the need to keep active Conservative groups in Labour strongholds. There is some correspondence on Womersley's various honours.

Such a small number of papers survived because Womersley lived at the Constitutional Club when in London; he had no room for storage there. His wife did not normally keep his letters. Womersley's grandson, Sir Peter Womersley, 2nd Bt, has no papers concerning his grandfather.

EDWARD FREDERICK LINDLEY WOOD, 1st EARL OF HALIFAX (1881-1959)

Edward Wood was Conservative M.P. for the West Riding of Yorkshire (Ripon) 1910-1925. He was Parliamentary Under-Secretary of State for the Colonies April 1921-October 1922, President of the Board of Education 1922-January 1924 and June 1932-June 1935, Minister of Agriculture and Fisheries November 1924-November 1925, Viceroy of India 1926-1931, Secretary of State for War June-November 1935, Lord Privy Seal 1935-May 1937, Lord President of the Council 1937-March 1938, Secretary of State for Foreign Affairs 1938-December 1940, and Ambassador to Washington 1941-1946. He was created G.C.S.I. in 1926, K.G. in 1931, and Baron Irwin in 1925; he succeeded his father as 3rd Viscount Halifax in 1934, and was created Earl of Halifax in 1944.

Wood's papers are held by his son, the present (2nd) Earl of Halifax, of Garrowby, Yorkshire. The papers are in the process of being listed; those papers already listed are described in the list of the Hickleton (Wood) papers, sections A4.410 and A7.8. Copies of this list are available at the British Library and the National Register of Archives. A card index of names is being compiled. A microfilm of some of the papers, particularly those relating to the period 1938-1939, and to Wood's term as Ambassador, has been deposited in the library of Churchill College, and will soon be available (ref. Halifax microfilm). Arrangements can be made for the papers to be read at the York City Library or at the Borthwick Institute, York, rather than at Garrowby.

The papers were divided by Wood himself into 21 divisions according to his terms of office as Viceroy, Lord President, Foreign Secretary, and Ambassador. Some of the divisions comprise Wood's speeches, lectures, articles, and letters to the press. Other divisions have a subject basis: papers on Wood's regiment, the Queen's Own Yorkshire Dragoons; papers on the Abdication crisis; notes by Wood on '. . . the present [1922] discontents of the Conservative Party'; papers concerning the 1938 resignation of Anthony Eden. Other divisions (nos. 14-21) consist of letters from Stanley Baldwin 1924-1947, C.R. Attlee 1955, R.A. Butler 1940, Neville and Mrs Chamberlain 1939-1956, Winston Churchill 1940-1956, and Anthony Eden

EDWARD FREDERICK LINDLEY WOOD (cont.)

1937-1957. Wood's diaries for the years 1922-1956 (in 41 volumes) are described in section
A7.8 of the list.

A further collection of Wood's papers as Viceroy was deposited in the India Office Library
(ref. MSS. Eur. C. 152). The collection consists of 38 volumes of correspondence, most of it
printed and indexed. There is a volume of correspondence with the King 1926-1931, five
volumes of letters and five volumes of telegrams exchanged with the Secretary of State, and
a further five volumes of departmental telegrams. There are also three volumes of letters and
telegrams exchanged with people in England, and six volumes of letters and telegrams exchanged
with people in India. There is a volume of correspondence with the Secretary of State concerning
the Statutory Commission on India 1926-1929, and another with Sir John Simon, the Commission's Chairman 1927-1929. There is a volume of correspondence from Wood's visit to
England June-October 1929, when he urged the establishment of the Round Table Conference,
printed proposals for Indian reforms by Wood and others 1930, and a volume of the proceedings
of the Round Table Conference 1930-1931. There are also various notes, Legislative Assembly
decisions, Orders in Council and a volume of correspondence with his father.

Twenty volumes of Foreign Office miscellaneous general correspondence 1938-1940 are
to be found in the Public Record Office (ref. F.O. 800/309-328). Further volumes are being
prepared for deposit in this class.

Many of Wood's papers, including his diary, are quoted in the Earl of Birkenhead, *Halifax:
the Life of Lord Halifax* (1965). Wood himself quoted from his papers and gave his reminiscences in *Fulness of Days* (1957).

SIR (HOWARD) KINGSLEY WOOD (1881-1943)

Kingsley Wood was Conservative M.P. for Woolwich (West) 1918-1943. He was Parliamentary Secretary to the Ministry of Health November 1924-June 1929, Parliamentary Secretary
to the Board of Education September-November 1931, Postmaster-General 1931-June 1935,
Minister of Health 1935-May 1938, Secretary of State for Air 1938-April 1940, Lord Privy
Seal April-May 1940, and Chancellor of the Exchequer 1940-September 1943. He was knighted
in 1918.

Wood's adopted daughter, Mrs Marjorie Brothers, informs us that she has no papers which
belonged to her father. His estate was administered by his law firm, Messrs Kingsley Wood &
Co. They have deposited a small collection of press cuttings in the library of Kent University
(ref. Kingsley Wood papers). The collection, the result of a subscription to a press cutting
agency, covers 1905-1940. There are fifteen quarto books for 1905-1923, ten folio books for
1924-1940, a volume on the 1918 Woolwich by-election, and a collection of unsorted cuttings
for 1940.

Some of Wood's Air Ministry papers are now available at the Public Record Office (ref.
AIR 19/25-72, 556). They include papers of the Air Defence Research Committee, correspondence with J. Moore-Brabazon, Sir Nevile Henderson, Winston Churchill, Lord Londonderry,
Sir Archibald Sinclair, Lord Trenchard, and others. There is also some correspondence 1938-
1939 with Conservative Central Office.

THOMAS McKINNON WOOD (1855-1927)

Thomas McKinnon Wood was Liberal M.P. for Glasgow (St Rollox) 1906-1918. He was
Parliamentary Secretary to the Board of Education April-October 1908, Parliamentary Under-
Secretary of State for Foreign Affairs 1908-October 1911, Financial Secretary to the
Treasury 1911-February 1912 and July-December 1916, Secretary for Scotland 1912-July
1916, and Chancellor of the Duchy of Lancaster July-December 1916.

A small collection of his papers has been given by his daughter-in-law, Mrs C. McKinnon
Wood, to the Bodleian Library (ref. MSS. Eng. hist. c.499-500; d.311-312).

The papers comprise one box of correspondence, a collection of pamphlets, two volumes
of press cuttings covering the years 1906-1908, and a book of cuttings collected on McKinnon
Wood's death. All the correspondence dates from the twentieth century apart from papers

THOMAS McKINNON WOOD (cont.)

concerning the burial of McKinnon Wood's parents. There is a letter from Harold Harmsworth 1901 on London County Council (L.C.C.) and Liberal Party politics; a letter from John Sinclair 1902 about McKinnon Wood's candidature for the Orkneys; several letters 1906 asking McKinnon Wood to stay on the L.C.C.; some notes for a speech to the L.C.C., and a solicitor's letter concerning a defamatory article in the *Standard* January 1907; a letter from Sir Henry Campbell-Bannerman 2 November 1907 offering a knighthood; letters of congratulation on McKinnon Wood's appointment to office at the Board of Education and the Foreign Office; several letters from Edward Grey on the conduct of Foreign Office business; a letter from McKinnon Wood to his Aunt Anne [?] 1911 relating the circumstances of his appointment to the Treasury and including a comment on his work by Grey: 'I have always felt quite safe all the time'. There is some correspondence May 1915 with John Gulland and Asquith on the Cabinet reconstruction, and whether or not the Secretary for Scotland should be in the Cabinet. There is another long letter to Aunt Anne in 1916 explaining why he had accepted an apparent demotion in returning to the Financial Secretaryship at the Treasury.

The collection of fifteen pamphlets consists of speeches and articles written by McKinnon Wood, mainly while he was a member of the L.C.C. 1892-1907. They put the case of the Progressive Party, for example, *The London County Council: Three Years' Progressive Work* (1901); *The Progressive Party, Past and Present* (1904); and *Under Moderate Rule, First Year of 'Municipal Reform'* (1908). There is one pamphlet concerning McKinnon Wood's work at the Foreign Office: *British Commerce and the Declaration of London* (1911); and one reflecting his post-war views: *Government Extravagance makes the People Poor* (Cheltenham, 1921).

ARTHUR WOODBURN (1890-   )

Arthur Woodburn was Labour M.P. for Stirlingshire and Clackmannanshire (Clackmannan and East Stirlingshire) 1939-1970. He was Parliamentary Secretary to the Ministry of Supply August 1945-October 1947, and Secretary of State for Scotland 1947-February 1950.

Mr Woodburn informs us that he never kept any notes, diaries, or other papers relating to Cabinet business for fear that they might get into the wrong hands. He has deposited five letters in the National Library of Scotland. The letters are from Keir Hardie, Ramsay Mac-Donald, David Kirkwood, Robert Smillie, and Alexander Wilkie (ref. MS. 7198, ff. 125-9). The library also has a list of articles by Mr Woodburn written for the *Labour Standard* 1927-1930 (ref. MS. Acc. 3693). Mr Woodburn was President of the National Council of Labour Colleges for over 30 years; the Council's papers are also in the National Library of Scotland.

GEORGE WYNDHAM (1863-1913)

George Wyndham was Conservative M.P. for Dover 1889-1913. He was Under Secretary of State for War October 1898-November 1900 and Chief Secretary for Ireland 1900-March 1905.

The bulk of Wyndham's papers are in the possession of the Duke of Westminster, The Grosvenor Estate Office, 53 Davies Street, London W.1. The papers form a part of the much larger collection of Wyndham's wife's papers (her first marriage was to the eldest son of the first Duke of Westminster). The papers have been partially arranged; they are not generally available.

Possibly the most interesting items in the collection are George Wyndham's letters to his wife. There are 21 files for the period 1887-1913; the letters have been arranged in chronological order and there is a brief note made by the Duke of Westminster's archivist on each file. Since no private office papers appear to have survived from Wyndham's term of office at the War Office and as Chief Secretary for Ireland, these letters form an important record of his activities and interests. Many of the letters, particularly from the earlier period, are purely personal; but there is some political comment, for example a description of Sir John Brunner as 'a bounder' who 'on account of his wealth' is 'somebody in the Radical Party', and a description of the formation of Arthur Balfour's government in 1902. Wyndham had been Balfour's private secretary 1887-1889 and, from the letters to his wife, he seems to have

GEORGE WYNDHAM (cont.)

remained a staunch supporter for the rest of his life. There are disappointingly few surviving letters from Balfour in this collection. Perhaps the major political event recorded by these letters is the passage of the Parliament Act in 1911: there is a good deal of information about Conservative tactics during that period.

Complementary to the series of letters from Wyndham to his wife are her own letters to him, as well as letters from his mother (ten files), his brother Guy, and his three sisters, Mary, Countess of Wemyss, Madeline, Mrs Adeane, and Pamela, Lady Glenconner, as well as some papers of Denis Hyde, one of Wyndham's private secretaries. The papers of another private secretary, George Fitzhardinge Berkeley, as well as those of Wyndham's Permanent Under-Secretary at the Irish Office, Sir Anthony (later Lord) MacDonnell, are in the Bodleian Library (ref. MS. Eng. hist. c.321 and MSS. Eng. hist. a.11-12; b.206; c.350; d.235-238; e.215-218).

There is also a large box of unsorted constituency papers and a small amount of material relating to Wyndham's literary activities: five folders of poems, some articles, and correspondence with Hilaire Belloc.

As these papers were only discovered in 1969, they were not used by John Biggs-Davison in his biography, *George Wyndham; A Study in Toryism* (1951); indeed he states that his 'supreme debt' is to the *Life and Letters of George Wyndham* by J.W. Mackail and Guy Wyndham (2 vols., 1924). These volumes include selections from letters from George Wyndham to his contemporaries, that is, letters which may be found in the papers of those individuals. The two volumes also drew on a more extensive, privately printed, edition of Wyndham's letters compiled by his brother Guy Wyndham: *Letters of George Wyndham 1877-1913* (2 vols., Edinburgh, 1915). Both the biography and the volumes of letters are available in the British Library, the Bodleian Library, and elsewhere. Some of the originals of these letters are in the possession of Guy Wyndham's son, Mr Francis Wyndham, 19 Lonsdale Road, London W. 11. Mr Wyndham has nine volumes of letters, five of which contain George Wyndham's letters to his parents 1877-1886, 1898-1905 (approximately 320 letters). There are also three albums of letters from all of the Wyndham children to their parents 1868-1879, and an album compiled after George Wyndham's death, containing letters of sympathy, photographs, and mementoes. The album includes letters from A.J. Balfour and Mark Sykes, and an obituary of George Wyndham published by Sykes in the *Saturday Review* 14 June 1913.

SIR EDWARD HILTON YOUNG, 1st BARON KENNET (1879-1960)

Edward Hilton Young was Liberal M.P. for Norwich 1915-1923 and 1924-1929, and Conservative M.P. for Kent (Sevenoaks) 1929-1935. He was Financial Secretary to the Treasury April 1921-October 1922, Parliamentary Secretary for the Department of Overseas Trade September-November 1931, and Minister of Health 1931-June 1935. He was created G.B.E. in 1927, and Baron Kennet in 1935.

Young's papers are in the possession of his son, the present (2nd) Lord Kennet, 100 Bayswater Road, London W.2. They have been listed in great detail by the National Register of Archives.

Young himself appears to have gone through his papers and his last arrangement has been maintained: an alphabetical arrangement by writer with the exception of some subject files. There are over 170 letters from his father 1882-1930 and over 70 from his mother. There are many letters from his political contemporaries though few from Lloyd George (Young was Chief Whip of the Lloyd George Liberals in 1922).

Young's subject files cover a wide range. Perhaps the most interesting to political historians is that concerning his resignation from the Liberal Party in 1926, because he felt Lloyd George's land proposals were too socialistic. The file contains correspondence with Lloyd George February 1926, and also a letter from Stanley Baldwin welcoming Young into the Conservative Party May 1926. There is a file of miscellaneous papers concerning the Department of Overseas Trade and two boxes of Cabinet memoranda, mainly on Health Ministry topics — rents, health insurance, maternity services, and town and country planning. On the latter subject there are notes of discussions with Lloyd George. There are files of speeches, broadcasts, and

SIR EDWARD HILTON YOUNG (cont.)

articles by Young, and volumes of press cuttings. There is also a draft autobiography 'In and Out', mainly written in 1959, and diaries for 1914-1918.

Young's wife's papers, included in the same collection, are an important source of information about her husband as well as about her own distinguished life. There are a considerable number of his letters to her 1919-1946, as well as her diaries for 1910-1946 and her correspondence with the leading figures of her time — including two volumes of correspondence with H.H. Asquith 1912-1926. Young edited selections from his wife's diaries: *Self-Portrait of an Artist* (1949).

COLLECTIONS IN INSTITUTIONS

This list is arranged in alphabetical order of institutions with cross-references from more commonly used names to the formal title. As in the main part of the guide, collections are listed by the family name of each minister. As well as a list of the collections in each institution, we have given the address, the officer to whom enquiries should be directed, and any special regulations. Most of these details have been taken from the Royal Commission on Historical Manuscripts, *Record Repositories in Great Britain* (5th ed., 1973). Several institutions specify that researchers should make a written application and appointment, sometimes enclosing a character reference. Researchers are strongly advised to make such written application, even where it is not specified: collections are sometimes kept in outside stores and are not immediately accessible. Advance warning is particularly necessary for unlisted collections, so that the library can try to arrange for the member of its staff who knows most about such collections to be at hand. Brackets ( ) round the name of a collection indicate that the papers are not those of a cabinet minister but that they are relevant to the study of the career of a cabinet minister.

AUSTRALIAN NATIONAL LIBRARY
See National Library of Australia

AUSTRALIAN WAR MEMORIAL
P.O. Box 345, Canberra City, A.C.T. 2601, Australia
The Director
Munro-Ferguson

BATTERSEA DISTRICT LIBRARY
265 Lavender Hill, London S.W.11
The Reference Librarian
Burns

BEAVERBROOK LIBRARY
33 St Bride Street, London E.C.4. tel (01) 353-2444
The Hon. Director
Hours: Monday-Friday 10-4. Closed bank holidays and other times at discretion of Trustees or Hon. Director
Application must be made in writing first.
Aitken; Davidson; Lloyd George, D.; Law, A.B.; Lee

BIRMINGHAM UNIVERSITY LIBRARY
The Main Library, P.O. Box 363, The University, Edgbaston, Birmingham B15 2TT.
tel. (021) 472-1301, ext. 171
The University Librarian
Hours: Monday-Friday 9-10 (MSS. reading room open 9-8.45); Saturday 9-12.30 (during term); Monday-Friday 9-5; Saturday 9-12.30 (during vacation). Closed all Saturdays during August.
Chamberlain, N.; Chamberlain, J.; Chamberlain, A.; Eden

BODLEIAN LIBRARY
Oxford OX1 3BG. tel. (0865) 44675
The Keeper of Western Manuscripts
Hours: Monday-Friday 9-7 (10 in full term); Saturday 9-1
Addison; Asquith; Balfour, A.J. (Sandars); Montague-Barlow; Birrell (Magill); Griffith-Boscawen; Bryce; Carrington; Chamberlain, J. (Dodson); Crookshank; Davidson; Worthington-Evans; Fisher, H.A.L.; Goschen; Grigg, E.; Harcourt; Creech Jones; Key; Mackenzie; Maclean; Macpherson; Marquis; Milner; Palmer, R.C. & W.W.; Pollock; Ponsonby; Sankey; Somervell; Stokes; Wallace; McKinnon Wood, T.; Wyndham (Berkeley and MacDonnell).

BRADFORD CITY LIBRARIES
Central Library, Prince's Way, Bradford BD1 1NN. tel. (0274) 33081
The City Librarian
Hours: Monday-Friday 9-9; Saturday 9-6.
Jowett

B.B.C. WRITTEN ARCHIVES CENTRE
B.B.C., Caversham Park, Reading
The Written Archives Officer
A charge of 50p per day is made for the use of the centre's records.
Chuter Ede

BRITISH LIBRARY, DEPARTMENT OF MANUSCRIPTS (formerly British Museum)
Great Russell Street, London WC1B 3DG. tel. (01) 636-1555
The Keeper of Manuscripts
Hours: Monday-Saturday 10-4.45
Balfour, A.J.; Campbell-Bannerman; Brodrick; Burns; Cave; Cecil, Lord Robert; Cooper; Cross, R.A; Chuter Ede; Arnold-Forster; Giffard; Gladstone, H.J.; Kitchener; Macmillan, H.P.; Ritchie; Robinson

BRITISH LIBRARY OF POLITICAL AND ECONOMIC SCIENCE
Houghton Street, Aldwych, London WC2A 2AE. tel. (01) 405-7686
The Librarian
Hours: Monday-Friday 10-9.20; Saturday 10-5.50; in August, Monday-Friday 10-5
Dalton; Lansbury; MacDonald, J.R.; Strauss; Webb, S.

BRITISH MUSEUM: see British Library

CALIFORNIA STATE UNIVERSITY, NORTHRIDGE
University Library, Northridge, California 91324, U.S.A.
The Chairman, Bibliography Department
Burns

CAMBRIDGE UNIVERSITY LIBRARY
West Road, Cambridge CB3 9DR. tel. (0223) 61441
The Librarian
Hours: Monday-Friday 9-10 (term), 9-7 (vacation); Saturday 9-1
Baldwin; Hoare; Crewe-Milnes; Smuts

CARMARTHENSHIRE RECORD OFFICE
County Hall, Carmarthen. tel. (0267) 6641.
The County Archivist
Hours: Monday-Friday 9-5
Campbell

CHRIST CHURCH, OXFORD
Oxford. tel. (0865) 42201
The Librarian
Hours: weekdays in term: 9-10.30; weekdays in vacation: 9-1 and 2-5; Saturday in term:
9-6; Saturday in vacation: 9-1
Cecil, R.A.T.G. (3rd Marquess of Salisbury)

CHURCHILL COLLEGE, CAMBRIDGE
Cambridge CB3 ODS. tel. (0223) 61200
The Keeper of the Archives
Hours: Monday-Friday 9-5, by appointment
A 30-year closure rule is usually applied to papers in their care.
*Alexander; Attlee; Bevin; Churchill; Maxwell-Fyfe; Grigg, P.J.; Hankey; Inskip; Cunliffe-Lister;
Lloyd; Lyttelton, A. & O.; McKenna; Margesson; Sinclair, A.; Weir, W.; Willink*

COLEG HARLECH
Harlech, Wales
The Librarian
Griffiths

CONSERVATIVE RESEARCH DEPARTMENT
24 Old Queen Street, London SW1H 9HX. tel. (01) 930-1471
G.D.M. Block, O.B.E.
Papers may be seen only by prior appointment.
Sanders

DOUGLAS LIBRARY
Queen's University Archives
Queen's University, Kingston, Ontario, Canada
The University Archivist
Bruce, V.A.; Grigg, E.

DUKE UNIVERSITY
Durham, North Carolina 27706, U.S.A.
Manuscript Department, William R. Perkins Library
The Assistant Curator for Cataloguing
Asquith; Balfour, A.J.; Brodrick; Noel-Buxton

DURHAM COUNTY RECORD OFFICE
County Hall, Durham. tel. (0385) 4411, ext. 576
The County Archivist
Hours: Monday 8.45-5.15, Tuesday-Friday 8.45-4.45; evenings by arrangement
Chaplin; Vane-Tempest-Stewart

EPSOM BOROUGH LIBRARY
Bourne Hall, Ewell, Epsom, Surrey
The Librarian
Chuter Ede

THE FAWCETT LIBRARY
Fawcett House, 27 Wilfred Street, London S.W.1
The Librarian
Emmott

FLINTSHIRE RECORD OFFICE
The Old Rectory, Hawarden, Deeside CH5 3NR. tel. (0244 53) 2364
The County Archivist
Hours: Monday-Friday 9-12.30, 1.30-5.30
Gladstone, H.J.

GLADSTONE LIBRARY
The National Liberal Club, P.O.Box 347, Whitehall Place, London S.W.1. tel. (01) 930-9871
The Librarian
Sinclair

GLOUCESTERSHIRE RECORDS OFFICE
Shire Hall, Gloucester GL1 2TG. tel. (0452) 21444
The County Archivist
Hours: Monday-Friday 9-5
Hicks Beach

GREATER LONDON RECORD OFFICE
County Hall, London SE1 7PB. tel (01) 633-8116
The Head Archivist
Hours: Monday-Friday 9.45-4.45; Saturday morning by arrangement
Burns

GUILDFORD MUNIMENT ROOM
Castle Arch, Guildford GU1 3SX. tel. (0483) 66551
The Archivist
Hours: Monday-Friday 9-4.45; Saturday (usually) 9-3.45; closed for an hour at midday
Brodrick; Onslow, R.W.A.; Onslow, W.H.

HAMPSHIRE RECORD OFFICE
20 Southgate Street, Winchester. tel. (0962) 63153
The County Archivist
Hours: Monday-Friday 9.15-1, 2-4.30
Ashley; Palmer, W.W.

HEREFORD COUNTY RECORD OFFICE
The Old Barracks, Harold Street, Hereford. tel. (0432) 5441
The County Archivist
Hours: Monday-Friday 9.15-5
James

HOUSE OF LORDS RECORD OFFICE
House of Lords, London S.W.1. tel. (01) 219-3000
The Clerk of the Records
Hours: Monday-Friday 9.30-5.30
Benn; Emmott; Gibson; Samuel

IMPERIAL WAR MUSEUM
Department of Libraries and Archives, Imperial War Museum, Lambeth Road, London S.E.1.
tel. (01) 735- 8922
The Keeper of Libraries and Archives
Hours: Monday-Friday 10-5
Stokes

INDIA OFFICE LIBRARY, EUROPEAN MANUSCRIPTS SECTION
Foreign and Commonwealth Office, 197 Blackfriars Road, London S.E.1.
tel. (01) 928-9531, ext. 16
The Archivist
Hours: Monday-Friday 9.30-6; Saturday 9.30-1
A 30-year closure rule is usually applied to papers in their care. A letter of recommendation
must be sent with applications for reader's tickets.
*Anderson; Brodrick; Bruce, V.A.; Casey; Cavendish, S.C.; Cecil, R.A.T.G. (3rd Marquess of
Salisbury); Cripps, R.S.; Cross, R.A.; Curzon; Dundas; Petty-Fitzmaurice, H.; Fowler;
Hamilton; Hoare; Isaacs, R.D.; Kitchener; Pethick-Lawrence; Montagu; Morley; Peel;
Smith, F.E.; Dorman-Smith; Thesiger; Wood, E.*

ISRAEL STATE ARCHIVES
Jerusalem, Israel
Samuel

KENT ARCHIVES OFFICE
County Hall, Maidstone. tel. (0622) 54321
The County Archivist
Hours: Monday-Friday 9-5.15
Akers-Douglas; Stanhope; Thomas, J.H.

KENT UNIVERSITY LIBRARY
Canterbury, Kent
The Librarian
Wood, Kingsley

LABOUR PARTY ARCHIVES
See Transport House

LANCASHIRE RECORD OFFICE
Sessions House, Lancaster Road, Preston PR1 2RE
The County Archivist
Cross, R.A.

LINCOLNSHIRE ARCHIVES OFFICE
The Castle, Lincoln. tel. (0522) 25158
The Archivist
Hours: Monday-Friday 10-1, 2-5 (by arrangement during lunch hour); Saturday 10-1; advance
notice of intended visits is requested. Closed for a fortnight in October.
Chaplin; Crookshank

LIVERPOOL CITY LIBRARY
City Libraries, William Brown Street, Liverpool L3 8EW. tel. (051) 207-2147
The City Librarian
Hours: Monday-Friday 9-9; Saturday 9-5
Stanley, E.

LIVERPOOL UNIVERSITY LIBRARY
Harold Cohen Library, Ashton Street, P.O. Box 123, Liverpool L69 3DA. tel. (051) 709-6022
The Curator of Special Collections
Birrell

LONDON SCHOOL OF ECONOMICS
See British Library of Political and Economic Science

MINISTRY OF DEFENCE LIBRARY (NAVY)
Empress State Buildings, Lillie Road, Fulham, London
The Librarian
Campbell; Marjoribanks

MITCHELL LIBRARY
The Library of New South Wales, Macquarie Street, Sydney, N.S.W., 2000, Australia
The Principal Librarian
Carrington

NATIONAL LIBRARY OF AUSTRALIA
Parkes Place, Canberra, A.C.T., 2600, Australia
The Manuscript Librarian
Baird; Carrington; Munro-Ferguson

NATIONAL LIBRARY OF IRELAND
Kildare Street, Dublin 2, Eire
The Director
Hours: 10-1, 2-5.30
Brodrick; Bryce; French

NATIONAL LIBRARY OF SCOTLAND
George IV Bridge, Edinburgh EH1 1EW. tel. (031) 225-4104
The Keeper of Manuscripts
Hours: Monday-Friday 9.30-8.30; Saturday 9.30-1. Closed on Christmas Day, New Year's Day
and the day following, and Good Friday.
Elliot; Haldane; Macmillan, H.P.; Woodburn

NATIONAL LIBRARY OF WALES
Aberystwyth. tel. (0970) 3816-7
The Keeper of Manuscripts and Records
Hours: Monday-Friday 9.30-6; Saturday 9-5
Lloyd George, D.; Thomas, D.A.

NATIONAL MARITIME MUSEUM
Greenwich, London S.E.10. tel. (01) 858-4422
The Custodian of Manuscripts
Hours: Monday-Friday 10-5.30; Saturday 10-5.30 (by appointment only)
Chatfield

NATIONAL REGISTER OF ARCHIVES
Quality House, Quality Court, Chancery Lane, London WC2A 1HP. tel. (01) 242-1198
The Registrar

NATIONAL REGISTER OF ARCHIVES (SCOTLAND)
P.O. Box 36, HM General Register House, Edinburgh EH1 3YY. tel. (031) 226 5101 ext. 38
The Registrar
Balfour, A.J. & G.W.; Bruce, A.H.; Munro-Ferguson; Hope

NEWCASTLE UNIVERSITY LIBRARY
Newcastle upon Tyne NE1 7RU. tel. (0632) 28511
The Librarian
Runciman; Trevelyan

NORTH RIDING COUNTY RECORD OFFICE
County Hall, Northallerton. tel. (0609) 3123, ext. 306
The County Archivist
Hours: Monday-Friday 9-1, 2-5
Dundas

NORTHUMBERLAND RECORD OFFICE
Melton Park, North Gosforth, Newcastle upon Tyne NE3 5QX. tel. (089 426) 2680
The County Archivist
Hours: Monday 9-5.30; Tuesday-Friday 9-5; (open 9-9 last Monday of each month)
Ridley

NUFFIELD COLLEGE LIBRARY
Oxford OX1 1NF. tel. (0865) 48014
The Librarian
Hours: Monday-Friday 9.30-1, 2-6; Saturday 9.30-1
Cripps, R.S.; Emmott; Lindemann; Pease; Seely; Shortt

PUBLIC ARCHIVES OF CANADA
Manuscript Division, 395 Wellington Street, Ottawa, K1A ON3, Ontario, Canada
The Chief of the Manuscript Division
Petty-Fitzmaurice, H.

PUBLIC RECORD OFFICE
Chancery Lane, London WC2A 1LR. tel. (01) 405-0741
The Keeper of Public Records
Hours: Monday-Friday 9.30-5; Saturday 9.30-1
*Anderson; Noel-Baker; Balfour, A.J. & G.W.; Montague-Barlow; Benn; Brodrick; Bryce;
Cecil, Lord Robert; Cecil, R.A.J.G. (5th Marquess of Salisbury); Chamberlain, J.;
Chamberlain, A.; Churchill; Cooper; Curzon; Chuter Ede; Worthington-Evans; Petty-
Fitzmaurice, H.; Geddes, E.; Grey; Hankey; Henderson, A.; Hoare; Isaacs, R.D.; Kitchener;
Law, A.B.; Cunliffe-Lister; MacDonald, J.R.; Macmillan, H.; Milner; Crewe-Milnes; Murray;
Runciman; Sinclair, A.; Stanley, E.; Weir, A.; Wood, E.; Wood, K.*

PUBLIC RECORD OFFICE OF NORTHERN IRELAND
66 Balmoral Avenue, Belfast BT9 6NY. tel. (0232) 661621
The Deputy Keeper
Hours: Monday-Friday 9.30-4.45
Carson; McNeill

QUEEN'S UNIVERSITY, KINGSTON
See Douglas Library

RHODES HOUSE LIBRARY
Parks Road, Oxford
A department of the Bodleian Library (*q.v.*)
Montague-Barlow; Creech Jones

ROYAL AIR FORCE MUSEUM
R.A.F. Hendon, The Hyde, London N.W.9. tel. (01) 205-2266
The Archivist
Archives may be consulted at present by appointment only.
Brabazon

ROYAL ARCHIVES
The Round Tower, Windsor Castle, Berks.
The Keeper of the Royal Archives
Written application is required; students enrolled for higher degrees are not admitted.

ROYAL COMMISSION ON HISTORICAL MANUSCRIPTS
Quality House, Quality Court, Chancery Lane, London WC2A 1HP
The Secretary

ST DENIOL'S LIBRARY, HAWARDEN
See Flintshire Record Office

SALOP RECORD OFFICE
Shirehall, Abbey Foregate, Shrewsbury SY2 6ND. tel. (0743) 52211
The County Archivist
Hours: Monday-Friday 9-5
Bridgeman

SCIENCE MUSEUM LIBRARY
South Kensington, London SW7 5NH. tel. (01) 589-6371
The Librarian
Hours: Monday-Friday 10-5.30
Pearson

SCOTTISH RECORD OFFICE
P.O. Box 36, H.M. General Register House, Edinburgh EH1 3YY. tel. (031) 556-6585
The Keeper of the Records of Scotland
Hours: Monday-Friday 9-4.45; Saturday 9-12.30
Kerr; Steel-Maitland

SHEFFIELD CITY LIBRARY
Department of Local History and Archives, Central Library, Surrey Street, Sheffield S1 1XZ.
tel. (0742) 734 756
The City Librarian
Alexander

SOUTH AFRICAN ARCHIVES
Staatsargief — Government Archives, Private Bag X 236, Pretoria, South Africa
The Director of Archives
Smuts

SOUTHPORT PUBLIC LIBRARY
Central Library, Lord Street, Southport, Lancs. tel. Southport 5523
The Librarian
Curzon

SOUTHWARK PUBLIC LIBRARIES
Newington District Library, Walworth Road, London S.E.17. tel (01) 703-3324, 5529, 6514
The Borough Librarian
The archives may be seen by appointment only.
Isaacs, G.A.

STAFFORDSHIRE COUNTY RECORD OFFICE
County Record Office, County Buildings, Eastgate Street, Stafford. tel. (0785) 3121
The County Archivist
Chaplin

STOKE CITY LIBRARY
Local Studies Collection, Horace Barks Reference Library, Pall Mall, Hanley,
Stoke-on-Trent ST1 1HW
The Librarian
Wedgwood

SURREY RECORD OFFICE
County Hall, Kingston upon Thames. tel. (01) 546-1050, ext. 158
The County Archivist
Hours: Monday-Friday 9-5; Saturday 9-12 by appointment only
Chuter Ede

TOWER HAMLETS: LOCAL HISTORY LIBRARY
Central Library, Bancroft Road, London E1 4DA. tel. (01) 980-4366
The Local History Librarian
Hours: Monday-Friday 9-8; Saturday 9-5
Buxton; Lansbury

TRADES UNION CONGRESS
Congress House, Great Russell Street, London WC1B 3LS. tel. (01) 636-4030
The Librarian
Burns

TRANSPORT HOUSE
Smith Square, London S.W.1
The Librarian
Henderson; Wilkinson

TRINITY COLLEGE, CAMBRIDGE
The Wren Library. tel. (0223) 58201, ext. 288
The Librarian
Montagu

UNIVERSITY COLLEGE, OXFORD
The Librarian   tel. (0865) 41661
Attlee

WILTSHIRE RECORD OFFICE
County Hall, Trowbridge. tel. (022 14) 3641
The County Archivist
Hours: Monday 8.30-12.30, 1.30-5.50; Tuesday-Friday 8.50-12.30, 1.30-5.20
Long

WREN LIBRARY
See Trinity College, Cambridge

ADDENDA

AUGUSTINE BIRRELL (1850-1933)

A small collection of the papers of Andrew Philip Magill, Birrell's secretary, is also in the Bodleian Library (ref. MS. Eng. lett. c.213). It includes several letters to Birrell from his contemporaries, as well as 29 letters from Birrell to Magill.

ALEXANDER HUGH BRUCE, 6th BARON BALFOUR OF BURLEIGH (1849-1929)

Bruce's papers are in the possession of his grandson, the present (8th) Lord Balfour of Burleigh. They are being listed by the National Register of Archives (Scotland). Arrangements can be made for them to be consulted in the Scottish Record Office. All enquiries about access to the papers should be addressed to the National Register of Archives (Scotland) (ref. MSS. *penes*), giving as much notice as is possible.

The bulk of the papers concern the split in the Unionist ranks over tariff reform 1902-1903. Perhaps the most important papers in the collection are Bruce's contemporary notes on the crisis for July-September 1903. He also wrote a nine-page memorandum on the events leading up to his resignation in September 1903, and a narrative of the events of those months. As well as Bruce's own impressions of these events, some of his correspondence with his cabinet colleagues has survived. At a critical stage in the crisis, Bruce was Minister-in-Attendance at Balmoral, and thus isolated from his colleagues. There are several letters from the Duke of Devonshire, Lord James of Hereford, C.T. Ritchie, and A.J. Balfour. There are also cabinet memoranda and manuscript notes of five '. . . questions put to Mr Chamberlain through A.J.B. in June 1903 by B. of B.'. Letters of regret at Bruce's resignation have survived, and also some correspondence with Lord George Hamilton in 1911 about Bernard Holland's account of the crisis in *Life of Spencer Compton, 8th Duke of Devonshire* (2 vols., 1911).

There are few earlier papers, though there are some letters from W.E. Gladstone on the disestablishment of the Church of Scotland in 1889, and more letters about Church affairs from A.H. Charteris 1881-1889. Bruce's continued interest in the Church is reflected in correspondence with A.V. Dicey in 1920 about the union of the Established and Free Churches of Scotland. The present Lord Balfour of Burleigh thinks that more papers relating to church union in Scotland were given to the then Moderator of the Church of Scotland, Dr White. The present Principal Clerk of the Church, the Rev. D.F.M. Macdonald, informs us that the Church has no such papers; however, the Church did deposit a small collection of the papers of Lord Sands with the Scottish Record Office (ref. CH1/10/1-6). The collection relates almost entirely to reunion matters; there are 73 letters from Bruce to Lord Sands 1911-1921.

Bruce's own papers include miscellaneous correspondence with his political contemporaries, e.g. correspondence with the 3rd Marquess of Salisbury 1886-1902. There are also several memoranda, pamphlets, and letters on the reform of the House of Lords and the 1911 Parliament Act.

Bruce was Chairman of the Royal Commission on Trade Relations between the West Indies and Canada 1909-1910. Some correspondence (including his letter of appointment 18 August 1909), reports, memoranda, and other submissions to the commission have survived.

From October 1915 to April 1916, Bruce investigated grievances among the Clyde munition workers. Correspondence, agenda, submissions from employers and employees, and transcripts of the inquiry have survived. Bruce also chaired a Board of Trade Committee to consider post-war commercial and industrial policy. The committee reported in 1918; reports, pamphlets, and memoranda survive.

Lady Frances Balfour, *A Memoir of Lord Balfour of Burleigh K.T.* (1924) was based on papers put at her disposal by Bruce's widow and son. Some, at least, of those papers have survived, e.g. Bruce's narrative, written in 1911, about the events of 1903 (item 191).

JOSEPH CHAMBERLAIN (1836-1914)

The papers of J.W. Dodson, 2nd Baron Monk Bretton, in the Bodleian Library (ref. Dep. Monk Bretton), contain much material relating to Chamberlain. Monk Bretton was Chamberlain's secretary at the Colonial Office 1900-1903. As well as letters addressed to Chamberlain, there are many Colonial Office papers annotated by him; in particular, there are many boxes of papers relating to Chamberlain's South African tour.

GEORGE JOACHIM GOSCHEN, 1st VISCOUNT GOSCHEN (1831-1907)

About 80 letters to Goschen and his brother Charles are in the possession of Goschen's great-nephew, Mr D.C. Goschen, P.O.Box 49, Rusape, Rhodesia. They are held for Mr Goschen by his London bank. Most of the letters, which cover the years 1846-1866, are from Goschen's father. They particularly concern Goschen's work for the family firm, Fruhling and Goschen; there are some 30 letters for the years 1854-1856, when Goschen was supervising the firm's interests in South America. There are also letters from Charles Goschen in February 1890 on Goschen's financial position, and several letters from Goschen's mother.

T.J. Spinner, Jr, *George Joachim Goschen. The Transformation of a Victorian Liberal* (Cambridge, 1973), uses all the available papers, including those in Rhodesia, and quotes from them. Professor Spinner also informs us that he was able to contact most of the Goschen family, but found no papers, other than those mentioned above.

ARTHUR AUGUSTUS WILLIAM HARRY PONSONBY, 1st BARON PONSONBY OF SHULBREDE (1871-1946)

Ponsonby's notes of impressions of Sir Henry Campbell-Bannerman are not included in the collection in the Bodleian. They are extensively quoted in F.W. Hirst, *In the Golden Days* (1947). Hirst says there that Ponsonby wrote about 20,000 words in 1920 for J.A. Spender, who was then writing his biography of Sir Henry. When Hirst used the notes, they were in the possession of Ponsonby's widow. The notes are not in the collection in the Bodleian, and Lord Ponsonby is unable to find them.

INDEX OF MINISTERS

Adamson, William — 1

Addison, Christopher, 1st Viscount Addison — 1

Ailwyn: see Fellowes

Aitken, Sir William Maxwell, 1st Bt,
  1st Baron Beaverbrook — 2

Alexander, Albert Victor, Earl Alexander
  of Hillsborough — 2-3

Alness: see Munro

Altrincham: see Grigg, E.

Alverstone: see Webster

Amery, Leopold Charles Maurice Stennett — 3-4

Amulree: see Mackenzie

Anderson, Sir John, 1st Viscount Waverley — 4-5

Arnold, Sydney, Baron Arnold — 5

Arundel: see FitzAlan-Howard

Ashbourne: see Gibson

Ashby St Ledgers: see Guest, I.C.

Ashfield: see Stanley, A.

Ashley, Wilfrid William, Baron Mount
  Temple — 5-6

Asquith, Herbert Henry, 1st Earl of
  Oxford and Asquith — 6

Attlee, Clement Richard, 1st Earl Attlee — 6-7

Avon: see Eden

Baird, Sir John Lawrence, 2nd Bt,
  1st Viscount Stonehaven — 7-8

Baker, Philip J. Noel- — 8

Balcarres: see Lindsay

Baldwin, Stanley, 1st Earl Baldwin of
  Bewdley — 8-9

Balfour of Burleigh: see Bruce, A.H.

Balfour, Sir Arthur James, 1st Earl of
  Balfour — 9-11

Balfour, Gerald William, 2nd Earl of
  Balfour — 11-12

Bannerman, Sir Henry Campbell- — 12-13

Barlow, Sir (Clement) Anderson
  Montague-, Bt — 13

Barnes, Alfred — 14

Barnes, George Nicoll — 14

Bayford: see Sanders

Beach, Sir Michael Edward Hicks, 9th Bt,
  1st Earl St Aldwyn — 14

Beauchamp: see Lygon

Beaverbrook: see Aitken

Belisha, (Isaac) Leslie Hore-,
  Baron Hore-Belisha — 14-15

Bellenger, Frederick John — 15

Benn, William Wedgwood,
  1st Viscount Stansgate — 15-16

Betterton, Sir Henry Bucknall, Bt,
  Baron Rushcliffe — 16

Bevan, Aneurin — 16

Bevin, Ernest — 16-17

Birkenhead: see Smith, F.E.

Birrell, Augustine — 17; 166

Blandford: see Spencer-Churchill

Bondfield, Margaret Grace — 17

Boscawen, Sir Arthur Sackville Trevor
  Griffith- — 18

Brabazon, John Theodore Cuthbert Moore-,
  1st Baron Brabazon of Tara — 18

Bracken, Brendan Rendall, Viscount Bracken — 19

Brentford: see Joynson-Hicks

Bridgeman, William Clive, 1st Viscount
  Bridgeman — 19

Brodrick, (William) St John (Fremantle),
  9th Viscount Midleton,
  1st Earl of Midleton — 19-20

Brown, (Alfred) Ernest — 20

Brown, George Alfred, Baron George-Brown — 21

Bruce, Alexander Hugh, 6th Baron Balfour
  of Burleigh — 21; 166

Bruce, Victor Alexander, Lord Bruce,
  9th Earl of Elgin, 13th Earl of Kincardine — 21

Bryce, James, Viscount Bryce — 21-22

Buchanan, George — 22

Buckhurst: see Sackville

Buckmaster, Sir Stanley Owen, 1st Viscount
  Buckmaster — 22-23

Burgin, Edward Leslie — 23

Burns, John Elliot — 23-25

Butler, Richard Austen, Baron Butler of
  Saffron Walden — 25

Buxton, Noel Edward Noel-, 1st Baron
  Noel-Buxton — 25-26

Buxton, Sydney Charles, Earl Buxton — 26-27

Cadogan, George Henry, Viscount Chelsea,
  5th Earl Cadogan — 27

Caldecote: see Inskip

Campbell, Frederick Archibald Vaughan,
  Viscount Emlyn, 3rd Earl Cawdor — 27

Carpenter, Sir Archibald Boyd Boyd- — 27

Carrington, Charles Robert Wynn-,
  3rd Baron Carrington, Earl Carrington,
  Marquess of Lincolnshire — 28-29

Carson, Sir Edward Henry, Baron Carson — 29

Casey, Richard Gardiner, Baron Casey — 29-30

Castlereagh: see Stewart

Causton, Richard Knight, Baron Southwark — 30

Cave, Sir George, Viscount Cave — 30

Cavendish, Spencer Compton, Lord Cavendish,
  Marquess of Hartington, 8th Duke of
  Devonshire — 30-31

Cavendish, Victor Christian William,
  9th Duke of Devonshire — 31

Cawdor: see Campbell

Cawley, Sir Frederick, 1st Bt,
1st Baron Cawley — 31-32

Cecil, (Edgar Algernon) Robert Gascoyne-,
Lord Robert Cecil, Viscount Cecil
of Chelwood — 32

Cecil, James Edward Hubert Gascoyne-,
Viscount Cranborne, 4th Marquess
of Salisbury — 33

Cecil, Robert Arthur James Gascoyne-,
Viscount Cranborne, 5th Marquess
of Salisbury — 33

Cecil, Lord Robert Arthur Talbot Gascoyne-,
Viscount Cranborne, 3rd Marquess of
Salisbury — 33-34

Chamberlain, (Arthur) Neville — 34-35

Chamberlain, Joseph — 36; 167

Chamberlain, Sir (Joseph) Austen — 36-37

Chandos: see Lyttleton, O.

Chaplin, Henry, 1st Viscount Chaplin — 37-38

Chatfield, Sir (Alfred) Ernle Montacute,
1st Baron Chatfield — 38

Chelmsford: see Thesiger

Chelsea: see Cadogan

Cherwell: see Lindemann

Chilston: see Akers-Douglas

Churchill, Charles Richard John Spencer-,
Earl of Sunderland, Marquess of
Blandford, 9th Duke of Marlborough — 38

Churchill, Sir Winston Leonard Spencer- — 38-39

Clanmaurice: see Petty-Fitzmaurice, H.

Clive, Robert George Windsor-, 14th
Baron Windsor, 1st Earl of Plymouth — 39

Clydesmuir: see Colville

Clynes, John Robert — 40

Coleraine: see Law

Collins, Sir Godfrey Pattison — 40

Colville, Sir (David) John,
1st Baron Clydesmuir — 40-41

Cooper, Sir Alfred Duff,
1st Viscount Norwich — 41

Cowdray: see Pearson

Cranborne: see Cecil

Cranley: see Onslow

Crawford: see Lindsay

Crewe: see Crewe-Milnes

Cripps, Sir Charles Alfred, 1st Baron Parmoor — 41

Cripps, Sir (Richard) Stafford — 42

Crookshank, Harry Frederick Comfort,
Viscount Crookshank — 42-43

Cross, Sir Richard Assheton,
1st Viscount Cross — 43

Cross, Sir Ronald Hibbert, Bt — 43-44

Crossley, Sir Savile Brinton, 2nd Bt,
1st Baron Somerleyton — 44

Curzon, George Nathaniel, 5th Baron Scarsdale,
Marquess Curzon of Kedleston — 44-45

Cushendun: see McNeill

Dalmeny: see Primrose

Dalton, (Edward) Hugh (John Neale),
Baron Dalton — 45-46

Davidson, Sir John Colin Campbell,
1st Viscount Davidson — 46-47

De La Warr: see Sackville

Derby: see Stanley, E.G.V.

Devonport: see Kearley

Devonshire: see Cavendish

Dingwall: see Herbert

Douglas, Aretas Akers-, 1st Viscount Chilston — 47

Downham: see Hayes Fisher

Duke, Sir Henry Edward, 1st Baron Merrivale — 47

Duncan, Sir Andrew Rae — 47-48

Dundas, Lawrence John Lumley, Lord Dundas,
Earl of Ronaldshay, 2nd Marquess of
Zetland — 48-49

Dunedin: see Murray

Dunrossil: see Morrison

Ede, James Chuter, Baron Chuter-Ede — 49

Eden, Sir (Robert) Anthony, Earl of Avon — 49

Edwards, Ness — 50

Elgin: see Bruce, V.A.

Elliot, Walter Elliot — 50

Elmley: see Lygon

Emlyn: see Campbell

Emmott, Alfred, Baron Emmott — 50

Ennismore: see Hare

Ernle: see Prothero

Evans, Sir Laming Worthington-, 1st Bt — 51-52

Fellowes, Sir Ailwyn Edward, 1st Baron Ailwyn — 52

Ferguson, Sir Ronald Crauford Munro-,
Viscount Novar — 52-53

Finlay, Sir Robert Bannatyne, 1st Viscount
Finlay — 53

Fisher, Herbert Albert Laurens — 53-54

Fisher, William Hayes, Baron Downham — 54

FitzClarence, Geoffrey William Richard Hugh,
5th Earl of Munster — 54

Fitzmaurice, Edmund George Petty-, Lord
Edmond Fitzmaurice, Baron Fitzmaurice — 54-55

Fitzmaurice, Henry Charles Keith Petty-,
Viscount Clanmaurice, Earl of Kerry,
5th Marquess of Lansdowne — 55-56

Fletcher, Reginald Thomas Herbert,
Baron Winster — 56

Forster, Hugh Oakeley Arnold- — 56

Fowler, Sir Henry Hartley, 1st Viscount
Wolverhampton — 57

French, Sir John Denton Pinkstone,
1st Viscount French, 1st Earl of Ypres — 57

Fyfe, Sir David Patrick Maxwell-,
    Earl of Kilmuir   57-58
Gainford: see Pease
Gaitskell, Hugh Todd Naylor   58
Geddes, Sir Auckland Campbell,
    1st Baron Geddes   58
Geddes, Sir Eric Campbell   59
George, David Lloyd, 1st Earl Lloyd-George
    of Dwyfor   59-60
George, Gwilym Lloyd, 1st Viscount Tenby   60
Gibson, Edward, 1st Baron Ashbourne   60-61
Giffard, Sir Hardinge Stanley,
    1st Earl of Halsbury   61
Gilmour, Sir John, 2nd Bt   61
Gladstone, Herbert John,
    Viscount Gladstone   61-62
Goderich: see Robinson
Gore, William George Arthur Ormsby-,
    4th Baron Harlech   62-63
Goschen, George Joachim,
    1st Viscount Goschen   63; 167
Gosling, Harry   63
Gower, George Granville Sutherland-
    Leveson-, Earl Gower, Marquess of
    Stafford, 5th Duke of Sutherland   63
Graham, William   64
Greame, Lloyd-: see Cunliffe-Lister
Greenwood, Arthur   64
Greenwood, Sir (Thomas) Hamar,
    1st Bt, 1st Viscount Greenwood   64
Grey, Sir Edward, 3rd Bt, Viscount
    Grey of Fallodon   64-65
Griffiths, James   65-66
Grigg, Sir Edward William Macleay,
    1st Baron Altrincham   66-67
Grigg, Sir (Percy) James   67
Guest, Frederick Edward   68
Guest, Ivor Churchill, 1st Baron Ashby
    St Ledgers, 2nd Baron Wimborne,
    1st Viscount Wimborne   68
Guinness, Walter Edward, 1st Baron Moyne   68
Hailsham: see Hogg
Haldane, Richard Burdon, Viscount Haldane   68
Halifax: see Wood, E.F.L.
Hall, George Henry, 1st Viscount Hall   69
Halsbury: see Giffard
Hamilton, Lord George Francis   70
Hanbury, Robert William   70
Hankey, Sir Maurice Pascal Alers,
    1st Baron Hankey   70-71
Hanworth: see Pollock
Harcourt, Lewis, 1st Viscount Harcourt   71-72
Hare, William Francis, Viscount
    Ennismore, 5th Earl of Listowel   72
Harlech: see Ormsby-Gore

Harmsworth, Sir Harold Sidney, 1st Bt,
    1st Viscount Rothermere   73
Hartington: see Cavendish
Hartshorn, Vernon   73
Hastings, Sir Patrick Gardiner   73
Henderson, Arthur   73-74
Henderson, Arthur, Baron Rowley   74
Herbert, Auberon Thomas, 8th Baron Lucas,
    11th Baron Dingwall   74-75
Hewart, Sir Gordon, 1st Viscount Hewart   75
Hicks, Sir William Joynson-, 1st Bt,
    1st Viscount Brentford   75
Hoare, Sir Samuel John Gurney, 2nd Bt,
    Viscount Templewood   75-76
Hobhouse, Sir Charles Edward Henry, 4th Bt   76
Hodge, John   76
Hogg, Sir Douglas McGarel, 1st Viscount
    Hailsham   77
Hope, John Adrian Louis, Lord Hope,
    7th Earl of Hopetoun, 1st Marquess
    of Linlithgow   77
Hopetoun: see Hope
Horne, Sir Robert Stevenson, Viscount Horne
    of Slamannan   77
Houghton: see Crewe-Milnes
Howard, Henry FitzAlan-, Lord Maltravers,
    Earl of Arundel, 15th Duke of Norfolk   77-78
Hudson, Robert Spear, 1st Viscount Hudson   78
Hutchinson, Sir Robert, Baron Hutchinson   78
Hynd, John Burns   78-79
Illingworth, Albert Holden, Baron Illingworth   79
Inman, Philip Albert, Baron Inman   79-80
Inskip, Sir Thomas Walker Hobart,
    1st Viscount Caldecote   80
Inverforth: see Weir, A.
Irwin: see Wood, E.F.L.
Isaacs, George Alfred   80
Isaacs, Sir Rufus Daniel, 1st Marquess
    of Reading   80-81
James, Sir Henry, Baron James of Hereford   81-82
Johnston, Thomas   82
Jones, Arthur Creech   82
Jowett, Frederick William   83
Jowitt, Sir William Allen, Earl Jowitt   83
Kearley, Sir Hudson Ewbanke, 1st Bt,
    1st Viscount Devonport   83
Kellaway, Frederick George   83-84
Kennet: see Young
Kerr, Philip Henry, 11th Marquess of Lothian   84
Kerry: see Petty-Fitzmaurice, H.
Key, Charles William   85
Kilmuir: see Maxwell-Fyfe
Kitchener, Sir Horatio Herbert, 1st Earl
    Kitchener of Khartoum   85-86

172

Lamb, Sir Ernest Henry,
　1st Baron Rochester　　　　　　86
Lansbury, George　　　　　　　　86-87
Lansdowne: see Petty-Fitzmaurice, H.
Law, Andrew Bonar　　　　　　　87-88
Law, Richard Kidston, Baron Coleraine　88
Lawrence, Frederick William Pethick-,
　Baron Pethick-Lawrence　　　　88
Lawson, John James, Baron Lawson　88-89
Leathers, Frederick James,
　1st Viscount Leathers　　　　　89
Lee, Sir Arthur Hamilton, Viscount Lee
　of Fareham　　　　　　　　　　89-90
Legh, Thomas Wodehouse,
　2nd Baron Newton　　　　　　　90
Lincolnshire: see Carrington
Lindemann, Frederick Alexander,
　Viscount Cherwell　　　　　　　90-91
Lindsay, David Alexander Edward, Master
　of Lindsay, Lord Balcarres, 27th
　Earl of Crawford　　　　　　　91
Linlithgow: see Hope
Lister, Sir Philip Cunliffe-,
　1st Earl of Swinton　　　　　　91
Listowel: see Hare
Llewellin, John Jestyn, Baron Llewellin　91-92
Lloyd, Sir George Ambrose,
　1st Baron Lloyd　　　　　　　　92-93
Londonderry: see Stewart
Long, Walter Hume, 1st Viscount Long　93-94
Longford: see Pakenham
Loreburn: see Reid
Lothian: see Kerr
Lucas: see Herbert
Lygon, William, Viscount Elmley,
　7th Earl Beauchamp　　　　　　94
Lyttleton, Hon. Alfred　　　　　94-95
Lyttleton, Oliver, 1st Viscount Chandos　95
McCurdy, Charles Albert　　　　95
Macdonald, Sir Gordon, 1st Baron
　Macdonald of Gwaenysgor　　　95
MacDonald, James Ramsay　　　96-97
MacDonald, Malcolm John　　　　97
McKenna, Reginald　　　　　　　97
Mackenzie, Sir William Warrender,
　1st Baron Amulree　　　　　　　98
Maclay, Sir John Paton, 1st Bt,
　1st Baron Maclay　　　　　　　98
Maclean, Sir Donald　　　　　　98
Macmillan, Hugh Pattison,
　Baron Macmillan　　　　　　　98-99
Macmillan, (Maurice) Harold　　99
Macnamara, Thomas James　　　99
McNeil, Hector　　　　　　　　　99
McNeill, Ronald John, Baron Cushendun　100
Macpherson, Sir James Ian, 1st Bt,
　1st Baron Strathcarron　　　　100-101

Mahon: see Stanhope
Maitland, Sir Arthur Herbert Drummond
　Ramsay Steel-, 1st Bt　　　　101-102
Maltravers: see Howard
Margesson, (Henry) David (Reginald),
　1st Viscount Margesson　　　　102
Marjoribanks, Sir Edward, 2nd Bt,
　2nd Baron Tweedmouth　　　　102
Marlborough: see Spencer-Churchill
Marquand, Hilary Adair　　　　102
Marquis, Sir Frederick James,
　1st Earl of Woolton　　　　　103
Masterman, Charles Frederick Gurney　104
Maugham, Sir Frederic Herbert,
　1st Viscount Maugham　　　　104
Melchett: see Mond
Merrivale: see Duke
Midleton: see Brodrick
Milner, Sir Alfred, Viscount Milner　104-106
Milnes, Robert Offley Ashburton Crewe-,
　2nd Baron Houghton, Marquess of
　Crewe　　　　　　　　　　　106-107
Mond, Sir Alfred Moritz, 1st Bt,
　1st Baron Melchett　　　　　　107
Monsell, Sir Bolton Meredith Eyres-,
　1st Viscount Monsell　　　　　108
Montagu, Hon. Edwin Samuel　108-109
Morley, John, Viscount Morley of
　Blackburn　　　　　　　　　109-110
Morrison, Herbert Stanley,
　Baron Morrison of Lambeth　　110-111
Morrison, William Shepherd,
　1st Viscount Dunrossil　　　　111
Mosley, Sir Oswald Ernald, 6th Bt　111
Mottistone: see Seely
Mount Temple: see Ashley
Moyne: see Guinness
Munro, Robert, Baron Alness　　111
Munster: see FitzClarence
Murray, Andrew Graham,
　Viscount Dunedin　　　　　　111-112
Nathan, Harry Louis, 1st Baron Nathan　112
Newton: see Legh
Norfolk: see FitzAlan-Howard
Norwich: see Cooper
Novar: see Ferguson
Ogmore: see Rees-Williams
Olivier, Sir Sydney Haldane, Baron Olivier　112
Onslow, Sir Richard William Alan, 10th Bt,
　Viscount Cranley, 5th Earl of Onslow　112-113
Onslow, Sir William Hillier, 9th Bt,
　4th Earl of Onslow　　　　　113-114
Oxford and Asquith: see Asquith
Pakenham, Francis Aungier, Baron Pakenham,
　7th Earl of Longford　　　　　114
Paling, Wilfred　　　　　　　　114

Palmer, Roundell Cecil, Viscount Wolmer, 3rd Earl of Selborne 114

Palmer, William Waldegrave, Viscount Wolmer, 2nd Earl of Selborne 114-115

Parmoor: see Cripps

Passfield: see Webb

Pearson, Sir Weetman Dickinson, 1st Bt, 1st Viscount Cowdray 115-116

Pease, Joseph Albert, 1st Baron Gainford 116-117

Peel, William Robert Wellesley, 2nd Viscount Peel, 1st Earl Peel 117

Pentland: see Sinclair, J.

Percy, Eustace Sutherland Campbell, Lord Eustace Percy, Baron Percy of Newcastle 117

Plymouth: see Windsor-Clive

Pollock, Sir Ernest Murray, 1st Bt, 1st Viscount Hanworth 117-118

Ponsonby, Arthur Augustus William Harry, 1st Baron Ponsonby of Shulbrede 118-119; 167

Portal, Sir Wyndham Raymond, 3rd Bt, Viscount Portal 120

Primrose, Albert Edward Harry Mayer Archibald, Lord Dalmeny, 6th Earl of Rosebery 120

Prothero, Rowland Edmund, Baron Ernle 120

Pybus, Sir (Percy) John, Bt 120

Ramsbotham, Herwald, 1st Viscount Soulbury 120

Reading: see Isaacs, R.D.

Reid, Sir Robert Threshie, Earl Loreburn 121

Reith, Sir John Charles Walsham, 1st Baron Reith 121

Rhondda: see Thomas, D.A.

Rickett, Sir Joseph Compton- 121

Ridley, Sir Matthew White, 5th Bt, 1st Viscount Ridley 122

Ripon: see Robinson

Ritchie, Charles Thomson, 1st Baron Ritchie of Dundee 122

Robens, Alfred, Baron Robens of Woldingham 122

Roberts, Frederick Owen 122-123

Roberts, George Henry 123

Robinson, George Frederick Samuel, Viscount Goderich, 2nd Earl of Ripon, 1st Marquess of Ripon 123-124

Robson, Sir William Snowdon, Baron Robson 124

Rochester: see Lamb

Ronaldshay: see Dundas

Rosebery: see Primrose

Rothermere: see Harmsworth

Rowley: see Henderson

Runciman, Walter, 1st Viscount Runciman of Doxford 124-125

Rushcliffe: see Betterton

Sackville, Herbrand Edward Dundonald Brassey, Lord Buckhurst, 9th Earl De La Warr 125

St Aldwyn: see Hicks Beach

Salisbury: see Cecil

Salter, Sir (James) Arthur, Baron Salter of Kidlington 125-126

Samuel, Sir Herbert Louis, 1st Viscount Samuel 126-127

Sanders, Sir Robert Arthur, Bt, Baron Bayford 127

Sandys, Duncan Edwin 127-128

Sankey, Sir John, Viscount Sankey 128-129

Sassoon, Sir Philip Albert Gustave David, 3rd Bt 129

Scarsdale: see Curzon

Seely, John Edward Bernard, 1st Baron Mottistone 129-130

Selborne: see Palmer

Selsdon: see Mitchell-Thomson

Shaw, Thomas 130

Shawcross, Sir Hartley William, Baron Shawcross 130

Shinwell, Emanuel, Baron Shinwell 130

Shortt, Edward 131

Silkin, Lewis, 1st Baron Silkin 131

Simon, Sir John Allsebrook, 1st Viscount Simon 131-132

Sinclair, Sir Archibald Henry Macdonald, 4th Bt, 1st Viscount Thurso 132-133

Sinclair, John, 1st Baron Pentland 133

Smith, Sir Ben 133

Smith, Sir Frederick Edwin, 1st Bt, 1st Earl of Birkenhead 133-134

Smith, Hastings Bertrand Lees- 134-135

Smith, Sir Reginald Hugh Dorman- 135

Smuts, Jan Christian 135-136

Snowden, Philip, Viscount Snowden 136

Somerleyton: see Crossley

Somervell, Sir Donald Bradley, Baron Somervell of Harrow 137

Soskice, Sir Frank, Baron Stow Hill 137

Soulbury: see Ramsbotham

Southwark: see Causton

Stafford: see Gower

Stanhope, James Richard, Viscount Mahon, 7th Earl Stanhope, 13th Earl of Chesterfield 137-138

Stanley, Sir Albert (Henry), Baron Ashfield 138

Stanley, Edward George Villiers, Lord Stanley, 17th Earl of Derby 138-139

Stanley, Hon. Oliver Frederick George 139

Stansgate: see Benn

Steel: see Steel-Maitland

Stewart, Charles Stewart Vane-Tempest-,
    Viscount Castlereagh, 6th Marquess
    of Londonderry 140

Stewart, Charles Stewart Henry
    Vane-Tempest-, Viscount Castlereagh,
    7th Marquess of Londonderry 140

Stokes, Richard Rapier 140-141

Stonehaven: see Baird

Stow Hill: see Soskice

Strachey, Sir Edward, 4th Bt,
    1st Baron Strachie 141

Strachey, (Evelyn) John St Loe 141-142

Strachie: see Strachey, E.

Strathcarron: see Macpherson

Strauss, George Russell 142

Sunderland: see Spencer-Churchill 142

Sutherland: see Gower

Sutherland, Sir William 142

Swinton: see Cunliffe-Lister

Templewood: see Hoare

Tenby: see Lloyd George

Tennant, Harold John 142

Thesiger, Frederic John Napier,
    3rd Baron Chelmsford,
    1st Viscount Chelmsford 143

Thomas, David Alfred, Viscount Rhondda 143

Thomas, James Henry 143-144

Thomson, Christopher Birdwood,
    Baron Thomson of Cardington 144-145

Thomson, Sir William Lowson Mitchell-,
    2nd Bt, 1st Baron Selsdon 145

Thurso: see Sinclair, A.

Tomlinson, George 145

Trevelyan, Sir Charles Philips, 3rd Bt 145

Tryon, George Clement, 1st Baron Tryon 146

Turnour, Edward, Viscount Winterton,
    Baron Turnour, 6th Earl Winterton 146

Tweedmouth: see Marjoribanks

Waleran: see Walrond

Walker, Patrick Chrestien Gordon 146

Wallace, (David) Euan 146

Walrond, Sir William Hood, 2nd Bt,
    1st Baron Waleran 147

Walsh, Stephen 147

Walters, Sir (John) Tudor 147

Walton, Sir John Lawson 147

Waverley: see Anderson

Webb, Maurice 147

Webb, Sidney James, Baron Passfield 148

Webster, Sir Richard Everard, Bt,
    Viscount Alverstone 148

Wedgwood, Josiah Clement, 1st Baron
    Wedgwood 149

Weir, Andrew, 1st Baron Inverforth 150

Weir, Sir William Douglas, 1st Viscount Weir 150

Westwood, Joseph 151

Wheatley, John 151

Wilkinson, Ellen Cicely 151

Williams, David Rees Rees-, Baron Ogmore 151

Williams, Sir Edward John 151

Williams, Thomas, Baron Williams of
    Barnburgh 151-152

Willink, Sir Henry Urmston, 1st Bt 152

Wilmot, John, Baron Wilmot of Selmeston 152

Wilson, (James) Harold 152

Wimborne: see Guest, I.C.

Windsor: see Windsor-Clive

Winster: see Fletcher

Winterton: see Turnour

Wolmer: see Palmer

Wolverhampton: see Fowler

Womersley, Sir Walter James, 1st Bt 152-153

Wood, Edward Frederick Lindley, 1st Baron
    Irwin, 3rd Viscount Halifax, 1st Earl of
    Halifax 153-154

Wood, Sir (Howard) Kingsley 154

Wood, Thomas McKinnon 154-155

Woodburn, Arthur 155

Woolton: see Marquis

Wyndham, George 155-156

Young, Sir Edward Hilton, 1st Baron
    Kennet 156-157

Ypres: see French

Zetland: see Dundas